The
Zombie Film

THE ZOMBIE FILM

from *White Zombie* to *World War Z*

ALAIN SILVER AND JAMES URSINI

APPLAUSE THEATRE & CINEMA BOOKS
An Imprint of Hal Leonard Corporation

This book is respectfully dedicated
to the memory of
Richard Matheson

Copyright © 2014 by Alain Silver and James Ursini

Published in 2014 by Applause Theatre & Cinema Books
An Imprint of Hal Leonard Corporation
7777 West Bluemound Road
Milwaukee, WI 53213

Trade Book Division, Editorial Offices
33 Plymouth St., Montclair, NJ 07042

Permissions can be found in the Acknowledgments on page 7.

Book and cover design by Alain Silver

Printed in the United States of America

Library of Congress Cataloging-in-Publication Data is available upon request.

ISBN No. 978-0-87910-887-8

www.applausebooks.com

Front Cover: *The Walking Dead*
Back Cover: *The Evil Dead, Resident Evil*
Frontispiece: *The Night of the Living Dead* (1968)
Contents pages: *Zombieland*; Legendre and his Zombie troop from *White Zombie*
Acknowledgments page: *Zombie Honeymoon*
Page 372: Linda Brookover's "Dirndl Apocalyse" (photo by Alain Silver)

Contents

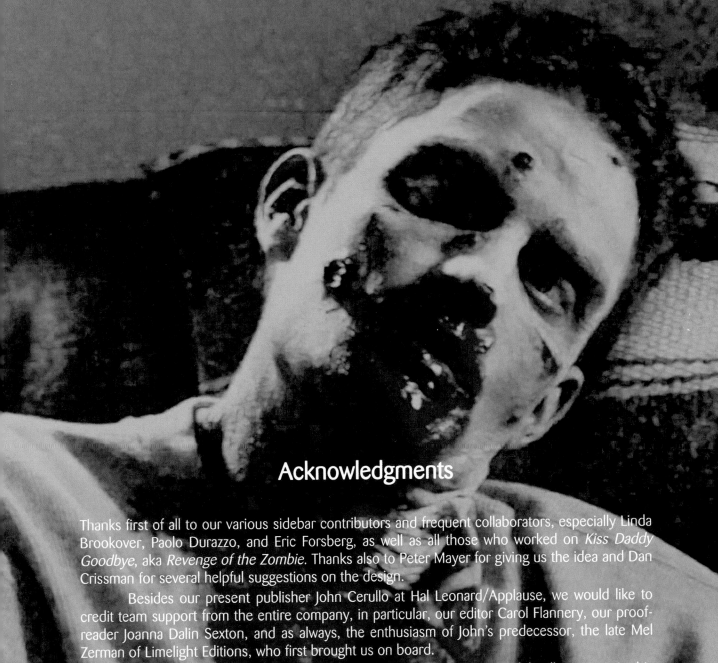

Acknowledgments

Thanks first of all to our various sidebar contributors and frequent collaborators, especially Linda Brookover, Paolo Durazzo, and Eric Forsberg, as well as all those who worked on *Kiss Daddy Goodbye*, aka *Revenge of the Zombie*. Thanks also to Peter Mayer for giving us the idea and Dan Crissman for several helpful suggestions on the design.

Besides our present publisher John Cerullo at Hal Leonard/Applause, we would like to credit team support from the entire company, in particular, our editor Carol Flannery, our proofreader Joanna Dalin Sexton, and as always, the enthusiasm of John's predecessor, the late Mel Zerman of Limelight Editions, who first brought us on board.

As with the *Film Noir Reader* series and *The Vampire FIlm*, most of the illustrations in this volume are from our personal collection, but for others we are grateful to several of our contributors, Timothy Otto, and visual archivists, too numerous to cite individually, who share their stills and posters on-line. Of the scores of on-line sources for illustrations, two that were particularly helpful are Wrongsideoftheart.com and Toutlecine.com.

Stills are courtesy of American International, Columbia, Hammer, MGM/UA, Monogram, Paramount, Republic, RKO, 20th Century-Fox, Universal, Warner Bros., and many other production companies and distributors; they are reproduced here strictly for historical and review purposes and to accompany critical refferences and expert commentary as permitted under fair use but remain as applicable under copyright to third parties.

Preface

After writing about and revisiting the vampire film genre for almost four decades—most recently in *The Vampire Film from Nosferatu to True Blood*—we have turned our attention to another type of "undead": the zombie. Although the zombie film did not really blossom until the arrival of George Romero and his low-budget *Night of the Living Dead* in 1968 and "apocalypse anxiety," it has existed in various forms on screen for over eight decades.

There are close relations to other supernatural myths and their movie variants as well. The Frankenstein myth, with its creature fabricated from body parts of exhumed corpses, is an obvious example. *The Mummy* (1932) was an original concept when filmed by Universal and transformed into a new myth when the title figure became, with Frankenstein's monster and Dracula, part of that studio's triumvirate of horrific beings. While Victor Frankenstein is the ostensible master of his creation, the mummified Imhotep returns to life in a dazed and almost innocent state but is soon driven to fulfill a destiny set in place in the time of pyramids, which is not the prototypical behavior of a zombie. At least until its post-modern examples in the new millennium, the zombie is usually a creature living purely off instinct that can be driven by a hunger and/or the will of a master, as in the earliest movie *White Zombie* (1932), but incapable of complex planning, let alone fulfilling a quest.

These early zombies of legend were hapless, reanimated corpses used as field workers and fed only vegetable scraps, as meat or salt would send them back to their cemetery homes. While the vampire also exhibits a bloodthirsty hunger, it is more subtle in its technique, more seductive in its manner, more likely to use its intelligence or supernatural powers, rather than the physical ferocity that characterizes the most powerful zombies.

While the number of zombie films produced before 1950 were few, the genre has grown exponentially since Romero's landmark *Night of the Living Dead*, making it a serious film genre with a substantial body of titles ripe for critical exploration and elucidation. The question we posed about the title character in *Jennifer's Body* and others like her in the 4th edition of *The Vampire Film* was "Are they vampires, zombies, or what?" The answer is still uncertain. As pictured, Jennifer (Megan Fox) has bodily presence and zombie-like teeth but savaging her victims can change her appearance. She also likes to drink blood and can float like a ghost. What is she?—we can't be sure. While we will not consider Frankenstein's monster and the Mummy that have defined their own myth, the world of zombies on film does encompass a wide range of variations, and in that regard we will strive to be most inclusive, if not in the text then at least in the Filmography.

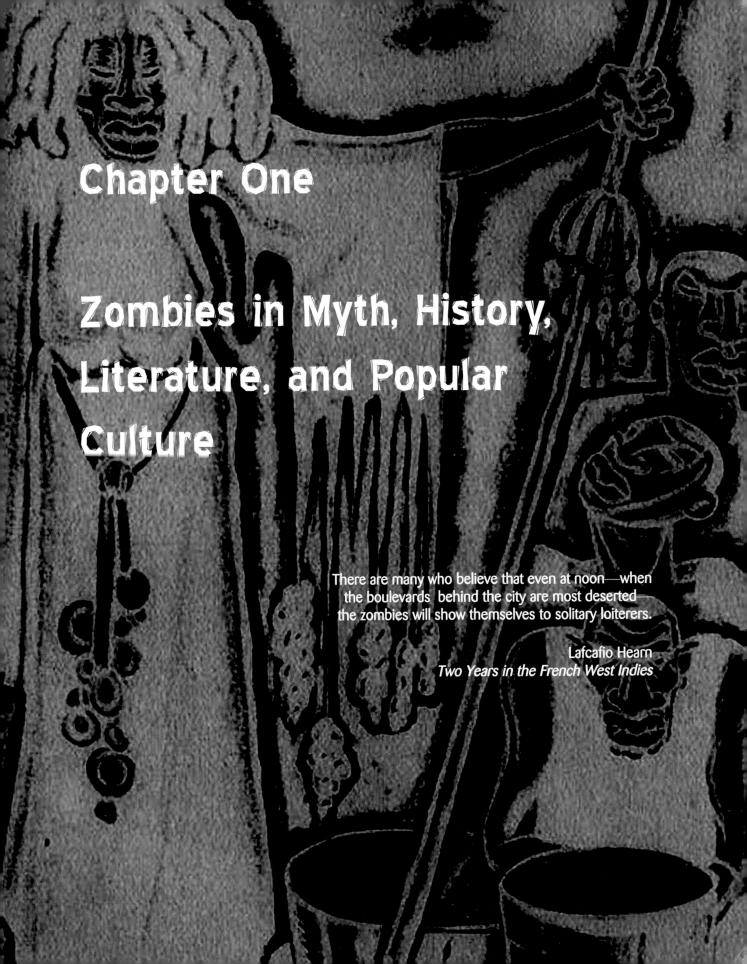

Chapter One

Zombies in Myth, History, Literature, and Popular Culture

There are many who believe that even at noon—when
the boulevards behind the city are most deserted—
the zombies will show themselves to solitary loiterers.

Lafcafio Hearn
Two Years in the French West Indies

Unlike the vampire archetype that exists in some form in most cultures in the world, the mythos and history of zombie (or *zonbi* in Creole) developed largely in the West Indies, particularly on the island of Haiti. Drawn from the beliefs and rituals of the West African tribes, whose members were forcibly enslaved and brought to the West Indies as chattel, the religion of vodou, vodoun, vodun, or voodoo posited the idea that individuals could be brought back to life. Alternately these unfortunates could be put into a near-death state and then controlled by a bokor or sorcerer, who performed the reanimation rite. The drug used in the transformation has been called "zombie powder." According to journalist and ethnobotantist Wade Davis (*The Serpent and the Rainbow*), the powder is a complex mixture of ingredients like puffer fish, blue lizard, and itching pea. According to lore of the period, zombies were often returned to the same position they had occupied in life, such as servants or plantation workers.

While the etymology of the term is itself vague, variants include the West African words *zumbi* meaning "fetish" and *nzambi, nzúmbe* meaning "snake god" or "dead spirit"; the Spanish *sombra* or French *ombre* meaning "shade" or "ghost," which in the West Indian language is *jumbe*[*e*]. The first discovered use of the word in the context of the supernatural dates from the early 18th century.

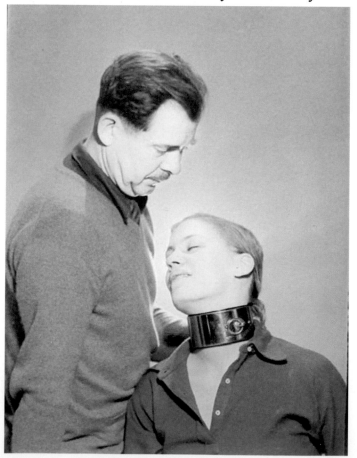

In terms of anthropological writing, the earliest is from Lafcadio Hearn, best known for his later writings in Japan but whose book *Two Years in the French West Indies* (1903), where he spent 1887–89, contained the first discussions about the zombi phenomenon in English [see Sidebar on pages 16–18], which Hearn also wrote about in 1888–89 articles for *Harper's* magazine. However, the book that moved the zombie into the mainstream of popular culture was *The Magic Island* (1929) by occultist/adventurer/journalist William Seabrook. Seabrook incorporated first-person

Left, author William Seabrook in a fetishistic pose.
Opposite, illustration and original caption from *The Magic Island*.

accounts of Haitian zombie-ism (including his own experience) into this mesmerizing study of myth and magic. His use of photos and art work (exotic woodcuts created by Alexander King) also enhanced the sensationalism of the book.

Prototypical zombies pop up here and there in literature beginning with the Middle Eastern cycle of tales *One Thousand and One Nights* (often called in the West *Arabian Nights*). In one of the tales a disgraced prince defeats an army of undead. Although some might consider it blasphemous, it could be argued that Lazarus, even Jesus Christ himself, are early examples of zombies. Two recent, very low-budget features actually exploit that hypothesis: *Zombiechrist* (2010, in which the mummified title figure is reanimated by a bevy of unclothed Druid priestesses) and *The Zombie Christ* (2012, in which a New Age redeemer comes to Texas to help end a zombie plague). Without creating any typical zombies, Edgar Allan Poe explored the netherworld between life and death in numerous stories, most notably "The Strange Case of M. Valdemar."

In Guy De Maupassant's "La Morte" (1887), a distraught narrator witnesses a rising of corpses who emerge from their graves to edit their own epitaphs. In Ambrose Bierce's

story "The Death of Halpin Frayser" (1893) the protagonist's mother rises from the grave to claim her son, which anticipates the psychosexual dimensions of some modern zombie films. Published in 1902 was W.W. Jacobs' timeless story "The Monkey's Paw," in which a family acquires a mummified talisman from a British army veteran just returned from India. After a first wish inadvertently causes her son's death, Mrs. White wishes him back to life but is stopped by her husband from answering the door when her mutilated zombie son comes knocking. The story has been adapted numerous times as a one-act play, an episode of a television horror anthology, and a short film. Some feature-length adaptations (such as the recent made-for-television movie) acknowledge their source. Other such as *Dead of Night* (aka *Deathdream*, 1972) or the Korean *Wishing Stairs* (2003) do not.

"Papa Nebo," Hermaphroditic Oracle of the Dead, Garbed as Half Man, Half Woman.

Cult horror writer H.P. Lovecraft also wrote stories, within his own unique mythos, which deal with zombie-like monsters: most notable "Herbert West–Reanimator" (1921–22), "The Outsider," and "Pickman's Model" (both 1926). "Herbert West" of course inspired the *Re-animator* films while "The Outsider" is novel in its use of a zombie as the first-person narrator of the story. Such pulp magazines as *Weird Tales, Ghost Stories*, and *Strange Tales of Mystery and Terror* occasionally published zombie stories. Among the most notable examples is "Salt Is Not for Slaves" (1931 in *Ghost Stories*) by Garnett Weston (as G.W. Hutter). Based on the strength of this story, Weston was hired to write the film script for the first movie in the genre—*White Zombie* (1932).

In "House in the Magnolias" (1932 in *Strange Tales*) writer August Derleth returned zombie-ism to New Orleans, always a hotbed for mysticism and magic. Besides the early Lovecraft, *Weird Tales* also published "Jumbee" (1926 by Henry S. Whitehead), "While

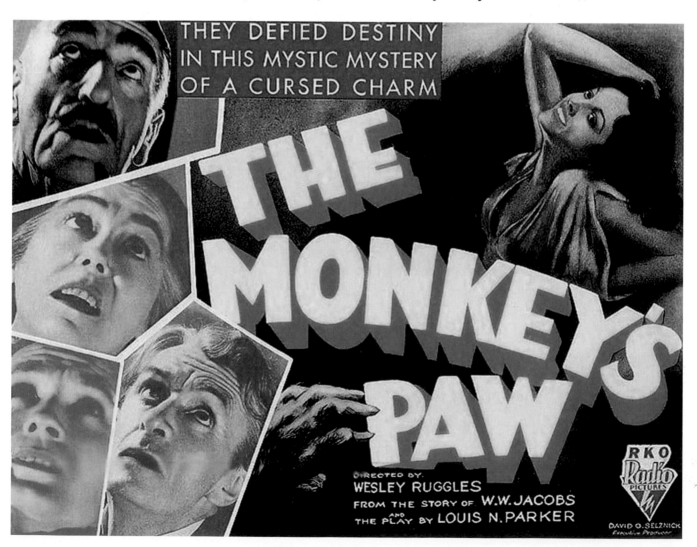

Pulp covers for Weston's "Salt is Not for Slaves" in *Ghost Stories* (left)
and Lovecraft's "Herbert West, Reanimator" in *Weird Tales*.

Zombies Walked" (1939 by Thorp McCluskey), and "Song of the Slaves" (1940 by Manley Wade Wellman). In 1954 Richard Matheson's seminal novel *I Am Legend* appeared. As will be detailed later, although Matheson's plague creatures were vampiric, the key concepts of barricaded humans struggling to survive the apocalyptic aftermath of a global pandemic first came together in this book. Published the following year, Jack Finney's *The Body Snatchers* uses the context of science fiction and alien invasion to explore the same terrain.

The next significant landmarks in zombie literature occur in the area of comic books, particularly in the pages of William Gaines' transgressive EC Comics. Before its evisceration by the Comics Code Authority, a self-regulating censorship organization formed by the large comic book companies, EC featured a number of gruesome zombie stories, some

Two Years in the French West Indies

—I ask, "what is a zombi?"

—"*Eti!*" answers old Théréza's voice from the little out-building where the evening meal is being prepared over a charcoal furnace, in an earthen canari.

—"*Missié-là ka mandé savé ça ça yé yonne zombi;—vini ti bouin!*"... The mother laughs, abandons her canari, and comes in to tell me all she knows about the weird word.

"*I ni pè zombi*"—I find from old Thereza's explanations—is a phrase indefinite as our own vague expressions, "afraid of ghosts," "afraid of the dark." But the word "Zombi" also has special strange meanings.... "*Ou passé nans grand chimin lanuitt, épi ou ka ouè gouôs difé, épi plis ou ka vini assou difé-à pli ou ka ouè difé-à ka màché: çé zombi ka fai ça...*" (You pass along the high-road at night, and you see a great fire, and the more you walk to get to it the more it moves away: it is the zombi makes that....)

—"How big is the fire that the zombi makes?" I ask.

—"It fills the whole road," answers Théréza: "*li ka rempli toutt chimin-là.* Folk call those fires the Evil Fires—*mauvai difé*;—and if you follow them they will lead you into chasms—*ou ké tombé adans labîme.*"...

And then she tells me this:

—"Baidaux was a mad man of color who used to live at St. Pierre, in the Street of the Precipice. He was not danger-ous—never did any harm—and what I am going to relate is true—*çe zhistouè veritabe!*

"One day Baidaux said to his sister: '*Moin ni yonne yche, va!—ou pa connaitt li!*' [I have a child, ah!—you never saw it!] His sister paid no attention to what he said that day; but the next day he said it again, and the next, and the next, and every day after—so that his sister at last became much annoyed by it.

"One evening he went out, and only came home at mid-night leading a child by the hand—a black child he had found in the street; and he said to his sister:

Images from St. Pierre, Martinique: "Capresse" (top) and another young woman in an elaborate headress (opposite). Left, the port marketplace; opposite, Mouillage Cemetery.

by Lafcadio Hearn

—"*'Mi yche-là moin mené ba ou! Tou léjou moin té ka di ou moin tini yonne yche: ou pa té 'lè couè—eh, ben! MI Y!'*" [Look at the child I have brought you! Every day I have been telling you I had a child: you would not believe me—very well, LOOK AT HIM!]

"The sister gave one look, and cried out: *'Baidaux, oti ou pouend yche-là?'*... For the child was growing taller and taller every moment....

"And the sister threw open the shutters and screamed to all the neighbors—*'Sécou, sécou, sécou! Vini oué ça Baidaux mené ba moin!'* [Help! help! Come see what Baidaux has brought in here!] And the child said to *Baidaux: 'Ou ni bonhè ou fou!'* [You are lucky that you are mad!] Then all the neighbors came running in; but they could not see anything: the Zombi was gone."

Zombi!—the word is perhaps full of mystery even for those who made it. The explanations of those who utter it most often are never quite lucid: it seems to convey some ideas darkly impossible to define—fancies belonging to the mind of another race and of another era—unspeakably old. Perhaps the word in our own language which offers the best analogy is "goblin": yet the one is not fully translated by the other. Both have, however, one common ground on which they become indistinguishable—that region of the supernatural which is most primitive and most vague; and the closest relation between the savage and the civilized fancy may be found in the fears which we call childish—of darkness, shadows, and things dreamed. One form of the *zombi*-belief—akin to certain ghostly superstitions held by various primitive races—would seem to have been suggested by nightmare—that form of nightmare in which familiar persons become slowly and hideously transformed into malevolent beings. The *zombi* deludes under the appearance of a travelling companion, an old comrade—like the desert spirits of the Arabs—or even under the form of an animal. Consequently the creole negro fears everything living which he meets after dark upon a lonely road—a stray horse, a cow, even a dog; and mothers quell the naughtiness of their children by the threat of summoning a zombi-cat or a zombi-creature of some kind.

Two Years in the French West Indies

"*Zombi ké nana ou*" [The zombi will gobble thee up] is generally an effectual menace in the country parts, where it is believed zombis may be met with any time after sunset. In the city it is thought that their regular hours are between two and four o'clock in the morning. At least so Cyrillia says:

—"*Dèezhè, toua-zhè-matin: c'est lhè zombi. Yo ka sòti dèzhè, toua zhè: c'est lhè yo. A quattrhè yo ka rentré;—angelus ka sonné.*" [At four o'clock they go back where they came from, before the *Angelus* rings.] Why?

—"*C'est pou moune pas joinne yo dans larue.*" [So that people may not meet with them in the street], Cyrillia answers.

—"Are they afraid of the people, Cyrillia?" I asked.

—"No, they are not afraid; but they do not want people to know their business" (*pa lè moune ouè zaffai yo*).

Cyrillia also says one must not look out of the window when a dog howls at night. Such a dog may be a *mauvais vivant* [evil being]: "If he sees me looking at him he will say, '*Ou tropp quirièse quittée cabane ou pou gàdé zaffa lezautt.*'" [You are too curious to leave your bed like that to look at other folks' business.]

—"And what then, Cyrillia?"

—"Then he will put out your eyes—*y ké coqui zié ou*—make you blind."

—"But, Cyrillia," I asked one day, "did you ever see any zombis?"

—"How? I often see them!... They walk about the room at night;—they walk like people. They sit in the rocking-chairs and rock themselves very softly, and look at me. I say to them:—'What do you want here?—I never did any harm to anybody. Go away!' Then they go away."

—"What do they look like?"

—"Like people—sometimes like beautiful people (*be. moune*). I am afraid of them. I only see them when there is no light burning. While the lamp bums before the Virgin they do not come. But sometimes the oil fails, and the light dies."

More images from Hearn's study: a "Young Mulatress" (top) and a "Coolie Servant" (immediate left).

included in the two infamous comic book series *The Crypt of Terror* and *The Vault of Horror*. Not to be outdone, in the mid-1970s Marvel Comics literally resurrected the Zombie/Simon Garth, a character created in 1953 (by founder Stan Lee and Bill Everett), as a quasi-tragic, quasi-heroic figure trying to find peace but compelled to kill to escape the control of his master after a ritualistic transformation by a voodoo priestess.

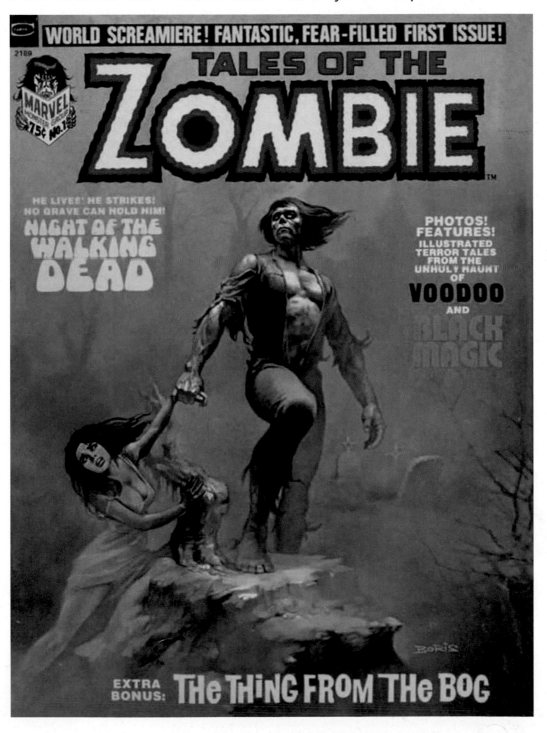

After the exponential growth of the zombie movie genre in the 1980s and 1990s, popular culture followed suit. In the 1980s video games opened the door to the zombie revival with gaming adaptations of movies like Sam Raimi's *The Evil Dead*. In 1983 Stephen King published *Pet Sematary*, clearly inspired by the thought of what would have happened had Mrs. White's husband not used the third wish on the monkey's paw to send their resurrected son away. King's novel progresses from animal to human resurrection and its emotional impact on the "normal" people. In 1989 the short story anthology *Book of the Dead* ramped up the zombie apocalypse theme introduced by director George Romero, who wrote a preface for the book, which features a set of stories by writers such as Stephen King and Les Daniels that detail a world overrun by zombies. *The Mammoth Book of Zombies* (1993) also pushed the zombie agenda further into the collective consciousness with its splatter-punk ethos.

The 1990s also saw the introduction of the influential video game *Resident Evil*, which lets players pit their gaming skills against a world infected by a zombie virus. The series in both video game form and several movie adaptations is ongoing. Stephen King wrote another influential zombie novel in 2006 *The Cell* (a pulse turns cell phone users into zombie-like creatures, a not too subtle critique of that pervasive technology). Seth Grahame-Smith's 2009 zombie satire *Pride and Prejudice and Zombies* innovatively grafts Jane Austen's classic novel onto a zombie template. It has inspired many similar mash-ups that turn classic literature into pulp horror.

Below, the urban zombie landscape: a frame capture from *Resident Evil* Game 1.
Background: Cover of Issue 2 of *Zombies! Feast* comic book.

Comic books and graphic novels have picked up the EC torch and resurrected the zombie tale in illustrated form. *Zombiepowder* (1999–2000), the first manga of Tite Kubo, made that material the reanimator's philosopher's stone. Current manga and/or their anime derivatives include *Zombie-Loan* (*Zonbi-ron*) and *The Corpse Princess* (*Shikabane Hime*). The most influential in this arena was Robert Kirkman's *The Walking Dead*, first published in 2003. Wounded in the line of duty, deputy sheriff Grimes awakens from a coma in the hospital to find his town filled with zombies. He travels to Atlanta to find his son and wife. There he becomes the leader of a group who are intent on surviving this zombie apocalypse. This tale became a current television series.

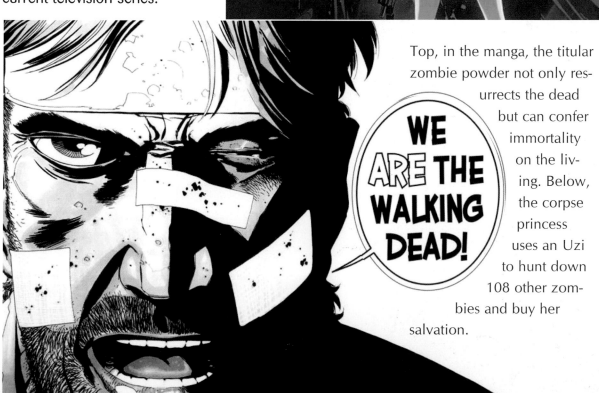

WE ARE THE WALKING DEAD!

Top, in the manga, the titular zombie powder not only resurrects the dead but can confer immortality on the living. Below, the corpse princess uses an Uzi to hunt down 108 other zombies and buy her salvation.

Zombie-mania in the last two millennial decades has seeped into current events. Books like Max Brooks' *The Zombie Survival Guide* (2003) and his sequel The *Zombie Survival Guide: Recorded Attacks* (2009) were instrumental in raising zombie-awareness in the public mind. There is even a zombie opera, *Evenings in Quarantine*, that in the spirit of Welles' *War of the Worlds* combines newscaster arias with pre-recorded footage of carnivorous hordes overrunning the city (of Romero's Pittsburgh, of course).

Beyond the hoaxes and mash-ups, there have been numerous instances of "real-life" zombie-ism that have repeatedly prompted headlines in tabloids and mainstream media alike. In the last few years a myriad of zombie marathons, zombie flash mobs, zombie festivals, and other zombie happenings have sprung up around the world. Several releases from the CDC on "Zombie Preparedness" have also raised awareness in the minds of the public and

The influential iconography of Matheson's solitary hunter in the novel *I Am Legend* (below, from the 2007 feature adaptation) is replicated (opposite below) in the television series *The Walking Dead*.
Opposite right, the solo shooter from *Resident Evil* the game is the typical pose for the individual confronting hordes of zombies.

Gerry Lane (Brad Pitt) contemplates the Zombie Apocalyse in *World War Z*.
Opposite insets; accused "Miami Zombie" Rudy Eugene (top) and Ronald Poppo, his homeless victim, before 75% of his face was chewed off and fearful cries of an actual "Zombie Apocalypse" echoed through the state of Florida.

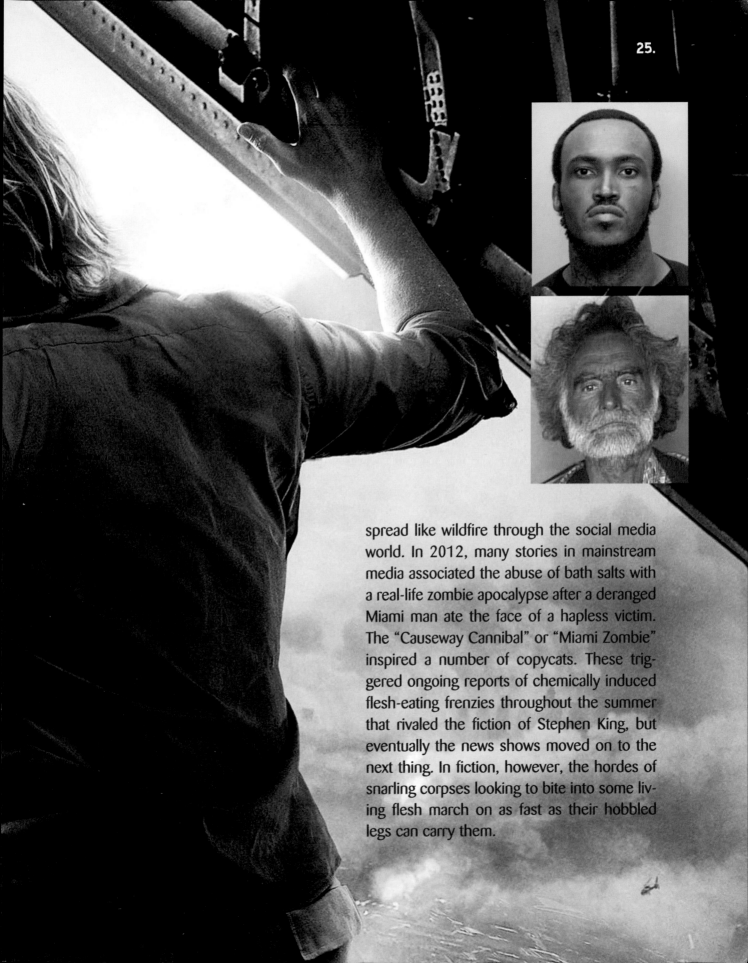

spread like wildfire through the social media world. In 2012, many stories in mainstream media associated the abuse of bath salts with a real-life zombie apocalypse after a deranged Miami man ate the face of a hapless victim. The "Causeway Cannibal" or "Miami Zombie" inspired a number of copycats. These triggered ongoing reports of chemically induced flesh-eating frenzies throughout the summer that rivaled the fiction of Stephen King, but eventually the news shows moved on to the next thing. In fiction, however, the hordes of snarling corpses looking to bite into some living flesh march on as fast as their hobbled legs can carry them.

Morlant (Boris Karloff) attacks Betty Harlon (Dorothy Hyson) in *The Ghoul*.

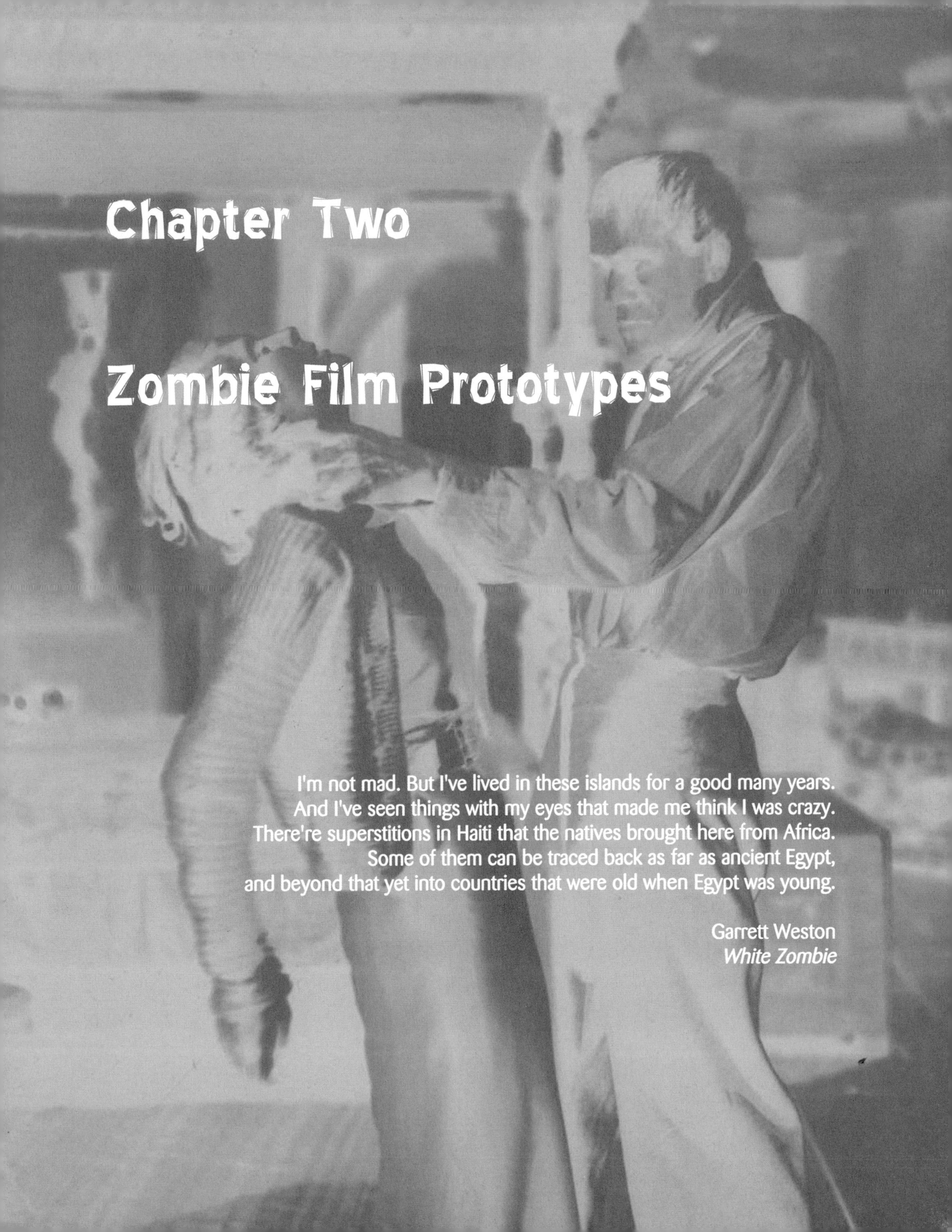

Chapter Two

Zombie Film Prototypes

I'm not mad. But I've lived in these islands for a good many years.
And I've seen things with my eyes that made me think I was crazy.
There're superstitions in Haiti that the natives brought here from Africa.
Some of them can be traced back as far as ancient Egypt,
and beyond that yet into countries that were old when Egypt was young.

Garrett Weston
White Zombie

Zombie movies shambled onto the screen in 1932 with Victor Halperin's independently produced *White Zombie*. Inspired by Seabrook's *The Magic Island* and coincident with Kenneth Webb's short-running Broadway play *Zombie*, Halperin's movie also owes much to the 1931 Universal incarna-

tion of Bram Stoker's *Dracula* for its story and style, not to mention its star, Bela Lugosi. Understandably Halperin and his brother Edward wanted to make their relatively low-budget ($50,000) enterprise resemble a studio-produced feature as much as possible. Garrett Weston's screenplay used various plot points that viewers had already come to expect from a horror movie. So it was money well spent to acquire the services of Lugosi and rent some pieces from Universal's scene dock of horror sets. Italian-born cinematographer Arthur Martinelli, who had worked at both Warner Bros. and MGM in the silent era, easily adapted some of the signature lighting and framing techniques used by Karl Freund in *Dracula*. The marketing campaign, as the 3-sheet opposite reveals, promised viewers that "Dracula" Lugosi would have an entranced, diaphonously gowned female "performing his every desire."

Lugosi as "Murder" Legendre (above) faces down John Harron as Neil Paker (right) and controls both Madeline (Madge Bellamy) and Beaumont (Robert Frazier, on previous page). Opposite, flanked by his zombie troop, Legendre orders Beaumont and his "prize" Madeline out of the crypt.

The film opens on a young, innocent couple—Madeline (Madge Bellamy) (the name is a reference to Poe's quasi-undead character in "The Fall of the House of Usher") and Neil (John Harron)—travelling to the Haitian plantation house of colonist Charles Beaumont (Robert Frazer). Like Jonathan Harker in Universal's *Dracula*, Neil has been lured by the promise of business connections. On the road they encounter "Murder" Legendre (Lugosi in a performance much more fluid and natural than in *Dracula*). There is an elaborate optical in which the backlit coach seems to drive between two eyes (lit as were Lugosi's in *Dracula* by small key lights) then the eyes pull back, left, and disappear to reveal a caped figure by the side of the road as the driver stops to ask directions. Lugosi's full face is finally seen when he leans into the passenger compartment: missionary hat raised to reveal a wide forehead, heavy twisted brows, and a devil's horned goatee immediately establish the character's demonic power and charisma. This is reinforced by repeated cutaways to his familiar or avatar, a vulture. As he unexpectedly meets a "white goddess" in a dark land—a trope of early

Hollywood adventure films like *King Kong* (1933), *Trader Horn* (1931), etc.–Legendre uses his mesmeric ability to pin Madeline to her seat and take her silk scarf as a memento, which are obvious visual links to Mina, the hapless heroine of *Dracula*.

After witnessing the driver's reaction to Legendre and his retinue, a shout of "Zombies! Allez vite!" before racing away, the emotionally unsettled couple arrive at Beaumont's mansion. The viewer soon learns that Beaumont had an ulterior motive in asking the young couple to his abode. He, too, is obsessed with this passive "white goddess" and wishes to seduce her away from her fiancé. In order to accomplish this objective, he solicits Legendre's aid; but he is singularly off-put when he witnesses the zombie master's slaves at work in his mill.

In a powerful scene heavily influenced by the German Expressionist classic *The Cabinet of Dr. Caligari*, the zombies, wide-eyed and expressionless, slowly and deliberately push the mill wheel. The only sound is the creaking of the wood as these figures, like Milton's "Samson Agonistes" ("eyeless in Gaza at the mill with slaves"), walk in endless circles, powering the gears of the mill. Even when one of their own falls into the murderous blades of the mechanism, they continue without pause.

Ultimately Beaumont's lust triumphs over his fear and repulsion. Shots of Madeline in transparent lingerie and floating down the stairs of his mansion sheathed in a silk dress reinforce for the viewer the compelling sensuality of Frazier's object of desire. So he makes a "devil's deal" with Legendre, who provides a "zombie powder" that will produce a death-like state in Madeline and allow the zombie master to impose his will. After the marriage ceremony at Beaumont's house, the happy couple attends a celebratory dinner arranged by Beaumont. There, as Legendre offhandedly carves a "voodoo doll" of the lovely Madeline out of candle wax, Beaumont spikes Madeline's wine with the zombie potion. Madeline slips into a catatonic state and is pronounced dead.

The distraught Neil finds scant solace at the bottom of a bottle. In a montage sequence Neil sits in a dimly lit bar as shadows bathe the background and visions of Madeline torment him. Desperate to see her again, Neil rushes to the graveyard while screaming her name, even as Beaumont and Legendre carry out the theft of her coffin. The zombies in silhouette like some expressionist woodcut carry off the still-beauteous Madeline (her sleeping face revealed with the coffin's top portion removed) to Legendre's castle on the cliffs above the sea (looking very much like Dracula's Transylvanian edifice). Neil arrives to discover her empty crypt.

The Dr. Van Helsing from *Dracula* is recalled here by Dr. Bruner (Joseph Cawthorn). Although

Opposite, Legendre strikes his side-lit, clasped hand mesmeric pose.
Below, with the former high executioner Chauvin (Frederick Peters).

played with greater levity than Edward Van Sloan's dour Van Helsing (Cawthorn is always rambling and looking for a light for his "smokes"), Bruner is the only one who can help Neil recover his love. After explaining to him the meaning of zombie-ism, including its place in the legal code of Haiti, Bruner guides Neil to Legendre's castle. When Neil is too distraught to continue, Bruner goes on intrepidly. In another montage the filmmakers again invoke amour fou. A series of wipes using varying geometric shapes connect Neil and Madeline as she stares out blankly at the ocean, as if posed in expectation of the arrival of her lost love.

When Beaumont becomes discouraged by Madeline's lack of response to him—she is, after all, a zombie—and begins to feel some guilt over his scheme, Legendre decides to pursue his own quasi-necrophiliac interest in the zombie bride. Legendre puts zombie powder into Beaumont's drink and watches sadistically as the man gradually slips into catatonia, taunting him by carving the voodoo doll that he will use to finalize Beaumont's "enslavement."

In the final scene Neil drags himself up to the steps of the Gothic castle while Legendre with his mesmeric powers forces Madeline to take a knife and hover above his reclined form ready to sever his jugular. Bruner, inexplicably dressed in a cape like a vampire, intervenes and knocks Legendre

Below, the caped (?!) Dr. Bruner (Joseph Cawthorn) prepares to club down Legendre whose zombie minion clearly does not have his back.

Opposite, with Legendre, Beaumont, and the zombie crew in the sea at the bottom of a cliff, the filmmakers permit a Hollywood ending and a final clinch for their star-crossed couple.

unconscious. This break in his control permits his zombies to march themselves off the cliff and into the sea. When Legendre comes to and tries to regain control of the situation, the semi-catatonic Beaumont emerges from the shadows to hurl himself and Legendre into the sea, thereby freeing the young couple and expiating his guilt.

In a sequence before the grave is robbed, the zombies themselves are introduced by Legendre to a horrified Beaumont. They include a former government minster, Legendre's mentor, and Chauvin, who was the high executioner; but none of them has the sentience to function as even a minor character. Instead in this first iteration, Halperin established the blank stare and the deliberate walk, the mute presence of the prototypical movie zombie.

The British-produced *The Ghoul* (1933) draws on the success of both Universal's *Frankenstein* (1931) and *The Mummy* (1932) in its casting of Boris Karloff as a sympathetic zombie. Karloff gives one of his most poignant performances as Egyptologist Professor Morlant, who plunders ancient tombs in search of a jewel of "eternal light" that will guarantee him entry into the afterlife. We first see him on his deathbed praying to the statue of Anubis to the disgust of his intolerant Christian servant Laing (Ernest Thesiger, better known for portraying Dr. Pretorius two years later in *The Bride of Frankenstein*). As the dying Morlant demands in a hoarse and breathless voice that Laing obey his dying wish to have his hand bandaged with the jewel inside, the battle between the ancient mystery religions and the Judeo-Christian ethic becomes the core theme of the movie.

When Morlant is entombed in a crypt displaying Egyptian hieroglyphs and icons, the mourners exit the scene while mumbling their disapproval of their friend's "paganism," immediately recapitulating that ethical conflict. Even the character of the duplicitous minister (who turns out to be simply a crook intent on stealing the jewel, played by Ralph Richardson) acts as ironic commentary on this

Below, Karloff (Professor Morlant) appeals to his priggish servant Laing (Ernest Thesiger). Opposite, post-zombification the dark-eyed Egyptologist has considerable brute strength.

theme with his deceptive sermons about the dangers of Morlant's worship of ancient deities.

The necessary twist in the film occurs when Laing decides to impose his religious strictures on the dead Morlant by stealing the precious stone from the corpse's hand. Inevitably this compels Morlant to rise from the grave in search of the jewel. Stumbling through the English countryside and attacking the odd assortment of characters gathered in his Gothic mansion, much like an Agatha Christie mystery, Karloff revisits his *Frankenstein* performance and uses his formidable pantomimic skills to convey the desperation and single-mindedness of this zombie to reinstate his plan for the afterlife.

When Morlant finally locates the jewel in the possession of his heir, he takes it and returns to his tomb. There he prays to Anubis wordlessly and carves an ankh on his chest. Placing the jewel in the statue's hand, he voluntarily reenters a death state, avoiding the grisly process by which most movies zombies are rendered completely dead. As a sop to Anglo-Saxon "rationalism" it is then revealed that the hand in the statue which received the jewel was not that of Anubis but of the hypocritical minister. Even the police try to dismiss the undead state of Morlant by claiming he was just suffering from "catalepsy."

The film boasts not only a chiaroscuro photographic style, that ranges from wind-swept country sides and foggy London at night to low-key interiors, but an underscore which mimics Wagnerian pomp, particularly in the early scenes around the death and burial of Morlant. The movie also draws on the wealth of British acting talent in its cast. Ralph Richardson is particularly effective and runs counter to viewer expectations as an apparently sincere if somewhat judgmental minister who becomes the villain of the piece. Cedric Hardwicke delivers a droll performance as the neurotic Broughton, who also lusts for the jewels and comically conveys that emotion through such mannerisms as a greedy pout and a tendency to bite his knuckles when thinking about the talisman. Thesiger is typically wildly expressionistic, with his thick Scottish accent, club-footed limp, and overwrought pleas to his master and later to his god after he steals the jewel.

The Scotland Yard Mystery (1934) was released in the United States with a title meant to exploit its zombie theme: *The Living Dead*. The movie's narrative centers on a police doctor who creates a zombie powder of his own with the intention of using undead to bilk their insurance companies. The plot is somewhat absurd. One cannot help thinking that there must be an easier way to commit insurance fraud.

Ouanga (1936 and re-released as *The Love Wanga*) is an independent exploitation film shot in Haiti and Jamaica, which trades on the era's taboo against miscegenation for its sensationalist appeal. The movie's lead is the light-skinned, gray-eyed African-American actress Fredi Washington, who had already demonstrated her talent as a femme fatale in Paul Robeson's *The Emperor Jones* (1933) and *Imitation of Life* (1934). As she does in all her performances throughout a movie career sadly truncated by her refusal to accept the studio preference of studio heads that she pass for White, Washington brings an aggressive sexuality and an emotional complexity to the character of Clelie, a Black Haitian plantation owner obsessed with White overseer Adam (Philip Brandon) with whom, it is implied, she had an affair.

Clelie's unabashed pursuit of Adam is unsubtle: "You belong to me, Adam, no one else but me." When speaking to LeStrange (played in black face by Sheldon Leonard), another overseer in love with Clelie, she reveals her determination and lack of inhibition, taunting him with her soft skin and full cleavage even as she says that she prefers the White man to him.

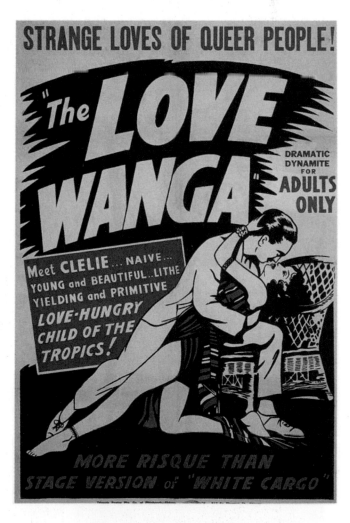

When Clelie finally sees that she cannot seduce Adam in the traditional way, she resorts to voodoo. She is a priestess; and using two of her zombie slaves, she kidnaps Eve (a character name that is perhaps a bit too on the money), Adam's most recent flame. Clelie begins a voodoo ceremony, but before she can complete it the jealous LeStrange intervenes and strangles her.

African-American actors Fredi Washington
(below) and Nina Mae McKinney (right).

Ouanga was remade in 1939 as *Devil's Daughter*. With the Holllywood Production Code now in full force, in order to obtain a certificate for exhibition in mainstream theaters, the story's sensational aspects had to be watered down. Gone was the inter-racial love triangle and even the elements of voodoo were soft-pedaled, to the point where the protagonist Isabelle (Nina Mae McKinney) suggests that her powers as a priestess were largely a hoax. It does, however, feature a striking and innovative scene in which Ida (Sylvia Walton) is returning from Harlem to her plantation in Jamaica. While in transit her vehicle is stopped by a group burying a loved one in the middle of the roadway. After asking, she is told that this practice helps prevent priests from raising their dead as zombies to work on plantations because the shamans fear being exposed publicly.

Revolt of the Zombies (1936) was another "Halperin Production" and promoted as a follow-up to *White Zombie,* that even recycled some superimposed shots of Bela Lugosi's eyes from the earlier movie. This rather tedious semi-sequel set in Cambodia has little of the visual panache of the original. Except for a few striking shots, such as an army of zombies marching in the trenches, it adds nothing to the evolving vernacular of the genre.

Below, the army of undead from the Halperin Production *Revolt of the Zombies.*

The Walking Dead (1936) brings back Karloff as another unconventional zombie. In fact, Ellman, the unjustly convicted victim who is reanimated by a cutting edge scientist, is one of the few sympathetic, quasi-articulate zombies among the early examples of the genre. Grafting the Warner Bros. gangster genre onto the Universal horror film, director Michael Curtiz (best known for mainstream A-projects such as *Casablanca* [1942] and *Mildred Pierce* [1945]) deftly moves in and out of the overlapping worlds of crime and horror.

A crime syndicate fronted by slick lawyer Nolan (Ricardo Cortez) flaunts the law repeatedly. When a courageous judge finally gives one of their members the sentence he deserves, Nolan devises a plan to eliminate the jurist as a warning to others. Loder (Barton MacLane) sets up Ellman, a non-violent and somewhat naïve ex-convict, as a patsy for the murder by hiring him to watch the judge's movements as part of a bogus divorce case. After the judge is murdered and his body dumped in the unsuspecting Ellman's car, Nolan volunteers to represent Ellman but puts on a sham of a defense. The dazed and confused ex-convict is convicted and sentenced to die in the electric chair.

At this point the film changes from fast-paced, hard-bitten Warner Bros. gangster fare into a zombie movie with direct references to the *Frankenstein* films. A young couple who had witnessed the dumping of the judge's body but were too frightened to report the incident beg the scientist for whom they work, Dr. Beaumont (Edmund Gwenn), to help them free Ellman. It is too late to save him: in a classic Warner Bros. proto-noir scene, shot from a low angle with shadows bathing the prison, Ellman is led down the "last mile" to the execution chamber. The lights dim, and the viewer understands he has been electrocuted.

Undeterred Dr. Beamont asks for Ellman's body in the belief that he can bring the innocent man back from the grave. Again the film shifts gears and becomes classic Universal horror. In a laboratory resembling those in James Whale's *Frankenstein* and *The Bride of Frankenstein*, low angles frame the electrical instruments, the flashes of current, the medical paraphernalia while Ellman lies on the operating table, made-up in a manner that resembles Dr. Frankenstein's monster. As Ellman begins to breathe, Beaumont declares, if somewhat less grandiosely than actor Colin Clive over Karloff's composite corpse in *Frankenstein*, that "he is alive."

Zombie Ellman walks with the increasingly traditional labored gait and speaks haltingly. He remembers little of his past or, and this is what interests Dr. Beaumont most, his sensations immediately after being executed. Only when Ellman finally reencounters his persecutors, the members of the syndicate, does his expression indicate that he may have memories, unpleasant ones. As he plays the piano at a gathering arranged by District Attorney Beaumont to get the men they believe are guilty of the judge's murder into one room, Ellman stares grimly at each of the conspirators in turn. Curtiz intercuts between Ellman's somber mien and point-of-view shots of the criminals, while bringing up a key light on each of them to symbolize the intensity of Ellman's emnity.

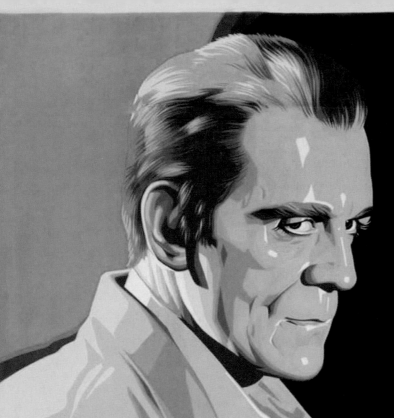

HE DIED a man with a hunger to love . . . and returned a *monster* with an instinct to kill.

BORIS KARLOFF

in

"The Walking DEAD"

with Ricardo CORTEZ

Edmund GWENN · Marguerite CHURCHILL
Warren HULL · Barton MacLANE
Henry O'NEILL · Joseph KING

Directed by MICHAEL CURTIZ

A WARNER BROS. PICTURE

Like any single-minded zombie, Ellman hunts these men down one by one. Although he never directly murders any of them, he precipitates their deaths via car crash, accidental shooting, and heart attack. While he acts as an angel of vengeance, Ellman takes no apparent joy in this. Rather he regards his victims with dispassion and even regret.

Sensing he does not belong in this world and explicitly wishing to return to the "peace" of the after-life, he haunts graveyards at night. It is there where the final scene occurs. Shot to death, again, by one of the syndicate, he expires even as the doctor still interrogates him about the nature of death. The movie illustrates two possible answers. First, Curtiz cuts to the car carrying the last two killers to their horrifying death careening off a hazardous roadway. This provides the audience with a con-crete answer. Then he cuts back to Ellman, who whispers the word "peace" as he expires, taking the edge off the tragic demise while putting forth a more transcendent possibility.

The last entry in Karloff's trilogy of zombie proto-types (released three years apart) is *The Man They*

Could Not Hang (1939). As obsessed scientist Henryk Savaard, Karloff's character is convicted and executed for the murder of a test subject that he planned to reanimate. When he is brought back by an eager assistant, his interest shifts from science to revenge. Whereas Ellman and even Morlant were somewhat tragic figures and those responsible for Ellman's death the true criminals, Dr. Savaard may be a man brought back from the dead but is much more psychopath than zombie, a methodical killer who lures his last victims to a location where he can torment them before ending their lives.

Opposite, Karloff as reanimated convict John Ellman attended to by Dr. Beaumont (Edmund Gwenn) and Nurse Nancy (Marguerite Churchill) in *The Walking Dead*.

Below, *The Man They Could Not Hang* and Karloff as yet another "mad" scientist, Dr. Henryk Savaard.

The Many Faces of Karloff

Unquestionably best remembered for other than his zombie-like protrayals, Boris Karloff at right watches the preparation of a prosthetic head (bottom right, opposite) on the set of *The Man They Could Not Hang.*

Frankenstein's Monster (1931).

Imhotep in *The Mummy* (1932).

More or less himself as
Dr. Niemann in *House
of Frankenstein* (1944).

Morlant in
The Ghoul (1933).

1939.

The Ghost Breakers (1940) is a comedy featuring Bob Hope and Paulette Goddard and set on a Caribbean island. The zombie in the movie (played by the estimable character actor and producer of Black films Noble Johnson) is simply a pastiche who comically menaces the characters portrayed by Hope and Goddard. Nonetheless the aspects of stereotype and parody in this confirm that less than a decade after *White Zombie* the traits of a film zombie were already established in the viewer's expectations.

King of the Zombies (1941) is a poverty-row production from Monogram, which like *The Ghost Breakers* mixes comedy and mystery. A plane caught in a storm lands on a small island near the West Indies. There the passengers encounter a strange doctor who employs zombies in a wartime espionage plot. In the resolution, these figures, some of whom dance, turn on their master.

Bowery at Midnight (1942) is another Monogram release, which features an already physically declining Bela Lugosi as a mastermind using a soup kitchen as a front for criminal activities. He also keeps a set of zombies in the basement just in case.

Opposite, Paul Lukas manages to keep a straight face while posing with Paulette Goddard and Bob Hope for *The Ghost Breakers*.

Below, Tom Neal (right) seems to have taken a detour into the horror mash-up *Bowery at Midnight:* despite holding a gat on Lugosi (in a dual role of Prof. Brenner and Karl Wagner),

Neal still has his better-known co-star's name sticking in his ear.

Right, Mantan Moreland is the stereotypical comic relief as the nervous manservant Jackson in *King of the Zombies.*

Along with *White Zombie*, producer Val Lewton's *I Walked with a Zombie* (1943) is the most significant zombie film of the early years of the genre. Still known for his B-budget but imaginative series of horror films at RKO, Lewton teamed with co-writer Curt Siodmak (who worked on *Son of Dracula* [1943] for his director brother Robert and 1941's *The Wolf Man*) and director Jacques Tourneur (who also helmed *Cat People* and *The Leopard Man* for Lewton) superimposed Charlotte Bronte's classic Gothic novel *Jane Eyre* onto the emerging template for a zombie film. Nurse Betsy (Frances Dee), seeking employment, is lured to the West Indies island of San Sebastian by promises of "palm trees" and "sunbathing." What she finds is a quite different landscape: beautiful during the day but haunted by strange sights and beings after nightfall. While still on the ship to the

Below, Jessica Holland (Christine Gordon, left) and her nurse Betsy Connell (Frances Dee) encounter a blood sacrifice along a jungle path.

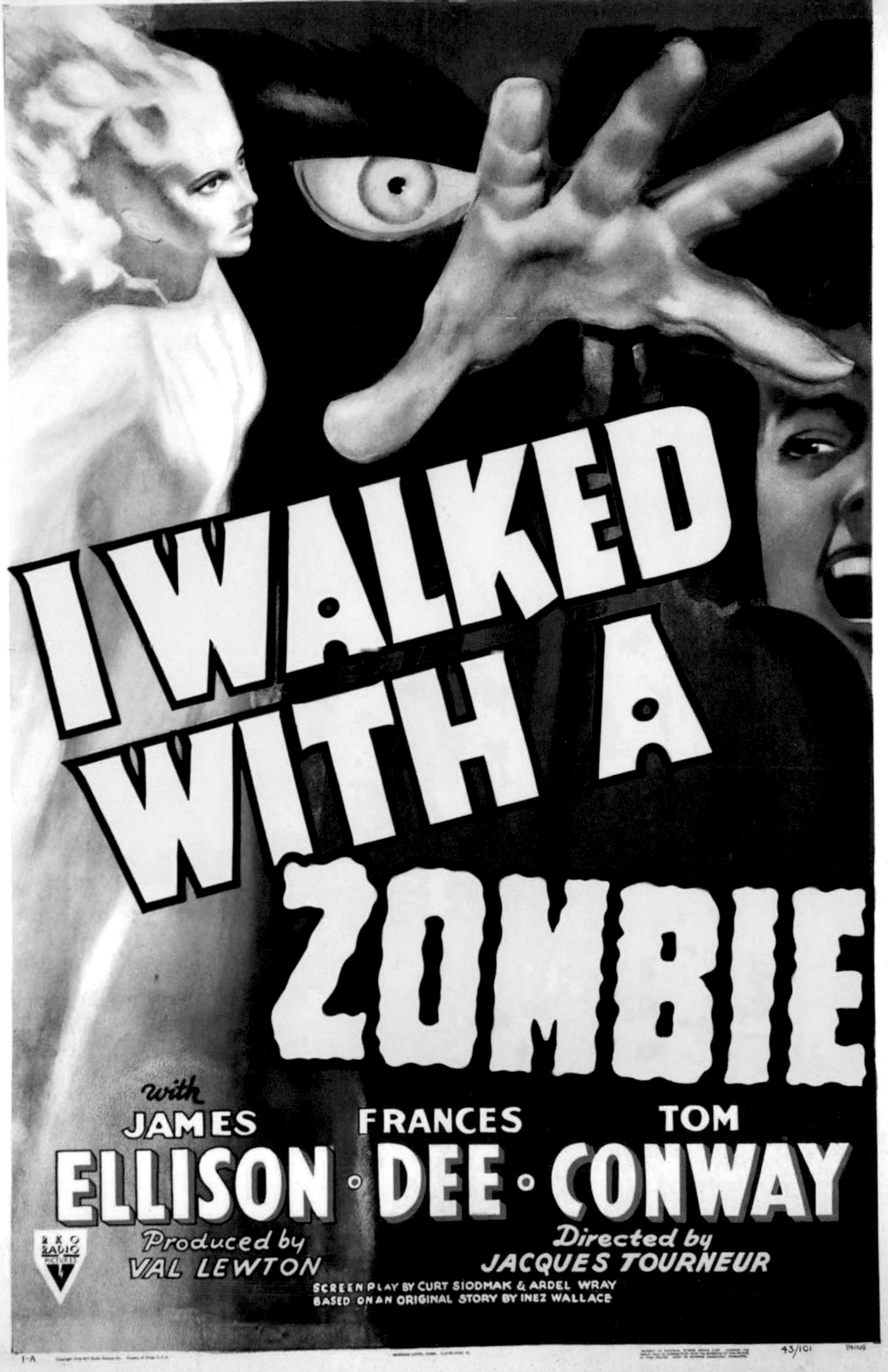
I WALKED
WITH A
ZOMBIE
with
JAMES ELLISON
FRANCES DEE
TOM CONWAY
RKO RADIO PICTURES
Produced by
VAL LEWTON
Directed by
JACQUES TOURNEUR
SCREEN PLAY BY CURT SIODMAK & ARDEL WRAY
BASED ON AN ORIGINAL STORY BY INEZ WALLACE
43/101

Early Visual Style at Lewton's RKO

The horror pictures made by Val Lewton at RKO in the early 1940s with directors Jacques Tourneur, Robert Wise, and Mark Robson were quickly recognized for their use of stylized lighting and settings to underscore the sense of dread felt by diverse characters being threatened by preternatural or uncanny beings. Despite their limited budgets, the ingenuity of Lewton and his director collaborators helped create classic set pieces in B-budget movies such as *I Walked with a Zombie*. Shot barely more than a dozen years after the publication of Seabrook's *The Magic Island*, the influence of artist Alexander King also seems evdent in the movie's production design, costuming, and make-up.

In this scene, the entranced Jessica Holland and nurse Betsy stumble across the striking sentinel Carrefour (Darby Jones) in the local back country.

Opposite are a frame capture of Jones as Carrefour and a King woodcut.

54.

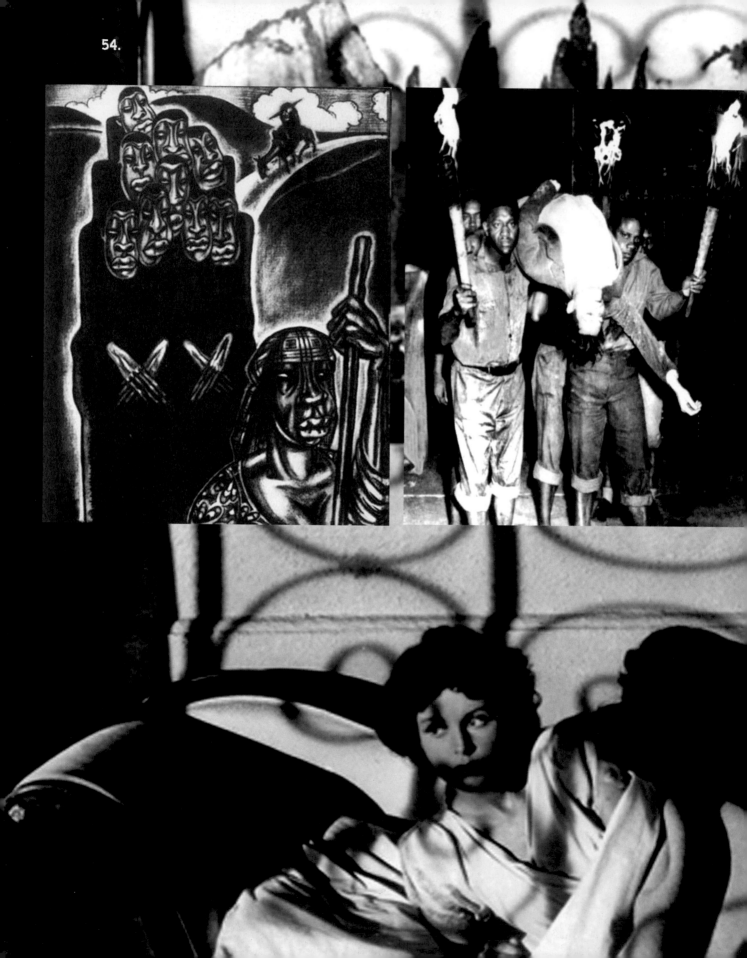

In the scene, Betsy awakens to find the menacing shadow of Carrefour looming over the foot of her bed.

Opposite, grisly processions drawn by King and staged by Tourneur.

Below, the physical attractions of a damsel in the moonlight could not be as explicitly drawn on film in 1943 as it was on paper in 1929. In contrast, compare the graphic image of the female figure on the poster from the pre-Code-enforcement release of *White Zombie* on page 28.

island, Betsy gazes out at the night sky in wonder only to be disabused of her illusions by her "Byronic" (his brother describes him that way) employer. Paul Holland (Tom Conway) tells her meteors are simply "dying stars"; and that she will find nothing but doom and depression at her new location.

Living in the sugar plantation manor house is a zombie-like patient, Paul's wife Jessica (Christine Gordon), who is confined to a tower (much like Bertha Mason in *Jane Eyre*). An aloof even rude Paul refuses to provide Betsy with needed information about her patient. In a scene typical of Lewton's horror films, after she hears crying coming from the tower, Betsy explores it. She walks through its maze of menacing shadows and is finally confronted by the disturbing mute figure of Jessica, looking like a model for a Modigliani painting: tall, gaunt, with a long curved neck. Lewton often referenced painting and literature in his productions, and *I Walked with a Zombie* reflects his intellectualism in its script and its cinematography.

Betsy finally learns Jessica's history through a dinner performance by a local calypso singer (portrayed by real-life troubadour Sir Lancelot). His lyrics reveal that Paul's bitter and alcoholic brother Wesley (James Ellison) also loved Jessica, who planned to spurn the cruel Paul and run off with Wesley.

The film's treatment of voodoo and the Blacks is among the most respectful and serious of early zombie films. Shortly after Betsy's arrival, a servant explains the sorrowful atmosphere of the island as symbolized by the black figurehead of St. Sebastian taken off the prow of a ship that brought their ancestors to work as slaves. Later when Betsy decides to try and help her patient by visiting the voodoo priest during a ceremony, the film tries to recreate the rituals with deference and some authenticity.

As they walk through the tall sugar cane, Betsy and Jessica are met by Carrefour (Darby Jones), a tall, sinewy zombie with protruding eyes, who at first terrifies them but later leads them to the priest. The priest, however, turns out to be a woman, the mother of Paul and Wesley, Mrs. Rand (Edith Barrett), who has adopted the traditional religion of the people in order to dispense medical aid. For Mrs. Rand later reveals that she has taken revenge on Jessica for disrupting her household and done this by using voodoo rituals to turn her into a living zombie. Although both Paul and the rationalist doctor refuse to believe her story (the battle between rationalism and the supernatural is a constant in Lewton films), Wesley is not so sure.

After a radical medical method suggested by Betsy fails to bring Jessica back to a functioning state, Wesley decides there is only one hope for his lover: her death. He takes an arrow from the statue of St. Sebastian and stabs Jessica while the drums of the ritual call her home. Carrefour now appears and stretches his arms towards Jessica, trying to return her to the "home fort" where the voodoo rituals are centered. Instead Wesley lifts Jessica into his arms and walks into the ocean to drown with her.

In *Revenge of the Zombies* (1943) Monogram strikes again, combining wartime propaganda with the walking dead. John Carradine turns in a remarkable performance under low-budget duress playing a Nazi sympathizer attempting to create a zombie army for the Third Reich. The film is most memorable for its strain of proto-feminism as the doctor's wife (Veda Ann Borg), whom he has turned into a zombie, fights her husband for control of his preternatural army. Another Carradine character dabbled with reanimation again for Monogram in the 1946 *The Face of Marble*. Dr. Charles Randolph, a figure closer to Karloff's portrayals of Morlant and Savaard, is another clinician who wants to raise the dead. He is so obsessed that he never notices the growing passion of his wife (Claudia Drake) for his handsome assistant Cochran (Robert Shayne). After failing with a

Opposite, much like Jane Eyre with Rochester, Betsy confers with her employer, Paul Holland (Tom Conway), in *I Walked with a Zombie*.

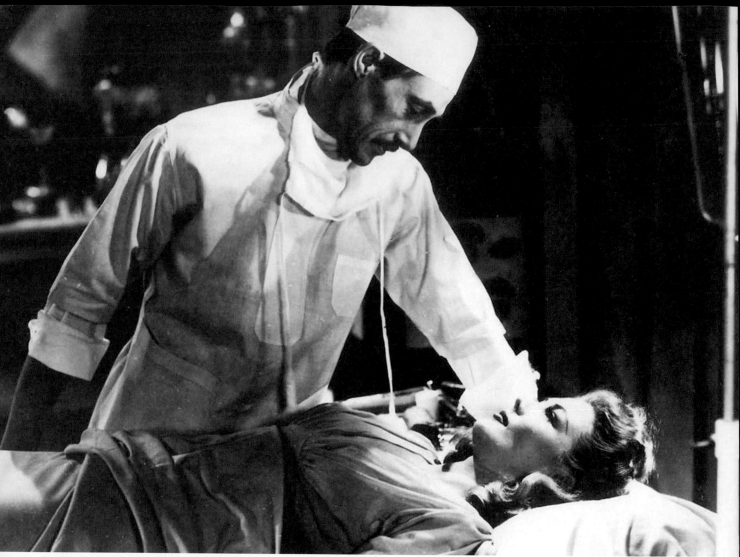

Above, in *Revenge of the Zombies*: Dr. Max Hein-rich von Alterman (John Carradine) reanimates his wife Lila (Veda Ann Borg).

Left, Carradine again takes up the mad scientist mantle of Karloff in *The Face of Marble*.

human subject, Randolph kills his wife's dog to attempt his scientific magic on a lesser species. This so incenses his wife's third-world servant Maria (Rosa Rey) that she put a zombie-powder-like spell on her mistress and her dog that sends them on a killing spree.

The Mad Ghoul (1943) is unique in that it is the first time the audience is presented with zombies hungry for human flesh (in this case, hearts), a staple of the post–George Romero zombie film. George Zucco plays a scientist who has discovered a Mayan nerve gas, which can turn live humans into zombies. He experiments on a lab assistant (few of these mad scientists spend much time looking for human guinea pigs), who then must find human hearts in order to return himself to a normal state.

In *Voodoo Man* (1944) Monogram brings together two horror icons: John Carradine and Bela Lugosi. Lugosi plays a doctor who uses a combination of voodoo rites and hypnotism to bring his

MONOGRAM PICTURES presents

BELA LUGOSI IN

"VOODOO MAN"

featuring

JOHN CARRADINE
GEORGE ZUCCO

Produced by SAM KATZMAN and JACK DIETZ
Associate Producer, BARNEY A. SARECKY
Directed by WILLIAM BEAUDINE
Original Story and Screenplay by ROBERT CHARLES

wife back from the dead and John Carradine plays his assistant.

Zombies on Broadway (1945) is RKO's attempt to capitalize on the success of Val Lewton's *I Walked with a Zombie*. It is in many ways a satire of the earlier movie, utilizing a low-rent Hope and Crosby duo named Brown and Carney, who land on an island with the objective of finding real zombies for a Broadway show. Elements of the sets of *I Walked* are recycled as are the performing talents of Sir Lancelot and Darby Jones.

Despite the pointed tie-in to Nazism in *Revenge of the Zombies* or the criminal exploitation of Ellman in *The Walking Dead*, like most horror films through the mid-1940s, the zombie genre stayed on point and away from social consciousness. Whatever their twisted reasons for wanting-to raise the dead, whether portrayed by Karloff, Carradine, Zucco, Lugosi, or any combination there-of, mad scientists were still just mad. No matter how they came to be zombies, like their vam-piric and lycanthropic cousins, they shared a need to prey on normal folks and that was reason enough to put an end to their afterlives. In the atomic age, as apprehension over nuclear war made the public aware of new threats to normality from radioactive mutations to extraterrestrials, the genre began to evolve, or mutate, into something more.

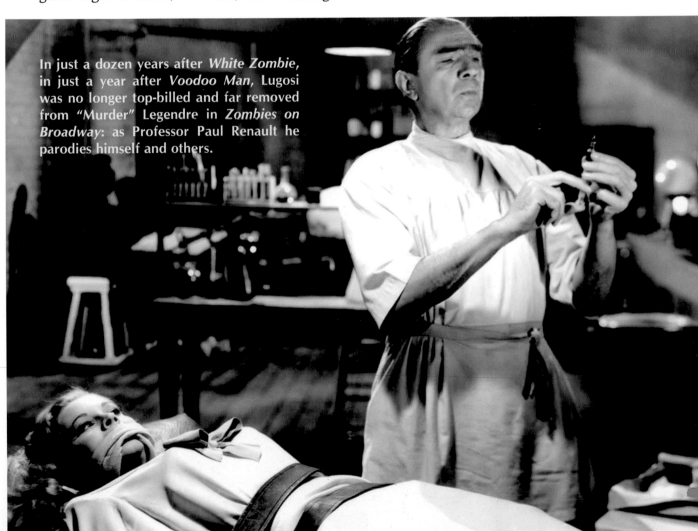

In just a dozen years after *White Zombie*, in just a year after *Voodoo Man*, Lugosi was no longer top-billed and far removed from "Murder" Legendre in *Zombies on Broadway*: as Professor Paul Renault he parodies himself and others.

The Druid ceremony in
Plague of the Zombies.

Chapter Three

The Second Coming:
The Postwar Zombie

And what rough beast, its hour come round at last,
Slouches towards Bethlehem to be born?

William Butler Yeats
"The Second Comng"

Don Siegel's *Invasion of the Body Snatchers* (1956)—co-written by film noir scenarist Daniel Mainwaring, whose novel *Build my Gallows High* became *Out of the Past* (1947)—is one of the first releases to transpose the emotionless zombie from its Haitian roots to a space age context. In the post-war era rough beasts from Godzilla to the giant ants in *Them!* (1954) did not slouch towards Bethlehem but Hollywood to be born. During that decade the zombie movie genre first dipped a decayed toe into waters that were higher tech and anticipated the apocalyptic mode that would supercharge the genre after 1968.

Invasion of the Body Snatchers is among the first to utilize a zombie-like figure as a metaphor for larger issues such as conformity, greed, violence, and paranoia. Invasion paranoia, in particular, derived from the 1950s anti-Communist hysteria worked against the conformist social behavior of the Eisenhower era. The attitude of complacent acceptance was reinforced less by explicit government policy than by the media particularly through television sitcoms like *Father Knows Best* and *Leave It to Beaver*.

While 1950s science fiction often visualized Cold War anxieties as giant monsters and invaders from space, *Invasion of the Body Snatchers* fashions a political allegory about infiltration and possession where exposure to dangerous ideas will transform a person into an agent of a conformist alien ideology. The conspiracy spreads until the pod contagion, through which the aliens fashion

Previous page, Miles (Kevin McCarthy) prepares to burn an alien pod.

Above, the two couples discover pods growing, appropriately enough, in their greenhouse and prepare to do a little pruning. In the lead with the pitchfock is Jack (King Donovan); cowering in horror behind him are Becky (Dana Wynter, left) and wife Teddy (Carolyn Jones).

Opposite, as the narrative progresses director Siegel underscores paranoia and tension as he progressively frames the characters and their faces more tightly within the widescreen Superscope.

emotionless zombie duplicates of sleeping or dead humans, is openly disseminated at street rallies while possessed lawmen victimize citizens in broad daylight. Behind the political threat is the personal fear of losing one's emotional identity. Awareness, however, brings no comfort; for the alienated town doctor Miles Bennell (Kevin McCarthy) and his love interest Becky Driscoll (Dana Wynter) become a hunted minority in a new order of conformity to a collective will. The "traditional value" Miles fights to retain is his essential individuality.

Miles had an awareness of an erosion of human emotions before the pods came: both he and Becky bore a sense of personal failure because of their recent divorces. This adds heavy social irony to a scene in which Miles observes an unnaturally tranquil pod family placing a fresh pod next to a baby's crib: after the duplication, there will be "no more tears."

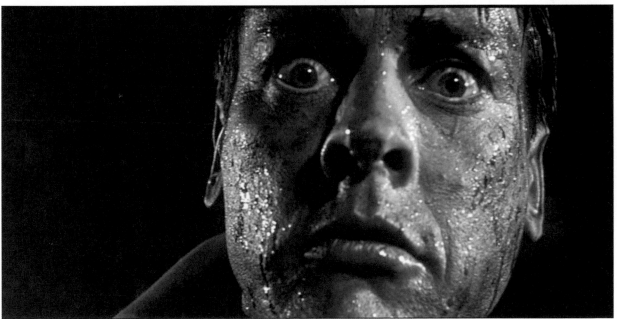

Director Siegel internalizes the struggle and confusion of Miles by having him frequently confess to his fear in his voice-over narration. This fear is also externalized through claustrophobic imagery such as dark closets, narrow hallways, tunnels, and other enclosures. Knowing that he is pursued by a relentless peril that threatens his very identity as a person, the only recourse for Miles is desperate: he must take "anti-social" action before his small town of Santa Mira is overrun.

Left, like many fugitive couples in film noir, Miles and Becky are compelled to flee the ostensibly safe confines of his doctor's office and ultimately end up dissheveled and exhausted in a cave.

Below, Siegel adds distinctive lighting to his clautrophobic framing to superimpose the noir style over his sci-fi saga of alien zombies.

Several emblematic scenes crystallize the narrative's aspect of nightmare and paranoia. First is the greenhouse sequence, in which seed pods burst open to reveal duplicates before the terrified eyes of Miles, Becky, and their friends Jack (King Donovan) and Teddy (Carolyn Jones). As Miles plunges a pitchfork into the chest of his duplicate, Siegel quickly cuts to the hallway telephone. This fast cut to the ringing telephone gathers the tension of the greenhouse scene and discharges it into the next scene as Miles takes Becky by the hand and says, "We're getting out of here right now."

In the tunnel scene, Becky is exhausted after running from the mob and falls asleep while Miles is momentarily absent. In the process she, too, becomes a pod person/emotionless zombie. Miles' realization that a moment's sleep has transformed the woman he loves into an inhuman enemy dedicated to his assimilation compels his voice-over, "I didn't know the real meaning of fear until I kissed Becky." Her "pod-scream" alerts their pursuers as he takes flight.

In what is perhaps the film's signature scene, Miles' attempt to escape from Santa Mira takes him to a busy highway at night. The frantic pace of the scene, with its cars, trucks, headlights, horns, and the angry shouts of impeded motorists, who come perilously close to running Miles down, become an objective correlative for his confused and disordered consciousness as he shouts, "You're next! You're next!"

At left, Corman regular Richard Denning (center) in *Creature with the Atom Brain.*

Low-budget professional Edward L. Cahn—whose *It! The Terror from Beyond Space* (1958) is the unofficial source for *Alien* (1979)—made two Z-budget alien-zombie movies in 1955 and 1959: *Creature with the Atom Brain* and *Invisible Invaders* respectively. The first film was written by Curt Siodmak (co-screenwriter of *I Walked with a Zombie*) and posits the outlandish premise that an ex-Nazi scientist and a deported gangster might join forces to take revenge on their enemies by resurrecting the dead and sending them on murderous missions.

In *Invisible Invaders* aliens inhabiting the moon take over the bodies of the dead in order to compel humanity to surrender or be annihilated. In both movies the zombies are usually dressed in suits and ties, which reinforce the idea of 1950s conformism epitomized by the deification of the "man in the gray flannel suit," the corporate executive critiqued in Sloan Wilson's 1950s novel of the same name.

In *Zombies of Mora Tau* (1957) Cahn returns to the Haiti-based voodoo mythos. Cult actress Allison Hayes, later the title figure in *Attack of the 50 Foot Woman* (1958), plays Mona, wife of a vulgar gangster. Mona spends the first part of the film taunting the men on a jungle treasure-hunting expedition with both biting sarcasm and ample displays of her body. In one scene indicative of the arrogance inherent in most of Hayes' femme fatale performances, she reclines in a bathing suit and suns herself on the deck of the ship, even as a distracted crew tries to prepare the divers for a dangerous mission to retrieve a stash of diamonds. In another sequence, after her husband promises to cover her body in diamonds, she dangles her foot in the men's faces and says provocatively, "Now what would I do with diamonds on my toes?" Even after she is kidnapped by the zombies, a

point at which the audience might think that this predatory female is about to receive her come-uppance, she gets herself declared queen of these zombies and leads them in an attack against her former comrades.

Low-budget auteur Reginald Le Borg, whose string of off-beat movies began with *Weird Woman* (1944), based his *Voodoo Island* (1957) on the performance of veteran zombie-film star Boris Karloff. As the supercilious and sardonic scientist Dr. Knight, Karloff's character arrives in the South Seas to debunk several local reports of zombie-ism for his book and television show. He also assists business-tycoon Howard Carlton (Owen Cunningham) in his attempt to "colonize" another island and turn it into a resort for the privileged.

In the first scene even after he confronts a "living zombie," who was one of the men sent to explore the island by Carlton, Knight pooh-poohs the superstition of the new exploratory team that he has arrived with and the core beliefs of the island natives. When in flight to another island, the plane loses its signal mysteriously and almost crashes, there is still no reason to worry. In Le Borg's world view Knight is the ultimate rationalist, who refuses to admit the existence of forces he cannot measure scientifically.

Genre veterans Elisha Cook, Jr. (at left as Martin Schuyler) and Boris Karloff (adjacent as Phillip Knight) looking sunburned and seedy in *Voodoo Island*.

Only after he witnesses man-eating plants devouring humans and voodoo dolls that transform men into zombies (or, as in the case of the avaricious landowner Schuyler, push them to their deaths) does Knight accept that something seriously off-kilter might be happening. In an unusually progressive scene for the era, Knight confesses to the tribal chief (Friedrich von Ledebur), who has used his powers as a shaman to protect his people from the relentless expansion of Western civilization, that he has been wrong in backing the politics of colonialism. After a promise to discourage Carlton from expanding the development to the island, he leads the survivors of his exploratory team back home.

In *The Disembodied* (1957) Allison Hayes again showcases her eroticism—and her dancing skills—as the voodoo priestess Tonda, who finds herself married to an impotent, aging doctor incapable of fulfilling her sexual or emotional needs. Rather than killing her husband outright, the frustrated Tonda performs various rituals that include dances in revealing leopard-skin outfits. Her ultimate goal is slowly torturing her husband to death then turning him into zombie as she has done to several other ex-lovers. Into this domestic nightmare marches virile Tom Maxwell (Paul Burke) who becomes the new object of Tonda's unsated desires. Tonda is eventually undone by one of her own followers, a jealous native girl who stabs the voodoo queen to death.

Night of the Ghouls (1959) is another film maudit by the legendary Ed Wood, Jr. *Night* was made in the same spurt of creative incompetence that resulted in the much more "celebrated" *Plan 9 from Outer Space* (begun earlier but also completed for release in 1959) featuring a resurrected police Inspector Dan Clay (Tor Johnson). *Night of the Ghouls* has zombies rising from the grave to bury alive the bogus medium Dr. Acula (Kenne Duncan), who

Above, the tortured Tor Johnson in *Plan 9 from Outer Space*.
Below, a less tortured "Dead One" John Carlton (John McKay) in *Blood of the Zombies*.

disturbed their sleep. Tor Johnson takes another zombie turn as Lobo, in this mish-mash of characters with names inspired by vampires and werewolves and monsters that spring from a supernatural con game gone wackily awry.

The Dead One (*Blood of the Zombies,* 1961) attempts to underscore its zombie foundations by situating its story in New Orleans and the bayous, a center for voodoo second only to Haiti. The film exploits the jazz and storied decadence of Louisiana to give the film some atmosphere. But the performance of Linda Ormond as the blonde priestess who resurrects her dead brother to short-circuit the attempt of a male relative to inherit the family land does not remind one of an Austen heroine. In a movie where most of the actors and their characters share the same first names, the Z- (and that is not for zombie)-budget enterprise barely rises above the level of an Ed Wood epic.

In *Doctor Blood's Coffin* (1961) an amoral doctor (who maintains a veneer of caring about his patients) experiments in a small Cornish town on freezing victims with the South American poison *curare* then reviving the dead with harvested organs. Shot back to back with *Snake Woman* (1961) and one of the earliest titles in the long filmography of Canadian-born director Sidney J. Furie, long before he helmed A-projects at Universal in the mid-1970s, *Doctor Blood's Coffin* is from a story and screenplay by another B-horror director Nathan Juran and also features Irish-born mainstream actor Kieron Moore as Dr. Peter Blood. Something of a victim of its own lurid advertising campaign, this movie is a serious variant on the themes of vivisection and reanimation originated in *Frankenstein*. Like the more celebrated doctor/experimenter, Blood finally succeeds only to be done in by the local town bum and a decomposing zombie corpse.

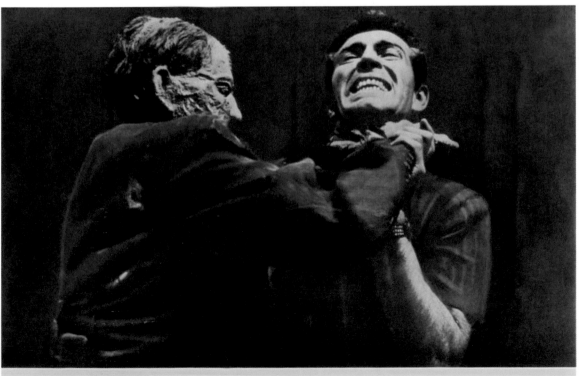

KIERON MOORE
HAZEL COURT·IAN HUNTER·Directed by SIDNEY J. FURIE
Produced by GEORGE FOWLER·A Canadian Production·Released thru UNITED ARTISTS

"The Case of M. Valdemar," based on the story by E.A. Poe, is an episode of the omnibus *Tales of Terror* (1962) directed by Roger Corman. It opens with a scene of mesmerism. Red, blue, and yellow lights cast by a revolving lantern pass rhythmically over a tight close-up of the face of M. Valdemar (Vincent Price). This close-up is intercut with matching shots of the hypnotist Carmichael (Basil Rathbone), who repeats in monotone the chant-like instructions that are to alleviate Valdemar's suffering, temporarily at least. For Valdemar's affliction is a terminal brain tumor. After entrusting his beautiful wife Helene (Debra Paget) to his friend Dr. James (David Frankham), Valdemar gives himself over to Carmichael who has promised to ease the pain of his transition to the "afterlife" through mesmerism.

But Carmichael has his own agenda: he wants to extend his control over the mind of Valdemar and capture the body of Helene. So after Valdemar's physical being expires peacefully, his mind stays under Carmichael's control. In that way he forces Valdemar to consent from the grave to a marriage to Helene. As with most of Corman's characters who "play God," punishment is not far behind. The

Vincent Price as M. Valdemar melts in *Tales of Terror* while his horrified wife (Debra Paget) looks on.

constant moaning of Carmichael's victim begins to wear down the mesmerist. As he sits at the writing table below, Valdemar's anguish reverberates from the bedroom above him. And when Carmichael finally physically presses his affections onto Helene, his power over Valdemar breaks and the outraged zombie rises from his bed, skin blue, hands frozen, and walks stilted but still capable of attacking and strangling the mesmerist. Once he does, Valdemar's body begins to decay until it is a "mass of putrescence."

I Eat Your Skin (*Zombies*, 1964) is a low-budget zombie movie shot in Florida (which stands in for a Caribbean island). A scientist discovers a cure for cancer drawn from the venom of snakes. Unfortunately it has a side effect as it turns his patients into zombies. And of course an evildoer tries to force the hapless scientist to raise an army of zombies to conquer the world. Another grade-Z effort from the mid-60s, this picture is perhaps best remembered for its reissue by aptly named schlockmeiste Jerry Gross on a double bill of ghastly gastronomy with *I Drink Your Blood*.

Opposite top, the jealous and avaricious Dr. Arrowsmith (Paul Muller) tortures his wife Muriel (Barbara Steele) and her paramour.

Below, although the disfigured Muriel makes a zombie-like, corporeal return, she also embroils her blonde sister Jenny in her revenge scheme.

In 1965 British cult actor Barbara Steele made one of the most sadistic horror films of her career: *The Lovers of the Outer Tomb* (aka *Gli amanti d'oltretumba*, *The Faceless Monster*, *Nightmare Castle*). As she has done several times in her career, Steele plays two characters. The first is Muriel, the verbally abusive and unfaithful wife of the sadistic scientist Dr. Arrowsmith (Paul Muller). After several scenes in which Muriel belittles her impotent husband, he pretends to leave on a journey. Instead he remains and witnesses his wife cheating on him with her lusty gardener David (Rik Battaglia). An enraged Arrowsmith drugs the couple and then takes them to his dungeon. There in a series of Inquisition-style tortures, he turns them into bloodied pulps. This long sequence of torture culminates in his electrocution of the couple as they lie in each other's arms in their bed of blood.

In order to secure his wife's fortune as well as relive the obsession he still carries for the virago Muriel, he marries her twin—the blonde-haired and mentally unstable Jenny. Locked in a double bind, the doctor alternates between amorous episodes with Jenny, who is slowly taking on the personality traits of Muriel, and attempts to disturb her mental stability by reinforcing her belief that her sister is haunting her.

In the final sequence we learn that her now disfigured and spectral sister, along with her lover-slave David, have somehow returned from the grave and are seeking revenge. Seemingly as beautiful as ever with her long black hair concealing one side of her face, Muriel approaches her husband, who becomes aroused as she tells him, "You taught me the pleasure of torture." Revealing her full face and her hideous disfigurement, she pushes him into a restraining device and begins torturing him. Laughing demonically, she then burns him alive, bringing this tale to its sadistic conclusion.

Hammer Studios was primarily responsible for reviving the vampire genre with its *Dracula* series in the 1960s. As with the independent *White Zombie*, Hammer attempted to apply its successful Dracula formula onto the zombie genre with *The Plague of the Zombies* (1966). A small village in Cornwall experiences an outbreak of mysterious deaths and resurrections. Dr. James Forbes (Andre Morell)—a surrogate version of *Dracula*'s Van Helsing—responding to the petulant urgings of his spunky daughter Sylvia (Diane Clare)—the Mina surrogate—heads for Cornwall to help his former student, Dr. Peter Tompson (Brook Williams), who is overwhelmed by the titled plague.

Forbes and his daughter encounter a cabal of voodoo practitioners on the road. This group of decadent, upper-class roués pursue and corner a fox, much as they will with Sylvia as their prey later in the movie. Rampaging through town they carelessly disrupt a funeral, knocking the coffin off onto

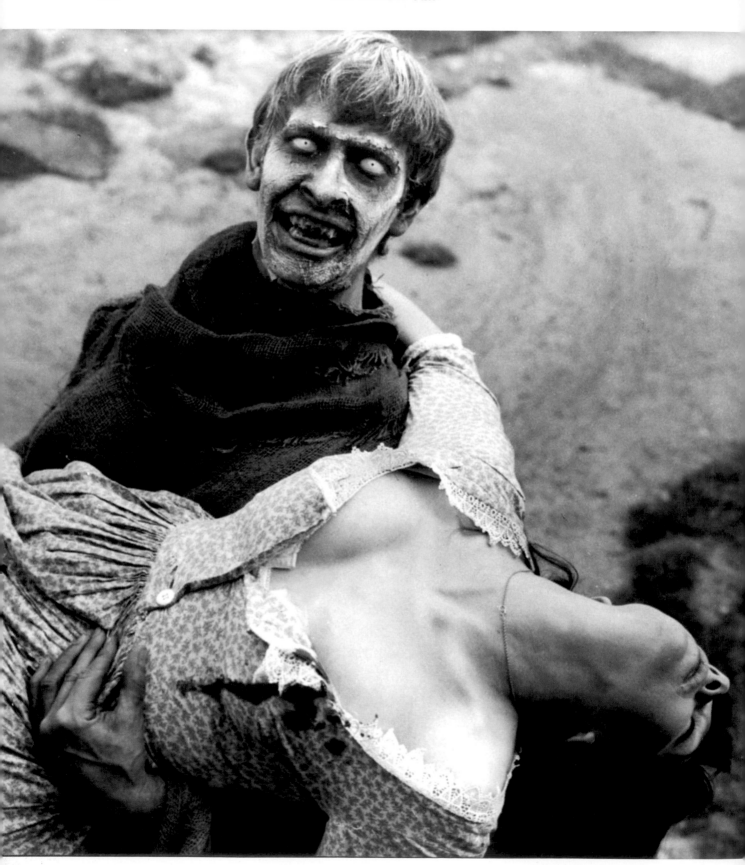

the road, thereby revealing to Dr. Forbes the form of a zombie.

Sylvia and her father find that Tompson has descended into depression and alcoholism, even as his wife Alice (Jacqueline Pearce)—the Lucy surrogate—shows evidence of possible affliction through her lethargy and anemia. During a voodoo ceremony overseen by the zombie master Squire Clive Hamilton (John Carson)—the Dracula surrogate—Alice leaves her bed and "sleepwalks" towards his mansion. Before she reaches her goal, she is attacked and killed. The climax of this attack is witnessed by the inquisitive Sylvia.

After consulting books on witchcraft and voodoo and performing an autopsy on Alice's body, Forbes comes to the conclusion that dead villagers are being transformed into zombies. His diagnosis is confirmed when Alice's body is exhumed and she turns into a decomposing zombie before

Plague of the Zombies: opposite, pre-cursor of Romero-type zombie and his hapless victim. Below, Sylvie (Diane Clare) brings her father Dr. Forbes (André Morell, right) and Local Dr. Thompson (Brook Williams, left) to the corpse of Thomson's wife Alice (Jacqueline Pearce).

Above, one of the group of grisly figures (apparently "Norman Ward") rising.

the eyes of Forbes and her husband Tompson. In a reworking of the destruction of Lucy in *Dracula*, Forbes decapitates Alice, while Tompson faints in horror.

During a nightmare sequence, Tompson imagines himself threatened by a group of grisly figures rising from their graves. In a scene that closely foreshadows Romero's vision of a zombie plague, the group of decomposing corpses emerges from the ground and surrounds Tompson.

The climax and resolution of the film occurs in Hamilton's mansion and the nearby tin mine in which he employs the zombies as worker slaves. Hamilton has by now used his charisma and blood ritual to seduce Sylvia as he did Alice. Hamilton lures her to his ceremony as a sacrifice and Sylvia marches off in a trance to the mine where the ritual (in costuming and accoutrements that appear more West African than Haitian) is proceeding. Meanwhile her father searches the mansion and while fighting off and killing one of Hamilton's henchmen, he accidentally starts a fire which burns the voodoo effigies of the zombies. As these are consumed, the zombies in the mine begin to combust spontaneously. After Tompson and Forbes accomplish the rescue of Sylvia just before the sac-

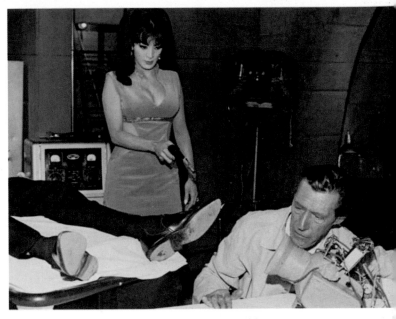

rifice, the flames from the zombies spread to the mill and burn it to the ground. As with horror tales and movies in general, purification through fire to remove the stain of evil from the world acts a trope in this fiery resolution.

Ted V. Mikel's *The Astro Zombies* (1968) features the cult icon Tura Satana (best known for 1965's *Faster, Pussycat! Kill! Kill!*) who, like Barbara Steele in *The Lovers of thc Outer Tomb* and Allison Hayes in her two zombie movies, is a proto-feminist character. She controls the erotic and horrific discourse of the movie whenever she appears, most often costumed in her personally designed Asian-style silk dresses slit well up a bare thigh. Satana is no simpering 1950s female-in-dis-

Tura Santana menaces John Carradine in *The Astro Zombies.*

tress common to horror and science fiction films of the period. Rather Satana gives her own name to the character of an Asian foreign agent intent on uncovering the secret of producing robotic zombies. "I am Satana and you must obey my commands" is her final line as she is electrocuted by one of the stray robotic zombies. Her desire to know the secret of their zombie state is as much for her own sake as for her government's. For she desires a zombie army of her own. In fact she complains several times that her own "servants," an effeminate psychotic who dresses impeccably and a foreign thug whom she humiliates and slaps around to keep in line, are not "subservient" enough.

Most often it is Satana who has to do the killing in the movie, smiling sadistically as she shoots victims repeatedly, the camera at a low angle enhancing her stature and voluptuous figure. Her final confrontation with the idealistic scientist (played solidly by an aging John Carradine), whose zombie experiments have spun out of control, compels her to take out a small horde of zombies before she can dispatch the recalcitrant scientist. Only a thousand-volt electrical charge can immobilize this "force of nature."

Even as mostly low-budget and/or exploitation filmmakers in the United States and England developed some new aspects of the zombie movie, underlying interest among filmgoers would still only support a limited number of releases. By the end of the decade, the genre was stagnant. About to be culled from these unappetizing waters by a group of young filmmakers based in Pittsburgh, Pennsylvania, were a confluence of narrative elements that would revitalize it.

I Am Legend
by RICHARD MATHESON

Of Beginnings and Bloodlines: Richard Matheson's Stake in Zombie History
by John Edgar Browning

In 2012, the Horror Writers Association presented Richard Matheson's 1954 *I Am Legend* with the "Vampire Novel of the Century Award," the first honor of its kind ever given. The novel's first years alone saw at least four American editions, and at least three international editions, but that's only a small part of the story. Indeed, the "Century Award" has less to do with *I Am Legend*'s print (and film) history and more to do with the "vampire" novel's profound influence on a different, but related, subgenre: zombies. Matheson's novel—more precisely, Matheson's *vampires*—broke utterly from tradition when they discarded many of the tropes on which literary vampires of the previous century had so depended, figures "derived from folklore but now bearing precious little resemblance to them," observes Paul Barber in *Vampires, Burial, and Death: Folklore and Reality* (Yale University Press, 1988). Instead, Matheson's un-dead would resemble the much older, pre-literary "revenant" of Central and Eastern Europe. Far removed from Europe's more "civilized" capitals, the revenant was, in general, the less-than-romantic corpse of a local villager, one who, after returning from the grave, proceeded to attack his family and neighbors in their homes at night. *I Am Legend* comes to us much in this same vein; however, the similarities between the 1954 novel and cinematic zombie pictures preceding it decidedly end there. The "proto-strain" of zombie films leading up to Matheson's conception, famously with *White Zombie*, portrays a distant, geographically isolated, and relatively surmountable (that is, single or few) zombie threat, much like its Eastern European cousin the revenant. Matheson's zombie-vampires (vampire-zombies?), on the other hand, abandon altogether this earlier design and, in doing so, help to birth the more familiar breed of zombie we recognize today.

While *I Am Legend* is perhaps the first work of fiction to graft dystopian elements onto the vampire and zombie mythos, the novel's principal narratological features generally go unnoted by scholars and enthusiasts. Indeed, it is Matheson's novel that forever infuses the zombie with mob-like tendencies; after *I Am Legend*, the zombie (singular or few) becomes *zombies* (an insurmountable, "multiple threat"), a new, heightened quality which began appearing on movie screens almost immediately following the novel's publication, one of the earliest examples being 1957's *Zombies of Mora Tau*.

Equally notable, the setting in Matheson's novel is an inversion of classical Gothic space and geography. That is, the central "threat" in the story is re-located around, rather than inside, the Gothic edifice or enclosure. These two features help *I Am Legend* over the next half a century to rake in three major motion pictures, beginning with the release nu American International Pictures of *The Last Man on Earth* (1964), starring Vincent Price, followed by Warner Bros. and their *The Omega Man* (1971), starring Charlton Heston, and 2007's *I Am Legend* starring Will Smith, and even a low-budget, straight-to-video picture with *I Am Omega* (2007), starring Mark Dacascos. This first strain of "straight" filmic adaptations attests to the enduring narrative framework of Matheson's novel, but what's more striking is Matheson's use of recognizably domestic qualities to distinguish his zombie-vampires from their more foreign brethren in the Caribbean. In doing so, Matheson in effect de-orientalizes the figure of the zombie by relocating it from its previously exotic locale to American suburbia where he merges the zombie with the bodies and faces of families, friends, and neighbors.

By the late-1960s, however, Matheson's novel helps to engender a vastly larger "second strain" of zombie narratives, a body of films that has become, by comparison, culturally and socio-politically more prolific than the "straight" filmic adaptations of the first strain. George Romero's *Night of the Living Dead* and sequel *Dawn of the Dead* (1978) have become the zombie films proper of the second strain, precisely because they signal a body of films that is consistent with, yet has mutated considerably from, Matheson's original narrative. Studies have often examined the business end of Romero's low-budget reconfiguration of the zombie archetype and its impact on subsequent zombie pictures, but narratologically his film achieves much more than this. Few writers, beyond "generally acknowledging Romero's indebtedness to Matheson," writes Deborah Christie in *Better off Dead: The Evolution of the Zombie as Post-Human*, have probed "this connection beyond assuming that it begins and ends with the obvious visual cues of the shuffling, blank-eyed dead banging on the doors and windows of a house, trying to get in and eat the inhabitants." Indeed, the second strain, which is first initiated by Romero's film, has consistently preserved two essential Mathesonian elements that have since defined nearly every zombie narrative since the late 1960s.

The first of these elements is Matheson's "multiple threat" (a term I borrow from the work of Gregory A. Waller). The second, and least recognized of these elements, is what I refer to as the "survival space," that is, the central enclosure in *I Am Legend* in which Neville—the world's only survivor—is forced to defend, fortify, and survive. It should be noted, however, that while the preservation of these essential elements of Matheson's work may be what founded the second strain, it's the creative license Romero took that has inevitably allowed the second strain to continue to speak to us through its numerous cinematic retellings.

In particular, *Night of the Living Dead*'s "survival space" is one in which a small group of survivors simultaneously occupies and defends against the "multiple threat" outside. Resulting from this minor alteration by Romero to Matheson's formula is an enclosure that has proven to be more socially and politically volatile and, by all accounts, more entertaining. While few critics point out that the zombie *en masse* in fact began with Matheson, scarcely is it acknowledged that the "survival space," too, is his conception, perhaps because critics rarely feel inclined to treat the predominantly monolithic construction of the "survival space" in the first strain—after all, it's just Neville occupying it.

However, the most significant elements here—the indiscriminate and voracious nature of the zombie-vampires' hunger and their advanced decompositional state, the impossibly vast numbers by which they threaten humanity, and the "survival space," whose occupant must fortify in order to protect the enclosure from what is "outside," coping all the while with a bleak sense of disparity and hopelessness—are distinctly Matheson's. On the other hand, what is unquestionably Romero's, and indeed the reason for the second strain's continued endurance, is the way in which he reconfigures the "survival space" through the introduction of multiple characters into its interior, transforming it, in effect, into a more socially dynamic and potentially turbulent space. The multi—rather than singly—defended "survival space" introduced in *Night of the Living Dead* has not only afforded the second

Opposite and left, *Night of the Living Dead*: Romero's version of Neville, Ben, uses fire and retreats within his survival space.

strain its longevity but, more crucially, seems to anticipate in its design and what Tony Williams in *The Cinema of George Romero: Knight of the Living Dead* calls "Romero's later attacks on the government/military/media, and scientific establishments." Thus, Romero's reconfigured "survival space" continues to lend the second strain its most fundamentally entertaining and dramatic qualities.

By the 1990s, the second strain's porosity and versatility even incites cross-pollinations with the video gaming industry. Thus emerge "survival horror" video game titles, whose players are tasked with reaching the end, finding a way out, working together, or simply surviving. In *The Living and the Undead: From Stoker's Dracula to Romero's Dawn of the Dead*, Gregory A. Waller places great importance on how normalcy is represented in the survival loci of zombie pictures once they are rendered safe again by their respective survival group. Here, "what is most important in and to the world" is defined. Waller holds that binding these narratives most often is "the threat posed by the undead and the defensive and retaliatory action undertaken by the living." It is in such narratives, he adds, that "the living must act to survive the threat posed by the undead, and through their actions in this life-or-death confrontation they demonstrate humankind's capabilities."

For Waller, resolution is here central: the ideological and psychological dimensions potentialed by the "destruction of the undead" and the "resumption of normality," as well as questions of whether or not "normality is worth saving or resuming," offer the second strain almost infinite socio-cultural flexibility. Thus, while Romero would be nothing without Matheson's design, Matheson's design would be far less remembered, and the zombie far

less potent a figure today, were it not for Romero's ingenuity.

Romero's *The Crazies.*

Chapter Four

Romero Reinvents the Zombie Film

They were dead souls...and you couldn't be bothered to pay attention to these zombies. Now their offspring ignore you, a fire that you did not make, lights and warms them. You keep your distance, furtive, in the dark, numb: your turn has come, and in the shadows from which another dawn will emerge, you find that you yourselves are now the zombies.

Jean-Paul Sartre
Preface to *Les Damnés de la Terre*

I. Slouching Towards Pittsburgh [co-written by Paolo Durazzo]

As many if not most of those reading are likely already aware, with the 1968 release of *Night of the Living Dead*, writer/director George A. Romero dramatically redefined the zombie film genre. For a genre that had always been multifaceted in terms of how zombies came to be but had never found a plot-line or single hit movie that rivaled the popularity of vampires, ghosts, or even were-wolves, Romero revived a moribund concept by expanding the "rules" about what it was to be a zombie. Over the course of almost two decades, pulling key constructs from various antecedents, most notably from Richard Matheson's novel *I Am Legend* and the post-nuclear science fiction/horror films of his youth, Romero subverted and modernized the graphic depiction and social symbolism of "the zombie."

Romero had struggled to survive as an independent filmmaker in the Pittsburgh, Pennsylvania, area, after attending Carnegie Mellon. This provided the aspiring filmmaker scant opportunities in the film industry. One essential moment was directing a segment for *Mister Roger's Neighborhood*, where Romero captured the show's titular host undergoing a tonsillectomy. Perhaps emboldened after probing Rogers' throat, Romero plunged into the horror world of *Night of the Living Dead*; but commercial success was certainly not overnight. One of the most horrific aspects of their ultra-low-budget first feature—the filmmakers, with two of the actors also producing, cobbled together a

budget just over $100,000, less than the Halperin Brothers had in 1932 when adjusted for 1968 consumer price index—was trying to keep others from siphoning off most of the profits.

Although the list of Romero-directed zombie feature films is certainly longer than any other filmmaker's; it stretched over more than four decades from *Night of the Living Dead* in 1968 to *The Crazies* (1973), *Dawn of the Dead* (1978), *Day of the Dead* (1985), followed by a twenty year hiatus from feature-length treatments to *Land of the Dead* (2005), *Diary of the Dead* (2007), and *Survival of the Dead* (2009).

Above and below, Barbra (Judith O'Dea) and her brother Johnny (Russell Streiner) arrive at the cemetery where he mocks her unease: "They're coming to get you, Barbra!"

Compelled by limited funds to espouse hard-core auteurism (besides directing and co-writing, he also photographed and edited), Romero expanded the horror subgenre with brutally graphic, socially reflexive, and cannibalistic twists. As noted in the first chapter, prior to Romero, film zombies existed in two forms: either solo mindless creatures or collective herds; both of which were centrally controlled

by an external force. The solo mindless creatures were often resurrected dead based on variants of the Haitian myth. They were conjured by a witch doctor (or doctoress) or some evil power that brought the dead back as soulless bodies capable of little more than clumsily scuffling forward in an apathetic existence, until commanded to do abominable deeds from *White Zombie* through *I Walked with a Zombie* with side-trips involving mad scientists and/or Nazi schemers through the postwar and atomic age. Even as these collective herds crossed over into 1950s science fiction, even as they got organized in their methods of systematically infiltrating, corrupting, and assimilating people in movies such as *Invasion of the Body Snatchers*, the zombie never found its core identity.

From the first, Romero presents his zombie uprising as a metaphor for the social unrest rife in the youth of the 1960s. The national unease left over from the 1950s Red scares and nightmares about the nuclear holocaust was heavy in everyone's daily lives. Nightly the nation watched newscasts overflowing with 16mm footage of American troops fighting in

Above, a horrified Barbra retreats from the sight of the first of countless Romero-style zombies to follow.

Below, rubber-faced actor Bill Hinzman as the ghoul that takes down Barbra's brother then sizes her up.

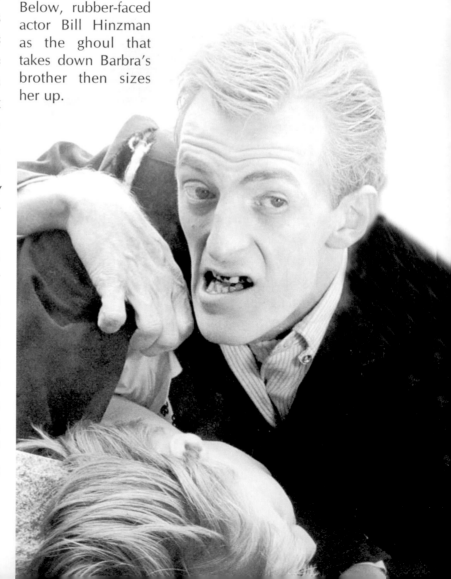

Vietnam and the backlash of protestors here at home. A loss of control and fractured understanding between generations, as well as the technical advent of smaller cameras and faster film stock, created a fertile ground for both independent filmmakers and social metaphors to flourish.

The milieu from which Romero introduces the new zombies is far removed from Lugosi leading his crew through the Caribbean cane fields and the schlocky experimenter sitting at a table of beakers and bubbling flasks. Romero recruits the chiaroscuro techniques of noir movies for a darker and more realistic approach. Most of *Night of the Living Dead* is hand held, so that the shaky, jagged-edge feel of cinema vérité stylistically reinforces the reality of its outlandish events. The stark shadows and Dutch angles in gritty black-and-white photography are eerily similar to the newsreel footage airing daily on television.

In *Night of the Living Dead,* as its title simply and starkly suggests, the viewer is thrown into a world hours after the dead have started re-animating as Barbra (Judith O'Dea) and Johnny (Russell Streiner—also one of the producers of the film) encounter the first zombie at the grave site of their father. It is here that that famous line, "They're coming to get you, Barbra!" is uttered by her brother Johnny as a joke. Within minutes, the two are attacked by the first unnamed zombie (Bill Hinzman). After witnessing her brother's demise, Barbra is forced to flee, making her way to a house on the outskirts of the cemetery. There she meets up with male protagonist Ben (Duane Jones), the first in a series of quasi-heroic figures in Romero zombie films who happen to be African-American. It turns out there are several additional humans hiding in the basement below. Father Harry (Karl Hadman), mother Helen (Marilyn Eastman), and their injured daughter Karen (Kyra Schon), who has been bitten by a zombie, as well as the young couple Tom (Keith Wayne) and Judy (Judith Ridley). The set-up is quick and uncomplicated: strangers fighting to survive an unimaginable assault, barricaded inside a far-from-impregnable structure, while Orson Wellesian *War of the Worlds* style radio broadcasts play in the background.

After those already inside begrudgingly accept Ben and Barbara, the group comes to terms with the car-

Left, Barbra framed within the clautrophoic confines of the house. As was the strategy of the Lewton unit at RKO, low-key lighting creates atmosphere and conceals the budgetary limits of set dressing.

Opposite, a low-budget zombie horde.

nage around them. We are informed that the Venus probe (in reference to 1962's Mariner 2) sent out to space has somehow returned and crashed somewhere in the Northeast, presumably contaminating the area with a mysterious radiation. Reports start to spread of marauding bands of mindless killers wandering in search of victims. The killers all seem to be dead, and while the mechanics of how they came back to life may not be clear, their singular purpose and overweening impulse certainly is to seize normal humans and eat their flesh. As had been variously depicted as the result of bites from vampires and/or werewolves, Romero posits that anyone who dies from a zombie attack will quickly reanimate as a zombie.

The only way to kill the zombie, referred to as a "ghoul," is a heavy blow or bullet to the head: "Kill the brain to kill the ghoul," the first iteration of a basic tenet that still holds true for the majority of modern zombies in movies, TV, literature, and comic books.

As the exponentially increasing number of ghouls gather in greater, ghastly force and pick off the characters one by one, the group learns there are rescue centers and an escape attempt might succeed. Tom and Judy attempt to procure a vehicle and are burned to death, which provides barbeque for the ravenous flesh-eaters. In one particularly shocking moment, Romero has Mother Helen descend to the cellar at precisely the moment that her daughter Karen has turned and begun feasting on Daddy Harry. Understandingly shocked and slow to react, Helen is then repeatedly stabbed by her own child with a garden tool, in ominous homage to such 1960s shock classics as Alfred Hitchcock's *Psycho*. Immediately after, another family member, Johnny from the beginning of the film, "comes to get" his sister Barbra, pulling her into the clutching zombie collective. Concurrent with these events is the continuous feed of reports from the outside world on the living room television about attempts to suppress the hordes of undead. Makeshift militias comprised of the local constabulary augmented by "redneck" volunteers follow the zombie trails with German-

Below, in the basement of the Cooper house are Father Harry (Karl Hadman), Mother Helen (Marilyn Eastman), and their injured daughter Karen (Kyra Schon).

Opposite, even low-budget filmmakers could afford to add graphic and sensational violence: Romero uses light to vignette the image of death by putty knife.

shepherd dogs and roam the roads with shotguns and hunting rifles intent on taking down every last ghoul. Embedded with one group led by a cigar-chomping police chief are a reporter and cameraman, armed only with a 16mm Eyemo but set to record the action as the zombie hunters take down their prey.

At the movie's end Ben is holed up in the basement and awakened by the gun shots and barking dogs of the militia. Hopeful that help is at hand, Ben moves out to meet the group only to be mistaken for a zombie and shot in the head. This bleak ending is made even more horrifying with the use of still images: the all White militia finding his body, swinging meat hooks into his lifeless carcass, dragging him out, and dumping him on a bonfire. These mimic contemporary newspaper photos that capture the White-on-Black violence and racial unrest of the late 1960s. Like many television viewers in 1968 who watched violent scenes from a Memphis motel balcony (the MLK assassination) to the kitchen of the Ambassador Hotel in Los Angeles (the RFK assassination) to Chicago's Grant Park (the 1968 Democratic Convention riots) to the revolutionary demonstrations in most capital cities of Europe, Romero intends for his audience to be left numb by the death of all the protagonists and by the vision of violence in the movie's final and markedly non-preternatural act of killing.

Night of the Living Dead clearly expresses Romero's response to the civil turmoil of the time. As commentary on the government's hubristic expansionism, exemplified by the war in Vietnam as well as the space/arms race with Russia, the filmmakers reflect the views of the civil rights movement and war protestors alike. The lead protagonist Ben, a Black man who took charge of the group with empathy, organized the plan of action, and survived the onslaught of dead would in a mainstream Hollywood movie more often than not be victorious. With grim irony, Romero deconstructs his triumph and brings him down by a bullet from White vigilantes that mirrors the assassination of Dr. Martin Luther King a few months prior to the film's release. As a 1960s independent, many

years and wars removed from the Halperin brothers, Romero recasts the horror genre and its zombie sub-set to denounce the dominant culture of the time. The authoritative older white males in charge, responsible for sending the Venus Probe into space, initiate a chain of events inciting the zombie menace and the demise of so many innocents.

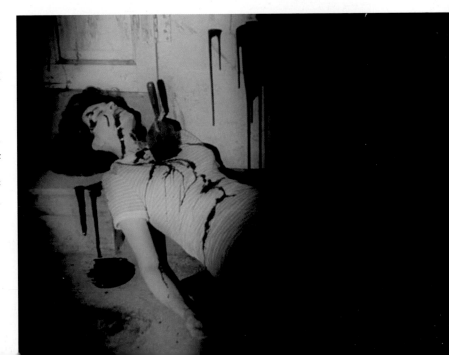

If there is an ultimate irony embedded in the drama of *Night of the Living Dead*, it is its profoundly unromantic core and anti-heroic posture. As they fight for their lives, the makeshift group inside the house represents the same struggle for survival which has been dramatized from human prehistory. No matter how they are brought down, whether swept away by the flood of ravenous undead or shot "between the eyes" by misguided rescuers, the last victims become mere detritus thrown onto a fire of anonymous corpses. On the one hand, the movie celebrates their desperate and doomed stand. On the other, the final statement of *Night of the Living Dead* echoes that of a "serious" film like the Masaki Kobayashi/Shinobu Hashimoto *Hara-kiri* (1964) where the remnants of one man's defiance of convention are swept up and discarded. Whether the protagonists died valiantly or ignobly, the result is the same, as all the dead are consumed by the flames and reduced to unnamed ashes.

Below, when thrown together to fight a common enemy, men of different races learn to work together. Ben (Duane Jones) keeps watch while Tom (Keith Wayne) works the gas pump.

By the time of his fourth full-length movie, *The Crazies* (1973), Romero had almost three times the budget (still a modest total, just under $300,000) and could afford color film stock and hiring someone other than himself as director of photography. The result of the latter was a rather flat-lit and garish Kodachrome look—the blood is no longer gray/black but bright red, almost orange—that again gave the overall movie a documentary or home-movie feel. Again using mostly handheld and appropriate tight close shots, the visual style was reasonably well integrated. But without more money for cast, Romero was again limited to local talent; and the best that Pittsburgh had to offer —Evans City, Pennsylvania, where the movie was shot is 30 miles to the north—more than occasionally resulted in wooden performances.

This is not to say that *The Crazies* is without interest in terms of its plot and staging. The pre-title opening sequence, in which two children watch as their father wreaks havoc inside the house with a crowbar and ultimately sets it on fire, is carefully constructed to draw the viewer into their point of view and add dramatic impact to the anomalous behavior of the semi-zombie-fied parent. It could be argued that *The Crazies* is not a zombie movie at all, that the strain of micro-organism which unhinges many of the town folk had nothing to do with zombie powders or voodoo or radiation from space. That makes its narrative more akin to the best-selling sci-fi novel and its studio

Above, *The Crazies* shot in Evans City, Pennsylvania.

Above, prologue from *The Crazies*: two children watch their father destroy the house.

adaptation, *The Andromeda Strain* (novel, 1969; film, 1971); and its infection is like the rabies virus. But this is a George Romero film, after all, and the bite of the undead, whatever made them that way in *Night of the Living Dead*, also spreads the zombie plague like a neurotropic agent. And, of course, this form of spreading zombie-ism, by virus or infection of some sort, will as in *The Crazies* often compel that the affected area be taken over by men in haz-mat suits and masks carrying automatic weapons. The plague, both literal and figurative, became the dominant source for the "disorder" in most zombie films within a decade and continues to this day with the recent novel (2006) and mega-budget film adaptation (2013) *World War Z.*

Romero still includes the political rhetoric of five years earlier. Like Vietnamese villagers the population of Evans City arms itself to oppose the occupying military force. When the local priest immolates himself, it is staged and photographed to recall the self-immolation of Buddhist monk Thich Quang Duc in protest of the Diem regime 1963 Saigon. There are bravura sequences that shock and surprise, as when a benign-looking old lady with a sweet smile kills a soldier by repeatedly plunging her knitting needle into his body and through the eye-glass in his gas mask, so that patches of red blood spread across his white haz-mat suit. But for every moment like this, there are a dozen others that miss the mark.

While not acting as DP on *The Crazies,* Romero still stages for maximum visual impact on a limited budget.

Ten years after *Night of the Living Dead,* with a still modest budget of just over half a million dollars but still many times what he had for his first foray into zombieland, *Dawn of the Dead* (1978) ratchets up the flesh-eating fervor and eviscerative carnage and continues to push against the stereotypes of contemporary mainstream cinema.

Romero not only permits his later zombies more agility but also permits them a vague awareness of and existential anguish over their past days as normal people. As they return in zombie mode and frequent familiar places from their human past, there is at least a semblance of conscious recollections, of memories however dim from of their own lives, which is quite different than the more elemental creatures in *Night of the Living Dead.* Romero also exploits the special make-up prowess of Tom Savini. With sanguine squibbing and flesh ripping that throws body parts all over the screen, Romero and Savini build on the gore effects of earlier 1970s films from *The Exorcist* (1973) to Dario Argento's *Suspiria* (1977).

Ten years after the release of *Night of the Living Dead* also means post-Vietnam and Watergate, post-Medicare, the civil rights act, and an après-Nixon reconstitution of attempts at the great society. But although the contemporary political scene for the third zombie film and second of the "Dead" titles is different, the social ideals of Romero's youth still resonate. Long lines at the gas pumps and a still wide chasm between the have and have-nots underlie the narrative arc of *Dawn of the Dead*. Any new "Barbra" could be liberated by the women's movement as well as by the sexual revolution (Romero's early *Season of the Witch*—1972— had already explored feminist themes). Romero expands on these themes while taking the time to create more naturalistic relationships between the four featured protagonists. Again, he places his characters in a confined and isolated space but one that reflects their desire (and that of a consumerist society as a whole) for upward mobility: an upscale suburban mall.

Dawn of the Dead is not a direct sequel to the original but more of an adjunct. The first frame is a deep blood-red 1970s shag carpet. The camera pulls back to reveal Francine (Gaylen Ross) slumped over, exhausted, in a corner of the control booth of a radio station. She awakes from a nightmare and gets up and back to work, as the whole studio is in a frenzy, feeding a stream of information about the zombie catastrophe, like those anonymous voices broadcasting in *Night of the Living Dead*. Francine's boyfriend Stephen (David Emge), a helicopter pilot, arrives to take her away from the city about to fall. The "emergency networks" are scheduled to take over broadcasting, so she agrees.

Meanwhile there is a massive police raid, led by a paramilitary force, on an apartment complex filled with Black and Latino tenants. An overzealous, racist policeman quickly escalates the engagement

Below, *Dawn of the Dead*; Stephen (David Emge) arrives to rescue Francine (Gaylen Ross).

into a shooting spree. The zombies that have been kept in locked in apartments are now free to feed. Another trigger-happy cop kicks down doors and shoots at anything moving, but he is taken out by Peter (Ken Foree), who befriends another officer, Roger (Scott H. Reiniger). After the two become allies, Roger informs Peter he knows a helicopter pilot that could get them out of the city, if he is willing to abandon his post. A one-legged preacher enters declaring that "many has died…you are stronger than us, but soon I think, they be stronger than you," which helps solidify their decision to run.

Roger leads Peter to the helicopter rendezvous point, where they discover a group of street cops trying to escape by hijacking the chopper from Francine and Stephen. The standoff is averted as the street cops take off on a boat, looking for an island to hold up on—and our four fly off. Soaring over the Pennsylvania landscape they witness the anarchy below: makeshift militias like those in *Night of the Living Dead* are comprised of part professional military personnel and part "redneck" beer-drinkers with shotguns, all of whom have itchy trigger fingers. They spot an apparently abandoned shopping mall and land to look for more supplies and equipment and sequester themselves to rest. While there they hear more about the scourge outside all around them: reports broadcast the particulars of an imaginary OEP—an Occurrence Exceedance Probability curve that is used in predicting the progression of catastrophes for insurance and contingency purposes—while the CDC in Atlanta theorizes that the "zombies" were created by an unknown viral outbreak. Despite the holocaust without, the four inside decide to sample the otherwise unaffordable delicacies offered by the mall's high-end stores: they feast on caviar and other exotic foods washed down by pricey wine. It is Peter who notices something wrong with Francine, that "she really looks sick, physically." Stephen explains that she is pregnant and suggests the mall might be just the kind of safe haven they were seeking when they took off. So they decide to barricade themselves inside by placing trucks in front of the entrances. In the process of setting these barricades, Roger gets so caught up in the run-and-gun action of blasting zombies and hot-wiring the trucks that a moment of inattention permits a dead walker to bite his arm and leg. After those wounds are tended to and the interior lockdown finished, another ghoul violently reopens Roger's leg wound. In the zombie world of Romero, the viewer must realize that his fate is sealed and a transformation into the walking dead is inevitable.

Alarmed by the attack on Roger, the group goes on a "zombie hunt" within the mall to make certain it's safe to walk around. Peter builds a camouflage wall to obscure their living area, in case unwanted people come around to plunder their resources. Once safe inside, Francine wonders aloud why the zombies hang around trying to get in. Peter responds with a Macumba tale from when his father was a missionary in Trinidad, "When there's no more room in hell, the dead will walk the Earth." Even as he ponders the reasons, Peter guzzles liquor in anticipation of having to

Above, Francine, Stephen, Peter (Ken Foree), and the wounded Roger (Scott H. Reiniger in the wheelbarrow) set out on their zombie hunt. Below, some results of their efforts.

destroy Roger once he dies and turns zombie. After Roger slowly slips away only to awaken as a saggy-skinned corpse intent on feeding, Peter does shoot his friend in the head.

Although the cool-headed African-American Peter completes the assumption of the role originated by Ben in *Night of the Living* and takes charge as the leader of the group, Francine is not like Barbra: she decides that she will not sit idly by and learns how to use a gun. The trio have a night out inside the mall, in a scene of interracial dystopia reminiscent of that in *The World, the Flesh and the Devil* (1959). Through the next few days, Francine also pushes for Stephen to teach her the basics of how to fly the helicopter. In a slightly odd turn of events, Romero anticipates his next, non-zombie movie *Knightriders* (1981) and imagines that a phalanx of well-armed and maniacal bikers spot the copter over the mall and decide to ransack the place.

The bikers break through the barricaded entrances, which permits a flood of zombies and Harleys (but no zombies on Harleys) to pour into the mall and ignite both a firefight and feeding frenzy. Rather than focusing on the undead, Stephen starts blasting at the motorcycle marauders and is shot by one of them as he enters an elevator. He manages to crawl out partially through the trap door atop of the elevator, only to have the doors spring open to admit a swarm of ghouls who assault his dangling legs. Since the bikers are disorganized and careless, this allows the plodding

Below, a Hare Krishna zombie: in Romero's sardonic vision of an egalitatian apocalypse, no one is immune from the zombie plague.

Opposite, the hungry ghouls swarm into the elevator.

zombies to gain the upper hand. A freshly turned Stephen heads towards the living quarters, leads his new zombie pals through the false wall, and makes his way towards Francine and Peter.

The ending is only slightly less bleak than *Night of Living Dead.* With the dead in pursuit, the last two humans reach the chopper and Francine prepares to put her flying lessons to use. Before they take off, Peter asks, "How much fuel do we have left?" His only riposte to Francine's "Not much" is "All right." In a situation far from being that, the two fly off into a bleak dawn, that is probably as advertised: of the dead.

Before the next "Dead" feature, Romero collaborated with Stephen King in the anthology *Creepshow* (1981) and directed all the episodes, some originals, and some adaptations by King of his own short stories, including the zombie-themed "Father's Day." The sardonic plot involved the inadvertent reanimation of evil patriarch Nathan Grantham (Jon Lormer) by his daughter Bedelia (Viveca Lindfors), who killed him after enduring decades of his torment and his murder of her fiancé. Years later en route to a family reunion Bedelia stops at the cemetery to visit Nathan's grave

Above, Viveca Lindfors as Bedelia Grantham in *Creepshow.*

and revel in her triumph over his abuse but spills some liquor on his grave. Nathan's seriously decomposed corpse rises up to extract revenge on all his descendants. Although brought back by a distilled version of zombie powder, Nathan is far from a typical Romero zombie.

Day of the Dead (1985) is the third of the the "Dead" series, and this continuation of the *Night of the Living Dead* and *Dawn of the Dead* begins mid-apocalypse. In fact, the zombie problem as the film opens is pretty far advanced. Again Romero pulls motifs from the past two films and appends expanded carnage, escalated scale of scenery, and social commentary but with a stylistically different approach. Despite the talky, slow-paced story (and the same often wooden acting that popped up in *The Crazies*), Romero broadens the zombie evolution by giving them not only a mental connection to their past but also the ability to form new emotional ties. The racial and gender animus is still in prominent in the subtext.

Day of the Dead opens with a dream sequence that introduces Sarah (Lori Cardille) against a gray cinderblock room, in flat, sterile lighting. She stares at a dateless calendar for the month of October just before a bunch of zombie limbs smash through the wall at her. She awakens and finds herself strapped into a helicopter, from which position she nevertheless demands the pilot set down to use a bullhorn in search for survivors. On the ground they find nothing but zombies, plus an alligator

Below, Lori Cardille as Dr. Sarah Howard in the opening sequence of *Day of the Dead.*

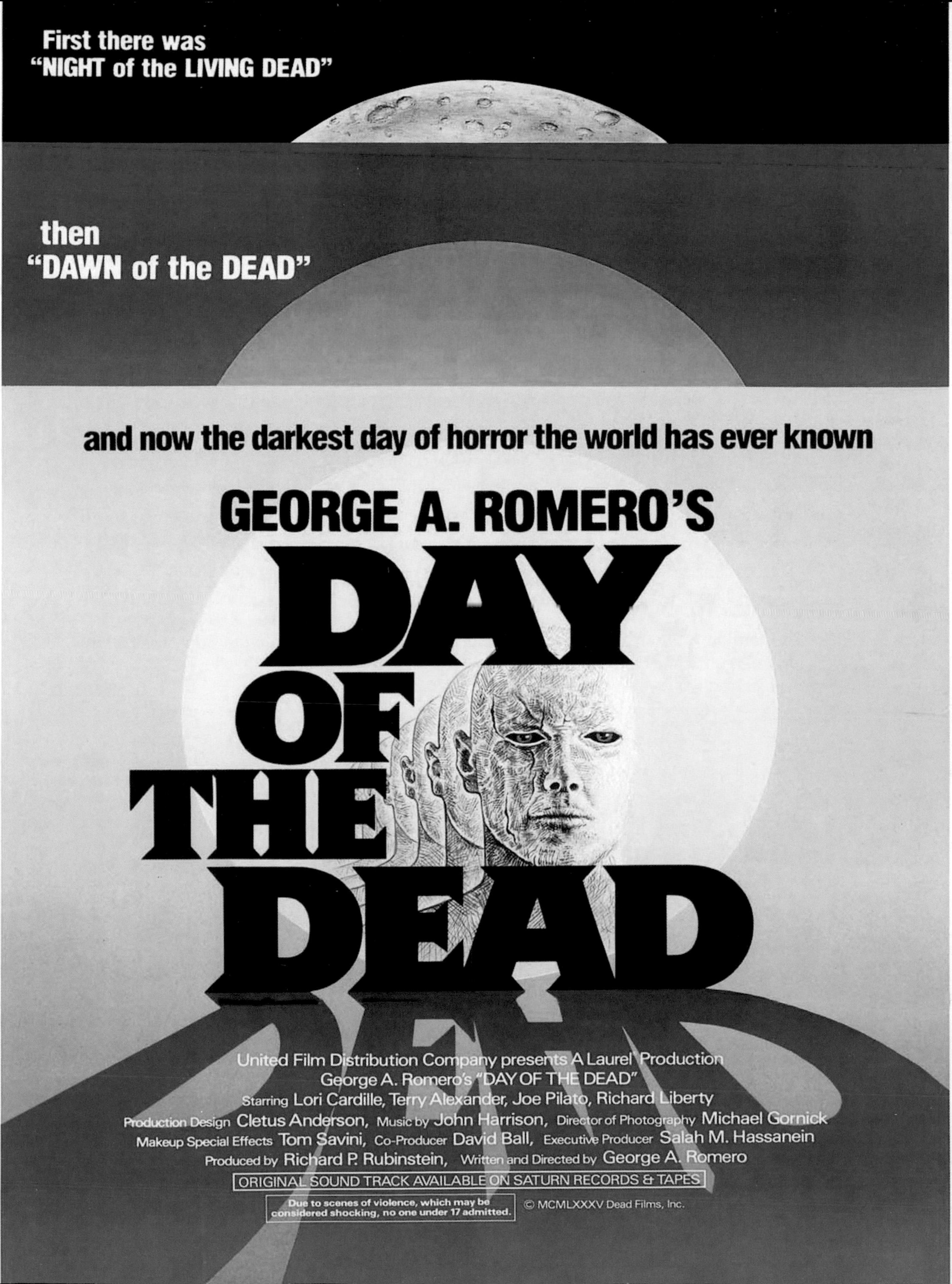

First there was "NIGHT of the LIVING DEAD"

then "DAWN of the DEAD"

and now the darkest day of horror the world has ever known

GEORGE A. ROMERO'S

DAY OF THE DEAD

United Film Distribution Company presents A Laurel Production
George A. Romero's "DAY OF THE DEAD"
Starring Lori Cardille, Terry Alexander, Joe Pilato, Richard Liberty
Production Design Cletus Anderson, Music by John Harrison, Director of Photography Michael Gornick
Makeup Special Effects Tom Savini, Co-Producer David Ball, Executive Producer Salah M. Hassanein
Produced by Richard P. Rubinstein, Written and Directed by George A. Romero

ORIGINAL SOUND TRACK AVAILABLE ON SATURN RECORDS & TAPES

Due to scenes of violence, which may be considered shocking, no one under 17 admitted.   © MCMLXXXV Dead Films, Inc.

and an over-sized tarantula. The pilot, a Black man from the Caribbean, and his brandy-swigging, Irish co-pilot, never cut the rotors. Also along for the ride is Sarah's Fidel Castro look-alike boyfriend, Miguel (Anthony Dileo, Jr.). They fly back to their research compound, which is described as 14 miles underground.

This massive facility is like a sewer stretching out in all directions with a mostly cavernous rock face and interior concrete walls to create built-in rooms throughout. Romero uses stark, hard light with an abundance of cookaloris shadowing to give little sense of detailed decor, which compels the viewer to share a claustrophobic sense of confinement and confusion throughout the movie. It is, in fact, nothing more than a massive underground tomb.

Romero uses his characters as stereotypical representations of humanity and its worse fears. There is a slightly unhinged, power-hungry military commander ready to blast anyone that doesn't follow his orders. A herd of mindless soldiers blindly follow him without a thought of their own needs. A blood-soaked "mad" scientist rambles on about a potential cure for the zombie plague without any particulars. Sarah, the female lead, is presumably also a scientist but behaves like a precursor to the warrior women of action films to follow such as *Aliens* (1986) and *Terminator 2: Judgment Day* (1991). Occasionally Sarah engages in rants that are self-righteous, scientific pontifications but never seems actually to do any scientific work.

Below, Sherman Howard as the sentient ghoul Bub. Opposite, the object of Bob's filial affection Dr. Logan (Richard Liberty).

While the visual constructs reinforce the underlying emotions of the situation, the superficial dialogue takes the viewer no deeper into either plot or character and barely pushes the plot forward. The only character that surprises the viewer with his behavior is the lead zombie Bub (Sherman Howard). Ironically he retains more humanity than the uninfected but feckless survivors. Bub's emotional connection to his past life compels him to form a filial regard for the lead scientist. He is hyper-aware of the nuances of "civilized behavior" and observes them in those that hold him captive. His incentive for carnage is as much moral imperative as it is craving for flesh. Consequently his behavior towards those around him is benign until his parental figure is brutally shot to death. His subsequent violence is an act of revenge directed at the perpetrators not an automaton-like zombie reaction. Bub tracks down the commander, shoots him repeatedly to immobilize him then sarcastically lures the injured man as he is descended upon by a gang of ravenous undead. He sputters, "Choke on it…choke on it!" as they feast on his disemboweled entrails.

Scenes such as this notwithstanding, there is scant zombie carnage in *Day of the Dead*. Rather the "horror" stems from the clichéd situation of entrapped and frustrated humans raging against one other. These ordinary people in blind conflict are responsible for the majority of killing and inadvertently open the facility to a marauding onslaught that consumes most of what remains of humanity. Nonetheless, as in *Dawn of the Dead*, this movie ends somewhat hopefully as Sarah, the helicopter pilot, and his dipsomaniac cohort manage to escape through a tube up to the surface, reach the aircraft and fly off to safety, presumably on some tropical island far away from the nightmare.

One can only wonder why they did not launch a search for such a place in earlier and less desperate circumstances.

In 2005, Romero returned to the zombie genre he had helped sculpt with his original vision. In the interim, he had directed a pilot for a cable series of adaptations of Edgar Allan Poe stories developed by Italian horror specialist Dario Argento, who, when the series was not picked up, came to Pittsburgh to shoot enough additional material for a feature. The end result was a costly flop. While Argento's adaptation was a free-wheeling riff on "The Black Cat," an add-on with the panache permitted by hindsight, Romero's adaptation of Poe's "The Facts in the Case of M. Valdemar" is rela-

Left, Jessice Valdemar (Adrienne Barbeau) recoils at the sight of her hapless husband (Bingo O'Malley, below).

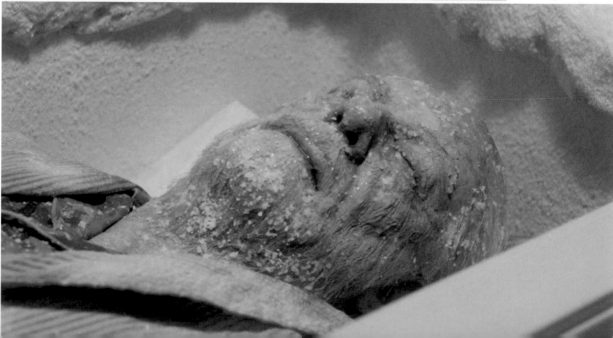

tively flaccid. Unlike Corman's period version of the Poe tale, Romero's re-situation of "the facts" to present-day Pittsburgh adds little visual interest to a staging that Romero clearly intended for the small screen. The straight-forward and leisurely paced narrative features a pallid rendering of Poe's Valdemar, a quasi-zombie character that never seems to spark the interest of Romero (who had wanted to make a pilot based on "The Masque of the Red Death"). The episodes were released in 1990 as *Two Evil Eyes*.

In *Land of the Dead* (2005), Romero had a larger budget ($16 million) than all his previous zombie projects combined but still returned to basics: he combined the new millennial interest in sentient zombies with his tried and true political and social themes. The protagonist, Riley Denbo (Simon Baker), is a for-hire special forces commando whose job is to bring back supplies from the devastated zombie zones in a special tank-like vehicle called "Dead Reckoning." In another post-apocalyptic dystopic universe, started by Romero in *Dawn of the Dead* and newly popular in millennial

films, survivors populate a high-rise fortress ("Fiddler's Green"). There the 1% live in luxury while the remaining 99%, which includes zombies, struggles to survive in a fortified urban downtown protected by rivers and an electric fence. Denbo, like many millennial action heroes, has become embittered and somewhat cynical. Although we later discover that Denbo had to shoot his own brother, who was on the verge of turning into a zombie (thereby giving the audience a reason for his anti-social behavior), at first glance he seems totally self-asorbed, interested only in money and finding a "way out" of the nightmare. As the film progresses, a less self-centered character emerges.

Two characters have the most positive influence on Denbo. His "retard" sharp-shooting buddy Charlie (Robert Joy) invokes Lenny in Steinbeck's *Of Mice and Men* in both performance and character. Charlie depends on his partner for moral and emotional support. Slack (Asia Argento) is an ex-soldier forced by the

Land of the Dead: zombies stagger way before the Dead Reckoning dreadnought.

all-powerful corporation headed by Paul Kaufman (Dennis Hopper) to become a prostitute for his rich friends. Denbo and Slack bond immediately when they save each other's lives during a "bread and circus" event staged to keep the masses happy. The spectacle includes nude dancers, tortured undead in bondage, and a death match between two zombies in which Slack, dressed in slutty fishnets and leather, is thrown in as bait. Before one of the zombies can take a bite out of her, Denbo shoots him. Then Slack returns the favor: she pushes Denbo out of the way and takes a bullet to her arm when the event's promoter tries to eliminate the spoil-sport mercenary.

Concurrent with the story of Denbo, Slack, and Charlie is that of the African-American zombie Big Daddy (Eugene Clark), another in a line of Black quasi-heroes in Romero films, who dresses in his garage mechanic overalls and leads his zombie followers in a workman-like and rather rapid evolution into sentience. Like early men, they begin to "use tools"—in this instance, automatic weapons—and to identify the source of their new society's problem: the fortified Fiddler's Green located across the river in a mythical Pittsburgh (but actually shot in Toronto, Romero's new home town). The performance of Eugene Clark is particularly striking as he uses facial expressions, action, and guttural utterances rather than words to express his growing empathy with his fellow zombies. In one early scene he exemplifies his heroic nature by saving several of them in an attack by commandos of the corporation and thereby begins to understand who the true enemy is.

Once Big Daddy and his followers finally spy the neon "shining city upon a hill," a favorite trope of the American right wing, they move with intelligence and deliberateness towards their goal. Attacking the mall area first, in a reference back to *Dawn of the Dead*, the "terrorist" zombies "eat the rich," while their leader goes directly to the top. In a scene filled with irony, Big Daddy traps Kaufman in his car, takes a handle from the nearby gas pump, and begins to pump gas like any old-school and proletarian mechanic. Except in this case once the interior of the rich dude's swanky auto is full, he sets it on fire.

In the final scene of the movie, Denbo, Charlie, and Slack decide to head north in Dead Reckoning to find refuge. In the distance they see Big Daddy and his troop crossing a bridge. A close-up of Big Daddy's face, as he looks out towards Denby, reveals how much of his pre-zombie cunning has been restored. Although Denby has the fire-power to eliminate the zombies, he refuses and tells his friends, "They're just looking for a place to go, just like us."

Opposite, Slack (Asia Argento) fights for her life in a "bread and circus" gladitorial event.

Below, Big Daddy (cEugene Clark) at the gas pump. Romero's sardonic humor includes a "May we clean your windshield" sign in the frame and explicitly informs the sideshow-like scene on the next page: "Take your picture with a zombie."

Although much more modestly budgeted (at $2 million), *Diary of the Dead* (2007) is among Romero's most complex movies. It is a wide-ranging critique of such social phenomena as "reality" TV and cinema, media's lack of conscience, desensitization of viewers to images of violence, the deceptiveness of authority, and even the worthiness of humans as a species—all of which have figured in earlier films.

With a nod to his own roots as a young filmmaker, Romero follows a group of University of Pittsburgh film students and their alcoholic faculty advisor as they document the spread of an ill-defined zombie virus. The film within the film is called *The Death of Death* and uses mixed media (high-definition cameras combined with low-definition surveillance devices and cell phone recordings), like many modern horror films, to tell the story of their road trip through the land of the dead.

In a rural Pennsylvania location the students shoot their own low-budget mummy film replete with a sexy female victim pursued by a none-too-convincing actor covered in the wrappings of the grave, possibly a wry comment on the graveyard scene that opens *Night of the Living Dead*. The students, particularly actress Tracy (Amy Lalonde), complain vociferously about how cliché, sexist, and cheap the movie seems. Like any group of youthful, would-be artists, they are argumentative and often antagonistic towards one another. The chief object for their disdain is, of course, the director Jason (Joshua Close). As we later learn from his girlfriend and fellow filmmaker Debra (Michelle Morgan), Jason is most comfortable behind the camera. In fact we see relatively little of

Diary of the Dead: Debra (Michelle Morgan) shoots.

him in the film, as he operates the camera for most of the footage. Even when they argue over emotional issues, Jason insists on having the camera running to record their own "reality show."

Soon a different kind of reality arises and alters the trajectory of the film Jason and his cohorts are creating. Watching images on-line of the dead rising and devouring their living brothers and sisters, the students notice that the official media reports are underplaying the seriousness of the situation. But in the internet age, it's hard to hide the truth. The students find sections of posted videos, which graphically reveal the horror around them. Jason wants to continue documenting their journey and create a record of the real situation. Although Debra ascribes less than altruistic motives to this, she agrees.

As the students move through the Pennsylvania countryside, they arm themselves and are forced to kill zombies by the score. The first serious encounter occurs on the highway when the religious and timid Mary (Tatiana Maslany) runs over a family of zombies. Wracked with guilt she shoots herself shortly thereafter. Her friends take her to a nearby hospital, where she dies and becomes a zombie. As the body count rises, the refugees become proficient if uneasy killers. In a particularly shocking scene, Debra returns to her home to find her family turned into zombies. As her small

More from *Diary of the Dead*: opposite, mummy actor Ridley (Philip Riccio) really attacks Jason (Joshua Close).   Above, Debra applies a zombie coup de gras with a defibrilator.

brother attacks her, the faculty advisor Maxwell (Scott Wentworth) pins the boy to the wall with an arrow through the head.

They finally let down their guard after reaching a purported "safe house," the Philadelphia mansion of their fellow student Ridley (Philip Riccio), who still sports his mummy outfit from the first scene. In a semi-comic reversal of the first scene, Ridley, now morphed into an actual zombie, attacks, this time more believably. Ridley bites Jason who, in an ironic affirmation of what Debra had always said, photographs himself dying. After the death of Jason, Debra decides to finish the "documentary" and to put it out on what remains of the internet in hopes that it may help humanity survive by knowing the truth. Her final words are pessimistic. As she watches a compilation of images of violence and horror perpetrated by humans, she pronounces in a melancholy tone, "Are we worth saving?"

Survival of the Dead (2009) opens with a statistical narration: "Last time anyone counted, 53 million people were dying every year. 150,000 every day, 107 every minute. And that was in normal times. Now every one of those dead people gets up and kills another person…and every one of those gets up and kills." The narrator is revealed, a sergeant dressed in camouflage, lighting a cigarette, waiting beside a body under a blood-stained sheet, waiting for it to get up and kill. Another soldier/zombie attacks a man responsible for his undead state and bites off the side of his face with his teeth. An M-16 blows that ghoul's head away, literally: the top of his skull falls onto the stump of his neck before his body crumbles out of frame. Forty years after *Night of the Living Dead* the technology permits more graphic effects, but the set-up is the same. Sgt. Crockett (Alan Van Sprang) discards his cigarette and gets back to business. In the next scene, the guardsman recalls how they became renegades, "held up a bunch of kids in a Winnebago shooting a documentary about themselves," and with that link to *Diary of the Dead* the pre-title sequence ends.

The twist is simple enough: Plum Island off the coast of Delaware is entirely populated by descendants of the two Irish immigrant families (although most of them sound as if they just got off a coffin ship from Queenstown). One clan wants to kill their zombie kin. The other wants to keep them imprisoned until a cure is discovered (or at least until the dead learn to eat something other than live humans). First they get their guns, then they get to feuding. So that we can tell them apart, one side, the Muldoons, wear cowboy hats. The others, the O'Flynns, wear knit caps. Eventually O'Flynn (Kenneth Welsh) is banished to the mainland where he circulates "y'all come visit" flyers for Plum Island on the internet. First O'Flynn tries to steal their ride then he forms an alliance of convenience with Crockett and the last of the guardsman. Together they hijack a ferry boat to return to Plum Island, O'Flynn to resume the feud, the

Opposite, Devin Bostick as the unnamed "Boy," Romero's most recent young zombie killer shoots with a gun not a camera. Right, ghoul-eyed Kathleen Munroe as Jane (or is it Janet?), one of two doomed equestriennes.

Above, shortly after they arrive on Plum Island, a rider interrupts the pointless scuffle between Patrick O'Flynn (Kenneth Welsh) and Sgt. Crockett (Alan Van Sprang). Opposite, as he escapes the horde at the ferry terminal, O'Flynn tosses some dynamite.

others to get away from the "deadheads," a new name for the original ghouls popularized by a late-night talk show host.

As with most of Romero's riffs on the zombie dance that he first choreographed in 1968, the steps have not changed much: die, get up off the ground, catch a bullet to the head, and fall back down. More bullets get fired and more brains fly but the bleakness of the zombie apocalypse remains the same, and the Hatfield/McCoy sub-plot adds little interest. On a few occasions, Crockett, who does his close work like a Western lawman with a pair of single-action Colts, shows some compassion. When the latest version of the "rednecks" in *Night of Living Dead* stake some still groaning zombie heads on poles, the Sergeant puts them out of their undead misery. A few scenes later, when the face of an undead is engulfed in flames, he lights a cigarette off of it. As one might expect from a Romero film, there are only the usual three survivors (two men and one woman) who flee the infested island at the end. Ironically, soon thereafter some of the deadheads acquire a taste for horsemeat. As for the head of the warring clans, their zombie selves fire away futilely at each other with long-empty guns.

II. Hinzman's Children

"Are these people alive or dead?"

"We don't know."

Dawn of the Dead (2004)

Even after the copyright issues on *Night of the Living Dead* were ostensibly resolved, digital technology permits unauthorized remakes, spin-offs, reimaginings, and other riffs to proliferate as fast as a horde of ghouls. There are a few authorized offspring of the original zombie incarnated by William Hinzman in that cemetery not far from Pittsburgh, as well as remakes of the other three original Romero's, the most recently released being *The Crazies* (2010).

The best one could say about many of those successors to the original *Night of the Living Dead* is that they probably earned George Romero some of the money he should have made in the early 1970s and no actual zombies were harmed in the making of these movies. As the quote above from a news conference scene indicates, we don't really know if Hinzman's children are alive or dead. We do know that in their ceaseless craving for flesh, they continue to lumber or even run through untold running times splattered with gore, in two or three dimensions, and express the full range of undead emotion with the traditional assortment of grunts, shrieks, chirps, and throat rattles.

In the 2010 edition of *The Crazies* an old-school ghoul confronts the local Sheriff David Dutton (Timothy Olyphant). The focus on the sheriff and his deputy, characters who were firefighters in the original, also recalls the fugitive couples in *Invasion of the Body Snatchers* and is the most recent and best of the Romero remakes.

In the inset, more zombie trouble for Dutton.

Romero's make-up designer Tom Savini directed the 1990 remake of *Night of the Living Dead*. The make-up is a little spiffier. Johnnie (Bill Moseley) is still a screamer but Barbara (Patricia Tallman) is a bit more engaged in the fight (maybe it's the extra "a" in her name).

Dawn of the Dead 2004 edition: after Vivian the little girl next door (Hannah Lockner, left) almost bites her. Ana (Sarah Polley) also picks up a rifle and becomes just as kick-ass as Kenneth (Ving Rhames). Opposite, Ana takes the point in protecting Andre (Mehki Phifer) and his pregnant wife Luda (Anna Korobkina).

Day of the Dead 2008 edition: Pvt. Salazar (Nick Cannon) is plenty tooled-up with two guns in hand, a spare in the belt, and a blade back-up and about to take a head shot. Opposite, Cpl. Sarah Bowman (Mena Suvari) could use a little help.

I Am Legend: George Romero's Transformations
by Tony Williams

Throughout many of his interviews, George A. Romero has often spoken of the genesis of his zombie films and the key inspiration *I am Legend* by Richard Matheson. "I…got very much into the socio-political through-line that's present in it, although it doesn't really follow through. Inspired by it, I wrote a short story which dealt with a revolutionary society coming into being in the form of a zombie society – people coming back to life as soon as they die—and it was a trilogy right from the jump." He elsewhere mentions that he replaced the novel's post-apocalyptic vampires with his "blue-collar monsters." The familiar story of Romero's ingenious transformation of the Richard Matheson original is so well known as to seem to require little repetition. Yet what is not really

> From out of the night they came — the
> living and the dead — banded together
> in a single obsession — to drink the blood
> of Robert Neville, the last man on earth . . .
> They came at sunset, snarling, screaming—
> some of them crouching on their
> haunches like dogs, eyes glittering, teeth
> slowly grating together back and forth . . .
> Once they had been his neighbours . . .
> his friends . . . Now they were
> VAMPIRES . . .

apparent is Romero's recognition of the tensions affecting its solitary protagonist Robert Neville, tensions he extends to all the human characters in *Night of the Living Dead* who parallel the devouring creatures who surround his home at night. As the back cover of my re-issued 1971 U.K. Corgi edition states, "Once they had been his neighbours…his friends…Now they were VAMPIRES…" Although Romero recognizes the necessity for a new society to take the place of the old in his film unlike the hesitancy expressed by Matheson, it is the role of the living dead expressing tensions within the human species that links both authors.

Matheson's hero is "The Last Man on Earth" as the title of the first film adaptation of his novel. Robert Neville has lost wife and daughter to the plague that has wiped out humanity and seemingly left only himself and vampires to rule the earth. Besieged in his home at night like a Western pioneer threatened by savage Indians centuries past in America's pioneering days, he feels himself under threat by former neighbor Ben Cortman, now a demonic Oliver Hardy to Neville's Stan

U.K.   25p. (5s.)
AUSTRALIA   80c
NEW ZEALAND   80c
SOUTH AFRICA   60c

CORGI BOOKS

I AM LEGEND

RICHARD MATHESON

Alone in the darkness...
one man against the
massed power of evil...

Laurel, whose relationship is not one of comedy but rather a new version of the American Nightmare. Before the Plague, Cortman had driven Neville to work, "talked about cars and baseball and politics with him, later on about the disease, about how Virginia and Kathy were getting along, about how Frieda Cortman was, about..." It takes little imagination to see the unhealthy role of American conformity within this supposedly friendly relationship involving materialism, shallow aspects of conversation, and family life with Cortman insidiously playing a key pitcher testing his vehicle companion as to whether he is a "regular guy" in the words of Kubrick's Clare Quilty in *Lolita* (1962), playing his version of one-upmanship and "keeping up with the Joneses." It comes as no surprise to learn later that the changed Cortman is Neville's most dangerous and elusive foe, often leading those outside at night who "walked and walked about in restless feet, circling each other like wolves, never looking at each other once, having hungry eyes only for the house and their prey inside the house." Among those he leads are those women who expose themselves feeding on Neville's hungry sexual desires and hoping their potential consumer will finally become a consumed item.

Several of these descriptions certainly anticipate *Night of the Living Dead* as those threatening living dead vampires in Sidney Salkow's *The Last Man on Earth* (1964) did. Although the infected in Matheson's novel are compared to vampires, they (like their first cinematic incarnations in Salkow's film) more resemble prototypes of the zombies Romero will later develop. Neville had also worked in a plant, one of those Californian Cold War industrial powerhouses that once offered gainful employment to William Bendix in *The Life of Reilly* during America's most affluent era of Empire. The plague itself may not be accidental, having suggestive contacts with that science fiction explanation unconvincingly offered in *Night of the Living Dead.* By day, Neville hunts as many vampires

as he can find, becoming a modern version of Robert Montgomery Bird's Nathan Slaughter in *Nick of the Woods* (1836), the ancestor of Herman Melville's "Indian hater" from *The Confidence Man* and John Wayne's Ethan Edwards in John Ford's *The Searchers* (1956). Like Ethan Edwards, the paranoid Neville may have secretly desired the end of conformist America and family life to become D.H. Lawrence's classic embodiment of the American male described in *Studies in Classic American Literature* as an isolate and a killer. The vampires also embody a new version of Indians as a monstrous embodiment of the id, both in terms of presumed libidinous sexuality and cannibalistic violence in that dark legacy deriving from the Puritan era of the Mather Brothers, one of whom had the first name "Increase." He left an inheritance that certainly became fruitful and multiplied as we have witnessed over the past four centuries. In *Dawn of the Dead*, the zombies circulate outside the Mall like their predecessors outside the farmhouse in *Night of the Living Dead* only to become temporarily displaced by those biker descendants of Simon Girty, the renegade who "went Indian." It is by no means accidental that Romero's subsequent bigger budget installment in his zombie chronicles (*Survival of the Dead*) takes the form of a Western. *The Big Country* is not the only influence there. Although the appearance of a dog offers Neville the type of loner companionship shared by John Wayne's Hondo and Brian Keith's Dave Blassingame in Sam Peckinpah's *The Westerner*, this hope is cruelly nipped in the bud. After this Cortman becomes his Scar and hunting for Cortman becomes "one of the few diversions left to him."

I am Legend is a study of human paranoia and suspicion. When Neville discovers the presence of

Below, zombies outside the mall in *Dawn of the Dead*; opposite, their predecessors outside the farmhouse.

a supposedly healthy woman, Matheson makes clear that the central problem of the novel lies in Neville himself not the battle between a human and vampires. "The present was enough. And he was afraid of the possible demand that he make sacrifices and accept responsibility again. He was afraid of giving out his heart, of removing the chains he had forged around it to keep emotion prisoner. He was afraid of loving again." It is this insight that Romero incorporates into *Night of the Living Dead* seeing the whole of humanity, not just one individual and certainly not the supposedly heroic Ben, as all sharing a common dilemma of hostility, suspicion, and refusal to work for the common good.

Although Neville recognizes that he has become an anachronism in the future new society he also understands that Ruth, whom he formerly thought was "the last woman on Earth," has "become a brainless convert to this new violence." Unlike Romero's qualified and tentative optimism for a potentially progressive new society, Matheson pessimistically sees it as a continuation of the old as seen in Ruth's description to the doomed Neville. For Matheson, there is really no difference between the new society and the later redneck hunters in *Night of the Living Dead*. The members of Matheson's new society share the same antagonism to outsiders as Neville does to his prey.

The following description anticipates the biker horde of *Dawn of the Dead* as well as the military survivors of *Day of the Dead* who emotionally devour each other in a manner similar to the zombies outside the compound. How soon will it be before they set up their own form of hierarchy designating even their own people as "other" in a manner envisaged in *Land of the Dead* and turn on their own kin as do the warring families of *Survival of the Dead*? Although Matheson does not go into detail, the future of survivors in *I am Legend* is not positive and as dangerous as that experienced in *Diary of the Dead*. "'Maybe you did see joy on their faces,' she said. 'It's not surprising. They're young. And they are killers—assigned killers, legal killers. They're respected for their killing, admired for it. What can you expect from them? They're only fallible men. And men can learn to enjoy killing. That's an old story, Neville. You know that.'"

Ruth's description is an uncanny echo of the codes of the Frontier Society that has dominated America since its very foundation. There is to be no positive change only a continuation of the old order in a changing of the guard where the outsiders become the new establishment and the establishment the new outsiders taking the place of Native Americans who barely survived extinction in America's history.

"'As far as we know,' she said casually, 'You're quite unique, you know. When you're gone, there won't be anyone else like you within our particular society.'" It is to Romero's credit that he recognizes the dangerous continuation of America's heritage of violence in his zombie films viewing it as "a pyramid of skulls," the title of the closing chapter to the first part of Richard Slotkin's monumental cultural-historical trilogy of American psychopathology that begins with *Regeneration*

Through Violence: The Mythology of the American Frontier 1600–1815 and ends with *Gunfighter Nation: The Myth of the Frontier in Twentieth Century America.* The first part deals exclusively with literature and the final part almost exclusively with film paralleling *I am Legend* as a dystopian science fiction text and Romero's cinema containing hesitant and qualified hopes for the future. Both Matheson and Romero interrogate different examples of the human psyche, seeing their monsters as projections of deeply contradictory and destructive tensions. Yet while Matheson concludes on a pessimistic note seeing his hero as embodying "A new terror born in death, a new superstition entering the unassailable fortress of forever," Romero offers a less deterministic vision of the future but one left for his audiences to resolve. At least some hope exists at the end of *Land of the Dead* when the human remnants of the zombie apocalypse decide to leave the retreating zombies alone. Matheson offers no such hope but Romero suggests a tentative possibility that only human survivors can realize should they decide to and leave aside both their internal dissensions and the psychological mechanisms that will only continue violent past behavior.

"The redneck hunters" and the local police
in *Night of the Living Dead.*

The Evil Dead.

Chapter Five

Zombies on a Shoestring: The 1970s and '80s

"For God's sake!—quick!—quick!—put me to sleep—or, quick!—waken me!—quick!—I say to you that I am dead!"

Edgar Allan Poe
"The Facts in the
Case of M. Valdemar"

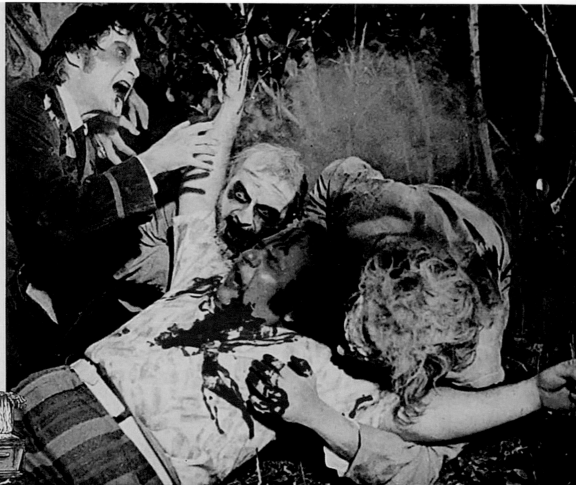

It is regrettable that writer/director Bob Clark's reputation is almost entirely based on two feature releases—the sophomoric *Porky* (1982) and the sentimental seasonal classic *A Christmas Story* (1983). Before he attained box-office success, Clark directed a series of horror films, which were both inventive and at times satirical, including two zombie movies. The first was *Children Shouldn't Play with Dead Things* (1973). The movie helped form the cabin-in-the-woods sub-genre, teenagers or college students trapped and tormented in a secluded location, a construct which would become so popular in the low budget horror revival of the 1970s–1980s and continuing to this day. In this movie, a theatrical troupe is led by a sadistic and pretentious director named Alan (Alan Ormsby, co-writer of this film as well as Clark's next zombie film). He has brought them to this island and its graveyard not only to frighten them but to humiliate them as well.

Alan pretends to raise the dead caretaker of the cemetery through use of a grimoire; but to his dismay, the resurrection actually happens. After humiliating the corpse of the caretaker—he dresses it as a woman and marries it to one of his actors—the dead rise around them. The zombies enact their revenge by breaking down the doors of the house in which the troupe is hiding, in *Night of the Living Dead* tradition. In the final scene the dead march off in slow motion to a boat waiting at the dock and, the audience assumes, toward the lights of Miami in the distance and beyond.

The second movie was far more serious in subject matter and metaphorical content. On the surface *Dead of Night* (aka *Deathdream*, 1974)—one of many film adapations of "The Monkey's Paw," as was Wes Craven's later *Chiller*—is a tale of a mother who wishes her son's safe return from the war. Her wish is granted, except that the

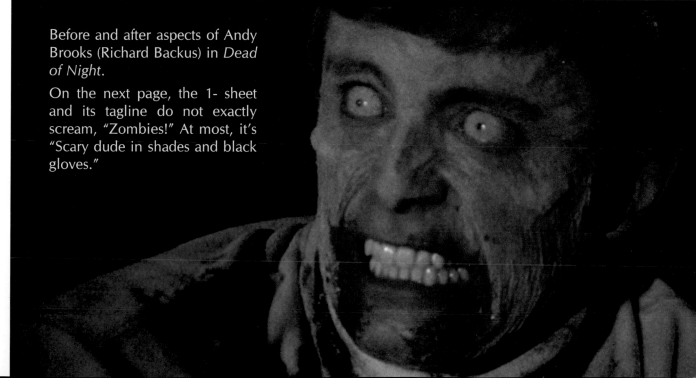

Before and after aspects of Andy Brooks (Richard Backus) in *Dead of Night*.

On the next page, the 1- sheet and its tagline do not exactly scream, "Zombies!" At most, it's "Scary dude in shades and black gloves."

IT WRINGS THE VICTIMS OUT.. AND HANGS THEM UP TO DIE!!!

DEATHDREAM

STARRING:
JOHN MARLEY • LYNN CARLIN WITH: RICHARD BACKUS • HENDERSON FORSYTH
Screenplay Written by: ALAN ORMSBY Music by: CARL ZITTRER Executive Producers: JOHN TRENT & PETER JAMES
Produced and Directed by: BOB CLARK

A QUADRANT IMPACT FILM

Color by: TECHNICOLOR
DEATHDREAM-76/195

An ENTERTAINMENT INTERNATIONAL PICTURES RELEASE

son is now a cross between a zombie and a vampire. On a figurative level the narrative, which is one of the few to deal with the Vietnam war while it was still being waged, uses zombie-ism to represent the post-traumatic stress disorder (PTSD) soldiers often suffer after the horrific experience of battle. (A more recent example of this trope from director Joe Dante came 31 years later in the "Homecoming" episode from the *Masters of Horror* cable series.)

After a brief prologue in which Andy Brooks (Richard Backus) is shot while fighting in the jungle, the scene shifts to the small-town home of the Brooks' family as they gather around the traditional dinner table. The setting is archetypically bourgeois: a patriarchal father (John Marley), an emotional and supportive mother (Lynn Carlin), and a sweet, obedient daughter (Anya Ormsby). As the father cuts the roast, the mother prays for her son's return, but a dark twist lurks beneath the Norman Rockwell surface, as it does in most of Bob Clark's dissections of bourgeois values. In the first indication that all is not well in Middle America, father finds mother performing a ritual in her rocking chair: pitching back and forth with a candle in her hand and summoning her son back from the war. This scene changes to a subjective camera with heavy breathing on the soundtrack as a trucker gives an unseen soldier a lift only to be murdered and drained of blood.

Although the audience had seen an officer deliver the notice of Andy's death in action in an earlier scene, Mother is somehow granted her wish. While in Jacobs' story the disfigured son is driven from the doorstep by a third wish, the reanimated Andy appears normal but is an emotionless shell unwilling to speak of the war or to relate to his friends and family in a customary way.

When a postman good-naturedly asks him about his experiences in combat, Andy cringes. When his father brings around some of his younger friends, their questions agitate Andy so severely that he strangles the family pet. When asked to smile he forms his mouth into a twisted rictus. Andy's only source of comfort seems to come from rocking compulsively in the chair. Driven to distraction at his son's behavior, the father gets drunk and abuses both his wife and daughter.

The emotional underpinning of Andy's PTSD is explicitly revealed when he kills the nosy family doctor: he died for all of them, he says, so now it's their turn to die for him. Zombie Andy completely loses control when he goes out on a date with his ex-girlfriend and murders her along with a few bystanders. He flees back to his house only to discover that his father has committed suicide and his mother wants to escape with her son. With the police in pursuit, a now decomposing Andy drives his mother to the graveyard. There he starts to bury himself, as his mother comes face to face with the horror that her counterpart in Jacobs' story was spared.

Sugar Hill (1974) is a blaxploitation film from low-budget studio and distributor American International Pictures designed for the same audiences as their *Blacula* (1972), which starred William Marshall, and *Coffy* (1973) with Pam Grier. Unfortunately the star of *Sugar Hill* Marki Bey lacks the charisma of either Marshall or Grier. The premise of *Sugar Hill* is over-the-top with all its

elements of the 1930s exploitation movie *Ouanga* as well as the zombies that were both in *Revolt* and raised to seek *Revenge* in the 1940s. In reaction to the death of her club-owner boyfriend at the hands of the White mob, Bey's title character Sugar Hill seeks assistance from a voodoo priest-ess and the voodoo spirit Baron Samedi–a key figure in voodoo mythology–to raise her own army of undead and destroy the mob-ster killers.

The Dead Don't Die (1975) is a TV movie directed by occultist/experimental filmmaker Curtis Harrington and written by Robert Bloch (best known for his *Psycho* novel). As he did in *Night Tide* (1961), Harrington paints this period zombie film (set in the 1930s) with an oneiric visual patina, particu-larly in the scenes situated in a mysterious dance hall, the promoters of which sponsor nightmarish dance marathons where the participants with their exhausted, stuttering steps seem more like zombies than the "real" undead of the movie.

Harrington opens the film with a homage to the style of Warner Bros. gangster films: the titles include inset images of the leading characters, a common technique in the 1930s, then transition into a death row cell block lit with deep chiaroscuro shadows. Here the protagonist Don Drake (George Hamilton, replete with a Clark-Gable-style mustache) tries to console his condemned brother about to be executed for the murder of his wife. Proclaiming his innocence to the end, this character is dragged out of his cell and led to the execution chamber. In an emotional and tense scene Drake watches as his brother whose head has been shaved to

Opposite, AIP had no compunction about using the Z word (and noting the featured song entitled "Supernatural Voodoo Woman") on their one sheet for *Sugar Hill. Below,* the video distributors of *The Dead Don't Die* were even less committed to understatement: "The Zombies are Taking Over the World!"

permit full contact with the deadly electrodes, is strapped to the chair and then "fried."

Intent on clearing the name of his brother, Drake seeks out his brother's former employer, Moss (Ray Milland, one of the many actors in the film from the classic period of Hollywood films), who runs the down-on-its-luck ballroom mentioned above. Armed with a few clues from Moss, the dreamscape atmosphere of the ballroom carries over as Drake moves through fog-shrouded streets and deserted graveyards like a classic noir detective. At a curio store he is attacked by its shopkeeper, who resembles Nosferatu (and is portrayed by Reggie Nalder, the vampire from the 1979 *Salem's Lot*). Drake believes he has killed this man in self defense (but will later discover that this shopkeeper can speak from his coffin in a mortuary), yet when he summons police to the scene, the shopkeeper appears alive and well at his job, although inexplicably wearing sunglasses inside.

Drake's befuddlement continues as he encounters a dark lady, a femme fatale named Vera (Linda Cristal), who alternately seduces him with her long dark hair and clinging 1930s dresses and repulses him with her revelation that she, like his brother, is a zombie, controlled by a Haitian-trained bokor named Varek. In order to prove it she unfastens her choker to reveal the scars of a decapitation. Before he can continue his investigation she spontaneously combusts.

Zombies now invade both Drake's waking and sleeping hours and soon both the viewer and Drake are unable to tell the difference between the real and unreal (a constant theme in Harrington's work). By the final scene in a meat locker where Varek (who is now revealed to be Moss) sends Drake's brother to murder him, the phantasmagoria has spun out of control. Drake breaks the spell on his brother by telling him that Varek is responsible for the death of his wife. Drake strangles Varek and then hangs him up on a meat hook. However, when the police arrive there are no zombies, no Varek, no blood. And so Drake is led away by a disbelieving cop (Ralph Meeker) to a quiet, restful "hotel."

In 1978 the first remake of *Invasion of the Body Snatchers* was released. The title itself was bifurcated to become *Body Snatchers* in 1993 and most recently *The Invasion* (2007). All were spun from the same source novel by Jack Finney. Presuming that most of the audience would be familiar with the story, new adapters W.D. Richter and Philip Kaufman open the 1978 film with a prologue in space that follows the alien beings from their dying planet to Earth where they rain down, then are assimilated by leafy plants and mutate into the pods. The narrative that follows is much like the 1956 version with Elizabeth Driscoll (Brooke Adams) falling asleep and transformed but with her lover Matthew Bennell (Donald Sutherland) apparently escaping. The twist from the original is that Nancy (Veronica Cartwright), the wife of the other couple, survives by behaving without

Opposite, a whole lot of snatched-body screaming going on in the first remake of *Invasion of the Body Snatchers:* the screechers Donald Sutherland as Bennell and Brooke Adams as Elizabeth compel Veronica Cartwright as Nancy (below) to cover her ears.

THEY THOUGHT THEY WERE
JUST KILLING SOME WEEDS

*Instead, they grew
a whole new kind
of crop!*

Toxic Zombies

Starring **CHARLES AUSTIN** • **BEVERLY SHAPIRO** • **DENNIS HELFEND** • **JOHN AMPLAS**
Music by **TED SHAPIRO** Director of Photography **DAVID SPERLING** Written, Produced & Directed by **CHARLES McCRANN**

A **BEDFORD ENTERTAINMENT** RELEASE

emotion, encounters Matthew on the street only to discover that he has also been zombiefied when his face contorts and he emits the warning scream of the pod people.

Above, tow-headed tykes who are actualy zombie masters: Nell and Patrick Regan as Beth and Michael in *Kiss Daddy Goodbye* and Rosalie Cole as Rosalie in *The Child*. Sending zombie Daddy and zombie friends out for revenge turned out to be the only star turn for these young thespians.

Low-budget maven Fred Olen Ray directed, with his customary tongue in cheek, *Alien Dead* (1980). A meteor strikes a Louisiana swamp and produces undead who eat alligators and later, as an afterthought, humans. Also in 1980 *Bloodeaters* (aka *Toxic Zombies*) was an early entry in the list of movies that would features zombies created by pollution rather than pathogen. As the rather wordy tagline on the poster says: "They thought they were just killing some weeds...instead, they grew a whole new kind of crop."

That same year on a very thin shoestring (and with a much shorter tagline), Alain Silver and his partners produced *Kiss Daddy Goodbye* [see the sidebar below], that. although they had never seen the movie, recalled the plot of exploitation producer Harry Novak's *The Child* (1977). In that film a young girl uses her supernatural powers to raise the dead and take revenge on the couple responsible for the death of her mother. Aside from the underlying concept, neither bring-the-parent-back-from-the-dead movie has much novelty or coherence. Of course, if Harry Novak were co-writing this book, perhaps there'd be a side-bar on *The Child*.

EVIL DEAD 2
DEAD BY DAWN

RENAISSANCE PICTURES Presents
EVIL DEAD 2
Starring BRUCE CAMPBELL With SARAH BERRY DAN HICKS KASSIE WESLEY RICHARD DOMEIER
Music By JOSEPH LO DUCA Special Makeup Effects MARK SHOSTROM Edited By KAYE DAVIS
Director of Photography PETER DEMING Executive Producers IRVIN SHAPIRO ALEX De BENEDETTI
Written By SAM RAIMI SCOTT SPIEGEL Produced By ROBERT TAPERT Directed By SAM RAIMI

ORIGINAL MOTION PICTURE SOUNDTRACK AVAILABLE ON VARESE SARABANDE RECORDS

Sam Raimi's own "Dead" series began in 1981 with *The Evil Dead*, followed by *Evil Dead 2 Dead by Dawn* in 1987 and *Army of Darkness*, 1992. Although marginally zombie movies but more in the tradition of demonic-possession films like *The Exorcist*, some genre enthusiasts see crossover in their undead style. Certainly their success was a significant influence on horror films in general, and all reflect Raimi's characteristic macabre humor arising out of his fan-like enthusiasm for the supernatural and mythic. The first and second moves in the series are almost identical—*Evil Dead 2* is simply costlier to make and flashier. The third in the series is a somewhat weathered rehash with little of the originality of the first two.

The Curse of the Screaming Dead (1982) is one of the early features of the East-coast exploitation mill Troma. A group of deer hunters disturb the swamp resting place of Confederate soldiers and the "South Shall Rise Again" as the tagline proclaims. Unlike Troma's signature *Toxic Avenger* (1984), their zombies are pretty run-of-the mill. *One Dark Night* (aka *Mausoleum*, 1983) is a teenage horror film in the tradition of *Halloween* (1978), in which a sorority pledge (Meg Tilly) must spend a night in a mausoleum in order to qualify for membership. Her satin-jacketed, big-haired sisters include singer/actress E. G. Daily who brings her smoky voice and Lolita demeanor to the

Below, some serious brain munching in *Evil Dead 2 Dead by Dawn*.

part. Unfortunately, coffins burst out of their niches and the dead rise, telekinetically controlled by a mass-murderer, Russian occultist Raymar. Raymar is neatly defeated in an oedipal struggle by his own daughter Olivia (Melissa Newman) in the final scene in which she reflects his own powers back on him with her hand compact.

In 1983 singer/composer and pop icon Michael Jackson brought Romero-style zombies to worldwide celebrity status with his music video for his album "Thriller." Dancing ghouls rise from their graves to pursue a young couple (the young male is also in a dual role). Gothic graveyards, undead executing choreographed twitches and turns, and a narration by horror legend Vincent Price, not to mentioned Jackson's song and performance, made this short a landmark event in the early history of music videos as well as zombie movies.

Night Shadows (aka *Mutant*, 1984) continues to extend the analogy between zombie-ism and pollution. Toxic waste in a small Southern town is turning its inhabitants into the undead. In a satire that starts with its title *Surf II: the End of the Trilogy* (1984; of course, there is no *Surf I*) Eddie Deezen, a low-rent Jerry Lewis look-and-act-alike whose career was en route from mega-budget *1941* (1979) to the spare-change effort *A Polish Vampire in Burbank* (1985), plays genius/nerd Menlo who takes revenge on arrogant surfers. He invents a soft drink, which turns them into punk zombies with a taste for garbage.

Night of the Comet (1984) exploits the 1980s fascination with "Valley Girls" (inspired by Frank Zappa's 1982 song and featuring his daughter Moon Unit), as well as a growing fear of approaching catastrophe and possible extinction at the end of the millennium. A comet tail sweeps the Earth with cosmic radiation causing most of the inhabitants to dissolve into multi-colored dust or, alternately à la Romero, to turn into zombie-like creatures with decomposing flesh and insatiable rage. The two teen heroines are Valley-Girl sisters Regina (Catherine Mary Stewart) and Samantha (Kelli Maroney). Regina works in a movie theater where she distracts herself from the boring routine of

Below, *Surf II*: soon-to-be zombie surfers Bob and Chuck (Jeffrey Rogers and a pre-*Mask* Eric Stoltz, right) staring at the waves and blissfuly unaware of the fate that awaits.

Above, *Night of the Comet*: sisters Regina (Catherine Mary Stewart, right) and Samantha (Kelli Maroney) get armed and dangerous to battle the newly hatched zombies, such as the one on the left on the streets of downtown Los Angeles.

her usherette duties by honing her skills as a video game player (she is also trained in martial arts) and as a sexually liberated femme by dallying with a hot young projectionist. Samantha, on the other hand, is a "girly-girl"—dressing, alternately, in spandex workout outfits, lingerie, or cheer-leader garb. During the comet collision both Samantha and Regina are preserved from harm by their locations: Regina is making love to her boyfriend in the fire-proof, cinder-block projection booth and Samantha is hiding out from her bullying stepmother in a metal tool shed.

The two sisters join forces to investigate the post-apocalyptic and barren cityscape of Los Angeles, its streets shot to create the illusion of emptiness. When not fighting off zombie survivors—both girls have training in the use of automatic weapons from their absent military father—they, like true Valley Girls, take a break by traipsing through now empty malls. In a shopping montage cut to the 1980s hit "Girls Just Wanna Have Fun," the sisters try on various outfits in order to assuage their post-comet blues. But even there they need to fight off a crew of zombie stock boys. The rest of the film devolves into a cat-and-mouse game between the sisters and a nefarious government agency, which is trying to use the few uninfected survivors to develop a serum to cure their own creeping zombie-ism. Of course, the sisters are triumphant. They save the human race and along the way Regina has even picked up a make-shift family to repropogate the planet. While Samantha, more interested in fun than responsibility, rides off in the sports car of another hot survivor.

Dan O'Bannon of *Alien* fame wrote and directed the zombie satire *The Return of the Living Dead* (1985). There are numerous references to *Night of the Living Dead* in the dialogue. The characters' initial reactions to the zombies are also based on the earlier movie's lead, which wryly leads them into more trouble. The zombies even speak among themselves, chatting about their decomposed state.

The Return of the Living Dead: the still caption reads simply "one of the ghouls making his way through the cemetery."

Among the most original and idiosyncratic independent horror filmmakers to emerge in the 1970s is Larry Cohen, whose break-out success was the killer-baby movie *It's Alive* (1972). Cohen worked his way into low-budget exploitation after a career writing for "serious" network television, was responsible for several neo-noir screenplays in the 1980s, and has a story credit on *Body Snatchers*. Like Romero Cohen often incorporates overt social commentary into his genre pictures such as *God Told Me To* (1976) and *The Stuff* (1985). The title substance in the latter feature is, in fact, a sweet and frothy version of the spores/pods in *Invasion of the Body Snatchers*. Cohen's frequent collaborator actor Michael Moriarty stars as a former F.B.I. agent turned investigator/industrial spy, David "Mo" Rutherford, who is hired by traditional frozen dessert executives to find what the makers of their new competitors put into the no-calorie but flavorful "stuff." Cohen's opening narrative includes commercials, prints ads, and matte shots of posters in Times Square hawking pint containers of "the Stuff," which parody the advertising industry almost as explicitly as *Will Success Spoil Rock Hunter?* (1957).

Ultimately Rutherford discovers that the mysterious substance is a real body snatcher, invading the brains of those who consume and turning them into zombies, much like the pod people, who encourage others to eat more stuff. When Rutherford and his ad-exec girlfriend Nicole (Andrea Marcovicci) visit a processing plant, the sentient substance feels threatened and launches a *Blob*-like attack on them at a local motel. With the help of a military unit, the plant is destroyed and with a perfectly straight face, Col. Spears (Paul Sorvino) broadcasts a warning: "We are under alien attack by a substance which represents itself as a popular dessert known as 'the stuff.' If 'the stuff' is in your house, do not eat it!" In the montage of "stuff" destruction that follows Cohen includes a shot of a McDonald's and an adjacent Stuff outlet—topped with a giant cone and strongly resembling a California Fosters Freeze franchise store—as angry citizens blow it up. In the end, executives team up to market a new product, "The Taste," a blend of ice cream with a small percentage of "the stuff" that is purportedly too little to induce zombie-ism. Rutherford quashes that plot, but, of course, he cannot prevent black marketers from selling the now-rare frozen treat out of automobile trunks on street corners.

Left, when the stuff oozes out of a pillow and latches onto Rutherford (Michael Moriarty) Nicole (Andrea Marcovicci) douses it with cologne and burns it off his face. Below, as Rutherford and Nicole watch the angry stuff swallows up an intruder and starts to fill the motel room.

Opposite, graphic from a television commercial.

Below, outraged consumers rampage against the no-longer-irresistible and tainted product and blow up one of its franchise stores.

Night of the Creeps (1986) is yet another riff on *Invasion of the Body Snatchers*: a variant type of body-snatching where aliens occupy humans and turn them into sci-fi zombies. It has a humorous tagline used in both the trailer and the movie: the cop says to the big-haired, newly primped teens waiting for their dates: "The good news is your dates are here. The bad news is they're dead." In *I Was a Teenage Zombie* (1987) toxic pollution produces another set of zombies. In this case there is a battle between a "good" zombie and a "bad" zombie. The film does feature some indie music of the period, including a title number by the Fleshtones. It also features an ample amount of sophomoric teenage humor. By the late 1980s Troma had carved out its niche in low-budget filmmaking by combining horror and broad comedy. In 1987 the company produced *Redneck Zombies* which featured stereotypical movie "rednecks" mixing radioactive material with their moonshine and then turning themselves into flesh-eating ghouls. *Working Stiffs* (1989) is a zombie comedy from Massachusetts. The head of a temp agency, after a visit to Haiti, decides to create a temp work force made up of reliable, subservient zombies, invoking the Haitian tradition of using zombies as workers on plantations.

The final, relatively low-budget ($2 million) success of the 1980s was *Pet Sematary* (1989). The set-up for this movie is full of cloying ironies. There are muted voices and a dirge-like chorus on the

Below, *Night of the Creeps*; an unwary moment can mean being blindsided by a teen zombie.

Opposite, the Indian graveyard in *Pet Sematary*.

underscore. As the camera moves through the title location, it floats past crosses with faded pictures of pooches and kitties, a rusted birdcage, and, right after a live skunk scurries through, a piece of old white-washed fence on which a childish scrawl that memorializes "Hannah, the best dog that ever was." Moments later, another epitaph, "Biffer, Biffer, a hell of a sniffer." The filmmakers could be as flippant as they wanted in their title sequence, as most moviegoers arrived at the theater already aware of Stephen King's grim novel of the same name. Still the prop crosses bedecked with no longer needed dog chains and collars with a touch of cobwebs or lichen around the edges cannot invoke the same level of grimness that characterized King's dark narrative, cannot even come close. In any case, the power of King's best prose does not reside in the evocation of the arcane or eerie but rather of the everyday into which the horrific intrudes so powerfully that no amount of reader expectation can blunt the impact. For this adaptation King wrote the screenplay, too; but he didn't dress the set.

While the boundaries of the zombie genre have always been fairly loose, neither King's novel nor this movie rely on the usual constructions—drums in the night, haunted figures back from the grave—to create the horror context. As noted earlier, the clearest line to any standard antecedent is all the way back to "The Monkey's Paw," with the myth of the magical Micmac Indian burial ground standing in for the talisman of an East Indian fakir. But where King the novelist paints a convincing picture of the Creed family that is already edgy when tragedy strikes, King's script and some over-the-top acting reduce the back story of *Pet Sematary* to cheesy melodrama with more schlock than horror underlying it.

The core event of the film, the death of young Gage Creed under the wheels of a semi, begins with the awkward posturing of the parents who must be inattentive enough to permit their toddler to run into the road, then maudlin cutaways to family snapshots as the reality sinks in, and finally the confrontation with a psychotic father-in-law at the funeral. All are staged in a way that verges on parody. The nadir is the flashback told by neighbor Jud Crandall (Fred Gwynne, playing it straighter than as Herman Munster) about the rebirth and redeath of Timmy Baterman 40 years before. Timmy eats dead things, has a zombie limp, and pathetically whimpers, "No, Dad, hate living" as townfolk

Above, cute little zombie child Gage Creed (Miko Hughes) seems like he just wants to play. That's a lot more than can be said for his pet cat, which preceded him in reanimation via the Pet Sematary.

stephen king's

Sometimes dead is better

PET SEMATARY

BASED ON THE BEST SELLING THRILLER

PARAMOUNT PICTURES PRESENTS · A RICHARD P. RUBINSTEIN PRODUCTION · A MARY LAMBERT FILM · PET SEMATARY · MUSIC BY ELLIOT GOLDENTHAL

EDITED BY MICHAEL HILL AND DANIEL HANLEY · DIRECTOR OF PHOTOGRAPHY PETER STEIN · CO PRODUCER MITCHELL GALIN · EXECUTIVE PRODUCER TIM ZINNEMANN · SCREENPLAY BY STEPHEN KING · BASED UPON HIS NOVEL

PRODUCED BY RICHARD P. RUBINSTEIN · DIRECTED BY MARY LAMBERT · READ THE SIGNET PAPERBACK

burn down his house. At least, that seemed like the nadir until the end title song, a kind of zombie's lament with a catchy lyric: "I don't want to be buried in a pet cemetery. I don't want to live my life again. Oh, no!"

The sequel to *Pet Sematary* opens in full Gothic mode: a white-gowned figure glides barefoot down the torch-lit stairway of a stone tower and across a wet floor to kneel in front of an ornate sarcophagus. A skeletal rubber arm grabs her in the wrong spot, so she breaks character and screams. The horror film set is revealed. We resume with the wildly exaggerated "take 33." From this relatively inane, menacing-then-not-menacing opening, a power cable is knocked into the water and in front of her teenaged son Jeff (Edward Furlong) and a horrified crew, actress Renne Hallow (Darlanne Fluegel) is electrocuted. After Jeff's veterinarian father Chase (Anthony Edwards) moves his estranged wife's body back to their Northeastern home town for interment, he takes over a seedy animal hospital with its yellowed hunting-dog wallpaper.

All these early scenes are accented by a needlessly creepy underscore and a second meeting with the even creepier local sheriff, Gus Gilbert (Clancy Brown). As this is *Pet Sematary II* (or on the posters *Two*), it is hard to imagine that any viewer is unaware that the pending narrative developments will center around reanimation. But first Jeff must run the gauntlet of unwelcoming peers at

the local junior high. While the expectation may be that dead Mom is a candidate for resurrection in the Indian burial ground behind the standard pet graves, the plot takes several turns, again beginning with a pet. Of course, there's more than a little Cujo in the dog with a zombie-like name, Zowie. A page from another of King's novels, *Stand by Me*, informs the behavior of the adolescent bullies, and one from *The Shining* underlies the attack by the zombie Sheriff, as he hammers his way through a door to get to his stepson Drew (Jason McGuire); but ultimately the filmmakers run out of literary material to plunder. This sequel is not without its sardonic highlights, as with the vet Chase's comment when he fends off a Zowie attack with a handgun: "I hate that dog." It still takes Chase a while to realize after encountering zombie Sheriff Gus that, as with the more traditional of his ilk, only a bullet to the brain will get the job done.

Over the course of two decades American movie zombies had barely changed from the standard established by Romero. There were occasional throwbacks such as *Sugar Hill* or *The Dead Don't Die*, some variants on environmental themes as underlying causes, and imaginative, sardonic variants on the genre as in *The Stuff*. But however they came to be animated dead people, they still shuffled, or "zombied," in and out of shots and remained mostly unaware of their perverse and pathetic conditions.

Pet Sematary II: opposite, Edward Furlong as Jeff, who wants his electrocuted Mom back. Below, Clancy Brown as the crazed undead Sheriff Gus.

"Daddy said, 'We shouldn't...ever again!'" Making *Kiss Daddy Goodbye* by Alain Silver

We didn't start out to make a zombie movie. We certainly had been inspired by the low-budget success stories in the horror genre. I had first seen *Night of the Living Dead* at a midnight show in Westwood while still a film student at UCLA in the early-1970s. But equally remarkable were *Texas Chainsaw Massacre* (1974) and *Phantasm* (1979). Most recently in May of 1980 *Friday the 13th* had cemented our plan. While many independent filmmakers have raised "doctor and dentist" money, small, discretionary investments from professionals who could afford the risk, we pitched the possibilities of *Ghost Dance* (the original title) to optometrists and realtors. Our tale was of an avaricious developer who wants to acquire some Indian land and hires some bikers to terrorize the locals before an old medicine man summons a guardian spirit to fight them. For that we needed a nearby desert location, so we drove south to the Anza-Borrego, where the temperature was 109 degrees on the 4th of July when director Patrick Regan and I, the co-writer and producer, scouted it with our proposed director of photography Peter Jensen.

A mere three weeks later, as we were poised to start work in earnest on the screenplay and aimed for a 15-day shoot in late October or early November, the Screen Actors Guild went on strike; and the entirety of Hollywood production shut down. Peter, who was a camera assistant on the television series *Fantasy Island*, was laid off. So were the crew people from every studio feature and television production. We needed a new idea, one we could write and shoot nearby and very soon.

So we made a list of what we had: a lead heavy on a Harley and a black Cadillac were carried over, and to those we added houses in Malibu and Encino, some offices in Burbank, my white Porsche, Patrick's two children, and his former brother-in-law Fabian Forte. We came up with a simple plot for *Caution: Children at Play* (the new title): a widower psychiatrist Guy Nicholas home schools his telekinetically gifted twins Michael and Beth. When Dad confronts and is killed by some trespassing bikers, his son and daughter, who have been repeatedly admonished never to reveal their powers lest they be taken away by scientists who would "stick needles" in their heads, reanimate him and send him out to silence the bikers. We broke the story in half, gave the second portion to our co-writers, and started typing as fast as we could. We didn't even think of it as a zombie movie until we came up with Beth's rebuke of her controlling brother: "You turned Daddy into a weird thing, a zombie!" That helped us decide how Nicholas would act as he lumbered about in his reanimated state. In the scene where he scares a local realtor to death, Patrick's stage direction of how to exit was "Zombie out," which the actor understood without need of further explanation.

Two weeks later we had a first draft. Before we could start casting we visited the headquarters of SAG in West Hollywood with a 40-page version of the script and a $30,000 budget (our actual budget was hardly more than that, we had tried to raise $75,000 but closed the offering when we got to 39) that would qualify us for the union's experimental agreement. All the staff were too busy making signs for the picket lines to pay much attention to us, so we left with our deal in hand and started casting.

Fabian was to be the local sheriff and then we had a chance to land Marilyn Burns, the sole survivor of the original chainsaw massacre. She would be the love interest, a teacher/welfare worker who monitors the home schooling. We added character actors Jon Cedar (with whom I had worked on *The Manitou* [1978]) and Marvin Miller best known for his role as the man with the check in the quirky television series, *The Millionaire*; a couple more bikers and a biker chick; one of the investors as Nicholas; two surfer/actors who had their own boards and wet suits; a policeman with his own uniform, etc. We did buy a few clothes, such as a generic sheriff's uniform and two identical, cheap polyester blue suits, one of which would get damaged as Nicholas was killed, reanimated, and sent out to extract revenge in zombie mode.

Most of the equipment came from a local purveyor who provided camera, grip, and electric loaded on a truck that towed a generator, a package that he usually rented to *Little House on the Prairie*. He also sold us a lot of film stock that he was afraid would become outdated before the strike was settled. Peter brought along grips and electricians from *Fantasy Island* (who also borrowed a few items from that show) and the rest of the crew came from *Mork and Mindy*, *Happy Days*, *The Bad News Bears*, and *Laverne and Shirley* (we knew a lot of people at Paramount), rounded out by an Emmy-winning sound crew from *Hill Street Blues*. As this production was not sanctioned by any guild or union other than SAG, many of technicians chose to be credited with colorful pseudonyms.

We broke off as much of the script as possible (in the end around 15 of its 85 pages) to be done by a second unit that consisted of me, a dipsomaniac Latvian DP, and whoever wasn't needed on the first unit. We finished in ten days despite being bogged down by enough people and equipment so that, as one visitor from Paramount put it, we "looked like a real show." Despite all our deals going in—we even promoted a few picture cars from Ford and some bags of chips from Frito-Lay—

and everyone working 100% deferred, film, food, and gasoline cost real money, so we had to maximize our limited resources.

On a day based at those free local offices in Burbank (which came courtesy of a friend), the second unit spent the morning shooting ins-and-outs and dodging local police, as we had no permits. After this while the first unit redressed it from metropolitan police to the county sheriff, I took the actor who portrayed the main biker heavy's lawyer, had him don his police uniform, and pointed the camera out the office door: the black front end of a camera's assistant's American sedan pulled into the foreground, the lawyer-turned-cop walked into frame and crossed the street to make it seem as if he had pulled up in his police cruiser, then with his back to camera he arrested the biker he had just represented. On our penultimate day of production, the strike was settled, so the following week our crew went back to their regular gigs.

"Daddy said we shouldn't. . .ever again."

PENDRAGON FILM LTD. presents

KISS DADDY GOODBYE

was it their turn to raise him?

STARRING FABIAN FORTE, MARILYN BURNS, JON CEDAR
WRITTEN BY ALAIN SILVER & PATRICK REGAN
AND RON ABRAMS & MARY STEWART
PRODUCED BY ALAIN SILVER   DIRECTED BY PATRICK REGAN

Then the real fun began.

First the lab scratched several thousand feet of our negative. We had purchased insurance; so our "accountant" Scott Adam, who was back in his production manager's office at Paramount, volunteered to use smoke and mirrors (after all our crew had not gotten any salary) and got us a $12,000 pay-out. Using this new money we re-shot the affected scenes and a few others.

Our post production was even more jerry-rigged than the shoot: looping in a garage, foley done to a video transfer in my living room, reverse printing added to the work order of a feature we were hired to supervise early the next year.

In 1982 we finally had a rough cut that we showed to the infamous Edward L. Montoro of Film Ventures International. He loved it. We can say that he did without fear of contradiction because, while we planned to approach him again about U.S. distribution after we made some

Making *Kiss Daddy Goodbye*

foreign sales, Montoro embezzled several millions from his company and disappeared. His whereabouts are unknown to this day. We needed some more money to finish post, so to find a foreign representative, we came up with the catchier title *Kiss Daddy Goodbye* and the tagline, "Was it <u>their</u> turn to <u>raise</u> him?"; cut a video trailer; and did a mini-one-sheet flyer, which, while we were in the hallway talking to a seller at the American Film Market, prompted a $30,000 offer for England and Scandinavia. Less the agent's commission, that was about what we needed, so we took it.

I had been warned repeatedly by Marilyn Burns not to let ourselves get ripped off by disreputable distributors as had been the creators of *Texas Chainsaw Massacre*. And, of course, we knew about the travails of the purportedly public domain *Night of the Living Dead*, a misappropriation that cost Romero and his partners millions. Filing for copyright was a lot more complicated in the early 1980s; but I did it. By the

Opposite, the original two-color mini-1-sheet that sold the movie at AFM 1983. Above, the French video art. Below and first page, Zombie Daddy emerges from the grave, the reason we had to buy two cheap suits.

time we made a provisional domestic deal, it was clear that our New York–based foreign sales person was not paying us all that he owed. He claimed, for instance, that the French buyers had stiffed us. When I went to their offices in Paris the following year, they showed me the cancelled check. They also gave me a VHS copy of *Au Revoir Daddy* that I screened, with some trepidation, for my grandmother, aunt, uncle, and cousins and discovered that the French-dubbed performances were a lot better.

We eventually got a new person for foreign sales; but, by that time, our domestic seller had gotten around the restrictions in our deal by purchasing a rejected answer print from the lab that had scratched our negative. That sold via several intermediaries to the producer of the *Elvira Mistress of the Dark* show. We only found out about that when Fabian, who used to date Cassandra "Elvira" Peterson, called to say he had been hired to do comic wrap-arounds. This copy of the movie ended up in the hands of a second foreign sales person, an even more unscrupulous one, who started selling it all over the world using a bogus copyright certificate (I had refused to provide a copy of the real one until a sale was reported to us).

I traded some budgeting services with an attorney to get some cease-and-desist letters, had an FBI agent visit my office (she said we had a good case but it was too small to warrant the agency's

Below, our star Fabian Forte used to date Elvira (Cassandra Peterson). He got paid by her; we never did.

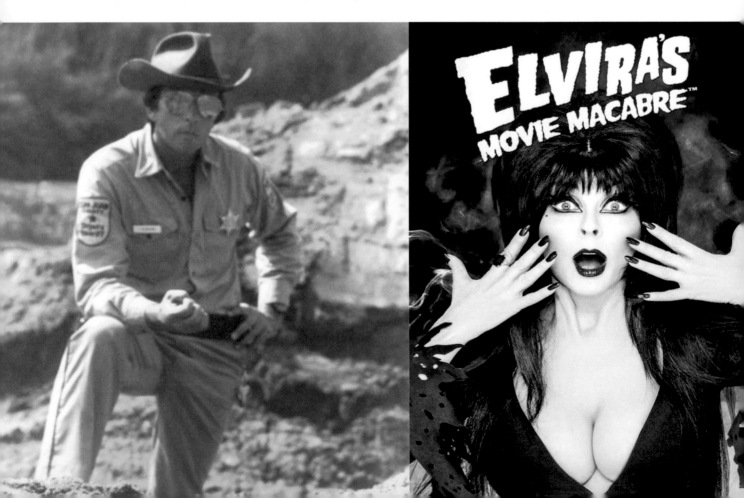

involvement), and made a few threatening calls on my own. That did not stop three pirated versions in Australia, while the bootleg *Revenge of the Zombies* migrated south from Canada and the French version for which we never got the check was released in Quebec. When the duped intermediary company that sold the picture to Elvira agreed to pay us directly, they got sued and went bankrupt, and compelled me to tell the trustee that I didn't care if Wells Fargo was a secured creditor, I would sell this repeatedly stolen movie on which we owned the legitimate copyright whenever and wherever I wanted. He tacitly acquiesced.

Eventually diminishing returns and the press of new projects compelled us to move on, to kiss *Caution: Children at Play, Revenge of the Zombie, The Vengeful Dead,* and a host of foreign titles goodbye. I estimated that our worldwide gross from all legitimate sales was just over three-quarters of a million dollars. Our net on that was less than $100,000. Who knows what money was taken in by the various film thieves who feasted on our celluloid flesh as if there were zombies. By the way there are still two versions out there. This left one is sanctioned and the other is a bootleg.

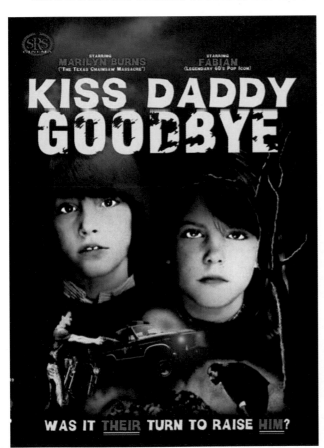 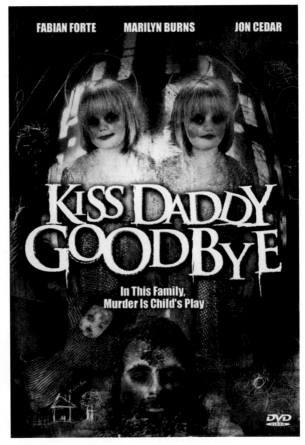

Afterword: in 2011 Patrick Regan and I did a Q&A following a screening of *Kiss Daddy Goodbye* for the patrons of a regular event in Hollywood known as "Horrible Movie Night."

JACOB TESS
FREUDSTEIN

*The House by
the Cemetery.*

Chapter Six

Zombies with an Old-World Flavor

"I will knock down the Gates of the Netherworld,
I will smash the door posts, and leave the doors flat down,
and will let the dead go up to eat the living!"

from Tablet VI
The Epic of Gilgamesh

The rise of zombie movies in Europe was a predictable result, conincident with the evolution of the manga in Japan, that accompanied the rising popularity of glossily illustrated sci-fi and horror adventure, typified by the French anthology magazine *Metal Hurlant* (beginning in 1974). The audiences for that print material developed and sustained a taste for zombie gore but with more style, with Gothic moods and settings. In addition, the official and unofficial European censors were considerably less puritanical than their American counterparts and allowed far more nudity that also increased the appeal worldwide of the Euro zombie movie.

Spanish filmmaker Amando de Ossorio's *Blind Dead* series remains the most influential of the early examples of this type of zombie film. The first in the tetralogy, *Tombs of the Blind Dead* (1972), showcases medieval locations (a resource Euro horror directors had readily available), ample bare flesh to be exposed and eaten, and mystical, murderous Templar Knights decades before Dan Brown imagined *The Da Vinci Code*.

Below, *Tombs of the Blind Dead*: a literary conceit not typical of American productions, as the mounted Templar ghouls lined up like the Four Horseman of the Apocalypse. Opposite, the Italian 1-sheet: a skeletal hand clutches the arm of a cringing, buxom victim.

LE TOMBE DEI RESUSCITATI CIECHI

JOHN BURNER · HELEN HARP
con
BRIGITTE FLEMING · GRAY THELMAN

The premise of the film, which is visualized in a period flashback, is that the infamous Templars returned from the crusades with occult knowledge from Egypt, which has some historical truth, and set up shop in a small town and monastery where they used the ankh as their sigil. The film then veers off into fantasy as the knight monks perform rituals of communion in which they drink the blood and eat the flesh of local virgins in order to obtain immortality. They are ultimately hung by the authorities and their eyes plucked out by birds.

In present time a young woman, Virginia (Maria Elena Arpon), disturbed after meeting her school-girl lesbian lover Bette (Lone Fleming) and miffed that her male beau Roger (Cesar Burner) is flirting with Bette rather than her, jumps off a rural train taking them to a vacation spot. She wanders into the deserted Templar town and spends the night in the monastery. As she tries to sleep, hooded, skeletal zombie monks rise from their graves. The scenes with the Templars are shot mostly in slow motion, giving the film its poetic, Gothic aura. In addition, the soundtrack mixes Gregorian-style chants with discordant, modern sounds to sustain an eerie mood. The Templars mount their horses and pursue Virginia, taking communion on her body when they bring her to the ground.

Bette and Roger identify her body in the morgue and determine then and there that they will discover the reason for her mutilation and murder. Meanwhile Virginia rises from the autopsy table to ravage a necrophiliac morgue attendant who was about to rape her body. She wanders to the mannequin factory where Bette is employed and attacks another worker there. In another striking scene, the worker throws a lamp at Virginia and sets her on fire. She burns surrounded by half-dressed mannequins.

Roger and Bette hire a smuggler for protection and return to the Templar town to find evidence. While waiting for the Templars to rise, the smuggler rapes Bette in the graveyard. In the aftermath of that, the Templars take revenge for Bette by devouring the smuggler. After Roger and the smuggler's girl are murdered, Bette attempts escape onto the passing train but the horsed Templars overrun it and devour all its passengers. When the train pulls into the station, Bette, her hair turned gray, stumbles onto the platform and the new passengers scream as they discover the bodies on board. De Ossorio's visual delineation of this grim narrative is certainly not Hollywood standard. The erotic and exotic imagery combines the medieval and the modern and uses the undercurrent of the both religious and sexual fervor for its social metaphor in which devout and deviant impulses alike are consumed by an atavistic power.

With *Return of the Blind Dead* (*Return of the Evil Dead*, 1973) de Ossorio had a slightly larger budget, which he uses to populate an entire town and add detail to the back story of the Templars. He reenacts their rituals involving young virgins, where the Templars appear to rely as much if not more on blood drinking than flesh eating in order to attain immortality. In this iteration, there is greater visual impact as the villagers burn them alive rather than hang them (which was shown only

The ancient Templars are considerably more skeletal than typical Romero-style ghouls. A bony hand, opposite, recalls the one holding a vial of poison in Carl Dreyer's *Vampyr*.

in an illustration from a book in the former film). And the Templar horde is larger, so that makes their resurrection more horrifying and the total destruction of the town more feasible. The scenes with the knights rising from their graves at night are shot with a blue tint. They ride their horses in slow motion with the hoofbeats echoing on the soundtrack—as they did in the original—both image and sound being part of de Ossorio's oneiric staging. There is also a more overt moral dimension to this film, that was understated in *Tombs of the Blind Dead*. All the characters in this *Return of the Blind Dead*, except the three who survive, two lovers and a young girl, are reprehensible on one level or another.

The film opens with a festival that celebrates the execution of the Templars: town people joyfully, with a morose delectation, burn the knights in effigy as fireworks fill the sky above. While this transpires the perverted and persecuted hunchback (Jose Canalejas), who was seen being pummeled by a group of children in the movie's prologue, kidnaps a young woman and eviscerates her in order to reanimate the blind dead. The mayor (Fernando Sancho) of the town is a stereotypical Euro-villain, both cowardly—he later uses the young girl as a diversion in a failed attempt to escape the Templars—and vengeful. He exerts total control over his "fiancée" Vivian (Esparanza Roy),

Return of the Blind Dead: in their blood-tinged cloaks Templars slash their way through town.

whom he treats as his chattel. When Jack Marlowe (Tony Kendall) arrives to supervise the fireworks, the mayor is unreasonably jealous and imagines that Marlowe and Vivian make a romantic connection. Consequently he orders his thugs to rough up Marlowe. The commissioner of the area is equally corrupt. He is too busy playing sex games with his young bedmate to respond to pleas for help when the Templars arise and start their massacre.

De Ossorio uses camera angles for the scenes of the mounted Templars slashing and cutting their way through the villagers that evoke how they might have acted during the Crusades where they honed their reputation as defenders of the true faith: they are like "arms of God" when they eliminate these "infidels," much as their historical counterparts did to Moslems and Jews with swords and pikes in the Holy Land centuries before. This moral ambiguity is at the core of a post-modern sensibility in de Ossorio's work. When simple natural events—the crow of the cock and the sunlight—eventually bring down the undead, who one by one fall to dust as they stand like sentinels around the town, only the innocent have survived the holocaust.

The Ghost Galleon (1974) is the weakest link in the series. De Ossorio complained about its minuscule budget and that the "magnificent" Spanish galleon was simply a paper model, burnt in the climax. It also features an array of swimsuit models, obviously added for pure exploitation value in anticipation of a titillating marketing campaign as evident in the Spanish and cheap two-color American ad art. Only the German poster focuses on the horror, as its lengthy tagline reads:

Below, prototypical Euro-trash horror in *Ghost Galleon*: the blind-dead Templars rise from the ocean to menace bikini-clad babes.

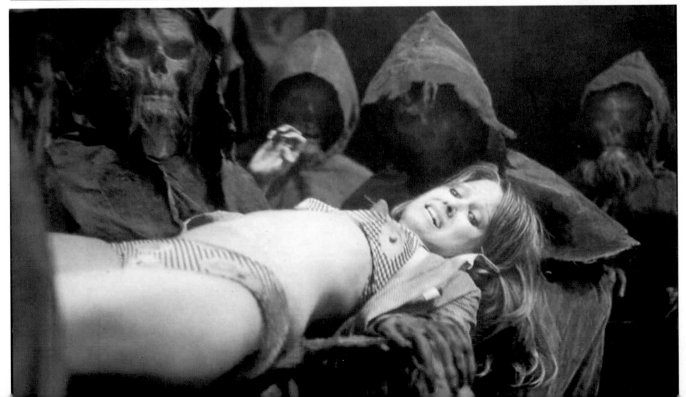

Mitternacht:
Wenn im bleichen Licht des Vollmondes
die modrigen Kajütentüren
von Leichenhand geöffnet werden,
beginnt die neueste
Geisterfahrt des Horrors.

Jack Taylor
Maria Perschy
Carlos Lemos
Barbara Rey

Farbfilm

Das Geisterschiff der schwimmenden Leichen

»The Ghostship of the Blind Dead«

Regie: Amando Ossori   Produktion: Ancla Century Film/Reelife Productions   Verleih

"Midnight, when in the pale light of the full moon the musty cabin doors are opened by corpse hands to begin the latest ghost ride of horror." By the final episode of the Templar zombie saga, even the German marketeers had gotten on board.

Night of the Seagulls (1975) owes much to H.P. Lovecraft's "The Shadow over Innsmouth" for its plot, symbolism, and archetypes. Like the narrator in Lovecraft's tale, a couple (a doctor and his wife) find themselves up in a small coastal village that worships and makes sacrifices to a fish god: Dagon, a fertility god from ancient Babylon and the environs. The image of that god figures prominently in the latest prologue set in the time of the Templars and resembles Lovecraft's Dagon, a hybrid of frog and fish. Just as Lovecraft had utilized the call of the whippoorwills in "Shadow," de Ossorio uses the sounds of seagulls, who represent the spirits of the virgins killed by the Templars, to herald the blood sacrifices and to evoke the undertone of horror that pervades the small town.

This is particularly so in the ritual scenes on the seashore: a procession of the inhabitants of the town, cloaked in black, leads a young woman to the rocks at the tideline. They tie her down as the seabird calls echo above them. The horsed Templars come out of the ocean, rising from the watery depths like Lovecraft's Deep Ones, and take the captive back to their castle. There, before the idol of Dagon and in demonic sacrament, they consume their victim's flesh and blood.

The newly arrived Doctor Stein (Victor Petit), and his wife Joan (Maria Kosty) learn of the cult

The seaside procession with the sacrificial victim in *Night of the Seagulls*.

A ravishing Templar in
Night of the Seagulls.

through their new servant Lucy (Sandra Mozarowsky) and the mentally challenged and abused town "fool" Teddy (Jose A. Calvo). When Lucy is finally called to give up her life to the Templars and their fish god, Stein and his wife refuse to permit her sacrifice. They rescue her from the rocks but are unable to elude the Templars. Lucy and the Steins take refuge in a house where, as the Templars batter down the doors, Teddy forfeits own his own life defending them. That is not enough for the implacable Templars. Although the three steal ghostly horses to attempt escape by riding off in the blue-tinted night, the ghoulish instinct of the horses prevents it. Lucy is caught by the knights, and the doctor and his wife are carried by their steeds to the castle. But when the Templars converge to consume Stein and his wife, the couple overturns the statue of Dagon. As the idol crashes and breaks into bits, so do the knights themselves. Their dying chants mix with the seagulls on the closing soundtrack.

La Orgia de los Muertos (*The Hanging Woman, Bracula Terror of the Living Dead,* 1973) is typical of Euro horror from the 1970s and 1980s in its multiple titles, versions, and even settings: one version of this movie proclaims the setting as Scotland rather than continental Europe. In some releases the European actors and behind-the-camera people are even given Anglo-sounding names (star Stelvio Rossi becoming Stanley Cooper) to give the audience the idea that this might be an American or British horror film in recognition of their greater popularity with local audiences than their national product. As do many Euro-horror productions, *La Orgia de los Muertos* features many actual Gothic locations. It also has putrescent zombies galore as well as a small part for Euro horror mainstay Jacinto Molina (Paul Naschy) as a necrophiliac gravedigger and Maria Pia Conte as a seductive older woman.

Vengeance of the Zombies (aka *Walk of the Dead*, 1973) was directed by Leon Klimovsky known for poetic and perverse vampire films such as *The Vampires' Night Orgy* (1974) and written by the star Jacinto Molina. The filmmakers transplant voodoo to England by way of India. As much about the depredations of English colonial rule as traditions of esoteric magic, the film deals with the vengeance of an Indian named Kantaka (Molina) who was burned alive by several English families because he had "deflowered" their daughter. The severely burned Kantaka survives the fire and manages to reach Great Britain where he transforms the racist families into his zombie slaves. With his scarred face hidden behind an array of Halloween-style masks, Kantaka uses occult fetishes, effigies, and blood to raise the bodies of the victims that he or his servants have murdered. Kantaka also has a twin, Krisna (Molina in a dual role), who has evolved beyond the pettiness of his brother and become a mystic. Krisna tries to foil his brother's plan but without success—in fact, he comes under his brother's mesmeric powers in the final scene of the movie.

Above, three of the numerous pieces of ad art used to promote *La Orgia de los Muertos* [see Filmography for a fourth].

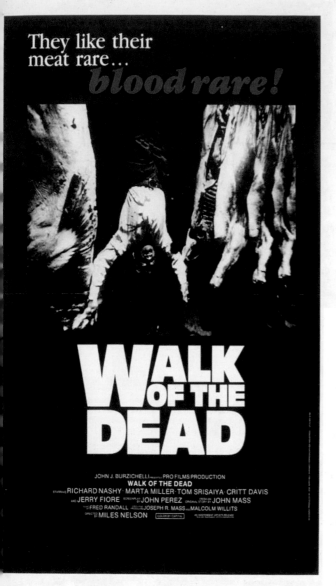

Many shots depicting the resurrection of these dead and their subsequent attacks on other members of the families are in slow motion, which imbues the scenes with much the same hallucinatory quality as in the Templar films. In certain ways, these attacks are more vampiric than what viewers may have come to expect from a post-Romero zombie film. The women ghouls—and most of Kantaka's victims are women—are dressed in diaphanous gowns and smile wickedly as they become predators and overpower their victims.

Even lower budget in 1974 was *Vudu Sangriento* (aka *Black Voodoo Exorcist* or *Bloody Pit of Horror*), in which a sword-wielding half mummy, half ghoul from

Africa (portrayed by Caucasian Spanish actor Aldo Sambrell) is reanimated in his coffin aboard a cruise ship and extracts revenge on the descendants of ancient enemies. Amazingly Sambrell is not the only performer in black face.

Jorge Grau's *Let Sleeping Corpses Lie* (*Don't Open the Window*, *The Living Dead at the Manchester Morgue*,

Above, *Let Sleeping Corpses Lie.*

1974), like director Jean Rollin's later zombie films, posits that zombie-ism is a genetic mutation and that its cause is environmental pollution. In this movie, it is a new form of pesticidal procedure, involving radiation and used in the fields around the English Lake District. Grau also indicts modern civilization in general with an opening montage of Manchester, where industrial pollution pervades the city and the inhabitants wear protective masks.

The rest of the plot is standard zombie fare with a few specific nods to Romero's *Night of the Living Dead* beyond its alternate titles. The zombies, affected by the pesticide, rise to feed off humans and lay siege to them at various locations, including a hospital. The art dealer protagonist of the movie, George (Ray Lovelock), tries to destroy the machine that is emitting the radiation, but his efforts are futile. He returns to the hospital to begin immolating zombies, including his female friend Edna (Cristina Galbo). The intolerant and arrogant police official (portrayed by Arthur Kennedy) refuses to listen to George's pleas and shoots him dead.

Devil's Kiss (*Wicked Caresses of Satan,* 1976) features Euro-trash star Syliva Solar as the raven-haired psychotic Countess Grandier. She conducts occult rites in order to raise the dead and send them on a mission to extract revenge for her. Solar approaches the performance with her usual sensuality and vigor, as her character recognizes no moral limits in her scheme to destroy a rival family. In one scene she saves a dwarf from a lynching in order to turn him into her slave. She seductively undresses before him to solidify his devotion on an erotic and emotional level.

Artistic exploitation director Jean Rollin, known for his erotic vampire films, delved into the zombie genre with three significant productions: *Grapes of Death* (*Les Raisins de la Mort*,1978), *Zombie Lake* (*Le Lac des Morts Vivants*,1980), and *The Living Dead Girl* (*La Morte Vivante*,1982). All three not only rework the zombie myth but also include the theme of environmentalism, which following Romero's lead was increasingly linked with zombie-ism by his European counterparts.

It would be atypical for a singular genre filmmaker such as Rollin to make a cookie-cutter zombie movie. His films are rife with painterly compositions and his personal meditations on amour fou, eroticism, and decadent sub-cultures. *Grapes of Death* opens on a row of masked farmers in various color coveralls and homemade masks walking in a line as they spray the blue insecticide over the vineyards. Their regimented movement and lack of emotion transform them, so that they seem like metaphorical harbingers of doom. And of course they are. This newly developed insecticide pollutes the grapes and turns the farmers into decomposing zombie-like killers.

The focus of the movie shifts to a young woman, Elisabeth (Marie-Georges Pascal)—many of Rollin's films are oriented around women's perspectives and feature one or two female protagonists—on her way to visit her fiancé, who is a supervisor at the winery. While en route by train, she and an acquaintance are attacked by an infected villager. She leaves the eerily deserted transport and makes her way on foot.

Les Raisins de la Mort: Brigitte Lahaie as La Grande Femme.

Above, *The Grapes of Death*: blind Lucie (Mirella Rancelot) is crucified, dismembered, and beheaded.

Like many of Rollin's works, *Grapes of Death* is constructed in the manner of a dark fairy tale spun off the Brothers Grimm, a trope reinforced here by its child-like calliope score. On her journey to the winery Elisabeth encounters various others, some infected, some not. Her first meeting is with a father and daughter who seem hostile to her. From the daughter, Elisabeth disoivers that the father is infected and has killed the mother—the viewer can see her body with its throat slit on a bed. The daughter wants Elisabeth to help her kill her patriarchal oppressor; but before they can act, the father strips his daughter naked in an incestuous fury and stabs her to death with a pitchfork. Elisabeth then steals his car and uses it to crush him to death.

The next character on the road to the winery is a blind woman, Lucie (Mirella Rancelot), who is wandering through the desolate countryside in her nightgown in search of her caregiver Lucas. Together the two women reach Lucie's village; but the inhabitants are all infected and walk about aimlessly, chanting and humming with ethereal voices. When Lucie meets the zombie Lucas, he crucifies her to a door and then decapitates her. He then dies with her head in his arms, as he kisses her bloody lips.

Next for Elisabeth is the beautiful and mysterious Grande Femme (portrayed by soft-core Euro-sex star Brigitte Lahaie). She displays the perfection of her body to prove that she is uninfected and then offers Ellisabeth refuge from the villagers. When two farmers arrive with guns and dynamite to destroy the plague victims, the Grande Femme takes her two mastiffs and confronts them. After again doffing her gown to reveal her unblemished white skin, which earns their trust as well as their awe, she eventually blows up herself and their dynamite-laden truck.

Elisabeth finally reaches the end of her quest at the winery. There she finds her fiancé. Although he is also infected, she refuses to leave him. When the two farmers kill him, she shoots them. Standing below his body, which hangs from the hayloft, she lets his dripping blood enter her mouth as a form of communion with the dead. Despite all she has witnessed, her emotional loyalty to her lover compels her to become an infected creature like him.

Although not without interest, *Zombie Lake* is the least effective of Rollin's zombie projects, which he took over from director Jesus Franco and tried to salvage despite its myriad production problems. From the original low-budget American conception in the 1943 *Revenge of the Zombies*, postwar examples of Nazi ghouls—in this case, as depicted in a flashback, killed and thrown into a lake by Resistance fighters during World War II—would carry on throughout the next few decades and reach a level of respectability in the mainstream 2009 Norwegian horror comedy *Dead Snow*. There are also some poignant and bizarre scenes between a young girl and her Nazi/zombie father.

Below, *Zombie Lake* yields up a squad of Nazi ghouls.

Above, Catherine Valmont (Françoise Blanchard) begins her disaffected, undead rampage in *Living Dead Girl*.

Opposite, zombie flesh eaters get down to their grisly business in Lucio Fulci's *Zombie*.

With his next film *Living Dead Girl*, Rollin moved into the realm of more traditional filmmaking with fewer instances of surrealism or non-linear structure. *La Morte* is a story of amour fou beyond death. While dumping toxic materials in an ancient catacomb, the workers "awaken" a corpse—because of, we can only assume, the toxic fumes in the barrels—that of the young heiress Catherine Valmont (Françoise Blanchard). She immediately attacks the three men: drinks their blood and devours their entrails.

Her hunger somewhat sated, the semi-catatonic Catherine, still dressed in her bloody burial gown, wanders through her ancestral chateau, which is now empty and up for sale. There various objects trigger a series of memory flashbacks. The viewer learns that as a child Catherine formed a romantic bond with her friend Helene (Marina Pierro). As a tearful Catherine listens to the haunting melody of a music box, the audience sees the two girls exchanging vows of eternal love, which they formalize by exchanging blood. Catherine is among the most tortured of protagonists in Rollin's oeuvre. She never fully adjusts to her environment, although it is physically restricted to the grounds of her own chateau. Her pangs of hunger cause her intense agony and prompt ear-piercing screams. Catherine finally manages to contact her childhood friend; and once Helene appears, she becomes her enabler. Helene first feeds Catherine from her own veins and then begins luring victims back for her. An anguished Catherine wants to die, but Helene refuses to let her lover return to the grave.

The film reaches its climax when a curious photographer named Barbara (Carina Barone) investigates this "living dead girl," whom she had observed from a distance. Helene tries to protect Catherine by putting an axe in the head of the Barbara's husband and setting the woman herself on fire. Intent on ending this bloody reign, Catherine now begs Helene to leave: "I am your death, Helene." When Helene reminds her of their childhood vow to follow each other into death, Catherine attacks her. As the camera zooms back slowly under a blue-tinged night sky, the sight of the two women lying dead on the castle bridge is revealed to the viewer. Then, after a moment's pause, Catherine's shrill screams ring out in the darkness.

Italian director Lucio Fulci upped the usual gore quotient in his Euro zombie films beginning with *Zombie* (1979) aka *Zombi 2*—to clarify *Zombi*, without an "e" or a "*1*," is the international title of Romero's *Dawn of the Dead*, and there is more below on the *Zombie/Zombi/Flesh Eater* series.

As with many of his movies, Fulci makes numerous allusions to literary sources. A boat with no live passengers drifts towards the shores of Manhattan. When the police go on board to investigate,

they are attacked by particularly violent and gory zombies, a scene and staging that harkens back to the arrival of the doomed ship *Demeter* in Bram Stoker's novel *Dracula*. A crack investigative reporter, Peter West (Ian McCulloch), joins forces with Anne Bowles (Tisa Farrow), who has received a letter, delivered via the zombie boat, from her father. He is on a Caribbean island doing research with a colleague, Dr. Menard (Richard Johnson). Together Pete and Anne fly to the Caribbean and hire a young couple to take them by boat to the isolated island where her father works. This time the allusion is to the horrifying core of Joseph Conrad's *Heart of Darkness*. At the end of a dangerous trek, which includes an encounter with underwater zombies, the couples discover a dissolute and megalomaniacal individual, who has sunken into a twisted and amoral morass while in a jungle hideaway.

Fulci had introduced the unidentified Dr. Menard in a prologue, his face in shadows, as he drew a revolver and shot a shrouded body in the head. Next he is depicted arguing with his addicted wife Paola (Olga Karlatos) about his mission on the island. He refuses to accept the reality of the native voodoo beliefs despite that fact that he has seen the zombies with his own eyes. Despite his wife's pleas, he also refuses to leave. When Paola is later attacked while showering—zombies in nudity-friendly Euro movies seem to prefer preying on naked women—and eaten alive by two zombies, the viewer easily makes the connection between his indifference to his wife's pleas and her fate. Even his reaction to her grisly demise seems detached. The climax of the movie is pure zombie holocaust. Menard and the two couples barricade themselves in the hospital as the zombies invade. It is particularly gory yet darkly elegiac: as the zombies shamble into the hospital and while the defenders throw Molotov cocktails at them, a dirge plays on the soundtrack.

While *Zombie* was more straight-forward genre action, in *City of the Living Dead* (*The Gates of Hell*)

(1980) Fulci moves into mysticism and metaphysics. Inspired by Lovecraft's "The Dunwich Horror"—in fact, the town in the story is named Dunwich—the film opens with the suicide of a demented priest, Father Thomas (Fabrizio Jovine) in the Dunwich graveyard as seen through the eyes of the psychic, Mary (Catriona MacColl), who is in New York City. The power of her vision causes her to fall into a catatonic state. She is pronounced dead and buried alive—this time the allusion is Edgar Allan Poe. In a tense and terrifying sequence, the camera is inside the coffin with Mary as she awakens and tries to claw her way through the lid. She is rescued by reporter Peter Bell (Christopher George), who is snooping around for a story.

Although cynical and disgruntled, Bell still decides to follow the lead given him by the rescued Mary. She and her psychic mentor tell him about the *Book of Enoch*, which stands in for Lovecraft's fictional *Necronomicon*, an ancient Jewish text that speaks of opening the gates of hell and releasing the undead. In Lovecraft's fiction, the book releases the Old Ones, ancient evil gods. Bell and Mary drive to Dunwich, where the undead have already started to rise and attack the living with typically gory aplomb.

The climax of the movie is a horror tour de force: Bell, Mary, and town psychiatrist Gerry (Carlo De Mejo) enter the catacombs below the graveyard to destroy the ghoul Father Thomas. The art direction, one of Fulci's fortes, is pointedly arcane and repulsive: skeletons seem to grow out of the walls of the blue-tinted catacombs, while huge rats scurry around the feet of the intruders. In the confrontation with Father Thomas, Mary's eyes begin to bleed as she faces off with him psychically. The psychiatrist delivers the death blow with a staff, and all the zombies burst into flame. With their demise, the incessant drum beat that has punctuated the soundtrack throughout the movie ends.

Opposite, *Zombie* investigator Peter West (Ian McCulloch) joins forces with Anne Bowles (Tisa Farrow).

Below, ghouls and power tools in *CIty of the Living Dead*.

In *The Beyond* (1981) Fulci situates the narrative in one of the traditional centers of voodoo, Louisiana—the movie was largely shot on location there. Fulci drives more deeply into the metaphysical with this tale of a ramshackle hotel situated smack dab on a portal to hell. The film opens in 1927 with an amber-tinted black-and-white sequence. Fulci intercuts three sequences: a painter named Schweik (Antoine Saint-John) working on a surreal canvas of a world beyond; young seer Emily (Cinzia Monreale) reading from the *Book of Eibon* (another *Necronomicon*-type text), and a group of solemn-faced locals arriving by boat with torches and tools. When this group reaches the hotel, they go directly to Room 36, which is Schweik's, and drag him to the basement where they crucify him against the wall, while calling him "warlock." In a reference to another Poe story, Schweik's ends up enclosed with the wall.

The film then shifts to the modern day where Liza (Catriona MacColl, again) is in the middle of restoring the dilapidated but moodily Gothic hotel. During the restoration she summons help for a flooded basement, and a hapless plumber releases the body of Schweik. This leads to the resurrection of the dead and the inevitable torture and vivisection of the living. By this movie Fulci had established his credentials as a purveyor of horror with a truly sadistic slant whose movies featured various forms of human torture, particularly those involving the eye.

The Beyond: Liza (Catriona MacColl) and McCabe (David Warbeck) fend off the horde of ghouls in the hospital.

Opposite, the couple find themselves inside the distorted yet painterly landscape that is the title's hellish beyond.

Above, The Beyond: even as his work in the genre ends Fulci continues to indulge in gore. Below, *House by the Cemetery* includes a macabrely humorous death by kitchen knife and, of course, more brains gaping from open skulls.

With the help of skeptical doctor McCabe (David Warbeck), Liza probes for the root of this mystery; but the body count keeps mounting and the zombies keep rising. In the climax in the hospital, the dead patients rise up and attack Liza and McCabe, who escape through a door leading to a basement. To their horror, they discover it is somehow the basement of Liza's hotel. In shock and awe they stare at a landscape right out of Schweik's painting of the hellish beyond. As they run forward in slow motion, a deep and disembodied voice pronounces their doom.

In *The House by the Cemetery* (1981) Fulci eschews the mysticism of his earlier zombie films and relies entirely on scenes of sadistic gore for dramatic impact. Like Romero, throughout his stories, Fulci does manifest a macabre sense of humor, particularly in his choice of character names and many of his killings. In *House*, the antagonist zombie is Dr. Freudstein, about which the audience is left to draw its own conclusions. An afterthought in the confusing chronicle of Fulci's undead oeuvre is *Zombi 3* aka *Zombie Flesh Eaters 2*, which suggests a direct sequel to Fulci's *Zombie* aka *Zombi 2* aka *Zombie Flesh Eaters*, except just as they morphed from Romero zombies in a shopping mall to ghouls on a sailboat in NYC, in *3*, humans in Southeast Asia are succumbing to a zombie bird flu that was introduced to avian carriers by toxic pollutants.

If this were not confusing enough *Oltre la Morte* or *Zombi(e) 4* returns (without Fulci's participation) to old-school magical zombies who over-run a jungle research facility. Ultimately the sole survivor, who is protected by a charmed necklace, returns for revenge but ends up a sentient zombie. Despite wielding AK-47s, everyone else in the party is slaughtered.

Top right, Fulci's participation is the largest selling point: "After *L'Enfer Des Zombies* [*Zombie*], a new film from..."
Right, *Oltre la Morte* or *Zombie 4*: Jenny (Candace Daly) prepares to rip off her charmed necklace.

Above left, Robert Vaughn as the disfigured and deranged Vietnam vet, Dr. Fred Brown, in *Zombie 5: Killing Birds*. Right, mimicking Fulci but without the panache: Brown's bayonet in a victim's head.   Opposite, the ongoing visual influence of *Metal Hurlant*: the cartoonish poster for another group of lecherous Nazi zombies, on which director Franco's pseudonym is among the largest creative credits.

Lastly there is *Uccelli Assassini* or *Zombie 5: Killing Birds*, which could just as well have been called *Louisiana Woodpecker Hunt*. Yes, there are zombies and a bird (that's not much of a killer), but mostly there's a sociopathic Vietnam vet lurking in a bayou plantation. By the way, number *5* in the series that is sometimes called Spaghetti Zombies was actually released in many Western European markets before either *3* or *4*.

After de Ossorio, Rollin, and Fulci, the Euro-zombie lost much of its distinction. The downturn begins with Jesus Franco's *The Treasure of the Living Dead* (*Oasis of the Living Dead*) (1982), which does make novel use of an African oasis as a setting. Still a long way from becoming a full-fledged sub-genre but already getting somewhat old-hat, there are Nazi zombies lurking in the

sands where they were left to protect a golden treasure from various interlopers. The zombie battles in the sand create a bizarre yet scenic aura. In *Le Notti del Terrore* (*Burial Ground*, 1981), a trapped in the country house by ghouls narrative, director Andrea Bianchi notoriously includes a scene in which a zombiefied "child" (a dwarf portraying a young boy) bites off his mother's nipple. None of the humans survives the undead rampage.

Right, old-school hooded ghoul in *Burial Ground:*

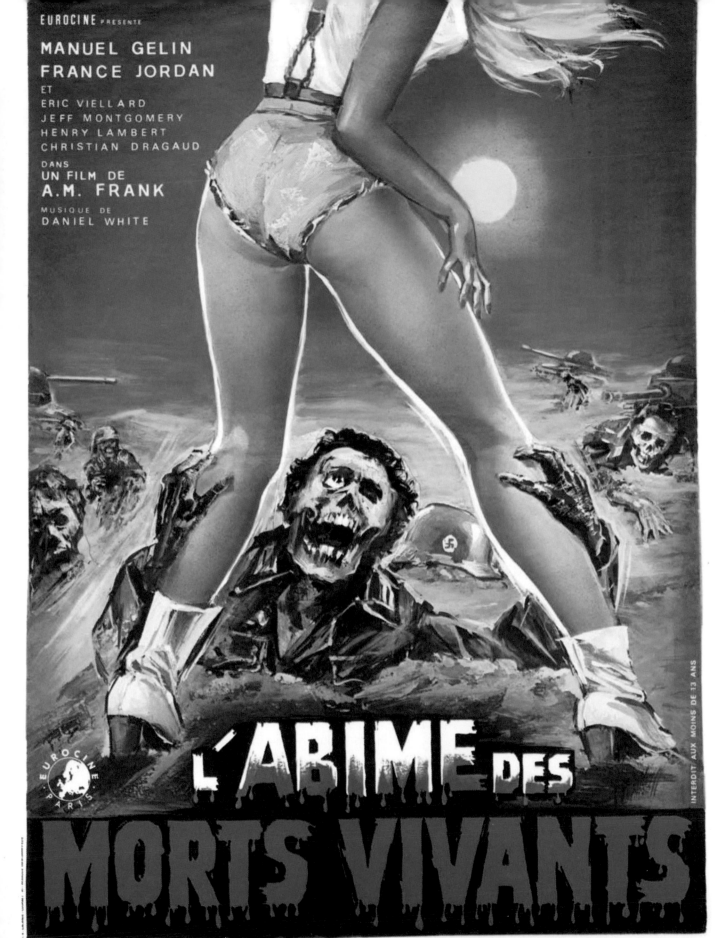

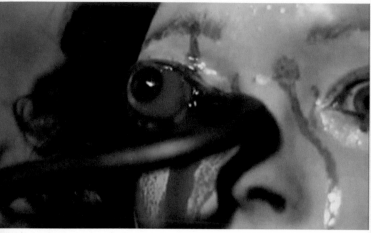

Carrying on the Fulci gore tradition: left, an eyeball is popped out in *Demoni 3*.

Right, a tablespoon of Fulci, a pinch of de Ossorio, and a soupçon of Rollin's *Living Dead Girl* in *Don't Wake the Dead* from Andreas Schnaas.

Further on in the Euro-zombies declining arc, *Demoni 3* (*Black Demons*) (1991) resurrects the voodoo aspect of the zombie myth. Set in Brazil a group of teens resurrect a slew of murdered slaves, who seek revenge on their reanimators for the atrocities they suffered.

In Germany in 1990 Fulci disciple writer/director/actor Andreas Schnaas started production of the shot-on-video "Violent Shit" series of gory homages to the Euro-horror filmmakers whose work he watched every week in the local cinemas as a child. Schnaas portrayed Karl the Butcher. Although unreleased for almost a decade, in *Violent Shit III: Infantry of Doom* (1999, aka *Zombie Doom*), Karl and his Dad are ensconced in an island laboratory and working on a strain of ghoulish super soldiers when interrupted by the arrival of castaways, much in the manner of Dr. Sangre in Monogram's *King of the Zombies* (Schnaas probably saw that on German television). The unexpected success of the first *Violent Shits* permitted a slightly larger budget for *Zombie '90: Extreme Pestilence* (1991): a zombie apocalypse is triggered by military experiments and leaked chemicals in this self-proclaimed "ultimate Gore-Film." In *Don't Wake the Dead* (2008)

Schnaas goes from full-on Fulci to outrageous Ossorio riffs, in which nubile college girls show up to help a friend's concert in a castle only to discover a basement full of combat hardened zombies that include both Templar Knights and Waffen SS. Of course, the women get naked a lot. Another German splatter specialist Olaf Ittenbach made his sole (to date) low-budget foray into the genre with *Born Undead* (aka *Garden of Love*, 2003) in which a journalist's murdered family returns as revenge-seeking, flesh-eating ghouls with predictable torrents of blood.

Above and below, *Garden of Love*: the film adopts some of the pictorialism of Rollin but still does not forget to paint with blood.

In Michele Soavi's *Cemetery Man* (1994), an erotic and surreal patina tinged with old-world myth replaces Romero style zombie-ism. The Italian version sports a more appropriate title: *Dellamorte, Dellamore* (*Of Death, Of Love*). This dark comedy's protagonist, Francesco Dellamorte (Rupert Everett), is suspended between life and love and death, as he laconically performs his job as cemetery custodian and killer of any zombies emerging therefrom. Set in the ancient graveyard of a small Italian village, Dellamorte and his mentally challenged assistant Gnaghi (Francois Hadji-Lazaro) are charged with attending burial of the dead as well as the destruction of the undead. As the sign over the gate says, "Resurrecturis" ("They will arise") and a week after being put in the ground for no particular rhyme or reason many do emerge from it.

Dellamorte narrates the movie with an ironic tone and tells the viewer that he is "indifferent" to death, love, or any life beyond his village. His actions seem to confirm that, as he blows the brains out of the newly minted ghouls, many still covered in freshly-dug earth, without a moment's pause. In town he is a joke, mocked by the young men for his supposed impotence and ignored by the officials as long as he keeps to his job. He tells the audience that his only friends are the dead.

All this changes when a beautiful widow enters Dellamorte's graveyard home to bury her aged husband. He stands awestruck by her aspect: black silk dress clinging to her voluptuous curves, full

pouting lips, smoldering eyes. In his sexually captivated state, he wonders whether he will see her again. Of course, as genre expectation dictates, he does. Having read the lust in his eyes, she returns to relate how her husband was a "tireless" lover. Possibly excited at the prospect of this morbid backdrop for a physical encounter, Dellamorte then invites the nameless widow (this character played by the statuesque Anna Falchi is only referred to as "She") to visit his ancient ossuary. Inside it, Dellamorte becomes aroused as she caresses the bones and tears her dress on a skeletal remnant. The man and woman finally couple on the grave of her dead husband.

During their orgasm, the cuckolded corpse arises and bites his unfaithful wife. She apparently dies; and, fearing that she has become undead, Dellamorte shoots her in the head when she sits up on the slab. Although distraught for a moment, he buries the widow and returns to the drudgery of his duties. But "She" is not through with Dellamorte. Like a symbol distilled from death, life, and love, she rises from the grave as a zombie. Entangled in branches and flowers like some Earth goddess, she beguiles Dellamorte again. When Gnaghi does what is required of them and puts her down, Dellamorte despairingly realizes that he is responsible for her fate.

Dellamorte receives yet another chance. She returns again (or seems to), when Falchi portrays the newly hired secretary to the venal mayor. This woman is particularly attracted to Dellamorte

Left and below, the power of obsession visualized in *Cemetery Man*: the aptly named Dellamorte (Rupert Everett) is enraptured by every aspect of every character portrayed by Anna Falchi.

because she has heard he is impotent and is disgusted by intercourse. He performs other acts of sex with her and becomes enraptured anew, so much that he visits a doctor and demands castration, reminiscent of the perversely motivated mutilation of Lon Chaney's character in Tod Browning's 1927 horror film *The Unknown*. The doctor will only consent to a chemical treatment that causes temporary impotence, after which Dellamorte is amazed to learn from his new object of desire that she is marrying the mayor, who raped her and in doing so restored her desire for sex. She would continue their relationship with Dellamorte as her sex slave, but he refuses.

This psychological blow pushes Dellamorte over the brink. He has hysterical visions of Death instructing him to "kill the living" and does so by gunning down the young male tormentors in town. In a last encounter with a Falchi character or "She Who Must Be Obeyed"—apologies to H. Rider Haggard—she is a college girl who seduces him and then turns out to be something of a coed hook-

Above, Dellamorte and Gnaghi (Francois Hadji-Lazaro) have a fairly simple charge: stop the dead people who return as ghouls, like the one at left, from overrunning the town. Apparently none the denizens of the cursed town have ever thought of starting a new cemetery somewhere else. Of course, where would be the fun in that.

er, trading sex for rent money. Although the girl professes her love, in a fury he sets the apartment on fire. In a desperate, last attempt to leave the world of death and find life elsewhere, he packs up and leaves with Gnaghi only to discover that the highway out of town ends abruptly at the edge of a cliff. Suspecting that there may be no life beyond the proscribed boundaries of the town, Dellamorte and Gnaghi are left staring out from the cliff's edge at the canyon below.

Overall these old-world zombies, though mostly fabricated in the Romero mold, took their audiences away from such proletarian settings as Evans City and the urban mall, and their replicas in the work of other American filmmakers, into a more picturesque world from old-growth vineyards to middle-age castles. But the evolution of the zombie character, from Caribbean figures to Templar monks or rogue priests, was not profound. With the exception of Rollin's angst-ridden living dead girl, Catherine Valmont, the existential zombie had yet to arrive on the scene.

The Top Ten Reasons Why I Hate Zombies (and the Movies About Them)
by Linda Brookover

10. They're ugly. Megan Fox in *Jennifer's Body* notwithstanding (was Jennifer really a zombie, after all), taken as a horde or as individuals with their swollen tongues, yellow eyes, skin that suggests much too long a stay in a tanning bed/grave, and sunken (or missing) cheekbones...I'll grant that "R" in *Warm Bodies* has a certain je ne sais quoi; but he gets de-zombified. Before that was someone actually considering sex with a zombie. *Deadgirl* may turn on some desperate jocks but, seriously, guys, could you really imagine getting it on with the lovely pictured below? These hideous creatures give the Frankenstein's monster and just about any ghoul that ever haunted the screen a shuffle for their money.

9. Speaking of that: **They can't dance.** Yes, yes, I've seen the "Thriller" video and that is

the exception that proves the observation.
Sure boyfriends may have come back from
the cemetery to attend the prom, but
they were still geeks with no sense of
rhythm.

8. They're undead <u>and</u> uncouth. They
have no sense of personal space
and constantly seek to violate that
of whomever they encounter
without compunction, such as
bashing their heads through
car windows. As for table
manners, well, if you have
seen just one of these
movies,
enough said.

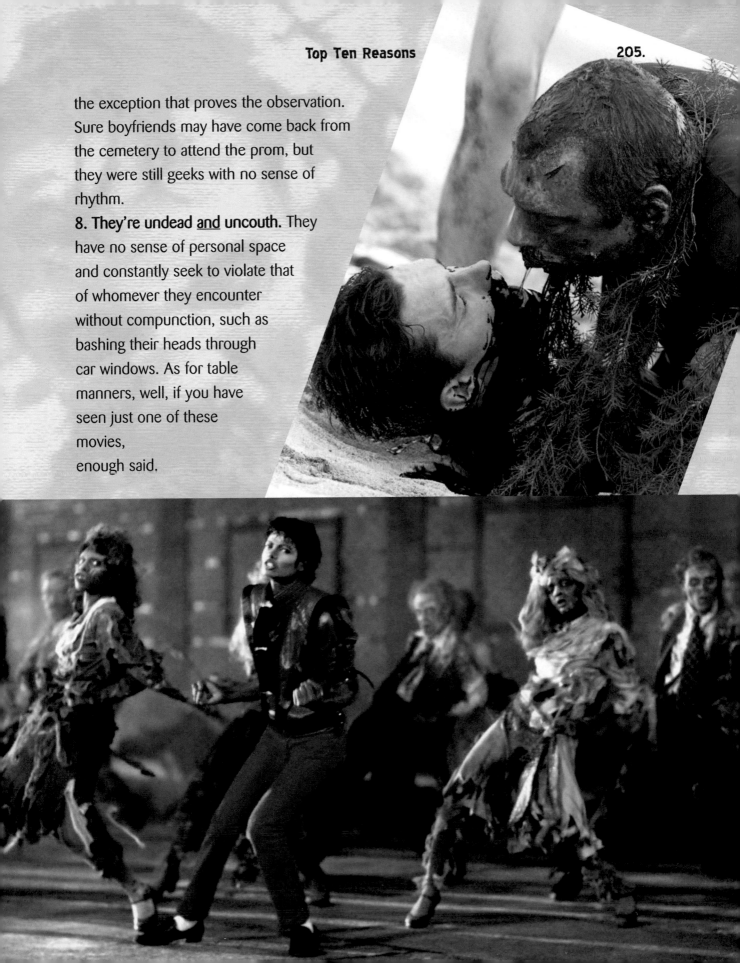

7. **They're not very romantic**—in the literal rather than the literary sense, but actually not in that sense either. Even in the misbegotten comedies that involve teen couples, they are simply never huggable. Can you imagine a zombie date, a zombie valentine, or, perish the thought, zombie sex? Even the most hardcore necrophile would have to be repulsed.

6. Despite no sex, **they breed faster than rabbits**. Sure you could argue that it is not actual breeding, but what else would you call it? It starts with just one zombie moving into the neighborhood, and before you know it the kids next door are inviting themselves to lunch…off your flesh.

5. They have no fashion sense. They look like they slept in their clothes. Even if they never spent time in a coffin but went right from ordinary life to zombiefied after being bitten, their previously unremarkable wardrobe is suddenly very shabby and somehow still looks like it was worn inside a freshly dug grave: it's dirty, shredded, and bloodstained. If vampires represent the height of movie monster fashion, zombies without question are the nadir.

4. They look like they smell bad. One can only presume that from the reactions and occasional comments of those who encounter them, so thank heaven Smell-O-Vision no longer exists. I mean *Scent of a Mystery* was one thing, can you really imagine *Scent of a Zombie*. **Eew!**

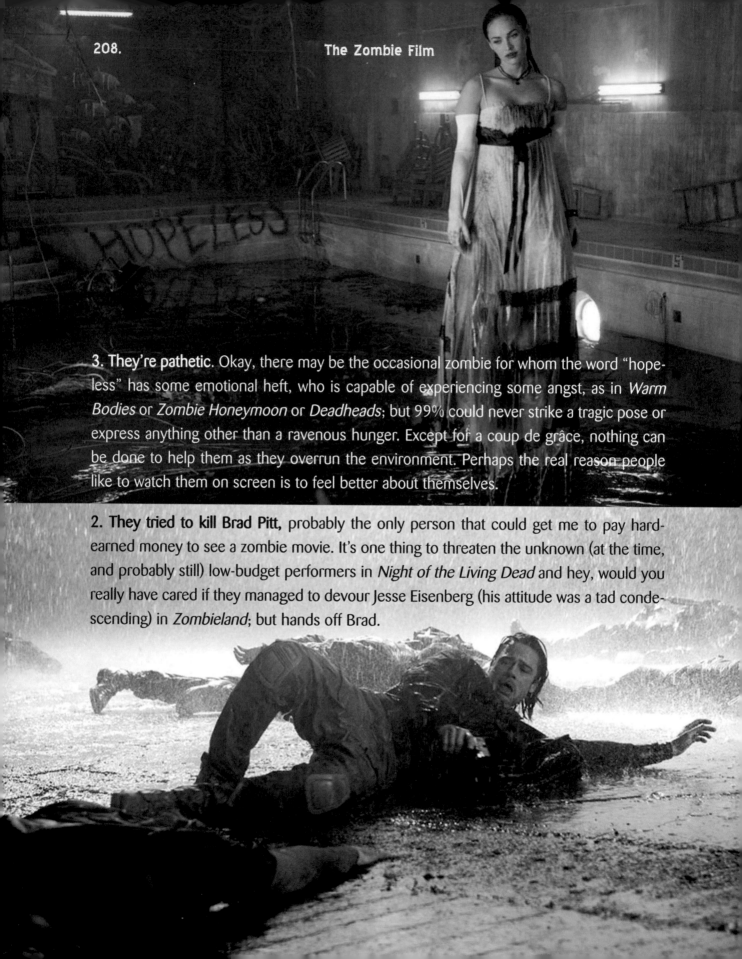

3. They're pathetic. Okay, there may be the occasional zombie for whom the word "hope-less" has some emotional heft, who is capable of experiencing some angst, as in *Warm Bodies* or *Zombie Honeymoon* or *Deadheads*; but 99% could never strike a tragic pose or express anything other than a ravenous hunger. Except for a coup de grâce, nothing can be done to help them as they overrun the environment. Perhaps the real reason people like to watch them on screen is to feel better about themselves.

2. They tried to kill Brad Pitt, probably the only person that could get me to pay hard-earned money to see a zombie movie. It's one thing to threaten the unknown (at the time, and probably still) low-budget performers in *Night of the Living Dead* and hey, would you really have cared if they managed to devour Jesse Eisenberg (his attitude was a tad conde-scending) in *Zombieland*; but hands off Brad.

And the Number 1 reason to hate movie zombies:

You can show me all the Zombie Strippers you want, like the one above and I'm sorry but **They're boring.** Conversation is limited to the occasional grunt or perhaps a rattle in their throat like a reverse hiccup, often accompanied by the clacking sound of their deformed teeth biting together in anticipation of finding your neck. If the "dissedents" in *Juan of the Dead* really had a political agenda, it might be something more than a biting satire about biting people. Tragically some of these post-persons were probably lively conversationalists when still were still breathing, but now…

Ali Larter as Claire Renfield and Milla Jovovich as Alice Abernathy in *Resident Evil: Afterlfe*.

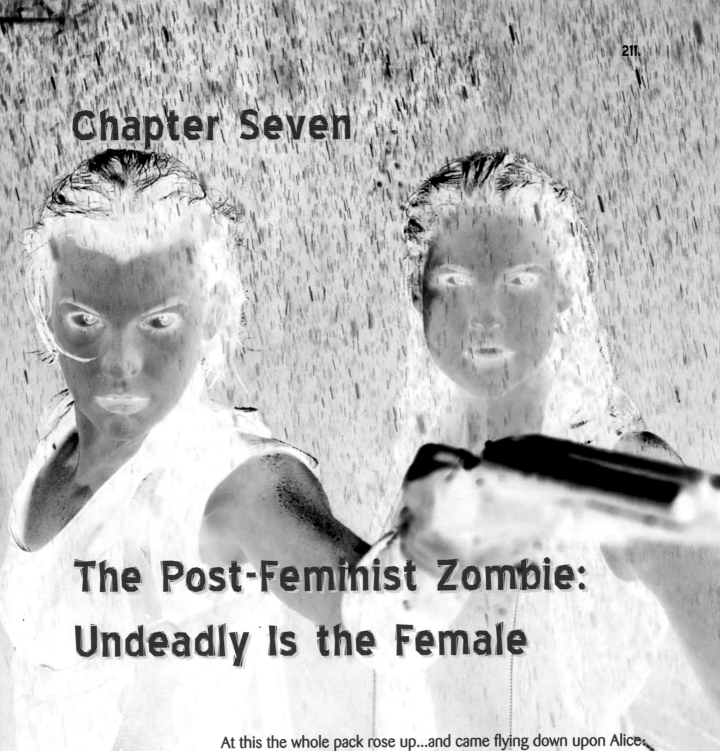

Chapter Seven

The Post-Feminist Zombie:
Undeadly Is the Female

At this the whole pack rose up...and came flying down upon Alice:
she gave a little scream, half of fright and half of anger,
and tried to beat them off.

Lewis Carroll,
Alice's Adventures in Wonderland

Post- or third-wave feminism of the early 1990s made inroads into all genres including zombie films, which resulted in transgressive female protagonists in both zombie and non-zombie mode. In fact many female undead were sentient and self-aware, setting them apart from their dim-witted and essentially asexual cohorts of the Romero type, craving flesh and seeing little with their dead eyes.

Since the *Night of the Living Dead* phenomenon transformed the genre two decades earlier, zombies had popped up here and there on television. The vampire soap-opera series *Dark Shadows* (1966–1971) featured a short-lived zombie who was ultimately "cured." As noted before, Curtis Harrington's *The Dead Don't Die* was a television move. In 1989 HBO launched its adaptation of the notorious EC Comic series *Tales from the Crypt*, which included zombie themes. But it was the ultimate "girl power" series, *Buffy the Vampire Slayer* (1997–2003), that reconfigured the zombie heroine. The darkest season of the show was undoubtedly its sixth, which opened with the "Scooby gang," unable to accept Buffy's mortal sacrifice at the end of season five. As her friends use a form of voodoo spell casting—a key component of which is purchased on eBay—the viewer sees Buffy awaken in her coffin then exploding through the wood and out of the earth with frightening dynamism. So Buffy returns in the series' penultimate season as a zombie, functional, intelligent yet essentially and miserably undead. As Buffy later explains to her cohorts, in their refusal to accept her death they have taken her from a form of "heaven" back to what for her is "hell," human

life. In an emotional condition that is reminiscent of earlier unwilling undead portrayed by Karloff, Buffy is unable to return to normality, to connect with anyone except Spike whom she uses as a toy for sadomasochistic, sexual interludes that give her a sense of being alive. There is even a musical number in which Buffy expresses her zombie angst. Gradually Buffy does come again to accept her friends and family and even her mission to save the world; but the human, female warrior is never the same.

Return of the Living Dead III (1993) is the film that brought actor Melinda Clarke to the attention of cultists. Julie (Clarke) is a thrill-seeking suburban teen. First seen on a cliff with her friends, dressed in combat boots, fishnet tights, shorts, see-through top, and a leather jacket, Julie places her hand over the flame of her cigarette lighter and smiles. When her more conservative boyfriend Curt (J. Trevor Edmond) arrives on his motorcycle, they begin a quest inspired by Julie to investigate a secret project Curt's father is heading. They sneak into a secret location on the military base, and Julie watches as Army scientists revive zombies with a chemical so that they can attempt to destroy them with a "magic bullet."

Back with Curt at his house, during sex Julie fantasizes about the frightening experiment she saw while making love to her boyfriend. When Col. Reynolds (Kent McCord) informs Curt that he is

Opposite, *Buffy the Vampire Slayer*: Spike (James Marsters) and the reanimated Buffy (Sarah Michelle Gellar). Below, a heavily pierced Melinda Clarke as Julie in *Return of the Living Dead III*.

being reassigned, Curt refuses to leave Julie. As they ride together, Curt tells Julie his decision. When she fondles him and causes him to swerve and crash, Julie is killed. Unable to accept her death, a distraught Curt takes her back to the army facility and uses the process he had witnessed to reanimate her.

Although the revivified Julie has the typical ghoulish hunger for flesh and brains, she is repulsed by her own impulses. During a botched robbery at a liquor store, where Julie is devouring junk food in order to alleviate her hunger, she attacks one of the perpetrators. When they escape, she turns on the store owner and devours his brains.

Disgusted, Julie attempts suicide by jumping off a bridge into the Los Angeles River; but Curt cannot "let her go." With the help of a homeless man (Basil Wallace), he finds her body once more. While concealed from view in an outflow pipe, Julie realizes that she can diminish the agony of her longing by inflicting pain on her own body. She inserts various pieces of metal and glass into her body and cuts her skin until she looks more like a 1980s punk than a zombie.

With her pain reduced, she makes love to Curt, whose desire for her knows no rational limit. Attacked again by the hoods from the liquor store hold-up, Julie entraps their leader, who thinks

Below, a hapless and emaciated zombie captive from *Return of the Living Dead III*.

Opposite, a Stacy, also hapless in her own way.

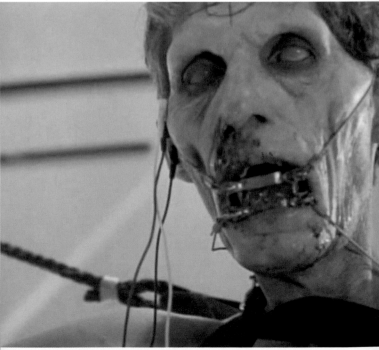

she is "kinky," and then rips off his head. Ultimately Julie is captured by Curt's father, who prepares to use her in more experiments. When Curt frees her for the final time, he is bitten by one of the zombies. The doomed couple decide on their own Romeo and Juliet scenario: they enter a furnace and they burn together, locked in an amour fou embrace.

Hot Wax Zombies on Wheels (1999) combines zombies with cosmetic waxing and motorcycle gangs in its attempt to satirize the genre as well as Middle American values. Gwen Somers portrays Yvonne Wayne, a dominatrix/biker chick/salon owner who moves from rural town to rural town turning uptight bourgeois women into sex-crazed zombies through her home brewed hair removal treatment. Fear of female sexuality runs throughout the film, as Yvonne's nemeses, a lingerie sales-woman and a barber, are as upset by all the wanton behavior and licentiousness as much as by the presence of zombies. In this way the film also functions as an allegory of heartland puritanism and the religious right's fervent opposition to the perceived sexual license of the 1990s.

As the Far East has very little of its own zombie tradition (as opposed to supernatural stories about ghosts or demons), genre films made there tend to follow the American model but tinged with explicit graphics and surreal sensibility. *Stacy: Attack of the Schoolgirl Zombies* (2001) explores Lolicom or "Lolita complex," the Japanese sexual idealization of young girls, and is outrageously serio-comic in its treatment of this cultural phenomenon, much like Takashi Miike's genre-bending zombie film *The Happiness of the Katakuris* (2001), which contains a fantasy musical number where its hapless title family sings and dances with its dead hotel guests.

Stacy: Attack of the Schoolgirl Zombies: above, Natsuki Kato as the doomed Eiko. Opposite, chainsaw TV commercial with a bunny-girl spokesmodel.

In *Stacy* teen girls are dying mysteriously after entering an N.D.H. state or "Near Death Happiness," where they represent the ideal Lolicom girl and are called "Stacies." They dress in schoolgirl out-fits, carry tinkling bells, and spread blue crystals, "Butterfly Twinkle Powder," all around, while speaking with a childish lilt and yearning for love, most often with older men. Of course, before any physical act can be consummated, the Stacies die and return as flesh-hungry Romero-style ghouls, who eat their families and friends. In this way the filmmakers demonstrate the dark side of Lolicom, the ferociousness of female sexuality even in its nubile form and the obsessiveness at the core of both *otaku* (asocial gamers) and *moe* (love for idealized forms, such as the anime *Sailor Moon*).

As a blustering scientist explains early on, the only way to kill Stacies is by cutting them into 165 pieces (as opposed to shooting them 165 times). In an opening that echoes King's novel *Stand by Me*, a horrified mother discovers three little boys in a field clustered around a dead schoolgirl. Her warning shout turns into a scream as the pigtailed Stacy rises up and attacks. Shortly thereafter, as she limps down a road, a red van filled with members of the pointedly named, Stacy-destroying "Romero Re-Kill Squad" pulls up and riddles her body with bullets.

This Stacy apocalypse drives several concurrent stories. One features a young RRK commando named Arita who remains entranced by his dead sister's friend Momo. She has turned and is kept

by the nefarious scientist at his "Art Institute" where he experiments on undead girls. Those Stacies are freed by a guilt-ridden RRK who gladly accepts their devouring of his body as a form of sexual consummation, and the young man is reunited with his obscure object of desire. He fetishistically gags her with a ball that prevents both screams and biting and saves her from the massacre.

There are also renegade private kill-squads such as the Drew Barrymore Re-Kill Squad. DBRS is a *Charlie's Angels* knock-off. Two of the young girls are traditional in garb and weaponry while their leader Nozomi (Tomoka Hayashi) dyes her hair blonde, prefers red vinyl mini-skirts and black boots, and packs an Uzi. Knowing they will inevitably become Stacies, they spend their remaining time as hunters.

The most elegiac of the stories is the love affair between a puppeteer named Shibukawa (Toshinori Omi) and Eiko (Natsuki Kato) who appears at his atelier, crystal bell in hand in the throes of NDH. Seeing that he is taken with her, Eiko demands his promise to re-kill. Like the DBKS women, Shibukawa focuses on the time that he has with Eiko before she becomes a flesh-eating Stacy. For her part, Eiko acquires a wrapped gift for him, which the viewer must suspect is a "Blues Campbell Right Hand 2" model chainsaw (in a homage to *The Evil Dead* star Bruce Campbell), seen advertised earlier in "a buy now and we'll include a deluxe carrying case" commercial.

In the climax of the movie, the puppeteer takes Eiko out to a garden area filled with blooming flowers where she dies in a wedding dress. When she begins to reanimate as a zombie, he unwraps the weapon. In a flash forward coda, the puppeteer as an old man returns to the field in which he had chainsawed his love. As he sits on the ground the camera pans up to a cubist style sculpture he

The Zombie Film

Alice Abernathy (Milla Jovovich) and Ada Wong (Bingbing Li) stride through an artificial New York City in *Resident Evil : Retribution*.

Opposite, compare a more demure and naive (and ten years younger) Alice in the original *Resident Evil*.

has erected of Eiko in order to memorialize his zombie "goddess."

As the new millennium turned, the movie *Resident Evil* (2002) and its counterpart video game reignited the zombie craze, both artistically and in terms of box office returns. The game, as was developed by Shinji Mikami as *Bio Hazard* and released in 1996, gave the player two possible avatars, both members of a military search-and-rescue team, the male Chris Redfield or female Jill Valentine, who has more weapons with which to kill zombies. In his first film adaptation writer/director Paul W.S. Anderson explicitly transformed Jill into a post-feminist Alice in Wonderland: the character's name is Alice Abernathy (Milla Jovovich) and her nemesis is the artificial intelligence named "The Red Queen." Unlike the Victorian heroine, she falls asleep, in this case because of a blast of nerve gas, and awakens to find her memory erased. She wanders through an eerie abandoned mansion, frightened by the emptiness, by the sound of a flock of birds taking flight, but most importantly totally disoriented by this unfamiliar location. Just as suddenly as she was awakened, Alice is kidnapped by a group of commandos. They transport the perplexed Alice, along with police officer Matt (Eric Mabius), who also stumbles into the mansion, to the Beehive, the genetic laboratory of the insidious multi-national Umbrella Corporation. The Beehive has been shut down by the Red Queen after the unit is infected by a powerful virus. Once there the team descends into a modern-day, high-tech rabbit hole and encounters riddle after riddle, all as complex as the ones in *Alice's Adventures in Wonderland,* but discovers creatures far more frighten-

The original *Resident Evil*: above, inside the Bee-hive, the infected multiply with exponential speed and quickly menace Alice (left).

Opposite, the painful transformation of Rain (Michelle Rodriguez) from zombie-killer to zombie.

ing than those in Lewis Carroll's surreal masterpiece.

For the first part of the movie, Alice, like her namesake, is largely passive while frightened and debilitated by the constant but incomplete memory flashes that are pieces to the puzzle of her identity. The commandos tell her that she is a security operative and with the man they pulled from the train, Chad (Martin Crewes), lived in the mansion above ground. More mental flash cuts corroborate this: she remembers having sex with Chad but also meeting with a woman from Umbrella and planning to subvert the operations of the Beehive. Was she responsible for the death of thousands of employees in the complex? Or did she betray her collaborator and remain faithful to her boss? These questions haunt Alice, creating an undertone of emotion that interferes with her ability to stay in the fight and escape from the maze.

As the movie progresses the group is attacked in video-game fashion by various mutants that have been infected by the release of the "T-virus," including zombies, some of whom are resurrected former humans and some of whom seem to be mutated forms. It is in the first battle with the undead that Alice begins to sense her power and prowess. She dispatches the zombies with martial arts kicks, snaps their necks with wrestling moves, and performs remarkable gymnastic feats. Once she has found her warrior persona, Alice takes the lead. She insists on speaking with the Red Queen, not merely to discover a way out but to obtain an antidote for the virus, the existence of which is lodged in her impaired memory. Like the one in Carroll's fantasy, the Red Queen is a cunning trickster, monomaniacal in her desire to control events. She is personified as a little girl bathed

Resident Evil: Alice's Weapons

Alice starts out by picking up a semi-automatic pistol and, over the course of five movies, progresses to (counter-clockwise from left) telescoping batons and sword in *Apocalypse*; *kukri* knives and auto pistols in *Extinction*; a pair of sawed-off, double-barreled shotguns in *Afterlife*; and finally (to date, that is) for the "ultimate battle" in *Retribution* a combo-pack.

THE ULTIMATE BATTLE BEGINS

MILLA JOVOVICH
RESIDENT EVIL: RETRIBUTION

Above and below, head-hunting Red Queens: illustration by Charles Robison from from 1907 edition of Alice and *Resident Evil: Retribution*.

Opposite, nastier zombies with bigger teeth in *Apocalypse*.

in red, creating a visual link to Jovovich's Alice, who wears a red mini-dress throughout most of the movie.

Alice manages to glean enough information to continue their way up the rabbit hole. When the Latina commando Rain (Michelle Rodriguez) becomes infected by a zombie and appears to die, Alice weeps and then prepares to shoot her in order to save her from the fate of the undead. Rain wakes up suddenly and announces she is "not dead yet." Alice laughs happily, grabs her, and says lustfully "I could kiss you, bitch," a line that crystallizes both sides of Alice, the traditional emotional "feminine" side and the harsher, blunter "male" side.

The final scene of the movie finds Alice in a brightly lit laboratory room, hooked up to IVs and semi-naked on a gurney. She has escaped the underground only to be captured by the Umbrella's scientists. She screams as she rips out the tubes and pounds angrily on the window. After discovering that she has been cloned for experimental use and with tears flowing down her face, Alice finally escapes the facility only to wander out into a city ravaged by plague and largely deserted.

In many ways *Resident Evil* is more akin to Gothic horror than a science fiction film. It follows a number of the conventions of the former: opening in an abandoned mansion, which the main character explores, frightened by every sound and shadow. Most of the settings are dimly lit and shadowy. With zombies and mad dogs, it focuses on horror archetypes. Finally the film employs black metal music, a hybrid of heavy metal and the Goth trance sound, like the cues from controversial rocker Marilyn Manson.

Alice has continued her battle against the Red Queen and Umbrella in the sequels *Resident Evil: Apocalyse* (2004), *Resident Evil: Extinction* (2007), *Resident Evil: Afterlife* (2010), and *Resident Evil: Retribution* (2012) with *Resident Evil 6* being prepared for release. In *Apocalypse* Alice is exposed to the T-virus, which actually gives her psychic ability. In *Extinction* she suffers some side

Above, Alice teams with Claire Redfield (Ali Larter) and Carlos Olivera (Oded Fehr) in *Extinction*. Below, sometimes it's best to live to fight another day: running from the horde in *Afterlife*.

Retribution: Alice in full regalia and decidedly unmerciful mode.

effects but still sharpens her skill set. In *Afterlife* her nemesis and former Umbrella head Wesker gives her an anti-viral drug that strips away the T-virus powers. In *Retribution* Wesker realizes that Umbrella and the Red Queen are indeed bent on world destruction and restores Alice.

Over the course of these shifting narratives, many of the allusions that had shifted the movie from the *Bio Hazard* game to Wonderland have been lost or abandoned. By the time of *Retribution*, the game architecture is more prominent than ever. There are virtual worlds within virtual worlds, protagonists and antagonists both magically empowered. Alice also acquires a daughter that had been with one of her clones, and some characters are as evanescent as the Cheshire Cat but without its charm. In the forthcoming installment, the announced narrative has the conflict between Alice and the Red Queen rejoined with all the surviving ancillary characters part of the fray and the location back at the Umbrella mansion, so that the possibility of a Wonderland sub-text is somewhat restored.

House of the Dead (2003) and its sequel *House of the Dead II* (2005) are also connected to video games of the same name. In the first film a group of ravers meet on a haunted island to party, only to be confronted by hordes of zombies who must be destroyed. Like most video-game-inspired movies whose target market remains young males and like *Resident Evil* before it, *House* features many scantily clad female characters.

Like many zombie killers Ona Grauer as the bustier-clad Alicia carries a big sword in *House of the Dead*. Below, Cynthia (Sonya Salomaa) has less defense against undead attacks.

The first female victim in the movie is a sexually liberated raver named Johanna (played by Erica Durance, later a regular on the series *Smallville*, here under the name Erica Parker) who strips but fails to lure her "wimpy" (her word) suitor into the lake and is attacked when she goes to look for him. Martial artist Penny Phang plays the spokesmodel Tyranny, dressed in a red, white, and blue patriotic spandex jumpsuit, who uses her fighting skills to take on the zombies. Ona Grauer, dressed in a bustier, is the true heroine of the film and ultimately the "last girl standing"—a convention that dates back to *The Texas Chainsaw Massacre* and *Halloween* (1978). She defeats the "monster," in this case by chopping off his head after she is impaled.

The filmmakers also insert frames from the Sega video game in the battle to connect it to its source as well as create a surreal atmosphere. For all its awkward stagings and miscues, *House of the Dead* contained enough zombies and nudity to turn a profit and inspire a sequel. In *House of the Dead II* Emmanuelle Vaugier (also of TV's *Smallville*) plays Dr. Alexandra Morgan who leads a team out to investigate the spread of a zombie virus.

Zombie Nation (2004) is somewhat like *Die-ner* in that it involves a serial killer, a favorite topic of exploitation director Ulli Lommel, whose filmography includes dramas about the Manson family, the Zodiac, BTK, and other actual figures. Unlike *Die-ner* this is not a comedy, the killer is a rogue cop, and the victims of his molestations and murders are women whom he arrested. These females rise from the grave to become a squad of zombie avengers.

Undead Pool (aka *Attack Girls' Swim Team vs. the Undead* or *The Girls Rebel Force of Competitive Swimmers*, 2007) is another example of the fetishization of young girls as sex objects particularly in Japanese movies and culture. Aki (Sasa Handa) is a teenager trained to be a killer by evil male twins. After escaping their abuse, which includes rape, she finds refuge at a girls' school. There she is befriended by Sayaka (Yuri Hidaka), one of the members of the formidable swim team. She has developed a girl crush on Aki. As they shower together Sayaka seduces Aki by revealing a bruise on her breast and the mole on her neck. Even though she believes that Aki, who has these marks, may be her twin separated at birth, Sayaka continues to pursue her sexually and romantically.

Meanwhile the authorities are testing an experimental virus at the school. While many of the students are protected from the microbe by the chlorine in the pool water, the teachers become virulent zombies. Understanding at some level that the teachers are part of the oppressive patriarchy that is attempting to use these young girls as guinea pigs, the swim team decides to do battle with them, and also a few of the students who are not immune. In a hilariously expressive scene, the swim team rips off their schoolgirl outfits to reveal their Speedo bathing suits, unfurl their attack flag then grab bats, pipes, and even swords and set off for combat. Aki participates but has her own patriarchal figure to fight in the persons of the evil brother twins—she is only aware of one of them initially—who sneak into the school and try to win her back to their side. The elder twin employs a

範田紗紗

The Girls Rebel Force of
Competitive Swimmers

懲女反亂軍

phallic flute to produce an orgasmic state in the brainwashed Aki; but now she has her Speedo suit as well as swimming ear plugs and cannot hear the tune. So she defeats him in battle.

Thinking that her beloved Sayaka is in danger, she runs to her side. In a conclusion as peculiar as anything in *Attack of the Schoolgirl Zombies*, Sayaka responds with a kiss, which contains a paralyzing fluid, as Aki and the viewer learn simultaneously that Sayaka had lied about her marks and was an agent of the twins.

But as Sayaka is about to kill Aki, she is shot by the younger twin. He then declares his own adoration for Aki and begins to molest her semi-mobile body. Aki, however, has more tricks in her arsenal and in typically bizarre Japanese fashion uses a laser hidden in her vagina to blow apart the second brother. Covered in blood she returns to the pool, the other members of the team are shown dead in another room, so once again alone, Aki enters the pool and swims.

Vampire Girl vs. Frankenstein Girl (2009, directed by Yoshihiro Nishimura and Naoyuki Tomomatsu, filmmaker of *Stacy*) is as much an exploration of Japanese girl power culture—which

A movie with many English-language titles, *Undead Pool*: if the above image is any indication there must be a lot of blood in the water. Opposite, it also seems as if among their tools is an extra-large model of the "Blues Campbell Right Hand 2" chainsaw.

includes extreme tanning, cutting, cosplay (using costumes and accessories, often in Gothic or Victorian style, to imitate a fictional character) and Lolicom as it is a zombie movie. In one scene Vampire Girl Monami (Yukie Kawamura) literally reduces a pedophile to blood corpuscles, which rain down on her, and although the antagonist is called a "Frankenstein girl" she fits most aptly into the zombie mythos.

Based on a popular manga, this film is female-directed, like a large part of Japanese popular culture. The "boy" of the film is simply that, a "boy" named Jyogon (Takumi Saito). Although he is the movie's off and on narrator and could be a subjective character, Jyogon is very much an object. As such he is the key to the conflict between the girls of the title. He is sensitive, handsome, the ideal for a schoolgirl crush; and as an added attraction to the young girls, he is malleable. Throughout the movie he is bounced back and forth between the school-girl-garbed transfer student, vampire girl Monami, and the cosplay Gothic mean girl of the piece, Frankenstein Girl Keiko (Eri Otoguro).

Early in the narrative Keiko and her posse of cosplay teens berate Jyogon for hanging around Monami and accepting her gift of chocolate on Valentine's Day. Obviously intimidated by Keiko (who threatens everyone including the teachers), Jyogon has no real riposte. But Keiko does not realize how far Monami has gone to win over the young man. She has laced the Valentine candy

Vampire Girl vs. Frankenstein Girl: apparently kimono-clad Frankenstein Girl (Eri Otoguro) is another zombie with power tools. Opposite, her titular antagonist vampire girl Monami (Yukie Kawamura) wears a schoolgirl uniform and has some serious fangs.

with her own vampire blood, which transforms Jyogon. When Keiko tries to get physical with Momani, she falls from the roof of the school and dies.

If these events were not bizarre enough, the main adult characters are Keiko's mad scientist/assistant principal Father (Kenji Furano), who dresses transformationally as a Kabuki shaman when working in his laboratory with the dominatrix school nurse Midori (Sayaka Kametani). He reanimates his daughter—there are several allusions to *Re-Animator*—with the addition of a few extra parts that give her zombie superpowers to fight the vampire girl. The rest of the movie is the fantastical battle between Vampire Girl and Frankenstein Girl, which ends with Monami as the bruised victor. Before he turns to dust, her aging slave Igor (Jiji Bu) puts the weary body of Monami in the arms of Jyogon. In the epilogue, the viewer sees Monami turning a few more antagonists into bloody messes and walking down the road with Jyogon in tow. As she tells him, he is now her new slave. Jyogon is momentarily taken aback but then obediently accepts his role and follows his new mistress.

Another J-horror variant on the zombie film is *Onechanbara, the Movie* (2008), which along with its sequel *Onechanbara the Vortex* (2009), is based on the video game of the same name. It features another larger-than-life female: a fur-bikini clad, tight-lipped heroine Aya (Eri Otoguro) who also wears a Western-style hat and poncho, a sexy teen variant of Clint Eastwood's nameless gunfighter from his spaghetti Westerns for Sergio Leone. Her blade glows like neon when she uses it and, as with many traditional samurai characters in traditional Japanese *chanbara* or "sword fight" dramas, her skill is matchless: in an early scene she easily dispatches a horde of zombies who have

overrun the country. Her only equal is the shotgun-toting, leather-clad motorcycle chick Reiko (Manami Hashimoto), who is initially an antagonist but joins forces with Aya to bring down the stereotypical real villain of the piece, evil scientist Dr. Sugita (Taro Suwa) who is, of course, responsible for the hordes of ghouls. In a typically non-standard complication, Aya's sister Saki (Chise Nakamura) has joined forces with Dr. Sugita after she killed their father to obtain his supernatural power. Comic relief is supplied by the rotund Katsuji (Tomohiro Waki), who is the more traditional whipping boy for the haughty warrior women.

The trio makes its way through zombieland, mowing down masses of undead in elaborate battle scenes with extensive CGI effects. Along the way Reiko picks up a daughter surrogate (her own daughter was turned into a zombie) and Aya confronts a mace-wielding zombie in the obligatory schoolgirl outfit—also a possible homage to adolescent assassin Gogo from Tarantino's *Kill Bill* (2003). Reiko is the sentimental core of the movie. She often expresses her grief as she empathizes with Katsuji's search for his own sister and with a lost girl, Maria, whom she adopts.

The most emotionally affecting scene of the film comes after Maria is infected by a zombie, and Reiko must shoot her as she did her daughter. Shot in slow motion, the staging captures Maria rising from her deathbed as other ghouls attack Reiko. When she is done with them, Reiko must turn to discover the transformed Maria and poignantly end the young girl's undead life. The final duel between the sisters is poetic and painterly at the same time. Their swords are like sci-fi light sabers, and both have the ability to turn into red and blue whirlwinds while fencing. Aya ultimately

Below, *Onechanbara* the game with its swordgirls. Opposite, the movie, "Frankenstein girl" Eri Otoguro portrays Aya in cowboy hat and bikini and Chise Nakamura as schoolgirl Saki.

姉さん…なんかたくましいのが…！

triumphs, but it is a bitter victory. She buries her sister and lays her sword on the grave.

There are new actors in *Onechanbara the Vortex*, where Saki (Rika Kawamura) is resurrected to fight alongside her sister Aya (Yuu Tejiima) rather than against her. Reiko (Chika Arakawa) is also back, this time in a leather Catwoman suit with a lot more cleavage and a pair of stylish eyeglasses. She runs a camp meant to protect children from the rampaging zombies. The antagonist is Himiko (Kaoru Yuki), a female zombie master, who much like the historical vampire figure Elizabeth Bathory wants the vitality of young girls from the certain bloodline shared by Aya and Saki to maintain her youth. Accompanied by a girl named Misery, whom the group picks up on the road, Saki takes a separate road in search of Himiko and inevitably discovers, when Misery is transformed before her eyes, that the aging Himiko has been her traveling companion. When Aya battles Himiko, she is armed with a huge, phallus-shaped shredding device. *Onechambara the Vortex* is not so anti-traditional as to let the villain triumph and ends as one might expect. Against the stronger performances of the original cast, the sequel is more of a pastiche of games sequence with much shabbier visual effects.

In the American, made-for-DVD release, *Doomed* (2007), the filmmakers construct a *Survivor*-type TV show set on an island of zombies. This unusual concept develops from the traditions of Romero and King—the production was shot in Bora Bora, which serves as the fictional, Italian-named Isola de Romero—and uses the genre for social commentary about the reality-TV generation and the sensationalist content producers of such shows must provide. As the ex-con Sybil, Mary Christina Brown uses her multi-ethnic sex appeal as well as her martial arts abilities to expand genre expectations. As a warrior woman under stress, Sybil is significantly evolved from *Night of the Living Dead*'s original Barbra.

Cadaverella (also made-for-DVD, 2007) takes the fairy tale "Cinderella" as its template and builds a sardonic zombie movie replete with a voodoo god and a sarcastic female narrator who, like Joe Gillis in *Sunset Boulevard* (1950), opens the film dead and then tells the viewer how she got there. As Cinder (Megan Goddard) relates the tale, she is an only child whose mother died and whose father remarried an "evil step-stripper" named appropriately Belladonna (Kieran Hunter) and adopted her two "mutant" children who never age. Belladonna repeatedly works her older husband into a sexual frenzy by taunting him with whips and long scissor-like legs, with the expected results: his collapse and early death.

Unlike her namesake, Cinder has a trust fund, to which she will gain access to on her twenty-first birthday. But her years of abuse by her spoiled and jealous step-relatives have made Cinder bitter, distant, and guarded. In the first glimpse of her as an adult, she pleasures herself while sitting on the lap of her trussed-up, paraplegic professor friend Justin (Ryan Seymour). Although Justin encourages her behaviors and buys her gifts, Cinder abuses and exploits his generosity and makes him an emotional slave, at whose home she shows up at all hours in expectation of his full and immediate attention.

Cinder's sense of anomie leads her to experiment with voodoo. She steals an idol of Baron Samedi, one of the Loa (or

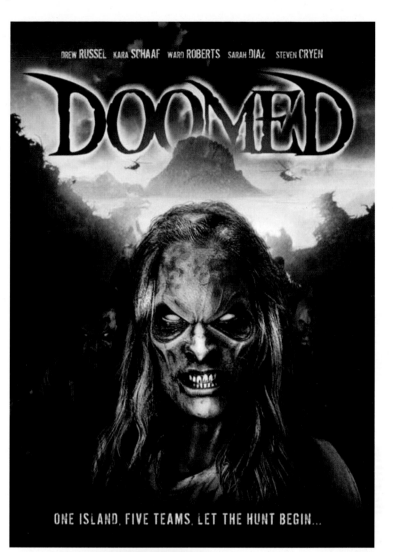

ONE ISLAND. FIVE TEAMS. LET THE HUNT BEGIN...

Right, Mary Christina Brown as Sybil one of the contestants in *Doomed*.

spirits) of voodoo, who is a gatekeeper to the underworld. Samedi appears in Cinder's bedroom and begins granting her morbid wishes, that include mutilating the bookish librarian who is obsessed with Cinder. But Samedi also grants one of her more "guilty pleasures": Cash (also portrayed by Ryan Seymour), the "bad boy" psychotic gardener whom we see worshipping photos of Cinder at a makeshift altar.

The husband-and-wife team who wrote, produced, and directed *Cadaverella* put both a post-modern and post-feminist spin on the Romero tradition with plot twists almost as eccentric as anything Japanese. As Justin, the sensitive male, has warned Cinder earlier, there are consequences when one accepts Samedi's favors. After being drugged, Cinder is lured to the forest on Cash's motorcycle and murdered. Awakened by Samedi, zombie Cinder sets out to take revenge. She smashes in the head of her step-mother, who had been bedding Cash in order to convince him to rape and murder Cinder. Then she tracks down Cash, who is very turned on by her zombie appearance and her ability to dispatch his friends in a blood massacre. When he attempts to seduce her again, she stabs him with her Samedi pin. Zombie-ism, however, has softened Cinder in one area at least. She visits Justin, apologizes for stealing items, kisses him tenderly, and gives him a hand job before she disappears.

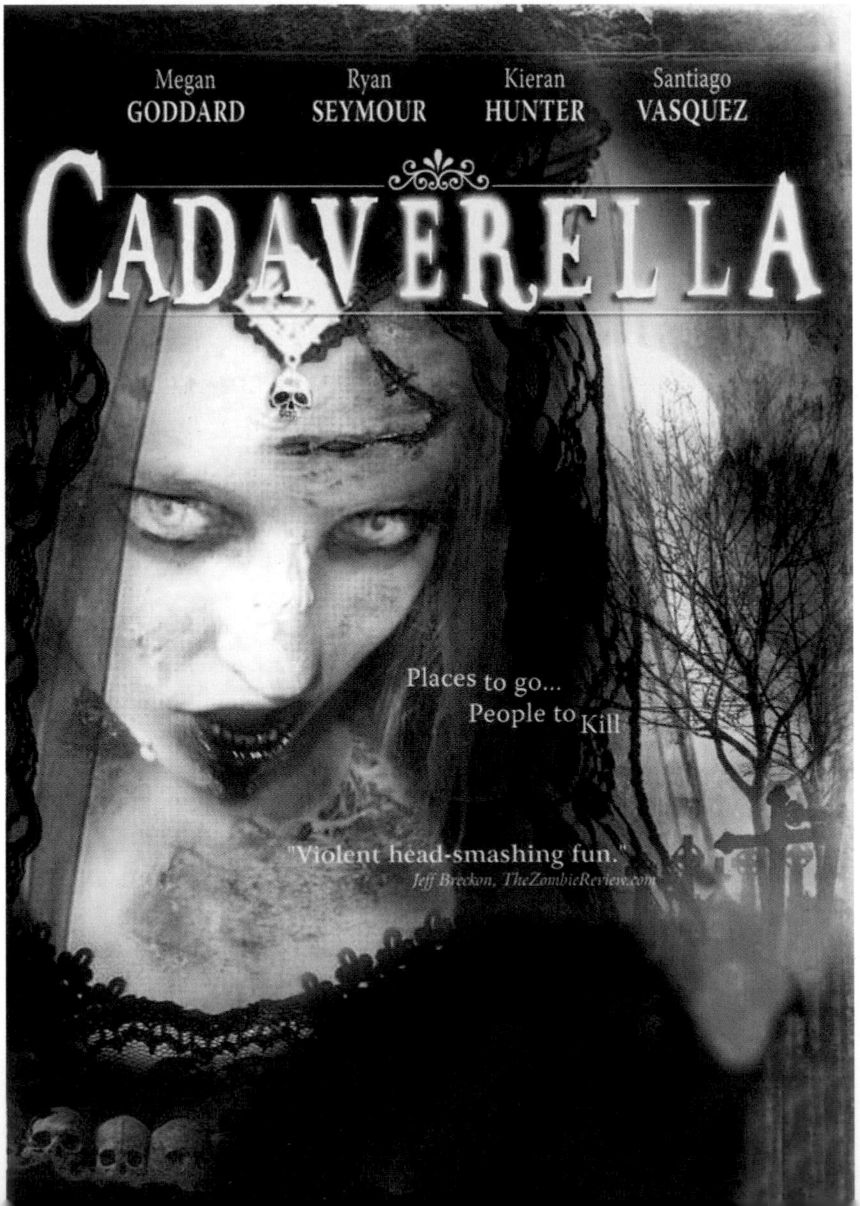

Robert Rodriguez's *Planet Terror* (2007) features Rose McGowan as Cherry Darling, a stripper who transforms herself with the help of her ex into a zombie-killing superwoman. After her leg is chewed off by a ghoul, Cherry replaces it with an automatic weapon. In an outlandish staging typical of Rodriguez, she uses her dancing skills to fly through the air and then manipulate her artificial leg in order to mow down rows and

Megan GODDARD   Ryan SEYMOUR   Kieran HUNTER   Santiago VASQUEZ

CADAVERELLA

Places to go...
People to Kill

"Violent head-smashing fun."
Jeff Breckon, TheZombieReview.com

Above, Rose McGowan as Cherry Darling, the woman with her very special prosthetic in *Planet Terror*.

rows of shuffling antagonists.

Trailer Park of Terror (2008), based on the Imperium comic series, alludes to the work of both Tobe Hooper and his original *The Texas Chainsaw Massacre* which set the standard for over-the-top, crazed slaughter and also to early gore-meister Herschell Gordon Lewis, maker of *Blood Feast* (1963) and *Two Thousand Maniacs* (1964). Despite its kitschy title, what gives this movie a patina of gravitas is the character of Norma (played with appropriate pathos and eerieness by Nichole Hiltz), a sexy trailer park teen with dreams of escaping the poverty and violence of her clichéd environment that is replete with both the standard trashy residents and pink flamingoes.

A flashback establishes Norma as she passes through a gauntlet of verbal abuse and catcalls from stereotypical redneck neighbors, who hint at past sexual escapades with her. When she finally meets her new sensitive boyfriend on the edge of the trailer park, the rednecks surround and taunt both her and the young man. When he tries to defend Norma, he is accidentally killed by one of the rednecks. Norma screams in rage and terror and runs off. Down the road she meets a man in black (singer Trace Adkins), the devil at the crossroads, a popular piece of Southern folklore. After the man in black promises to facilitate her revenge, Norma returns to the trailer park, armed with an automatic weapon and blows away her tormentors.

In present time, the idealistic minister Pastor Lewis (Matthew Del Negro) is driving a group of teen miscreants home from a retreat, gets lost in a rainstorm, and smashes the bus into one of the trailers at Norma's park. She has now been resurrected by the devil to rule over the zombie rednecks, who tormented her as a teen and are now not only sentient but very talkative. A seemingly normal Norma welcomes the pastor and his charges and tells them—in another flashback—more details of her story of abuse and the death of her mother.

Besides fleshing out her character, these flashbacks from her point of view reinforce the audience's identification and sympathy for Norma, which is important before the audience witnesses her commit a number of atrocious acts. To expose the hypocrisy of the minister, Norma undresses in front of him and, of course, he is easily seduced. Even as she appears to enjoy the sexual encounter, Norma's outrage at his hypocrisy boils over and she casually rips off his head.

The narrative context, in which ostensibly innocent characters pay for their moral turpitude, continues as Norma's fellow zombies attack the rest of the teens in ways that reflect the teens' individual faults. The addict finds drugs and is using as one of the zombies enters and saws off the victim's arm. A porn-obsessed teen hears the siren call of Miss China (played by martial-arts actress Michelle Lee), whose promise of a "happy ending" parodies Asian massage-parlor speak. Her face is a stylized kabuki mask as she "dances" on his back; but when he is on the brink of the "happy ending," Miss China rips out his spinal cord with her feet and for good measure castrates him with her toes.

Left, denizens of the *Trailer Park of Terror*. Above, a terrified and angry April (Sandra Louise Douglas) in *The Dead Outside*.

After extensive carnage, at dawn the zombies face down the last teen standing, the Goth "chick" Bridget (Jeanette Brox). When Bridget screams out about her own demons, her promiscuity, and her desire to escape to a better life, Norma is moved by the parallels to her own life and lets her survive, a closing reaffirmation of Norma's basic, wounded humanity even though she is a movie monster.

In a world of almost exclusively male directors of post-modern zombie movies, who are often fixated on nudity and sadism, Kerry Anne Mullaney's *The Dead Outside* (2008) is a refreshing exception. In this British independent, shot in the sparsely populated western uplands of Scotland with a mostly unknown cast, the gore level is dialed down even as the character complexity is enhanced. Daniel (Alton Milne) drives through the lonely border country of Scotland, hoping to escape the infection and the ravenous infected. After running out of gas near an apparently deserted farm, he decides to stay the night. In the low-budget tradition, Mullaney effectively adds suspense in this scene and many others that follow through the pointed use of cutaways.

As the film opens, only glimpses of the ghouls are allowed, as when one throws herself against Daniel's car then disappears. As Daniel investigates the dimly lit interior of the house, the film cuts to a short shot of someone standing with a rifle. Shortly thereafter, Daniel discovers that he is not alone. April (Sandra Louise Douglas), who suspects Daniel is one of the infected, confronts and threatens to shoot him. When he proves to her he is "clean"—which may or may not be the case—she begrudgingly permits him to stay the night. April's mysterious moodiness and anger, as in Boyle's *28 Days Later*, suggests that she may be harboring the virus and adds another layer of narrative tension, especially after Daniel finds her in the field with blood on her mouth. She has just killed an invading zombie, a possible sign of her own lust for flesh. April also reveals that she murdered her own infected grandparents after they allowed her to be taken to a hospital for research. Daniel is also dealing with his own demons, having visions of his young son around the farm and haunted by dreams of his wife, both of whom were infected by bites from ghouls.

The arrival of nurse Kate (Sharon Osdin), who wanders onto the farm seeking protection, triggers an intense action scene. Although April is suspicious of everyone, this time she's right. Kate kidnaps a debilitated April and in a twist reminiscent of Matheson's *I Am Legend* presumably takes her to a research facility because she may carry in her blood some antigen or other element that has kept her from fully succumbing to the effects of the virus. When the nurse's van is attacked by the mindless infected, April escapes and hides under the vehicle, until Daniel arrives with a rifle to rescue her. Kate, who has now been bitten and turned, attacks Daniel but a weakened April stabs her and saves him. In an ambiguous ending Daniel shoots his infected son, who may or may not be an illusion, and drives off with April into an uncertain future.

Deadgirl (2008) is a graphic independent film that brutally dissects young male attitudes and anxieties concerning females. The film, which is firmly within the tradition of suburban teen-angst movies stretching all the way back to *Rebel without a Cause* or *Blackboard Jungle* (both 1955), opens on the brooding Latino Rickie (Shiloh Fernandez) who daydreams of empty schoolrooms and the red-headed "vixen" Joann (Candice Accola of TV's *The Vampire Diaries* fame) with whom he has been obsessed since childhood. Unable to express his feelings to Joann, he takes to stalking her: watching her as she plays sports, staring at her while she works on her computer.

The alienated Rickie, who is being raised by a neglectful single mother, finds solace in his one close friend, the carefree J.T. (Noah Segan). After ditching school one day, they decide to vandalize an abandoned hospital, where they encounter a seemingly "deadgirl" wrapped in plastic and tied up in the basement of the hospital. Soon they realize that she is not really dead but is a ghoul girl, much to their horror and delight. Rather than report their finding to the police and over the strenuous objections of Rickie, J.T. turns the dead girl (Jenny Spain) into a love doll. Even though he is

Deadgirl: above, the plastic-wrapped body in the hospital basement. Below, the zombie-pandering jocks. Next page, the Deadgirl.

disgusted by J.T.'s physical and sexual abuse of the dead girl, Rickie follows the contemporary male code of "bros before hoes" and keeps quiet. Rickie does rather ineffectually try to free her several times but is simultaneously stimulated by her submissive behavior. In a daydream he imagines the distant Joann performing fellatio on him, when she is suddenly transformed into the growling dead girl performing the same act.

J.T. expands his growing sadistic behavior with the dead girl, whom he throttles while he penetrates her various orifices, by pimping his undead object to other teens. When while performing fellatio she bites the penis of Joann's jock/bully boyfriend and infects him, events begin to spin out of control.

However, this does not stop J.T.'s exploitation. Instead he comes up with the idea of creating more zombie love dolls. The theme of male objectification of women is further reinforced when J.T. and his "stoner" friend begin a search for another female victim. While sitting and waiting in an isolated gas station, the pair casually assess the "juggs" and "ass" of passing candidates, until they find one who is acceptable and ineptly attack her. She beats them off and even steals their money, wounding their macho pride.

As they recover from this humiliation, they are verbally attacked by Joann, who blames them for her boyfriend's "disorder." They abduct her and string her up back to back with the dead girl, a fitting metaphor for their inability to differentiate between live or dead females. Intent on finally freeing the pathetic dead girl, Rickie arrives with machete in hand, only to find Joann. Emotionally empowered by the male role of savior, Rickie cuts off the hand of the stoner so that the dead girl may free herself; but before she flees the hospital into the night, she infects both J.T. and Joann.

Deadgirl drives its theme home in the final scenes. Richie is back in school. But his demeanor has changed significantly. He seems less brooding, more lighthearted as he walks on the road to the abandoned hospital. The filmmakers then shift to a subjective camera as Rickie enters the under-

ground of the hospital and approaches a gurney on which a woman is tied. It is Joann, now also a dead girl, who has become Rickie's immobilized and undead love slave.

In 2005 the zombie genre was cross fertilized with another favorite icon of the new millennium: strippers. The cable series *Masters of Horror* adapted a 1954 zombie story by Richard Matheson entitled "Dance of the Dead." Always on the cutting edge of fantasy/horror/sci-fi literature, Matheson has woven a non-linear narrative set in a post-World War III society devoted to pleasure and violence, especially when dealing with "loopies." Somewhat like "Stacies" these creatures are all LUP, "lifeless undead phenomenon," the government acronym for zombies created by chemical-based viruses released during the holocaust of the war. Peggy, an innocent teenager dominated by the repression of her mother, sneaks off with some friends to a club which features sensual female loopies who perform bizarre exotic dances for sadistic audiences. There she physically and spiritually confronts a dancer and as a result finds herself liberated sexually and morally.

Adapted by Richard Christian Matheson, the author's son, *Masters of Horror*'s version expands the original plot by filling in the back story of Peggy (Jessica Lowndes) and focusing somewhat more on the sadistic club owner and MC (Robert Englund). The loopies here are naked rather than wearing diaphanous gowns and are stimulated by the use of electronic cattle prods into spasmodic exotic dances set to blasts of heavy metal music. Peggy has her epiphany when she simultaneously discovers her own innate sadism but realizes that the principal loopy is her long lost sister, who had been sold by their mother after the war to the MC. In the sardonic ending Peggy completes her journey to the "dark side" by selling her own morally culpable mother into bondage as a loopified exotic dancer.

Zombie Strippers (2008) is perhaps the cleverest in the sub-genre of zombie stripper movies that also include *Strippers vs. Zombies* (2008) and *Stripperland* (2011). Also situated in an ambiguous and somewhat dystopic future and in a variant on the zombie Nazi narratives, the film takes place after President George Bush has seized absolute power in the United States and funded scientific research to create an army of zombies as cannon fodder for his foreign adventures. As inevitably happens in movies (and the filmmakers satirically imply perhaps on occasion with actual reactionary political action), the project goes awry and the virus spreads beyond the confines of the lab, in this case to a small "gentlemen's club" in Sartre, Nebraska, run by a greedy germophobe named Ianna Esco, another role for Robert "Freddy Krueger" Englund.

Besides the obvious use of names from existential and absurdist literature, there are many conscious and post-modern cultural references in the movie which underscore its humor to the point where the production wears its hipness on its sleeve. The star stripper Kat (portrayed by adult film superstar Jenna Jameson) reads Nietzsche while preparing for her next number. In addition she pontificates to the other performers her "philosophy of stripping" like any true philosopher. As she

Above, adult-film star Jenna Jameson performs as Kat in *Zombie Strippers*, which ironically is a much classier (and bigger budget) production than *Zombies vs. Strippers* (below). To further confuse the title issue *Strippers vs. Zombies* also saw release as *Zombies Zombies Zombies* (opposite), with a girls-and-chainsaw pose that recalls the key art for *Undead Pool*. *Stripperland* has no aka, perhaps because Cheezy Flicks Productions could not afford to register more than one.

tells her sister strippers, particularly the religious fundamentalist newbie Jessie (Jennifer Holland) who is performing to earn enough money to buy her grandmother a colostomy bag, they have to be "warriors" to go onstage and battle the adolescent-like males and their mindless lust.

Consequently when Kat is bitten by a real zombie, she becomes even fiercer as a stripper and now enjoys the total power she has onstage, because as she pointedly informs her fellow workers she finally and totally understands what Nietzsche meant when he said "that which does not kill us makes us stronger." When dragging selected customers to the back rooms for lap dances, Kat no longer panders to their fantasies but uses them as food. As final commentary on the strip club milieu, rather than run in horror at the other decomposing ghouls whom Kat has transformed into "super-strippers" like her, even more eager patrons crowd the club each night to watch the dancers' increasingly erotic and violent acts and then to be eaten or turned into ghouls themselves.

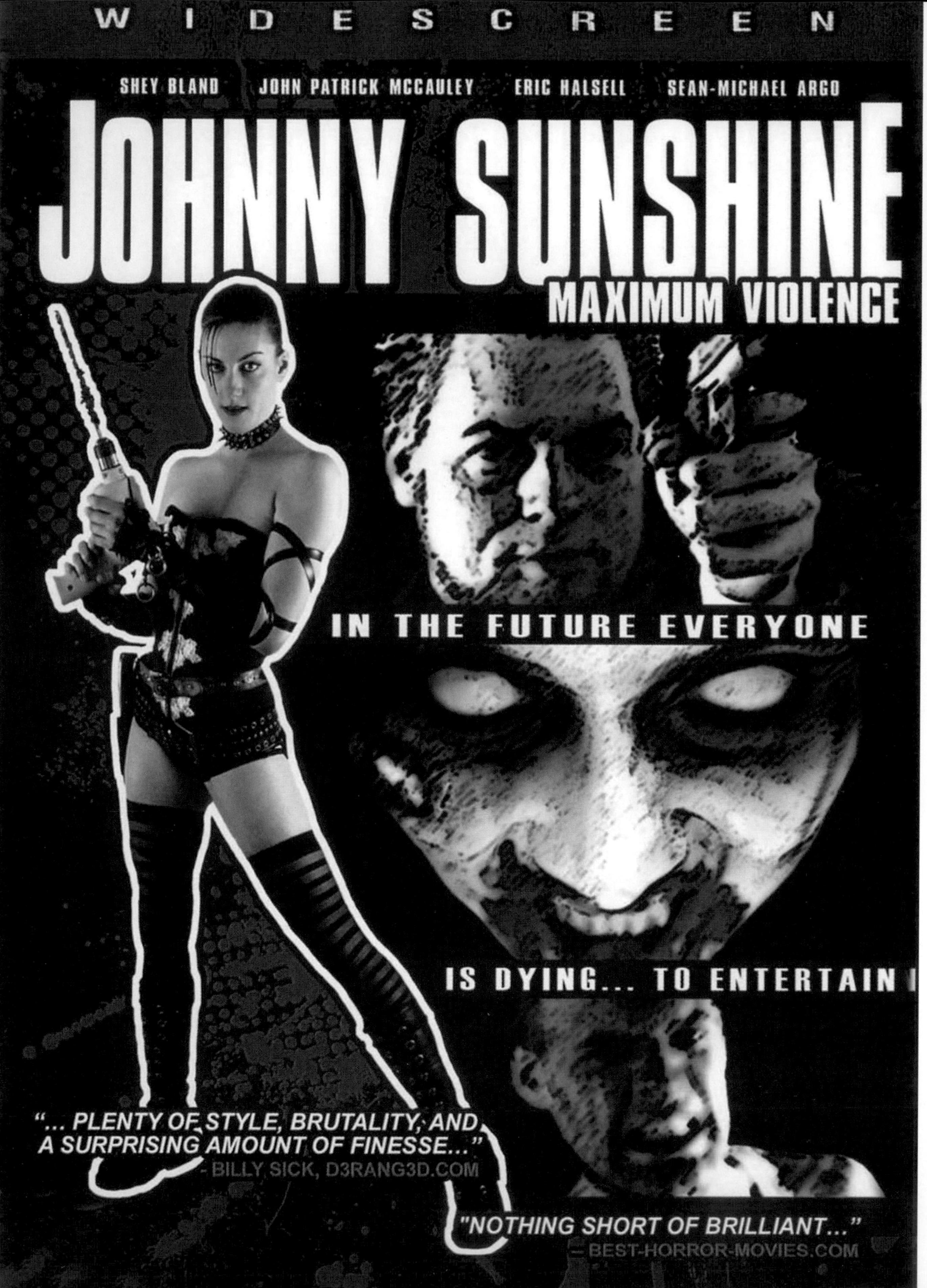
WIDESCREEN
SHEY BLAND JOHN PATRICK MCCAULEY ERIC HALSELL SEAN-MICHAEL ARGO
JOHNNY SUNSHINE
MAXIMUM VIOLENCE
IN THE FUTURE EVERYONE
IS DYING... TO ENTERTAIN
"... PLENTY OF STYLE, BRUTALITY, AND A SURPRISING AMOUNT OF FINESSE..."
- BILLY SICK, D3RANG3D.COM
"NOTHING SHORT OF BRILLIANT..."
– BEST-HORROR-MOVIES.COM

Johnny Sunshine: Maximum Violence (2008), an independent, micro-budget production out of Arkansas, is another Goth/dark metal exploration of a future world where zombies have overrun the "sprawl" (the unprotected areas), and the most popular form of entertainment is "zombie snuff" films, where zombies are raped, tortured, and re-killed for the entertainment of wealthy viewers barricaded in walled fortresses.

The opening titles include a montage of fictional newspaper clippings that set up the apocalyptic context. Over these a slow, minor key version of "You Are My Sunshine" plays eerily on the soundtrack. The viewer is then introduced to the female Johnny Sunshine (Shey Bland) of the title: she is part dominatrix, part zombie slayer, part snuff film star, dressed in leather, corsets, black stockings, studded metal collars, and combat boots. There is one long sequence in which the filmmakers fetishize Johnny's attire in a series of pans up her body as she dresses. Johnny is modeled on a better-known warrior woman (or, at least, much bigger budget), Violet Song, the vampiric title character created two years earlier in *Ultraviolet* (2006), portrayed by Milla Jovovich, and itself spun from a British series and the actor's better known alter ego Alice Abernathy of *Resident Evil.* Johnny paraphrases Violet's self-description: "Killing is what I do. It's what I'm good at. I am a titan, a monolith. Nothing can stop me." She prowls the dark streets in search of victims to "co-star" in her snuff shows. The viewer witnesses one of these films being made as Johnny overpowers a zombie, shoves a knife into his solar plexus, and reacts orgasmically as the zombie ejaculates blood through his mouth onto her skin.

Johnny works for Max (Eric Halsell), a sociopathic mogul who exploits everyone around him, including Johnny. Coincidentally a noir-style rogue cop, Stein (John Patrick McCauley), has become obsessed with Johnny. He tracks her and photographs her compulsively during her "kill-fucks" and her violent performance art, in which she dismembers zombies with chainsaws with more aplomb than Leatherface—all set to the sounds of heavy metal music.

Intent on increasing his sales and gaining entry into the armed fortress of the plutocrats, Max plans a snuff masterpiece that will capture Johnny's demise on screen. He hires Stein to kill her necrophiliac "boyfriend" then torture and rape Johnny with her on-screen death as the cinematic climax. Stein agrees to this, so he can experience what Johnny talks about in the narration, the orgasmic rush of maximum violence. Like any adept and deadly female, Johnny one-ups this plan. She outwits and kills Stein then, in an unforeseen turn worthy of the most twisted J-horror, returns to Max's studios and compels him to photograph his own suicide and releases it as his final product.

Jennifer's Body (2009)—written by Diablo Cody and directed by Karyn Kusama, previously known for *Juno* (2007) and *Girlfight* (2000) respectively—revamps the zombie myth and, according to the creators, makes the undead transformation into a metaphor for the tumultuous physical and emotional changes all modern teenage girls experience.

The movie opens in a mental institution where the narrator, Anita "Needy" Lesnicky (Amanda Seyfried), speaks of her ongoing change and how it came about. She exemplifies her intensity by cold-cocking a condescending nurse. Being thrown into solitary however triggers a meditative mood in Needy, and she begins her tale.

Anita of the flashback fits her nickname "Needy," as she stares at the camera with her thick glasses and stooped posture. As she admits to the viewer, she is a "dork," cheering for her best friend from childhood, the stellar "mean girl" of the title Jennifer (played with precision by Megan Fox). Jennifer is both her BFF and the object of her girl crush. While nothing explicit is established, a friend accuses Needy of being a lesbian ("You're totally lesbi-gay") and there is an implication that she and Jennifer may have had light sexual encounters over the years. Jennifer epitomizes the qualities that Anita, as a normal but needy teenage girl, wishes to possess. Jennifer is desired, independent, and sexually self-assured, or as Jennifer herself declares, she is "scrumptious." This prototype of teen-queendom is also manipulative, dismissive, and flirts shamelessly with Anita's boyfriend Chip (Johnny Simmons), even as she advises Needy on how to dress and comport herself, so as to not lose him.

On an outing to a "redneck" road house to catch a set by Jennifer's favorite indie band, Low Shoulder, Jennifer elaborates to Anita on her lessons about boys. As she details how to manipulate them, Jennifer calls them "morsels," which will take on an even grimmer tinge when she later

Jennifer's Body: Jennifer (Megan Fox) and Needy (Amanda Seyfried) at the bar. Opposite, after the ghoulish transformation Jennifer flashes sharp teeth and a plus-size mouth.

begins actually to devour boys. At one level, Jennifer seems to have preternatural powers even before she becomes a zombie—or whatever one might call Jennifer's altered self that combines aspects of ghouls, vampires, demons, and ghosts. As she clutches Anita's hand and watches the lead singer of the band, Jennifer falls into a trance state. Suddenly the roadhouse spontaneously combusts and the flames force the patrons to run for their lives.

Against the pointed advice of Anita, Jennifer goes off with the singed band members. What is revealed later as flashback is that, to insure their commercial success, the band tie Jennifer to a rock above a mysterious sinkhole called Devil's Kettle and make her body a blood sacrifice; but Jennifer returns as a flesh-hungry zombie. Unlike most zombies, each time Jennifer eats a boy her power and beauty increase. Whenever she stops feeding, she begins to take on the defects of a normal teen: her skin blotches; her hair becomes dull, etc. Symbolic references to menstrual periods, blood discharges, and hormonal changes in adolescence are numerous.

When Jennifer threatens Chip, the obligatory sensitive male endemic to post-feminist movies, Anita must find her own inner warrior. She summons the courage to confront Jennifer, who has taken Chip to an abandoned pool, overgrown with vegetation and a green tinge that give it a tropical feel. In this artificial jungle Anita and Jennifer face off. Unfortunately, Chip has already been bitten and dies. Anita pursues Jennifer to her house. There she stabs Jennifer not in the brain but in the heart, a method normally reserved for vampires. When Anita is also bitten, some of Jennifer's power is passed to her. As the flashback ends, a no longer needy Anita levitates to the ceiling of her cell, kicks out the window, and escapes into the night intent to take revenge against the band that killed her BFF.

Making *Night of the Dead: Leben Tod*
by Eric Forsberg

Numerous incarnations of zombies over the decades have influenced me and my work in one way or another. My first exposure to ghouls, as they were often called when I was a kid, was through comic books. The illustrations depicted high velocity action, intense violence, and zombie characters who were desperately insane. The cause of zombie transformation varied, from terrible voodoo ceremonies, to mad scientific experiments, to mass viral infections. Whatever the reason, a few panels later in the comic book there were zombies tearing through the shrieking crowds. Some of the zombies even shouted out garbled words, suggesting that they still had minds. Those early comic book images of ravenous cannibal undead compelled me and a friend when we were just fourteen to sneak into a private screening of George Romero's *Night of the Living Dead*. We expected to see one of the most terrifying films ever made. The showing took place in a dusty old church for an audience of hard-core horror fans, students, and a few art-film misfits. The movie not only gave me the creeps but it also made me want to pick up a camera and make a zombie film of my own. So my friend and I bought some rubber hands, made a quart of fake blood from corn syrup, grabbed my mother's super 8mm camera and filmed our own zombie epic. It was nothing but a series of shocker scenarios: someone doing homework while hacking off a hand or a person being attacked by plastic snakes that sucked out their eyes. When we showed the movie to our friends, it all worked. Everyone groaned and laughed and wanted more.

Zombie films are essentially creature films, and one of the goals of a creature film is to have fun. *Return of the Living Dead* directed by Dan O'Bannon is a great example of Zombie-Film Fun, and it was a huge influence on my own movies. *Return of the Living Dead* was also the film that introduced the idea that zombies must eat brains: and what's more fun than that. There have since been other zombie films that crossed over into comedy, like *Shaun of the Dead*, and the recent movie,

Warm Bodies. Both films were clever and comedic, but also a little self-conscious in their humor. *Return of the Living Dead* was deadly serious in its approach, even though the material was so over-the-top. My movie *Night of the Dead (Leben Tod)* was as much influenced by *Return of the Living Dead* as by any other picture. And *Return of the Living Dead* also had zombies that could talk; my favorite kind.

Night of the Dead was my second professional film as a writer/director. When I came to Los Angeles in 1997 to make movies I was pleased to find that genre films were booming and that most of the companies that were making films with new directors were making horror. I fell in with a young production company called The Asylum, and was hired to write and direct a science fiction horror, *Alien Abduction*. It was a great script with a real twist, filled with aliens and gore and brain-washing and synthetic humans who think they are real: a very ambitious film for being low budget. I realized that I had written a movie that was too big for the budget; but I knew I could write something for the next project that would be easier to shoot within very limited means. I needed a good story with a lot of action set in a single location, with a lot of blood and costumes that I could buy at a thrift shop, and that seemed to be a recipe for a zombie film. So I wrote *Night of the Dead*.

The original title for *Night of the Dead* was "Leben Tod," which means "Life-Death" in German. I lived in Vienna in 1986 and speak German, so I wanted to have all of the scientists be "Aus Deutschland," just to spice the story up with multiple languages and cultures. The set up follows Dr. Gabriel Schreklich as his experiments with cellular life-extension fail to achieve complete success. But when the doctor's own wife and daughter are killed by a hit and run, he uses the serum to partially revive them. Flash forward to a year later and the doctor is running a full blown hospital where he is desperately trying out different versions of his serum in order to perfect it. Meanwhile his wife and child are only half alive, blood drinking ghouls locked in a room, still human, but also zombies. I wrote the part of Schreklich's child for my own daughter Lola to play, so the role offers a very tender relationship between her and her on-screen father. She loves her dad, but she must eat flesh, and all she wants to do is go out and play (where she will kill everyone in sight). To make matters more complicated, the doctor's nephew Peter is assisting him in his work, in exchange for Schreklich taking care of Peter's pregnant wife (who we later find out is also on the serum because she died before delivering the child, but she does not know it). Of course, all of the doctor's failed experiments escape. Peter is bitten and becomes a zombie-ghoul, but he does not eat his pregnant wife, instead he saves her, massacring the other zombies in an act three bloodbath. It was a fun film to write and to shoot, and the requirements of production were right in line with the budget.

We ended up pre-selling the film to The Asylum in a deal called a negative pick-up. That means that my wife and I had to come up with the money to make it in order to complete the sale. So we sold

our house. Not a great idea in most cases but in ours it worked. We made the film, sold it, made our money back, and moved on. One casualty was that the name was changed from *Leben Tod* to *Night of the Dead*. I unofficially call it *Night of the Dead: Leben Tod*. Whatever the title, the movie has won numerous awards, had critical success, and keeps making money. It plays regularly on *Chiller* and is also available on Netflix and Amazon. Although it was shot in regular def and not HD, it is fun, gross (very bloody), and filled with action. With the new surge in zombies (*28 Days Later*, *World War Z*, etc.), I am hopeful that I will be producing and directing my next zombie film very soon.

Right, Lola Forsberg as Dr. Schreklich's daughter Christi. Below, Schreklich (Louis Graham) prepares to clean up bucketfuls of gore.

NIGHT OF THE DEAD
VOM MEISTER DES HORRORS ERIC FORSBERG
1 2 3
SIE LEBEN, ABER SIE
SIND NICHT LEBENDIG!
"So muss ein Zombiefilm aussehen -
Grausam und doch anspruchsvoll!"
-George A. Romero -

Cillian Murphy as Jim alone
in London in *28 Days Later*.

Chapter Eight
The Post-Modern Zombie

She watched the mouth jerk to a gaping cavity then a twisted scar that split into a wound again. She saw the dark nostrils twitching, saw the writhing flesh beneath the ivory cheeks, saw furrow dug and undug in the purple whiteness of the forehead. She saw the lifeless eye wink monstrously...

Richard Matheson,
"Dance of the Dead"

After years of Romero rip-offs, fake remakes and sequels, and repetitive formulas using pollutions or pathogens as plague starters, the zombie genre began to change. It adopted a more post-modern and hip attitude towards its subject, like that of the popular culture around it. The metaphors became more elaborate, the irony and satire more twisted, and the self-reflexive stance more pronounced. Concurrently, as the turn of the millennium approached and apocalyptic anxiety increased, what with Y2K, worldwide economic downturns, the seemingly endless war on terrorism, the ongoing influence of fundamentalist religion, and the pervasiveness of social media, the zombie's popularity ballooned. Literature and comic books reconsidered them which prompted segues into rock songs, fashion shows, performance art, and in summer 2013 a commercial zombie character thinking about changing his cell phone plan to Sprint. Spurred on even further by recent "zombie killings," the zombie apocalypse is the newest craze and its adherents are everywhere, most deeply rooted in graphic art and film.

With early post-modern verve Stuart Gordon's *Re-Animator* (1985) mixes gore and humor with bloody fervor. What holds this very loose adaptation of H.P. Lovecraft's story "Herbert West: Reanimator" together is the grand-guignol turn by actor Jeffrey Combs in the title role. With biting sarcasm he projects the arrogance, amorality, and non-specific personality disorder of Lovecraft's original protagonist. Whether haughtily dismissing the scientific theories of his colleagues or fighting off zombie attacks, including one from a cat he has reanimated, Combs' performance never loses its sense of humor.

Combs' and director Gordon's sense of theater of the macabre carries through the entire movie. West's repeated experiments in reanimation become more and more bizarre. As in the Lovecraft story, the event that opens the narrative, which had already inspired Stephen King's then recent best-seller *Pet Sematary*, is a beloved house cat that turns vicious after his revival. It is not entirely unexpected that its claws attach themselves first to the distressed West's back then later to the dean of the medical school (Robert Sampson), who has expelled both West and his reluctant assistant Cain (Bruce Abbott), the equivalent for the narrator character in Lovecraft's story. The dean takes his action after discovering their unorthodox experiments and the involvement of his own daughter Megan (Barbara Crampton). After the dean is accidentally killed by a rampaging ghoul, West and Cain reanimate him. Of course, he becomes another angry, screaming zombie, who does not recognize his own daughter until the end of the film.

The most bizarre reanimation is that of the nefarious Dr. Hill (David Gale), the movie equivalent of Lovecraft's Major Clapham-Lee. After Hill tries to steal his formula, West decapitates him, then with great relish reanimates Hill's head and body separately. To West's dismay, his antagonist returns as a sentient zombie who can use his brain to direct his detached body, which attacks West and kidnaps Megan, with whom Hill is obsessed and on whose bound body, in a truly outrageous moment, his head performs oral sex.

Re Animator. opposite, Jeffrey Combs as Herbert West with the living head of Dr. Hill (David Gale). Below, Megan (Barbara Crampton) with the lecherous head of Hill.

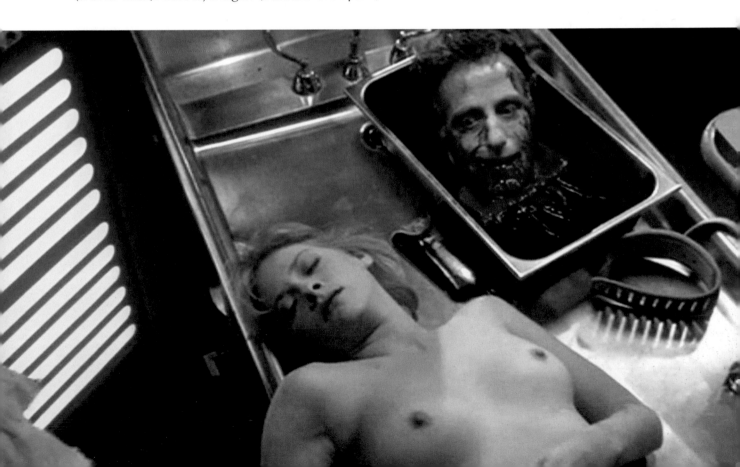

West interrupts Hill's bodiless rapture and initiates a bloodbath as his zombies wake up and attack blindly. The filmmakers, in the Hollywood tradition, add a love interest to the Lovecraft by making Cain and Megan a couple. So when she dies in the climactic bloodbath, Cain uses West's formula to bring his love back. As the movie fades out all that is heard over the blackness is Megan's scream as, we assume, she returns unhappily from the dead.

In *Bride of Re-Animator* (1990) the filmmakers continue their bloody adaptation of Lovecraft's phantasmagoric story. The film opens during a civil war in Peru where Cain and West are continuing their experiments in the battlefield. Lovecraft's setting is World War I. After their lab is destroyed by invading forces, they return to Arkham and Miskatonic Hospital and reconstitute it in the basement of Cain's house. Cain is still in the thrall of West and remains an assistant rather than being a partner. For his part, West remains controlling and somewhat possessive of Cain. He makes sarcastic comments when Cain flirts with their South American compatriot Francesca (Fabiana Udenio) and looks genuinely distressed when Cain seduces her. West, however, does possess an object that he knows will keep Cain close: the heart of his fiancée Megan. West has kept the tissue and promises to create a new, better Megan from it for Cain. So when not "doodling" (Cain's words) by grafting incongruous parts onto each other (an eye on a hand, a hand on a leg), West works on this female creation and finally succeeds. West presents his creature to Cain, who falls to his knees before the statuesque form of the "new Megan" (Kathleen Kinmont).

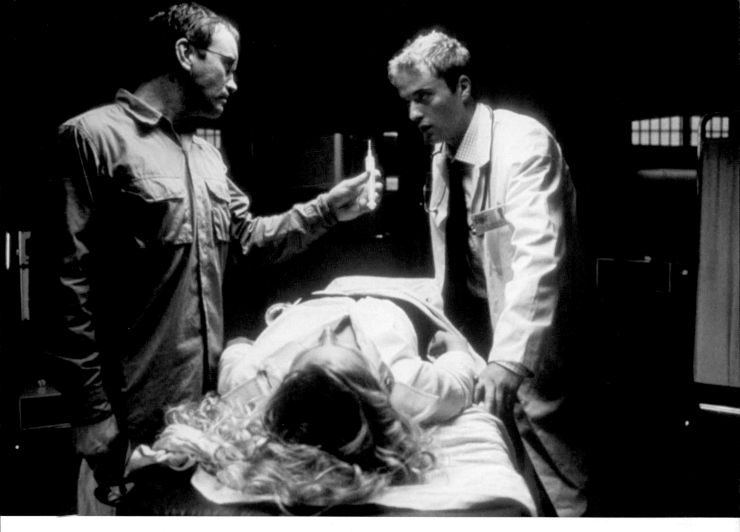

Opposite, *Bride of the Re-Animator*: Kathleen Kinmont as Megan channelling Elsa Lanchester from *Bride of Frankenstein* as she rips out her heart. Above, Combs as West shows Dr. Philips (Jason Barry) that he still has the hypodermic full of yellow fluid in *Beyond Re-Animator*.

Cain's reunion is shortly interrupted by the arrival of Francesca, who is pursued by zombies including his monstrous mutations and the flying head of another character from the first movie, Dr. Hill, the telepathic leader of the other ghouls. In another climax of carnage, the new Megan tries to defend Cain against the zombies while seducing him away from the influence of Francesca. When unsuccessful, Megan literally rips out her heart and offers it to Cain, even as she begins to dissolve before his eyes. With his usual sang froid, West remarks that Cain should make a note regarding the tissue rejection. The apocalypse leads to the collapse of the cellar and the burial of West and the zombies. Only Francesca and Cain escape. West somehow manages to disentangle himself from the rubble to make a final appearance in *Beyond Re-Animator* (2003), which opens with the character in prison. Although incarcerated he continues his experiments with the same insouciance and arrogance and the predictable catastrophic and deadly results. In 2011, the series spawned *Re-Animator the Musical*.

Wes Craven is perhaps more responsible than any other horror filmmaker for the transformation of the horror genre in America from Gothic-tinged with stylized action to ridden with graphic violence. From the impact of his breakthrough grisly re-imagining of Ingmar Bergman's *Virgin Spring* with *The Last House on the Left* (1972) through his commercial successes with *The Hills Have Eyes* (1977) and *A Nightmare on Elm Street* (1984), Craven established his prominence more than a decade before the *Scream* series.

Craven's contribution to the zombie genre is limited to two projects. *Chiller* (1985) is a television movie inspired by "The Monkey's Paw." The plot is modernized: wealthy Marion Creighton (Beatrice Straight) has cryogenically preserved her dead son Miles (Michael Beck) in the hope that at some point future medical technology will permit him to be unfrozen and re-animated. As the film opens a malfunction in the chamber accidentally thaws the body; and Marion comes to regret "calling" her son back from the grave. As with many of Craven's horror movies, the sub-text of *Chiller* is social and political allegory, in this case regarding the Reagan era of greedy and unfettered capitalism. Miles returns to life as an unemotional zombie interested only in power and money. After his pet dog turns on this "soul-less" reincarnation, Miles smothers it. He then takes over his family enterprise and transforms the ethos. He cuts costs by eliminating donations to charities. He runs roughshod over his employees in order to guarantee total control. He even humiliates the family's

longtime advisor and friend (Dick O'Neill), and then forces the ailing man to follow him up several flights of stairs in order to keep his job, leading to his heart attack and death. The only voice of opposition among the company's officers is vice-president Laura Johnson (Leigh Kenyon). On her, Miles uses a different control technique, a much too common occurrence for women in the corporate world. He meets her for drinks, sexually harasses her, forces her into sex, and lets her return to her job, chastened and fearful.

The only person who can bring down this Oedipally tinged "monster" is his mother, the person who brought him into the world twice. At first Marion refuses to believe the evidence that her priest (Paul Sorvino) presents her regarding her son's sociopathy; but when she discovers Miles about to rape her niece (Jill Schoelen), she

Opposite, *Chiller* repackaged after Craven's later successes. Above, a tearful Christophe (Conrad Roberts) inside his coffin in *The Serpent and the Rainbow.*

must take responsibility for her twisted creation. After luring Miles into a meat locker, she padlocks the door and summons the authorities. But not even the police can bring down this zombie. After Miles strangles one of the officers, his mother grabs the service revolver and shoots him repeatedly. Emotionally broken, she caresses her dying son's face, only to see his eyes flash open and reveal still-active demonic eyes.

With *The Serpent and the Rainbow* (1988), Craven directly explores the phenomenon of traditional and definitely pre-Romero zombie-ism. The film credits indicate that it was "inspired" by Wade Davis' best-selling book of the same name, but the author disowned the film. This could have been anticipated, as Craven left out most of the anthropology and science in favor of straight-up horror and political analysis. The movie opens a decade earlier—a title reads "Haiti 1978"—with men polishing a coffin in a shantytown at sunset. Other men arrive and haul it off on a boat. That night several members of the Tonton Macoute—the paramilitary units who employed murder, torture, and voodoo to enforce the rule of the Duvalier family—led by a man dressed as the lord of the underworld Baron Samedi arrive with a burning coffin and leave it in the roadway as a warning to the local populace. Sometime later, mourners gather at a small cemetery to bury another victim of the Tonton, Christophe. Inside his coffin, a tear runs down his cheek.

From this Craven cuts to eight years later, as protagonist Dennis Alan (Bill Pullman) is in the

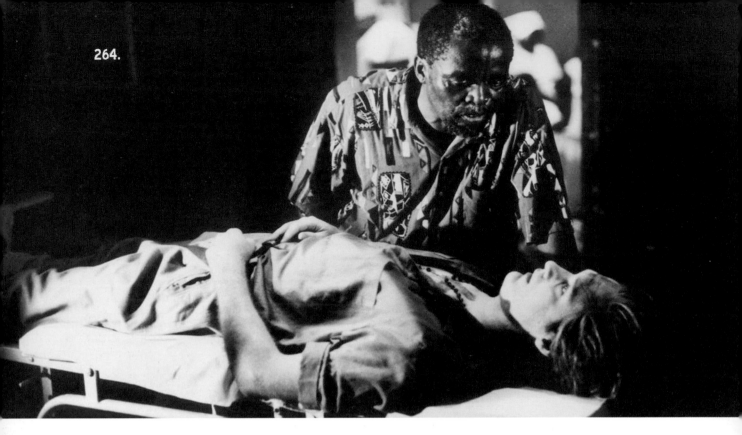

The Serpent and the Rainbow: above, Alan (Bill Pullman) under the effect of zombie powder administered by the *bokor* and Tonton Macoute Dargent Peytraud (Zakes Mokae). Opposite, the pieta pose with Marielle (Cathy Tyson)

Amazon and is coaxed into trying out a shaman's potion. He collapses and enters a trance state, in which he wrestles with a spirit guide, a jaguar. Then for the first time Alan sees the face of the *bokor* (or voodoo priest) Peytraud (Zakes Mokae), who will turn into his chief antagonist when he is hired to travel to Haiti in search of ingredients for another elixir, the infamous "zombie powder." As noted in the first chapter, Wade Davis believed he had discovered those ingredients. In Haiti Alan enlists the help of a psychiatrist Marielle (Cathy Tyson), who is also involved in the movement to overthrow the Duvaliers. She promises to shows him several zombies, including Christophe.

Dargent has been watching Alan since his arrival and sees him with Marielle in a voodoo nightclub where she performs while entranced. To stop his investigation, Dargent openly harasses and persecutes Alan. Much like Freddy Krueger in Craven's A *Nightmare on Elm Street*, the *bokor* even invades the anthropologist's dreams and triggers a series of terrifying visions in which Alan imagines himself being buried alive. After reconstituting the zombie powder with the aid of a trickster shaman, Alan returns to the U.S. to present his findings to a pharmaceutical corporation seeking to market it as an anesthetic with the improbable name "Zombanol." Although no longer in Haiti, Alan's disturbance continues as a powerful spell cast by the *bokor* follows him. Just as Legendre had in *White Zombie* but without need of the voodoo dolls and over great distances, Dargent invades and controls the bodies of others. When Alan has dinner at the home of the company president, Dargent invisibly sends a black zombie hand, which emerges from the soup then compels the hostess to slash Alan with a carving knife.

Fearing that Marielle is in danger and despite his colleague's warning that he has opened the doors to the mystical, Alan returns to Haiti, where he is framed for the murder of a woman: he awakens to find her decapitated corpse in his bed. Dargent infects him with zombie powder and, in a truly unsettling scene, the camera accompanies this prospective ghoul, as he is placed in a coffin and buried in the ground. Alan's screams as he awakens while buried alive reverberate through the graveyard until Christophe—a fictionalized version of the actual Clairvius Narcisee, a reputed Haitian zombie—digs him up. Alan returns to battle the *bokor*, as the Duvaliers fall from power and the streets of Port au Prince erupt in chaos and celebration.

Craven shows great respect for the culture and people of Haiti, where the film was partially shot. Besides portraying the struggles of the Haitians to overthrow their oppressive regime, the film incorporates many details about their native religion. In one scene Marielle explains how Catholicism and voodoo have merged and shows Alan an image of the Catholic Virgin Mary who has been conflated, as with many saints, with her corresponding figure in voodoo, the goddess of love and beauty Erzulie. As Marielle leads Alan on a procession which winds its way up the mountain to a magic grotto, Erzulie and Marielle, whose club owner friend had equated with the goddess, become one. Alan and Marielle embrace in a secluded area and she heals him sexually. Later, Craven even further emphasizes the mystical link in the personality of Marielle when a half-naked and wounded Alan is thrown at her door by the Tonton: she holds his torso in her lap in the traditional pieta pose seen in Michelangelo's sculpture.

Before *The Lord of the Rings* series or his break-through feature *Heavenly Creatures* (1984), New Zealand director Peter Jackson made *Braindead* (aka *Dead Alive*, 1992) a "splatstick" zombie movie in the tradition of Sam Raimi's *Evil Dead* series. Without the panache of Raimi's movies or the outlandish quirkiness of later commonwealth zom-coms such as *Shaun of the Dead* (2004) or *Fido* (2006), Jackson's mixture of slapstick and gore repeatedly falls flat. The only mildly effective aspect of the movie is the oedipal knot between mild-mannered son and overbearing mother, as she attempts to keep him tied to her umbilical cord even after she becomes a zombie. Its most notably creepy and outlandishly Freudian moment occurs when zombie mom grows to gargantuan proportions and then stuffs her son back into her womb in order to keep him "in place." An American studio picture, *Death Becomes Her* (1992) is a rather perverse zom-com, which used star power rather than an endearing narrative as its audience hook. While the reanimated rivals for the affection of a mad scientist (Bruce Willis) are technically zombies, portrayed by Meryl Streep and Goldie Hawn, they don't regard themselves as undead aberrations, even as they require more and more plastic surgery and cosmetics to mask the effects of their decomposition.

Along similar lines to *Braindead* and released the following year is *Ed and His Dead Mother* (1993), which features Steve Buscemi as a loser with a mother complex who falls into a depression after her death. Ed meets a mysterious man in white (played by John Glover) who offers to raise his mother from the dead for a small fee. Still wearing the apron in which she was buried the mother

Below, *Braindead*, pre-Tolkien monsters and a lot of blood from Peter Jackson. Opposite, among the first big-budget "zombies" Goldie Hawn and Meryl Streep suffer from early CGI.

(Miriam Margolyes) returns to take up where she left off, that is, dominating Ed's life. Mom has, however, developed some odd new habits: chasing dogs down the street with knife and fork in hand, preparing dinner while inside the fridge, and dancing seductively on her bed. Mom's taste for violence is also new. She tries to mow down a seductive neighbor who has put the moves on her beloved son ("She's a tramp") and chainsaws an ex-con who makes the mistake of visiting her. In order to live his life Ed realizes he has to re-inter his mom but that is easier said than done.

Also released that year without much fanfare is *My Boyfriend's Back* (1993), a groundbreaking release in that it presents—albeit in a hybrid zom-rom-com context—a sympathetic and sentient zombie Johnny Dingle (Andrew Lowery), who wants nothing but to reunite with his girlfriend. After being murdered while trying to stop a robbery, he returns from the dead by force of will in order to continue to court the "girl of his dreams," the popular but spoiled Missy (Traci Lind). Although he does have a craving for flesh, he is in most ways the perfect, sensitive boyfriend, with whom Missy falls in love all over again. Understandably the townspeople and Missy's other teen suitors object to this relationship, which they believe makes Missy a "zombie whore." The couple resist the physical threats and end up dancing together at their high school prom.

The comic-zombie trend crossed over into animation with *Scooby-Doo on Zombie Island* (1998), the first feature based on the popular children's TV show. The animation is sophisticated, zombies appropriately scary if cartoonish in the Romero mode. *Idle Hands* (1999) is a teen comedy that draws on the classic horror movie, *The Beast with 5 Fingers* (1946), for its premise. The main character is stoner Anton (Devon Sawa), whose right hand is somehow possessed by a demon serial killer, perhaps because he had used it in the way most right-handed teen boys do. Whatever the

cause, Anton is forced by his hand to kill his best friends (Seth Green and Elden Henson), driving a beer bottle into the forehead of one. They, however, are too lazy to go "into the light" and return as helpful zombies.

The upside of this demonic hand is that Anton now has the courage to be forthright with his nubile neighbor Molly, played with Lolita-like overtones by Jessica Alba, whose character is perennially dressed in nighties. In the middle of lovemaking, his hand becomes sexually adventurous to which Molly responds, "Umm kinky, I like that." When, however, the hand becomes too fond of Molly, Anton must rein it in. With the help a voodoo priestess (Vivica A. Fox) and his zombie pals, Anton destroys the offending hand before it can overreach with Molly.

Also released in 1993 was the second remake of *The Body Snatchers* (directed by Abel Ferrara) that uses the novel's actual title even as it reinvents the plot and characters with a move to an Army base in the South. In the fourth iteration, *The Invasion*, a fungus clings to debris from a space shuttle explosion and except for the alien invasion that produces

Above, the by-now familiar screech of alarm in *Body Snatchers*. Below, as Dr. Carol Bennell in *The Invasion*, Nicole Kidman channels a Stepford Wife and blends into a crowd of fungal zombies by displaying no emotion.

a zombie-like behavior as part of a collective consciousness most of the constructs of the novel, including the body snatching, are gone; and the crisis ends when antibodies from an immune person are used to create a vaccine.

I, Zombie: The Chronicles of Pain (1999) takes a fresh approach to the zombie in that it tracks the disintegration of an ordinary man from human to zombie. After being bitten by an infected undead, the protagonist tries to conceal his condition and repress his desire for human flesh. Soon he breaks down and tormentedly feasts on his fellow humans. The film is shot on 16mm, so it has a documentary patina, which adds to the existential reality. The British director/writer Andrew Parkinson of *I, Zombie* revisited the world of the angst-ridden ghoul in *Dead Creatures* (2001). This movie centers on a group of young women who have contracted a virus, which leaves them with a taste for human flesh. The women attempt to maintain a normal existence while tempering their flesh lust and avoiding a zombie bounty hunter. *Wild Zero* (1999) is an off-the-wall Japanese production, which includes animation. It features the Japanese garage band Guitar Wolf as zombie-fighting musicians who also ride motorcycles.

Below, the motorcycle-riding, zombie-killing garage band Guitar Wolf in *Wild Zero*.

It was not until after the turn of the millennium that critically acclaimed director Danny Boyle (then best know for *Trainspotting--1996*) gave the post-modern zombie respectability in the eyes of film critics. His *28 Days Later* (2002) is widely regarded as a substantive and serious attempt to rework a genre that festers so frequently in the realm of splatter-gore. This is not to say that Boyle neglected the naturalistic and exploitational elements of the past zombie film and ignored audience expectations; but rather than envision the zombie plague–here, as sometimes in zombie films before, caused by a virus that turns humans into ravenous beasts–as an opportunity for social commentary about racial or cultural prejudices, Boyle constructs a metaphor for basic human defects, for mankind's tendency towards violence and, linked to it, unreasonable and uncontrollable rage.

Boyle establishes his metaphor in the first scene when a group of animal rights activists raid a facility dedicated to animal experimentation. A chimp is tied down to a gurney with electrodes in his brain, and images of everyday violence throughout the world surround the animal. The activists free these test subjects; but instead of friendly chimps smiling at them in gratitude as they expected, they bare their teeth and viciously attack.

Because these creatures have been pumped full of an experimental virus inducing rage, within moments of being bitten, the activists themselves make the expected transformation into rabid, flesh hungry zombies. While the virus spreads throughout the country over the next four weeks, a

Opposite and below, while trying to escape London Frank (Brendan Gleeson), Jim (Cillian Murphy), and Selena (Naomie Harris) confront the horde in the tunnel in *28 Days Later.*

patient named Jim (Cillian Murphy) lies in a post-operative coma at a local hospital. On the 28th day, he awakens to an empty ward and steps outside into a post-apocalyptic London where the infected have formed cohorts and pursue him frenziedly. Unlike those in most earlier zombie films, these ghouls move swiftly, almost like sprinters or greyhounds chasing a mechanical rabbit. Wandering into a church filled with bodies, Jim barely manages to debilitate a fast-moving infected priest and later a young child.

Eventually Jim links up with two other survivors: Selena (Naomie Harris), a Black warrior woman, and Mark (Noah Huntley). They orient him to their survivalist ethic, which includes immediately killing anyone who seems infected and never going back for a straggler. Jim, who is good-natured and laid back, is uncomfortable with these new rules, but he quickly realizes that he must follow them or die himself. When a fast-moving mob surprises and overwhelm Mark, he is left behind by Selena and Jim and shortly thereafter they make contact with a father and daughter who have erected a fortress in an apartment block. Frank (Brendan Gleeson) and the teen-aged Hannah (Megan Burns) have created a fantasy island in a sea of chaos, a middle-class apartment filled with Christmas decorations and piped-in music. In many ways, Frank is a Santa Claus figure, with his wide girth and sense of humor.

Boyle's subtext on the emotional importance of the extended human family is introduced early on and reinforced. While not perfect, the de facto brothers and sisters are far removed from the bick-

Despite his cautious approach, Frank is done in by a stray drop of blood and never makes it to the promised safety of the compound.

ering and suspicious survivors thrown together in *Night of the Living Dead*. Unable to sustain their life in the apartment, the ad hoc family loads up Frank's taxi and plots a course for an army compound they have learned about through a repeated announcement broadcast over an emergency frequency. On the way the group grows closer, and even Selena lowers her defenses and allows herself to form an emotional attachment to both Hannah and Jim. A "family" of black and white horses seen running through a field symbolizes this new unity. As the horses prance away, the always-sentimental Frank blows them a kiss.

When the group finally reaches the compound it is apparently deserted. In disappointment Frank throws a rock at a cawing crow. A drop from an infected corpse falls from the tree above and enters his eye. While his horrified daughter watches, he metamorphosizes into a ravenous ghoul; but before he can attack, he is riddled with bullets by a commando team hiding in the compound.

The soldiers take the remaining members of the family to an abandoned country mansion where Major West (a nod to the Lovecraft's reanimator, played by Christopher Eccleston) meets them and promises safety. As with many portrayals of the military and/or police authority in post-modern zombie movies, particularly in Romero's films from *Night of the Living Dead* on, the army men are unreliable and as callous as the zombies. Gripped by the impulse that comes with infection and incapable of forming intent, the zombies the viewer sees are no more culpable than the chimps were while the soldiers are venal and morally debased. This fact is confirmed when the viewer learns why Major West has lured them there, particularly the women: he has promised his men that he will help satiate their sexual needs while they rebuild human civilization, whether or not their prospective "mates" consent. When Jim objects, he is knocked out and transported to be executed in the forest. Isolated, Selena and Hannah dress up in red gowns and feign interest in mating in order to buy time for either escape or suicide.

In the fast-moving climax, shot and edited, as are many scenes in Boyle's films, in a frenetic style, Jim transforms himself into a killer, equal to the infected, reinforcing Boyle's theme of the inherent violence in human nature. During a thunderstorm he escapes the soldiers, who are attacked by the infected, and returns to the mansion. Releasing a zombie soldier who is kept on a chain and starved, chaos reigns as the infected soldier makes his way through the remaining members of the troop while the half-naked Jim kills one of the soldiers. He then pounces on the roof like an animal and finds Selena who is about to be raped. He jumps through the window and grabs the soldier, pushing his thumbs through his eyeballs. Selena, now convinced Jim is infected, grabs a machete. But she cannot do the deed. Jim's face changes suddenly and the gentle Jim returns. In the resolution Jim, Selena, and Hannah have formed a new family unit and live in a small house in the country as they wait to be rescued. With this resolution Boyle comes down on the side of love as the only antidote for the violence in all of us.

28 Weeks Later: his wife's kiss tranforms Don (Robert Carlyle) into a ghoul with blood-red eyes.

The unexpected success of his zombie film in the United States prompted Boyle to become an executive producer of the sequel, *28 Weeks Later* (2007). In this narrative, most of the infected have perished from hunger and the small, armed camp of the original has become a heavily forti- fied military safe-zone in the heart of London. There Don (Robert Carlyle) is reunited with his two children who were in Spain when the outbreak began. When they sneak out into the city to search for family mementos in their former home, they discover their mother Alice (Catherine McCormack) is living there. As Don learns when she is brought back and he kisses her, Alice is an asymptomatic carrier of the rage virus.

Instantly zombiefied by Alice's kiss, Don becomes a ravaging ghoul who quickly infects most of the people in the safe zone. Although made for more than twice the budget, this follow-up barely grossed half as much as the original, possibly because it relied on techno-props rather than the simple insular intensity of *28 Days Later* and went for flashy effects more than flash mobs. Ironically, it reversed Boyle's subtext of where newly formed family ties enhanced one's survival chances and made a teenager's longing for his lost mother the precipitating factor in a second plague.

The British-American co-production *Doomsday* (2008) is quasi-follow-up set in a dystopic future still dealing with the threat of the ravenous infected. In this movie's extended prologue, the "Reaper Virus" overruns Scotland and a 60-foot tall, high-tech version of Hadrian's Wall is constructed to isolate the entire country. In 2035, with Britain long ostracized from the rest of the civilized world for their de facto genocide, infected persons are found in London, so the mechanical-eyed Major Eden Sinclair (Rhona Mitra in the semi-bionic role) is dispatched by Prime Minister Hatcher (yes, that is the character's name, portrayed by Alexander Siddig) and his sycophantic cronies including Capt. Nelson (Bob Hoskins) to breech the wall and sort it all out.

As Fulci did in *Zombie*, writer/director Neil Marshal uses Conrad's *Heart of Darkness* as a scratch pad, where Marlow becomes Sinclair, Kurtz is Kane (Malcolm McDowell), but the cannibals are her nemeses rather than the crew of her packet steamer. As it is primarily an action movie with a car chase peopled by villains cloned from *The Road Warrior* (1981), *Doomsday* does for the zombie plague what *Van Helsing* (2004) did for Dracula, that is reduce a legendary evil to the foil of a superhero, a role Mitra would shortly revisit as the warrior vampiress in *Underworld: Rise of the Lycans* (2009).

Released shortly after the commercial success of *28 Days Later*, *Shaun of the Dead* was a critical hit that fueled the zombie comedy trend. It is little wonder that Universal put its clout behind this project, as it fulfills many of the criteria for millennial "bro-mance" comedies. The two main characters, Shaun (Simon Pegg) and Ed (Nick Frost), are "child men" of the type so familiar to post-modern movie and TV audiences. Shaun works a dead-end job as an electronics salesman and cringes before his nagging girl-

Right, *Doomsday*: Major Eden Sinclair (Rhona Mitra) peeks around a wall with her non-bionic eye.

friend—read: surrogate mother—Liz (Kate Ashfield), another staple of "man love" comedies, and finds satisfaction in hanging out with Ed. Together they play videos, indulge in "fart" games, and drink themselves into a stupor at the local pub. So out of it are these two characters that they do not even notice that without explanation many of the people around them are turning into zombies.

In fact, it takes an actual zombie invasion of their house to convince them something is awry. As is typical of this sort of social comedy, once Shaun realizes the danger he displays a side to him that the audience would never expect (or could expect based on the mixed genre expectations). Shaun becomes a heroic action figure, even if his methods are often bumbling. He motivates Ed to accompany him on his quest to save his mother and girlfriend, which he does. When they take refuge in his favorite sanctuary, the pub, he is the one who uses the smell of his flesh to lure the zombie mob away from the bar—of course they immediately return. As the zombie body count mounts in the city, so does that of his friends and loved ones. His mother is bitten and Shaun himself, in a truly touching moment, saves her from zombiehood by shooting her in the head. Later he has to leave his best friend Ed behind with a gun. In a final prank, even while turning, Ed plays the "fart game," ironically undercutting the pathetic quality of these types of scenes in other zombie movies. Shaun and Liz rise in an elevator to an exit as Ed places the gun to his face.

In the coda the zombies have been destroyed or domesticated, as in the later comedy *Fido*, and Shaun has moved to a new place far more stylish than his former "man cave"; but Shaun has not abandoned all his childish ways. With Liz's consent he happily strolls off to a shed in the backyard where Ed, now a domesticated zombie, plays video games with a contented Shaun.

The same year *Dead Clowns* (2004) plays upon the paradoxical fear of clowns many people exhibit—it even has a clinical name, coulrophobia, and is a constant gag in sitcoms. But in this case the fear is not unreasonable when clown ghouls are resurrected in the state of Florida after a hurricane. The film does include some grisly humor and the talents of "scream queens" Debbie Rochon and

Opposite, Shaun (Simon Pegg in the old-school tie) and companions part the zombie sea in *Shaun of the Dead*. Above, the no-money riff on *Shaun*, *Cockneys vs. Zombies*.

Brinke Stevens.

The clown motif is also used in the British *Zombie Women of Satan* (2008), an early entry in a spate of ultra-low-budget (perhaps more than spare change but well under $50,000) United Kingdom zombedies that has grown to include such titles as: *A Grave for Corpses* (2008, a crazed detective and a zombie master named Davro, meant to be in the manner of Legendre, but more likely to spend two minutes imitating the laugh of Dwight Frye as Renfield); *Knight of the Living Dead* (2005, technically Icelandic, but the actors all attempt British accents in a folk allegory with papier-mâché props); *Attack of the Herbals* (2011, a self-described *Shaun* variant where apparently not every tea is calming and some can create undead in Scotland as quickly as a reaper virus); *Harold's Going Stiff* (2011, no, it's not hardcore); *Gangsters, Guns, and Zombies* (2011, a triple threat rife with possibilities but not exactly Guy Ritchie does zombies); *Stalled* (2013, a peeping-tom plumber finds the zombie apocalypse is happening in the ladies room); *Zombies from Ireland* (2013, Irish convicts from a botched swine flu test invade Wales, hence the title); *Convention of the Dead* (2013, there are so many now, it was time to get organized); and the ultimate, no-money riff on *Shaun of the Dead*, *Cockneys vs Zombies* (2012, presumably the audience must decide which of two groups is more frightening). Upcoming in 2014 is *The Curse of the Buxom Strumpet* (one suspects that title might change), a pastiche of Hammer and Henry Fielding about a ghoul outbreak in the early 18th century. Also slated (and hard to believe for anyone who has seen the original) is *Zombie Women of Satan 2.* Contemporary with *Shaun* but outside the UK, *Choking Hazard* (2004) is a zombie comedy from the Czech Republic. A group of intellectuals, rather than nubile teens, gathers at a resort to discuss existentialism, life, and death. Once there theoretical dissertations are interrupted by hungry zombies.

For the first third of its narrative, *Boy Eats Girl* (2005)—an Anglo-Irish comedy released a year after *Shaun*—is a standard yet clever teenage sex comedy, with only a hint of the horror to come in a brief prologue set in a crypt. Nathan (David Leon), the protagonist, is a sensitive, angst-filled Irish teenager in love with the seemingly unattainable Jessica (Samantha Mumba). He and his two socially inept buddies muse in traditional movie geek manner, avoid being attacked by school bullies, and make awkward advances on popular girls, which are inevitably rebuffed. The film also posits a trio of mean girls who taunt and humiliate the three boys.

After Nathan *thinks* he sees his idealized love Jessica performing oral sex on the high school Lothario, he gets drunk and sticks his head into the noose he keeps in his bedroom as a reminder of his teen alienation. But before he can complete the suicide on his own, his mother bursts into

the room and knocks him off the chair. His neck cracks. In a rapid montage Nathan's mother runs back to the crypt seen in the prologue, retrieves a book on voodoo, and resurrects her son from the dead.

Nathan now experiences even more angst as a zombie than he did as a hormonally imbalanced teen. (The parallel between zombie-ism and adolescent instability is made a more serious sub-text in *Jennifer's Body* a few years later.) After he bites the school bully who is beating him up for desiring his crush Jessica again, zombie-ism spreads through the town in classic, gore-fest style. Particularly gruesome is a scene where Jessica takes the controls of her father's farm machine and threshes through a crowd of zombies. But all is resolved happily in the final scenes with a zombie holocaust—they are burned alive...or dead...or whatever they are. Nathan's mother finds the antidote to zombie-ism: the bite of a snake from the crypt. After helping Jessica and his friends conflagrate the zombies, a snake-bit Nathan returns to his normal state. In the final shot, he reconciles with Jessica and they end up in a standard clinch.

In contrast such American ultra-lows as *Zombie Honeymoon* (2004), a movie with a title that suggests complete comedy, combines humor with tragic romance. In the set-up a pair of young, vibrant, and sexy newlyweds are attacked by a zombie rising out of the ocean. Only the husband, Danny (Graham Sibley), becomes infected. He dies and returns to life in the hospital. But when he goes back home with his wife, Denise (Tracy Coogan), he begins to decompose: bits of him drop off continually, even during dinner. The newlyweds try to stay together, as Denise supports him

Young Zombie Love:
left, *Boy Eats Girl*.
Below, *Zombie Honey-
moon: he's not going
for her neck...yet.*

while refusing to enable his desire for flesh, drawing a connection between the impact of addiction on a family and the horror of gradual zombie-ism.

In *Shadows of the Dead* (2004) a man named John (Jonathan Flanigan) is bitten by an infected zombie in the woods during a weekend getaway with his lover Jennifer. He gradually transforms into a zombie while Jennifer tries to nurse him back to health. His lust for flesh increases, however, and eventually he infects his beloved so they can be together "forever" as zombies. Beverly Hynds of the noteworthy vampire film *Apocalypse and the Beauty Queen* (2005) plays the woman who alternates between sympathy and recrimination in dealing with her flesh lust and with a lover who has infected her—the similarity to HIV seems pointed.

Tim Burton created a stop-motion zombie film in 2005 called *Corpse Bride*. In the story, set in Victorian England, an awkward young man (the voice of Johnny Depp) accidentally resurrects a corpse while rehearsing his marriage vows. The corpse bride (modeled after the always Gothic actress Helena Bonham Carter, who also does the bride's voice) assumes that he is her new groom and takes him to the land of the dead to live happily ever after. However, the young man finds himself still drawn to his live fiancée and so the corpse bride makes the grand sacrifice, by letting him return to his bride. In the final scene she dissolves into a flock of butterflies, as her soul is released. *Tokyo Zombie* (2005) is another unconventional satirical zombie movie from the Japanese. It features zombies rising from piles of garbage all over Tokyo (apparently there is a landfill shortage in Japan). Two over-the-top jujitsu experts take on the zombies in various ways, many non-conventional, including letting one zombie give them oral sex. Tadanobu Asano stars and delivers another idiosyncratic performance worthy of his lead role in Takashi Miike's violent and iconoclastic 2001 release *Ichi the Killer*.

Zombie comedies moved farther off-center with *Fido* (2006). The film is both a satire on the conformist and repressive 1950s and a Romero-style metaphorical examination of zombies as symbols of an oppressed minority, an analogy more and more common in millennial zombie films. The film begins with a black-and-white Eisenhower-era newsreel/infomercial for Zomcon Corporation. The company boasts of its role in defeating the zombie invasion that resulted from cosmic radiation and then "containing" them in a wild zone, while turning others by means of an electronic collar into slaves for the suburban middle class. The narrative relocates to a suburban town named Willard, where the filmmakers utilize a palette of bright, primary, high-key colors to give the town a sheen that is surreal. Unlike *Pleasantville* (1998), which the film resembles in some ways, the town itself is real, but the retrospective allusions to television sitcoms of the period are numerous. The young protagonist Timmy Robinson (Kesun Loder) is named after the boy in TV's *Lassie* series, and Timmy's zombie faithful servant Fido saves him several times just like Lassie did for his master. Timmy's mother, Mrs. Robinson (Carrie-Ann Moss), is a cocktail-dressed housewife in the *Father Knows Best* tradition while his father (Dylan Baker) in his gray-flannel suit and obsession with funer-

Opposite, *The Corpse Bride* broke ground for the critical success of *ParaNorman*. Below, the heavily collared Fido (Billy Connolly, center) dutifully holds up a parasol for his family.

als represents the corporate man of the period.

Unlike standard sitcom families, there is dysfunction underlying this bourgeois town. In school Timmy questions the conventional wisdom about zombies and the total control Zomcon Corp wields over their lives. His form of rebellion erupts when he forms a bond with the family's new servant zombie Fido (Billy Connolly). While his father and mother ignore him, Fido takes an interest in him, even saving him from gun-toting children (who are issued weapons at the age of 12 to kill rogue zombies) and murderous school bullies.

When Fido's collar malfunctions, he kills and partially consumes Mrs. Henderson, the neighborhood voyeur/curmudgeon. Timmy, inspired by his affection for his "pet," covers up the crime. Moreover Fido's child-like innocence and empathy has also inspired sympathy and sexual interest in Timmy's mother, who is neglected sexually by her neurotic, asexual husband—like any self-respecting 1950s couple they sleep in separate beds.

When war hero and Zomcon exec Bottoms (Henry Czerny) discovers the culprit in the zombie crime, he confiscates Fido and reprimands the family, particularly Mrs. Robinson (yes, more pop culture allusions, this time to Anne Bancroft's portrayal in *The Graduate*) who he feels must be "contained" like the zombies themselves. For Bottoms, Mrs. Robinson is much too bossy in a world with a Stepford Wives mindset. Unwilling to conform and live without Fido, Timmy enlists the help of the town pervert Theopolis (Tim Blake Nelson), who keeps his own teenage sex slave named Tammy (Sonja Bennett). Together they travel to the Zomcon factory where Fido has been reassigned. The Robinsons, newly motivated by their son's actions, follow; but it is not Mr. Robinson

A child ghoul in
Wicked Little Things.

who saves his son from Bottoms. After all it's not really the 1950s but a modern rendering of it. He does *try* to assert his manhood and prevent Bottoms from releasing Timmy into the hands of the zombies in the wild zone but to no avail. While he is largely ineffectual, in conjunction with a sharp shooting Mrs. Robinson Fido saves the day.

The final scenes of the movie balance the opening. Willard has returned to its idyllic self but with one significant difference: zombies and humans have achieved a rapprochement. One human plays chess with a zombie. Theopolis serves Tammy, now in a sun dress rather than sexy cheer-leader outfits. Finally Fido smiles contentedly at a radiant Mrs. Robinson, as he stands lovingly over the crib of her new baby, leaving the audience to draw its own conclusions.

The Wicked Little Things (2006, aka *Gravedancers* aka *Zombies*) of the title are not really *that* wicked. You could say they are gravedancers, and they are certainly zombies: the corpses of chil-dren buried alive while working in a sweatshop mine in 1913. In the present day, the children return to take revenge on the descendants of the mine owners who exploited them. Chloe Grace Moretz (who would later portray a child vampire in *Let Me In--2010*) gives an appropriately melan-choly performance as Emma, the descendant of one of the mine children. Mary (Helia Grekova) and Emma become friends, even though her mother believes zombie Mary is imaginary.

Last Rites of the Dead (*Zombies Anonymous*, 2006) is a serious attempt to "humanize" zombies. The ghouls of this unusual film walk among the living, some even "pass" in the larger society with the help of "look alive" make-up (a conceit used most recently in the British television series *In the Flesh*). Others have formed self-defense groups to protect themselves from vigilantes, outraged

Angela (Gina Ramsden) and her fellow ZA members at a meeting.

humans who kill zombies at will. The protagonist of the movie is Angela (Gina Ramsden), an abused woman who is knocked around and then murdered by her insanely jealous boyfriend Josh (Joshua Nelson). After returning from the dead, Angela loses her job because of her "smell," is beaten by a group of thugs, but finds solace at last in a self-help group (the "zombies anonymous" of the alternate title). The meetings themselves are staged like a parody of AA, with everyone expressing too much consideration for each other even as the issues are literally life and death and life again. Discovering Angela is undead, Josh begins stalking her, alternating between declarations of love and vile insults, which escalate when she begins seeing a member of the ZA group. Acting out his anger at Angela, Josh joins a paramilitary group, headed by an overbearing and sadistic Commandant (Christa McNamee) who relentlessly humiliates her male recruits, while prodding them into more violent action against zombies.

Desperate to escape the harassment by Josh, Angela joins a zombie cult led by Good Mother Solstice (Mary Jo Verruto). There she participates semi-consciously in an orgy of drugs, bondage, and eroticism designed to make her a "sister" to the other women members. As a result of a wound during one of their raids, Josh dies and also is transformed into an undead. Although he leads the Commandant to the cult, he still will not reveal the presence of Angela. In a psychotic frenzy, the Commandant shoots herself in order to penetrate the cult compound. During the massacre that ensues, Josh finds Angela and reaffirms his love. A hardened Angela first blasts him with a shotgun then castrates him. In the last shot of the movie, Angela stares into the mirror, throws away her "look alive" make-up, and smiles enigmatically at her reflection.

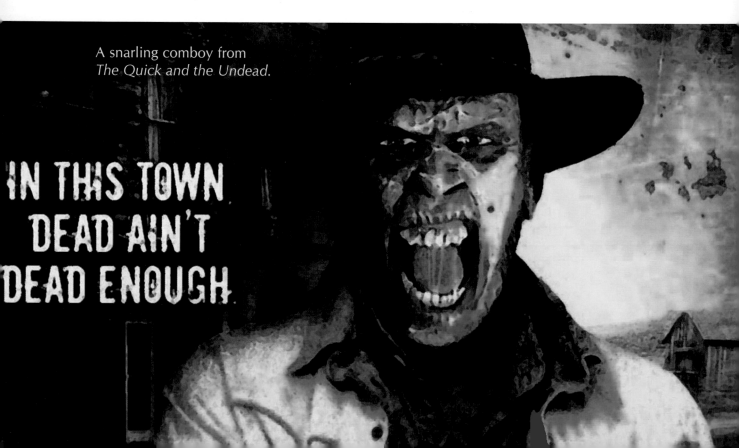

A snarling comboy from
The Quick and the Undead.

IN THIS TOWN, DEAD AIN'T DEAD ENOUGH.

Above, *Gallowwalkers*: Aman (Wesley Snipes) takes a scalp...and then some.

In *The Quick and the Undead* (2006) the filmmakers attempt to marry the Western genre to its zombie sister without much success. Even though the film is set in the future the characters wear Western outfits and use period weapons as a group of warring bounty hunters set out to gun down the zombie population. *Undead or Alive: A Zombedy* (2007) is a parody Western zombie pastiche. *Saturday Night Live* graduate Chris Kattan plays a bumbling cowboy who joins with his thieving buddy and the sassy niece of Geronimo (played fetchingly by Navi Rawat) to fight zombies. The niece wants to take revenge on the American army for the capture of her uncle. But Geronimo's curse beats her to the punch, as Anglos are turning into zombies. Of course, no send-up prevents newer productions that venture seriously in the same vein such as the more recent *The Dead and the Damned* (2010, and retitled as *Cowboys vs. Zombies* rather than *Aliens* for DVD release), which recruits aspects of Romero and *Body Snatchers*, as gold-seeking 49ers stumble across a meteorite that releases toxic spores that create...zombies. This film's bounty hunter must team up with a renegade Apache to survive a 19th-century apocalypse. If there is key stakeholder in this niche market within the zombie film, it would be the Adrenalin Film Group that began with a $500, contemporary Romero rehash entitled *The Second Death* (2005) and jumped all the way to 5-figure budgets with a trio of ghouls-in-the-West movies. Despite the titles, *Fistful of Brains* (2006), *Forever Dead* (2007), and *A Few Brains More* (2012) are not comedies, although their deadpan

Gallowwalkers.

performances and meager production values may elicit some chuckles. While meager by studio standards, it would take many more fistfuls of micro-budget projects such as these to total the $17-million cost of *Gallowwalkers*, shot back in 2006 but only released directly to DVD in 2013. All that time did not help make sense of the narrative that presents Wesley Snipes as the dreadlocked and resurrected gunfighter Aman, who was brought back to life by his mother, a rogue nun. Aman's problem, or rather curse, is that all those whom he has ever killed come back also, lea by the plat-inum-haired Kansa (Kevin Howarth), who pointedly notes that "Dead ain't what it used to be." Against this posse of ghouls, that includes an antagonist wearing a cast iron helmet reminiscent of Ned Kelly's to protect his zombiefied brains [see frame above] from a kill shot, Snipes is the same sort of killing machine that he was in the *Blade* series. That his targets are zombies rather than vam-pires is merely incidental. In Japan the same genre blending led to *Samurai Zombie* (2008).

American Zombie (2007) is a clever mockumentary directed and co-written by Grace Lee, which deals with the various types of zombies living among humans. They are respectfully called "Revenants" and are subdivided into various groups from the violent, flesh-eating types to the total-ly sympathetic, functional ones. The filmmakers interview the zombies in their homes and work-places and allow them to speak for themselves about their situation, hopes, and dreams. More recent "documentary" treatments on various cable television channels, such as *Zombies: A Living History* (2011) or *Zombie Busters: Outlive the Undead* and *Surviving Zombies: The Apocalypse Field Guide* (both 2012) discuss the history of zombies and their persecution, even offering satir-ic hints on how to eliminate them. If that's not enough serious combat shooters can sign in for var-ious role playing exercises that revolve around zombie hunting. *Deadheads* (2011) returns to the tradition of *My Boyfriend's Back* with a lot of *Dude, Where's My Car?* (2000) thrown in, as two sen-tient young undead males Mike (Michael McKiddy) and Brent (Ross Kidder) initiate a road trip through zombie-killer country to find the latter's former girlfriend, whose father it turns out, murdered him.

In *Outpost* (2008), a corporate rep hires a crack team of mercenaries to retrieve a mechanism from World War II, which, of course, turns out to be more Nazi experiments with the occult and zombie-ism. This concept has evolved from the hypothetical in *Revenge of the Zombies* and *The Creature with the Atom Brain*; through the semi-practical in *The Frozen Dead* (1966, where an American scientist portrayed by Dana Andrews plans to reanimate some dead Nazi leaders); *Shock Waves* (1977, wherein Peter Cushing's SS Commander is putting together a ghoul squad); or *Night of the Zombies* (1981, with the more explicit alternate title *Night of the SS Zombies*); to Franco's Africa Korps Undead in *Treasure of the Living Dead* or Rollin's ironic *Zombie Lake* or the more recent *Dead Snow*.

A few years before *Outpost,* there was *Operation Nazi Zombies* (released in 2003 as *Maplewoods*) and the Canadian micro-budget *War of the Dead* (2006), which imagined a Nazi Zombie Death Squad hunting down Allied veterans in North America. "The Soldier," a 2007 short film about Joseph Mengele creating German shock troops, has just been made into the feature *The 4th Reich* (2014), which co-stars German horror/gore filmmaker Andreas Schnaas. Now a full-fledged sub-set of the zombie film, *Outpost* spawned more Nazi ghouls in the sequels *Outpost: Black Sun* (2012) and *Outpost: Rise of the Spetznaz* (2013) and cheap spin-offs such as *Battlefield Death Tales* (2012, which in case anyone could not figure it out is also known as *Nazi Zombie Death Tales* or *Nazi Zombie Battleground*) and *Dead Walkers: Rise of the 4th Reich* (2013). Of course, the crate of killer-making tea in *Attack of the Herbals* also turns out to be leftover from a Nazi experiment.

Dead Snow.

A larger budgeted enterprise also called *War of the Dead* (2012) features another secret Nazi, this time uncovered in a Russian forest by the U.S. and Finland (former ally of the Third Reich) with much the same result. Perhaps wackiest of all is *Nazis at the Center of the Earth* (2012), another legacy of Mengele movie where the word "zombie" is thrown around, but these aren't really ghouls just old Nazis that keep running with replacement parts like used cars. Unlike the camp classic. The *Madmen of Mandoras* (1963), these 4th Reichers chose a cavern under the Antarctic rather than a tropical island. They also save Hitler's head but attach it to a bad knock-off of the second generation Robo-Cop with predictable results when they try to reconquer the world.

By 2008 and the release of *Colin*, many filmmakers had lost interest in the reasons why humans are turning into zombies: voodoo, a virus, cosmic radiation, herbs. That is mostly irrelevant. All that's important is the existential dilemma of the zombie and those he/she meets to greet or eat. Shot in a documentary-style "shaky cam," *Colin* tries to capture a character in transition from human to zombie in an apocalyptic London landscape. The audience meets the title character (Alastair Kirton) just after he has been bitten by someone the viewer does not see until the conclusion of the movie, the rest of which details his painful transition into zombiehood. Gradually he loses his memories as well as his empathy then wanders off into the city.

In many ways Colin is simply an observer, rarely participating in the feeding and violence going on around him. He acts as the viewer's guide to the apocalypse. Once in a while he will partake of an ear (which might happen still to have an earphone in it) or a piece of stray flesh; but mostly he dete-

Above, Alastair Kirton as *Colin.* Opposite, Columbus (Jesse Eisenberg) and Tallahassee (Woody Harrelson) stride down a trashed main street in *Zombieland.*

riorates mentally and physically while he and the audience witness the horror all around him. A family defends itself against invading zombies; an undead quietly feeds on the entrails of a man who sits numbly without resisting; a serial killer takes a new victim even as his old ones are turning into ghouls.

Ultimately, Colin's sister Linda (Daisy Aitkens), who has been bitten by Colin, kidnaps him with the help of her husband and takes him home to their mother (Kerry Owen). She holds to the belief that Colin can be re-humanized if he is exposed to memories. But not the grief of his mother, nor an array of photographs, nor familiar surroundings can bring back his humanity. In the end his mother sorrowfully locks him into a small room, puts newspaper over the windows, throws his now zombiefied sister in with him, and leaves. But somehow Colin escapes and finds his way through the chaos to an apartment, which stops Colin in his shambling tracks. Now the viewer learns how Colin became a zombie. His girlfriend was infected and he chose to try to save her. But eventually she bit him and he was forced to destroy her. This memory is so powerful that it can shake Colin to his core, even in his new animal-like existence. It is on this memory that the film concludes.

When it was released *Zombieland* (2009) became the largest grossing zombie to that date. It is easy to see why. It has an A-level cast, a slick script with an engaging voiceover narration, and well-timed humor. The chief protagonist of the movie is "Columbus" (Jesse Eisenberg), as the characters in this post-virus zombie land are named after the cities they came from. On the road back home in hopes of finding his parents, Columbus is a classic post-modern movie nerd: socially maladjusted, garrulously intellectual, and painfully timid, except in the face of an undead threat. Along the way he meets his first road mate, Tallahassee (Woody Harrelson), his polar opposite. Tallahassee, who we later learn has lost his child to zombies, is on a nostalgic quest for the perfect "Twinkie," the symbol of the mundane and normal in the face of the apocalypse. He is macho, gruff, taciturn, and armed to the teeth.

Columbus joins forces temporarily with Tallahassee, even though in many ways he finds him as terrifying as the marauding ghouls. For his part, Tallahassee thinks Columbus is mildly annoying and way too talkative. In one of the many markets where Tallahassee stops at to forage for provisions and possibly that elusive Twinkie, the unlikely partners encounter a pair of con-artist sisters, Wichita (Emma Stone) and Little Rock (Abigail Breslin). Both are experts in manipulating men who are often charmed into unguarded behavior by their winsome ways. These two men are not immune to that, so the sisters steal their car and weapons, not once but twice.

Columbus negotiates a truce and, after discovering that his home city has been destroyed, agrees to travel with the sisters and Tallahassee to Hollywood and its rumored zombie-free amusement park "Pacific Playland." Along the way they take a detour to star Bill Murray's mansion. In a self-por-

This encounter does not go exactly as Columbus had hoped it would: she's not the living dead girl of his dreams.

trait, Murray plays himself and is still living in his fictional home, surviving by adopting a zombie disguise when he goes out to play golf. During their stay in the mansion, Tallahassee bonds with Little Rock, whose manifest spunk compels his admiration and turns him into a surrogate father. Wichita seduces the virginal Columbus but cannot control her rebellious temperament.

After Columbus accidentally shoots Bill Murray dressed in his zombie outfit, the sisters take off by themselves for Playland. Once there, they ride the various attractions, including a tower-drop ride. However, in powering up the rides and their lights, they attract the attention of all the nearby undead. As the sisters defend themselves from besieging zombies, Columbus and Tallahassee arrive and mount a rescue. Despite the ongoing chaos all around them, in the movie's comic context, Columbus finds a happy ending with a newly constructed family, not exactly the one he was looking for but good enough. In 2013 *Zombieland* inspired a spin-off, a web series called, appropriately, *Zombieland the Series*. It was produced by Amazon.com with a new relatively unknown cast and did not survive the apocalypse beyond the pilot.

A more proximate follow-up (in the same year) to *Zombieland* is the low-budget *Die-ner (Get it?)*—sometimes called *Kentucky Fried Zombies*—a dark comedy about a serial killer named Ken (Joshua Grote), who is surprised to find his most recent victims coming back for him while he tries to get a decent meal in a diner modeled after the iconic image in Edward Hoppers' "Nighthawks." Although protagonist Ken is a serial killer, his irony in the face of the zombie apocalypse creates a personality with which both the audience and fellow characters can identify. He enlists a young

Joshua Grote as serial killer Ken in *Die-ner*.

couple Rob (Parker Quinn) and Kathy (Liesel Kopp), who amble into the diner, to help him figure out how to make the dead stay *dead*. The filmmakers seem to come down on the side of the zombies who are attempting to take a somewhat justified revenge for being pushed into an early grave by the glib serial killer.

The most significant development in the wake of *Zombieland*'s success is cable series *The Walking Dead* (2010–present [see the sidebar]). One of the highest rated shows on television, cable or broadcast, *The Walking Dead* is adapted from the popular graphic novel of the same name and with the same set-up: Rick Grimes is a former cop who has been in a coma for several months after being shot while on duty. When he wakes, he discovers that the world has been taken over by zombies and that he seems to be the only person still alive. Returning home to discover his wife and son missing, he heads for Atlanta to search for his family.

By the end of its third year episodes, *The Walking Dead* had refocused on the same ironies Romero had suggested in 1968. The core group of survivors, with whom the audience had traveled through zombie land for two seasons, has taken refuge in a prison guarded by implacable ghouls. It's a bit

larger than the farmhouse in *Night of the Living Dead* but the emotional situation and the bickering amongst themselves is much the same. What's more their main conflict is no longer with the "walkers" or "biters" but another, larger group of humans ensconced in a fortified town, who are more numerous, better armed, and lea by a sociopathic control freak that needs to kill them so that he can continue to rule his little world unchallenged. While that character may not yet have become Dennis Hopper's Kaufman in *Land of the Dead*, he is getting close.

Zombie Apocalypse (2010), *Zombie Apocalypse* (the television movie), and *Zombie Apocalypse: Redemption* (both 2011) reflect and exploit the growing millennial anxiety around an increasingly dangerous world and the fascination with zombies on the Internet as well as in the news. All three rely heavily on the same low-budget rendering of a dystopic future, the zombie world established from *Night of the Living Dead* through *28 Days Later* in which humans are outnumbered by zombies and in a continual state of anxiety and outright combat, much like the "war against terrorism." In a period context, *Abraham Lincoln vs. Zombies* (2012) hoped to coat tail on the success of the bigger-budgeted *Abraham Lincoln: Vampire Hunter* in the same year. Unfortunately neither met with either critical or financial success.

Even as a spate of ultra-low-budget projects over the last decade have infested the genre (and our filmography) as thoroughly as the aimless hordes in *The Walking Dead* have overrun the Deep South, some filmmakers have found an alternative to the standard "don't get bitten before you shoot those snarling zombies in the head" scenarios without needing a lot more money. *State of Emergency* (2011) uses the six-decades-old approach of Arch Oboler's *Five* (1951)–and the quite

Opposite, *The Walking Dead*. Below, a solitary zombie from *State of Emergency*.

THE WALKING DEAD

by Todd K. Platts

Based on viewer numbers, AMC's *The Walking Dead* (2010–present) is as the most watched show in cable television history, a key indicator that the "post-millennial," "post-9/11" interest in all things zombie is ongoing. Before premiering on the network associated with such "standard," that is non-supernatural, dramas as *Mad Men* (2007–present) and *Breaking Bad* (2008–2013), the serial story of a handful of humans struggling to survive in a world infested by undead had built up a loyal fan base through Robert Kirkman's graphic novel of the same name.

While some might assert that *The Walking Dead* is revolutionary, it is not unique nor even particularly novel. At the heart of its narrative lies a prototypical plot as first imagined by George Romero and revisited by scores of filmmakers since the debut of *Night of the Living Dead*.: the recently dead awaken with an inborn and insatiable craving for flesh and/or brains. Their contagious cannibalism precipitates an exponential spread of the zombie plague and societal collapse, so that the few remaining uninfected persons are compelled to band together in defensive cliques or become zombies themselves. Unlike its antecedents, however, *The Walking Dead* novel and series has a simple catch: the story is open-ended. It never ends.

The first few episodes of the television series, as in the original, center on small town sheriff's deputy Rick Grimes (Andrew Lincoln), who awakens from a coma and sets off to locate his family. As if an zombie apocalypse were not enough drama, Rick's narrative unfolds like a soap opera from the triangle with his wife Lori (Sarah Wayne Callies) and best friend Shane (Jon Bernthal), who thought he was dead, through the near-death of his son Carl (Chandler Riggs) to Lori's most recent pregnancy and death in childbirth. The series has a large ensemble cast of contrasting personality types, which is fertile ground for diverging storylines and character arcs. With the serial context audiences can invest emotionally in

ROBERT KIRKMAN • TONY MOORE

the survival characters (or, perhaps, root for one's death), as writers, actors, and directors can add new layers and nuance to the protagonists and antagonists. This series component is lacking stand-alone zombie films, where narrative closure occurs within two hours. Sequels that were not part of the original plan may be generated by a commercial success; but a different creative mix of cast and crew is usually the case with those.

Viewer attachments to the show's characters can become very strong. When the elder of the survivors, Dale Horvath (Jeffrey DeMunn), died in season two, publications like the *Los Angeles Times*, *Time*, and *The Atlantic* eulogized the character and even fretted for his surrogate daughter Andrea (Laurie Holden), as did fans on message boards devoted to the series. So strong are the sentiments that executive producer Gale Anne Hurd revealed that she receives death threats when a popular character gets axed. In one of the best-known examples of fan over-zealousness, actor Laurie Holden got such threats after her character accidentally shot at Daryl Dixon (Norman Reedus), one of the most popular figures. Holden and Reedus had to pose together and remind viewers that they are simply actors playing parts. Dixon, a character created for the series, is so popular that he has his own fan site (dixonsvixens.com) and is the key protagonist in a 2013 videogame adaptation, *The Walking Dead: Survival Instinct*.

As both television and comic series *The Walking Dead* has become a multimedia juggernaut. Besides the videogame, AMC licenses an array of show-related products including t-shirts ("I ♥ Daryl"), bobble-head dolls, a board game, action figures, a calendar, and DVD collector's sets with elaborate packaging. Season two includes a zombie bust with a screwdriver impaled through its eye socket. Given this overwhelming success, few would suspect that the show and comic almost never got made. It began with Robert Kirkman's misrepresentation to Image Comics, when he pitched the idea of a never ending zombie narrative in 2003. Without a stronger hook, the publisher doubted the comic's readership potental and rejected the concept. At the time zombies were perceived as moribund genre. So Kirkman famously lied and said he intended to tie the zombie apocalypse to an alien invasion. This was not in the first issue of *The Walking Dead*, but despite the ruse, Image agreed the book told a strong story. Still, the initial print run was limited to 7,500 copies. To everyone's surprise, *The Walking Dead* became an unmitigated success. Coincidentally zombies began a resurgence. *28 Days Later* and the *Dawn of the Dead* remake scored at the box office. Max Brooks' tongue-in-cheek *The Zombie Survival Guide* became a bestseller. Soon potential adaptors were inquiring about the adaptation rights to Kirkman's comic. As creator and copyright holder, the author retained certain copyright privileges in

Below text, this page, Norman Reedus as Daryl Dixon. Next page, the Walking Dead.

regards to his work, which included veto power over any offer.

In early-2006, after spurning several pitches, Kirkman got a call from Frank Darabont—the big-budget Hollywood director behind such studios projects as *The Shawshank Redemption* (1994) and *The Green Mile* (1999). Serendipitously the director had found a copy of the *The Walking Dead* while browsing in a Burbank, California, comic book store. He saw the graphic novel as the perfect vehicle for his long-standing desire to work in the zombie genre. When Darabont told Kirkman, "It's not about the zombies," the Dead's creator was sold. Even as the project went into development, the zombie film got hot. Yet, the odds were, as with most ideas, long in an industry where most shows never even make it to a pilot let alone past that. In order to secure a network backer *The Walking Dead* creative team would have to demonstrate to industry gatekeepers that it could reliably deliver desired audience segments to controversy-shy advertisers—no small feat for a show with such a gory premise. Kevin Reilly, then president of entertainment at NBC, decided to have Darabont develop a pilot script in 2006; but when he read the violent content of the completed draft, NBC backed out.

Ironically, programs like those belonging to the CSI franchise contain just as much, if not more, violence. The stigma of horror, as a disreputable genre, however, creates the potential for greater public backlash in a milieu that relies on repeat viewers. Though the Federal Communication Commission lacks specific guidelines for the management of television violence, the traditional networks (NBC, CBS, ABC, and Fox) avoid controversy as much as possible. Even the CW, home of *The Vampire Diaries* and *Nikita*, cannot overstep the standards and practices at the core of broadcasting. So the hard-edged horror of *The Walking Dead* was too much for NBC.

By Darabont's account, he then shopped the pilot concept to virtually every free and pay cable network. All rejected it. Even HBO—oddly considering the network's recent programming history of gangster shows and the vampire series *True Blood*—rejected it as too violent. HBO's conclusion can make sense by considering two programming and production protocols. First, the economics of premium cable permits the capitalization of fewer scripted series per annum and permits its executives to be extremely selective. Second, an increasing amount of revenue for product that initially airs on premium cable channels derives from syndication markets, where content with explicit language, sex, and violence must be altered to meet more stringent standards.

Daunted by the reactions Darabont took the project out of active development, until 2009 when Gale Anne Hurd—a fan of the comic from the beginning—learned of the script and convinced Darabont to take it to AMC. Having evolved from a network pre-1950s black-

and-white films into an innovator in original programming, a special set of circumstances made AMC the ideal network for *The Walking Dead* and *The Walking Dead* the ideal show for AMC. The network's foray into original programming purposely mimicked that of HBO. As a success in the comic medium with a built-in audience and with several feature projects in the works at studios, but on the heels of the network's newfound critical acclaim, AMC was inundated with pitches. Fortunately, for *The Walking Dead*, AMC wanted a show to play alongside its popular Halloween-period horror movie marathon, Fearfest.

Importantly for The Walking Dead, Fearfeast had been rebranded by AMC from Monsterfest in 2008 to reflect the addition of newer and often gorier horror films from the 1970s and 1980s. The change of tone had resulted in the highest ratings in the marathon's history, so an original zombie series could fit perfectly and hold those large audiences for additional advertisements. Not only were there zombies aplenty, but there was abundant human conflict as well. Everything aligned with the network's slogan at the time "Story Matters Here." So AMC did more than just green-light the pilot, they committed to financing a six-episode mini-season. To conform to the method of their existing hit shows, AMC executives even requested that the pace of the pilot be slowed to allow for more character development. AMC also gave the pilot episode a 90-minute time slot to cap off 2010's Monsterfest.

AMC's primary promotional campaign deemphasized zombies, choosing instead to focus on the image of Rick riding horseback into the Atlanta cityscape. AMC screened several scenes from "Days Gone Bye" at the 2010 San Diego Comic-Con, where cast and crew fielded audience questions to promote the show and generate greater anticipation among the comic's dedicated readers. As the debut inched closer, AMC strategically sprinkled ad-spots into its Fearfest lineup. Despite the buzz generated by *The Walking Dead*, no one connected with the show could be certain it would click. The ratings shocked everyone: 5.35 million viewers was a record for a basic cable season premiere. Episode two reached 5.07 million viewers, prompting AMC immediately to renew the series for another season. Seasons two and three drew even greater numbers, AMC's put out a new tagline "Something More" and logo, which debuted during *The Walking Dead*'s Season three finale with its record-setting 12.4 million viewers.

The Walking Dead replete with its images of mangled and sometimes oozy corpses, close-ups of blood and chunks of brain matter projecting out of gunshot heads, and zombies turning humans into roadside meals continues to push the boundaries of accepted series television. The series demonstrates that such fare can not only survive but thrive, that undiluted horror can work on television, that zombies are not just for movies anymore.

Above, the titular Juan poses atop a pile of his dead.

recent one of *The Walking Dead*—wherein a small group of survivors tries to find some sense of order in a post-apocalyptic landscape. But while *The Walking Dead* does have crowds of stumbling, craving undead, *State of Emergency* focuses on four people hiding inside an abandoned tractor factory and is mostly about distant, solitary figures, whose menace is exaggerated by the sound of helicopters, distant gunfire, and emergency broadcasts. In fact, the movie flashes back from an opening of the quartet trapped in a small room, outside of which the viewer may believe is a ravenous throng but which ultimately turns out to be just one particularly nasty ghoul. Then there's the helpless old lady whose pleas for help sound reasonable until her dead, red eyes reveal her true nature. So they shoot her, presumably in the head, but these filmmakers take a non-gore approach and cut to a long shot of a building, so that nothing is seen, and only a gun shot, no screams, reverberates on the soundtrack.

Juan de los Muertos (2011) is a Cuban/Spanish co-production shot in Havana, an infrequent locale for horror movies. Its post-modern filmmakers distill the Romero formula into a satirical narrative that draws parallels between zombie-ism and the country's ongoing scourge of political dissidence, as the government blames both on subversive activities by the United States. Trapped in a country that retains many physical and social vestiges of the last century, the opportunistic title character is both malcontent and ne'er-do-well, unable to find a regular job before the plague of undead hits Cuba, who puts his services in high demand and lives the capitalist dream when he becomes a zombie removalist.

One of the longest lived current series of zombie features, which began in 2007, is entirely Spanish in origin: the four installments in the *[REC]* saga from filmmakers Jaume Balagueró and Paco Plaza, who use the context of found footage in all the movies—[rec] stands for recording. The first movie, and its American remakes *Quarantine* (2008) and *Quarantine 2: Terminal* (2011), center on a female television reporter and her cameramen who are shadowing a fire brigade. Of course, the building on fire turns out to be crammed full of zombies. The "trapped in an infested building" concept borrowed from *Resident Evil* is redeployed in the French production with the on-the-money title: *La Horde* (2009), which could also be called Cops vs. Zombies. After burying a murdered colleague, four corrupt lawmen sneak into a gang HQ bent on armed revenge and end up in the middle of something entirely different, a gun battle where the dead rise up with a taste for brains and "You can't kill them because they're dead already."

The second *[REC]²* covers the official response to the infestation by health authorities. The third installment is a parallel story that actually opens with a fictional website that celebrates the nuptials of Clara and Koldo. Unfortunately there are wedding crashers, and they're ghouls. Again the *Blair Witch/Cloverfield* conceit (or more in context as if from the viewpoint of the filmmakers in Romero's *Diary of the Dead*) is in play but rather than footage from a news cameraman, this installment opens with amateur video shot by the groom's young cousin. Soon, however, the professional videographer shows up and pointedly invokes cinema verité and Dziga Vertov. He also

Clara (Leticia Dolera) is another woman with a chainsaw in *[REC]³*

decries the shaky-cam effect, and at times the cousin's footage rivals *Paranormal Activity* (2007) with its wild vertical and horizontal jerkiness. Hopefully the audience does not mind waiting for its zombie fix, since the first hint of trouble is Uncle Pepe puking on the veranda a full 15 minutes in. Shortly thereafter the conceit is abandoned, and third person camera kicks in. Having seen the cake cut with an *espadón*, viewers might expect that weapon to come into play (and it does); but what Clara finds in the basement is a chainsaw. The fourth and final chapter (forthcoming in 2014) again focuses on reporter Ángela Vidal (Manuela Velasco), who is found and placed in quarantine with consequences reminiscent of *28 Weeks Later.*

Inevitably it seems the zombie film attained the stuffy mainstream heights of critical and commercial success when the Academy of Motion Picture Arts and Sciences nominated one of the genre for best picture, an accolade received by the stop-motion animation film *ParaNorman* (2012). Heavily influenced by the work of Tim Burton, *ParaNorman* is a Gothic-styled fairy tale in which a young "freak," Norman of the title, confronts the supernatural witch Agatha, and saves himself as well as the intolerant inhabitants of his town of Blithe Hollow. It is poignantly ironic that Norman becomes the savior, as he is also the victim, regarded as a misfit and sociopath by most of the people in the puritanical town. They are after all the actual descendants of "real" Puritans who brought on the town's curse by condemning to death the young Goth witch Agatha. Norman suffers not only at the hands of town bullies but also acts as an object of mistrust within his own family.

ParaNorman it is the latest fable where outcasts including the zombies themselves are treated with the most sympathy. Resurrected from the grave by Agatha—they are her original jury—their decomposing corpses are only mildly frightening. Although they are pursued by a vicious mob of townspeople intent on the destroying these undead annoyances by any means necessary, it is clear that the real threat to peace in a zombie world is the ongoing intolerance of a civilized town that had originally condemned Agatha to the stake.

Summit Entertainment's *Warm Bodies* (2013) is based on the successful teen/supernatural romance novel of the same name by Isaac Marion. Particularly since the success of Stephenie Meyer's *Twilight* series where high school means vampires or werewolves sitting at the adjacent desk, paranormal romance tales have become a sub-set of young adult fiction. With an eye towards replicating the mega-box-office of the movie versions of the *Twilight* series, a Summit franchise, the filmmakers cast a look- and act-alike for Kristen Stewart, Bella of the *Twilight* films, in the role of the commando Julie (Teresa Palmer), who is saved by and then falls for a "corpse" named R (Nicholas Hoult). As with *Twilight*, *Warm Bodies* is rife with numerous allusions to the classic literature of young love. Although Hoult's performance as R—as was Robert Pattinson's as Edward Cullen in the *Twilights*—is certainly as brooding as any Heathcliff, in this movie it's less *Wuthering Heights* and more that staple of freshman English, Shakespeare's *Romeo and Juliet*. Although Julie without the "t" is older, hence a lot more self-assured and far less whiny than Bella, she still responds to zombie R's brooding "Romeo" much like Bella did to her vampire love Edward

The movie opens with a voiceover by R as he wanders the ravaged parts of the city in search of human brains and maybe human affection. His irony-ridden narration is underscored by his

Warm Bodies.

appearance, a slightly degraded "hot boy-toy" whose physical charisma cannot be concealed by graying flesh and stray flecks of victim blood. He is a physically appealing sentient zombie who finds himself alienated from his living dead comrades, except for a monosyllabic buddy named M (Rob Corddry, who also appears in *Rapture Palooza* [2013], a scatter-shot satire, that has everything apocalyptic from loquacious locusts to a lawn-mowing zombie.). The normal humans, like the survivors in Romero's *Land of the Dead*, have walled themselves up in the rest of the city.

R has his epiphany when he first spots the woman warrior Julie, who is the daughter of Grigio the military commander of the live zone (played by John Malkovich). She has been dispatched with her troop, which includes her boyfriend Perry (Dave Franco), to retrieve much-needed supplies from the zombie zone. As she fights off R's comrades, R is attacked by Perry. Responding instinctually, R takes Perry down and eats his brains—the "tastiest" part as he tells the viewer. Immediately Perry's memories infuse R's, and his awe for Julie turns to love. He saves her from his ghoulish cronies and takes her to the safety of the airport where he had converted an abandoned jet into a home. R saves Julie from the zombies several more times—actually whenever she tries to escape. Eventually, however, his gentleness and protectiveness overcomes Julie's understandable aversion to loving a "corpse," particularly one who has dined on her boyfriend's gray matter. *Warm Bodies* aspires to be more than a story about two people from different factions finding love; it is also about the regenerative properties of that emotion. As the zombies witness Julie and R holding hands, they begin to transform much as R has done. Their hearts beat and they remember their pasts, specifically those they loved. As this feeling spreads the zombies themselves begin to fight the "bonies," skeletal zombies who have no human feelings left.

R penetrates the living zone and performs an impromptu balcony scene with Julie at her house. Knowing what her intolerant father will do, Julie runs away with R. In a battle with the bonies, R saves Julie once again by jumping from a high building into a shallow pool of water. This dangerous act of selfless love seems to be enough to complete R's regeneration: his heart now beats normally and he bleeds when Julie's father shoots him. Unlike the original R&J, Julie and her zombie boyfriend live happily ever after. They kiss as the wall dividing the zombie world from the human world comes crashing down. The filmmakers use this image as an appropriate metaphor for the theme of the movie and the novel before it: love overcomes all, even zombie-ism.

A latent but obsessive paternal love underlies the latest adaptation of the *The Monkey's Paw* (2013). The filmmakers do use the viewer's genre expectations, as Munro's original plot becomes back story, the results of which are seen from the perspective of a boy in a brief, period prologue that introduces the titled totem. The new narrative that follows centers on a sentient and powerful if monomaniacal undead named Tony Cobb (Stephen Lang), who is reanimated with wish number 2 after a fatal car crash. As a zombie his craving is not for flesh. "All I wanted was to take my boy fishing" is his lament when he realizes six murders have not done the trick, so he self-immolates with a bullet to the brain (because at some level he must know what he is). Of course, the paw does end up in the hands of his young son, who could bring him back again.

Most zom-coms have restricted themselves to black humor, understandably since they lacked the monetary resources to make or market a movie at the level of Summit. Released in 2008 was the low-budget blend of Romero and *My Boyfriend's Back*. In *Dance of the Dead* zombies spew from a graveyard to assault high schoolers at a prom, but complete catastrophe is averted when the band discovers that the ghouls respond to music and would rather dance then dine on brains. The saviors are nerdish members of the Sci-Fi Club, several of whom succumb to attack and instantly join the ranks of the undead. One of the darkest and funniest moments involves Steven (Chandler Darby) and cheerleader Gwen (Carissa Capobianco). She has fallen for Steven, so when she is infected she bites him and they consummate their new-found love by devouring each other.

In the more recent Canadian-made *A Little Bit Zombie* (2012), a pre-wedding trip to the family cabin in the woods results in disaster when the groom Steve (Christopher Turner) is bitten by a zombie mosquito. As he becomes a little bit zombie and fantasies of brain-flakes cereal for breakfast dance through his head, the bickering between his fiancée Tina (Crystal Lowe) and sister Sarah (Kristen Hager) continues. Eventually they cross paths with ghoul hunters, Penny the tech/tracker (Emilie Ullerup) and Max "the muscle" (Stephen McHattie). Steve actually gets the shotgun-wielding Max down on the ground but can only bring himself to slobber on him. Steve's stoner brother-in-law suggests "Dude, we'll put you on an island somewhere...we'll come visit you at Christmas

Opposite, *The Monkey's Paw*: the newly resurrected Tony Cobb (Stephen Lang) looms behind Jill (Jessica Garvey) who will shortly become the first of his six victims.

A Litte Bit Zombie: Penny (Emilie Ullerup) and Max (Stephen McHattie) with the crystal ball-style zombie tracking device.

and shit, right?" But Steve is ready for the head shot. As he levels his weapon, even Max concedes "Of all the zombies I've encountered you're the most human." Because she wants to use Steve for research, Penny intercedes and inadvertently blows out Max's brains ("I was aiming for his leg"). When Tina blasts Penny's face off, the wedding is back on, and the still photos in the end titles capture the hi-jinks before the couple drive off in an ambulance for their zombie honeymoon.

After the Oscar nomination for *ParaNorman,* 2013 continued as a break-through year for the zombie film with the release with *World War Z* that catapulted the genre into the empyrean realms of the summer blockbuster. Although zombies had reared their ugly heads in a few big budget movies, most notably *Pirates of the Caribbean: On Stranger Tides* (2011) where Blackbeard commands an army of zombie pirates, *World War Z* is, as the "Z" in the title suggests, a "pure" zombie film. Considering those types of movies only (namely "pure" zombie films), *World War Z's* $190 million production budget is arguably greater than the combined cost of every other zombie film ever made. To that were added millions more in marketing costs greatly raising the stakes for Paramount. Since the movie has already, as of this writing, grossed more than half a billion dollars worldwide, it is now the highest earning movie in which Brad Pitt has even starred. Apparently there was more appeal in those hordes of ghouls than in the hapless Trojans he mowed down as Achilles. All the more remarkable: in *World War Z* Pitt's character didn't even carry a sword much less a gun.

The film is based on the best-selling novel *World War Z: An Oral History of the Zombie War* by Max

Brooks. Reputedly inspired by Studs Terkel's oral history of World War II, *The Good War*, Brooks' work consists of fictional interviews with survivors of the world-wide battle against zombie-ism, which brings multiple perspectives to this apocalyptic tale. While the movie *World War Z* eschews those shifting points of view for the sake of narrative directness, it does maintain the progressive political subtext of Brooks' original. In a suspenseful opening montage, the filmmakers present a world on the brink of collapse, much as Romero did, but on a much grander scale. Concerned prophets of ecological doom like scientist Michio Kaku are intercut with images of polluted cities, popular uprisings, ravaged nature, mindless talk shows, and conservative commentators who deny climate change. The pace of the intercutting quickens as the music rises to a crescendo, and the audience is swept into a spin that disparages lamestream and reactionary media alike.

If the audience has any doubts left about the project's political bent, the protagonist of the piece, Gerry Lane (portrayed by Pitt), is an ex-troubleshooter for the United Nations who is, it is implied, a burnt-out case. In order to rebuild his psyche, he has retired from his altruistic and dangerous work to spend more time with his wife and two daughters. The first few scenes establish Gerry as a house-husband who is prepared to do whatever it takes to safeguard his family. The zombie plague spreads exponentially and attacks on major cities begin as soon as the Lane family leaves their home, which compels Gerry to become a version of the cliché hero in modern action films, a remnant of the Bush-era's attempts to rehabilitate the image of the "patriarch" in American media usually embodied by a Sylvester Stallone or a Bruce Willis. But in keeping with the progressive politics of this film, Gerry is neither buffed like them nor a resilient gun-toting cop, who takes a licking and keeps on ticking à la Bruce Willis in the *Die Hard* series. He is a sensitive guy who works for a "world government" not some crypto-fascist black op.

The zombie horde sacks Jerusalem in *World War Z*.

The filmmakers also extend the political metaphors through several key scenes. When under duress—he does it to guarantee the safety of this family—Gerry agrees to help the U.N. find the source of the virus that is creating millions of ravenous ghouls. So he begins a global journey following leads. In Israel, where the government has erected a wall to keep the zombies out of Jerusalem, Gerry watches as the fast-moving zombies pile onto each other to overrun the wall and scurry like cockroaches to infest the "holy city" completely. The parallels to the political conflict between Israel and the Palestinians, particularly in respect to the siege mentality of the Israelis, are hard to miss. Another scene rife with the black humor that underscores the original by Brooks occurs on the last plane out of Jerusalem, which is to take Gerry to a World Health Organization lab in Wales. Unbeknownst to the passengers in first class some zombies, who clung to the plane's underbelly as it took off, have emerged from the baggage hold and infected all the coach section passengers. The cramped coach passengers now fight their way into first class, in search of, one presumes, better food and more leg room.

The resolution of the movie is open-ended—if less epic than its jettisoned Battle of Moscow finale more typical of mega-budget action films—and allows for a sequel. Having noticed that the ravaging zombies avoid the ill, such as an obvious chemotherapy patient in Jerusalem, Gerry and the surviving scientists at the World Health Organization building concoct a serum. It's a blend of dead viruses that send a too-ill-to-eat signal to the undead, with Gerry acting as the bait. As Gerry finally re-unites with his family, cutaways to images of inoculated soldiers continuing to battle the zombies, but with more success, are inserted. On the soundtrack Gerry haltingly and with a lack of confidence in his voice delivers his final message of hope for the future of a violent world.

Opposite, armed only with a fire axe an apprehensive Gerry prepares to peek around the corner of a hallway in an infested apartment building.

Below, the teeth-clacking zombie (Michael Jenn) reacts to Gerry's "spoiled" aura created by the inoculation.

The HBO series *A Game of Thrones* brought to life novelist George R.R. Martin's fantastic creatures: "The white walkers of the woods, the cold shadows, the monsters of the tales...hungry for blood...." However, visualization of the ghoulish, blue-eyed white walkers changed somewhat between the first and second seasons. Above, the most subtly disturbing aspect is the mouth: frozen and chapped lips with bits of flesh and a trickle of blood. Below and opposite, a full-blown monster, a horseman of the Apocalypse astride his mount and holding an icy spear.

When there's no more room in HELL the dead will walk the EARTH

First there was 'NIGHT OF THE LIVING DEAD'

Now GEORGE A. ROMERO'S

DAWN OF THE DEAD

HERBERT R. STEINMANN & BILLY BAXTER PRESENT A LAUREL GROUP PRODUCTION in Association with CLAUDIO ARGENTO & ALFREDO CUOMO

Starring: DAVID EMGE   KEN FOREE   SCOTT H. REINIGER   GAYLEN ROSS

Director of Photography: MICHAEL GORNICK   Music By: THE GOBLINS with DARIO ARGENTO

Produced By: RICHARD P. RUBINSTEIN   Written and Directed by: GEORGE A. ROMERO

READ THE ST. MARTIN'S BOOK   TECHNICOLOR®   ©DAWN ASSOCIATES MCMLXXVIII   Released by UNITED FILM DISTRIBUTION CO.

There is no explicit sex in this picture.
However, there are scenes of violence which may be considered shocking.
No one under 17 will be admitted.

Filmography

There are over 530 titles in this Filmography, which makes it the most complete ever compiled to date. While, as per the criteria indicated in the Preface, there are some gray areas about what constitutes a true zombie film, with few exceptions we have restricted ourselves to movies that feature reanimated corpses. While most of those beings since Romero are from interaction with some germ or toxin, some continue to be created through voodoo or "mad" science. Notable variants are the alien body snatchers and a few of their sci-fi kin, who preponderantly lack emotion but are otherwise sentient. Nor are all post-Romero zombies slow moving flesh eaters.

Films are listed alphabetically by their primary titles, which may be English or another language, in bold italics. This is followed by the significant alternate titles under which the movie may have been released in normal italics. These alternate titles, which are more abundant than ever as DVD and VOD releases and re-releases proliferate, are all listed in the Index. Our release year is based on the method of the Academy of Motion Picture Arts and Sciences that looks to the first release date in the country of origin.

Given the significant number of titles. our listings include only main technical credits and major cast. Pseudonyms and alternate spellings are Included based on the significance of the person. Running times and their reliability still vary greatly depending on the source. When possible we use the timing of the main release whether theatrical, DVD, VOD, etc. Otherwise we have used a consensus and/or opted for the source that we believe is the most reliable. Key to abbreviations: "Dir" is Director; "Scr" is Screenplay ["Tel," Teleplay]; "Mus" is Music; "DP" is Director of Photography; "Ed" is Editor; "AD" is Art Director; and "PD" is Production Designer.

As this book goes to press several movies are scheduled for release. While they are in this Filmography, we have opted not to include projects that are in production or merely scheduled to begin shooting soon.

Â! Ikkenya puroresu (*Oh My Zombie Mermaid*, 2004) Japan. Dir: Naoki Kudo. Scr: Izô Hashimoto, Naoki Kudo. Cast: Shinya Hashimoto (Kouta Shishioh), Sonim, (Nami), Shirô Sano (Yamaji), Nicholas Pettas (Ichijo). 100 min.

Abraham Lincoln vs. Zombies (2012) USA. Dir/Scr: Richard Schenkman based on a story by Karl Hirsch, J. Proctor. Mus: Chris Ridenhour. DP: Tim Gill. Ed: James Kondelik. PD: Bobbie Harley. Cast: Bill Oberst, Jr. (Abraham Lincoln), Kent Igleheart (Thomas Lincoln), Rhianna Van Helton (Nancy Lincoln), Brennen Harper (Young Abe Lincoln), Josh Sinyard (Aide), Debra Crittenden (Mary Todd Lincoln), Bernie Ask (Edwin Stanton), Chris Hlozek (Maj. John McGill). 96 min.

Ace the Zombie (2012) USA. Dir: Giles Shepherd [as The DeVille]. Scr: Rob Fox, Pat Bell, Melissa Shepherd, Rey Shepherd. Mus: Adam Fligsten, Rotem Moav. DP: Rory Gordon. Ed: Joshua Gohlke, Giles Shepherd. PD: Erin Jones. Cast: Mark Drum (Ace), Sarah Simmons Turner (Colleen Wells), Toryah Pugh (Brenda), Brandon S.N. Butler (Jesse), Jevocas Green (Keeper Ellis), Daniel Diaz (Stanley), Mike Yow (River Powers), Ondie Daniel (Carriane DeBeers), Lesley E. Warren (Rep. Elizabeth Wells). 110 min.

The Alfred Hitchcock Hour (1962, television series: "The Monkey's Paw" episode) USA. Dir: Robert

Stevens. Tel: Morton S. Fine, David Friedkin, Anthony Terpiloff based on the story by W.W. Jacobs. Cast: Alfred Hitchcock (himself), Leif Erickson (Paul White), Jane Wyatt (Anne White), Lee Majors (Howard White). 47 min.

Alien Dead (1980) USA. Dir: Fred Olen Ray. Scr: Fred Olen Ray, Martin Nicholas. Mus: Franklin Sledge, Chuck Sumner. DP: Peter Gamba, Gary Singer. Ed: Mark Barrett. Cast: Buster Crabbe (Sheriff Kowalski), Ray Roberts (Tom Corman), Linda Lewis (Shawn Michaels), George Kelsey (Emmet Michaels), Mike Bonavia (Miller Haze), Dennis Underwood (Deputy Campbell), John Leirier (Paisley), Rich Vogan (Krelboin), Martin Nicholas (Doc Ellerbe), Norman Riggins (Mr. Griffith). 74 min.

Alien Zombie Invasion (2011) USA. Dir/Scr/Ph/Ed: Joey Evans. Mus: Jonathan Hoop. Cast: Larry Jack Dotson (Derek), Renee Wiggins (Blake), Christopher Cassarino (Barry), Shane Land (Norv), Dana Wokas (Vel), Scott Evans (Fred), Audrey Elizabeth Evans (Polly), Bridgot Wolf (Cindy), Juan Rodriguez (Zombie), Katie Krewall (Mom), Tor Lono (Zombie Hitchhiker), Emma

Zuckerman (Hot Zombie Daughter). 84 min.

All American Zombie Drugs (2010) USA. Dir/Scr: Alex Ballar. Scr: Alex Ballar. Mus: Evan Goldman. DP: Chia-Yu Chen. Ed: Brett Register. PD: Chelsey Reynolds. Cast: Beau Nelson (Sebastian), Wolfgang Weber (Vinny), Susan Graham (Kara), Natalie Irby (Melissa), Alex Ballar (Michael), Bobby Burkey (Spider), David Reynolds (Big Al). 99 min.

Amanti d'oltretomba (*Nightmare Castle*, 1965) Italy. Dir: Mario Caiano [as Allen Grünewald]. Scr: Mario Caiano, Fabio De Agostini. Mus: Ennio Morricone. DP: Enzo Barboni. Ed: Renato Cinquini. PD: Massimo Tavazzi. Cast: Barbara Steele (Muriel/Jenny Arrowsmith), Paul Muller (Dr. Stephen Arrowsmith), Helga Liné (Solange), Marino Masé (Dereck), Giuseppe Addobbati (Jonathan), Rik Battaglia (David). 101 min.

Ame-agari no kimi (*Rain for the Dead*, 2013) Japan. Dir: Bishop Koyama. Scr: Bishop Koyama, Waita Uziga, from the manga. Mus: Ayumu Kitamura. Cast: Jin Chikamatsu, Marie Ono, Masaya Adachi.

American Zombie (2007) USA/South Korea. Dir: Grace Lee. Scr: Grace Lee, Rebecca Sonnenshine. DP: Matthias Grunsky. Ed: Tamara Maloney. PD: Nathan Amondson. Cast: Austin Basis (Ivan), Jane Edith Wilson (Lisa), Al Vicente (Joel), Suzy Nakamura (Judy), John Solomon (himself), Grace Lee (Herself), Andrew Amondson (himself), Amy Higgins (Dr. Gloria Reynolds). 90 min.

Angel (2001, television series, Season 2, Episode 14: "The Thin Dead Line") USA. Dir: Scott McGinnis. Tel: Shawn Ryan, Jim Kouf. Mus: Robert J. Kral. DP: Herbert Davis. Ed: Michael Stern. Cast: David Boreanaz (Angel), Charisma Carpenter (Cordelia Chase), Alexis Denisof (Wesley Wyndam-Pryce), J. August Richards (Charles Gunn), Elisabeth Röhm (Detective Kate Lockley). 42 min.

Aqui huele a Zombie (*Smell of a Zombie*, 2012—present, Web series) Argentina. Dir/Ed: Juan José Betz. Scr: Juan José Betz, Javier Viñuela. Cast: Juan José Betz (German), Flavia Ceballos (Pilar), Emilia Nahim (Laura), Milagros Pintos (Julia), Fernanda Porcel (Sofia), Martin Porcel (Pedro).

Army of Darkness (*Evil Dead III,* 1992) USA. Dir: Sam Raimi. Scr: Sam Raimi, Scott Spiegel. Mus: Joseph LoDuca. DP: Bill Pope. Ed: Bob Murawski. Cast: Bruce Campbell (Ashley J. Williams), Embeth Davidtz (Sheila), Marcus Gilbert (Lord Arthur), Ian Abercrombie (Wiseman), Richard Grove (Duke Henry). 89 min.

The Astro-Zombies (1968) USA. Dir: Ted V. Mikels. Scr: Ted V. Mikels, Wayne Rogers. Mus: Nicholas Carras [as Nico Karaski]. DP: Robert Maxwell. Ed: Ted V. Mikels. AD: Wally Moon. Cast: Wendell Corey (Holman), John Carradine (Dr. DeMarco), Tom Pace (Eric Porter), Joan Patrick (Janine Norwalk), Tura Satana (Satana), Rafael Campos (Juan), Joe Hoover (Chuck Edwards), Victor Izay (Dr. Petrovich), William Bagdad (Franchot), Vincent Barbi (Tyros), Egon Sirany (Sergio Demozhenin). 91 min.

El ataque de los muertos sin ojos (*Return of the Evil Dead*, 1973) Spain. Dir: Amando de Ossorio. Scr: Amando de Ossorio. DP: Miguel Fernández Mila. Ed: José Antonio Rojo. Cast: Tony Kendall (Jack Marlowe), Fernando Sancho (Mayor Duncan), Esperanza Roy (Vivian), Frank Braña (Howard), José Canalejas (Murdo), Loreta Tovar (Monica), Ramón Lillo (Bert), Lone Fleming (Amalia), Maria Nuria (Nancy, Amalia's daughter), José Thelman (Juan, Monica's boyfriend), Juan Cazalilla (Governor), Betsabé Ruiz (Governor's maid). 77 min.

Attack of the Herbals (2011) UK. Dir/Ph/Ed: David Ryan Keith. Scr: Alisdair Cook, Liam Matheson, David Ryan Keith. Mus: Leah Kardos. Cast: Calum Booth (Jackson MooCrogor), Steve Worsley (Russell Wallace), Richard Currie (The Roadrunner), Liam Matheson (Bennett Campbell), Lee Hutcheon (Danny the Pincer), Claire McCulloch (Jenny Robertson), Margaret Bramwell (Granny MacGregor), Jimmy Lynch (Grandad MacGregor), Alan Fraser (Aldof Frankenfurter). 81 min.

Attack of the Psychedelic Zombies, Man! (2013) USA. Dir/Ed: Aaron Hilden. Scr/Ed: Aaron Hilden, John Luedtke. Mus: Aaron Hilden, John Luedtke, Aaron Moe. DP/Ed: Aaron Hilden. Cast: Klaus Von Hohenloe (Scotty), Jon Yeske (Dong), Traci Fick (Topless Chick), Kevin Krause (Dirk), Aaron Hilden (Kevin), Aaron Moe (Sheriff), John Luedtke (Deputy Beuford), Jason Ranker (Bearskin Butch), Dennis Fick (Denny).

Attack of the Vegan Zombies! (2010) USA. Dir/Scr: Jim Townsend. DP: Max Fischer. Ed: Jay Lee. Cast: Christine Egan (Dionne), H. Lynn Smith (Audra), Jim Townsend (Joe), Kerry Carns (Jenny), Natalia Jablokov (Lee). 77 min.

Automaton Transfusion (*Zombie Transfusion*, 2006) USA. Dir/Scr: Steven C. Miller. Mus: Jamey Scott. DP: Jeff Dolen. Ed: Steven C. Miller. PD: Jerry Eller. Cast: Garrett Jones (Chris), Juliet Reeves (Jackie), William Bowman (Scott), Rowan Bousaid (Tim), Ashley Pierce

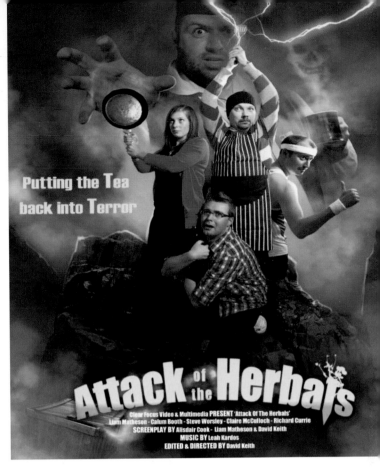

(Simone), Kendra Farner (Melissa). 75 min.

Autumn (2009) Canada. Dir: Steven Rumbelow. Scr: David Moody, Steven Rumbelow based on the novel by Moody. Mus: Craig McConnell. DP: Stephen Crone. Ed: Steven Rumbelow, Anthony Valenti. AD: Leanne McDonald. Cast: Garrett Jones (Chris), Juliet Reeves (Jackie), William Bowman (Scott), Rowan Bousaid (Tim), Ashley Pierce (Simone), Kendra Farner (Melissa). 110 min.

Awaken the Dead (2007) USA. Dir: Jeff Brookshire. Scr: Jeff Brookshire. Mus: Nathan Bonell, Ashkon Stone. DP: Melissa Holt. Ed: Jeff Brookshire. PD: Michelle Brookshire. Cast: Gary Kohn (Father Christopher Gideon), Lindsey Morris (Mary Payne), Nate Witty (Stanley), Michael Robert Nyman (Jeremiah Payne), Paul Dion Monte (Nick), Will Harris (Grin), Dominiqua Alexis (Delilah). 102 min.

Awakening (*Zombie Night*, 2006) Canada. Dir: David J. Francis. Scr: David J. Francis, Mike Masters. Mus: Roman Zebik. DP: Robert Scarborough. Ed: Chris Bellio. Cast: Steve Curtis (Keith), Sharon DeWitt (Shelley), Dan Rooney (Basil), Kari Grace (Crystal), John Paris (Derek). 90 min.

Bath Salt Zombies (2013) USA. Dir/DP/Ed: Dustin Mills. Scr: Dustin Mills, Clint Weiler. Cast: Josh Eal (Agent Forster), Ethan Holey (Bubbles), Jackie McKown (Rita), Dave Parker (The Chet), Brandon Salkil (Ritchie). 70 min.

Batoru gâru: Tokyo crisis wars (*Battle Girl: The Living Dead in Tokyo Bay*, 1991) Japan. Dir: Kazuo Komizu. Scr: Hitoshi Matsuyama [as Daisuke Serizawa]. DP: Kazuo Komizu. 73 min.

The Battery (2012) USA. Dir: Jeremy Gardner. Scr: Jeremy Gardner. Mus: Ryan Winford. DP: Christian Stella. Ed: Michael Katzman, Alicia Stella. AD: Kelly McQuade. Cast: Jeremy Gardner (Ben), Adam Cronheim (Mickey), Niels Bolle (Jerry), Alana O'Brien (Annie), Jamie Pantanella (Egghead), Larry Fessenden (Frank), Kelly McQuade (Laura), Eric Simon (Basement Zombie), Ben Pryzby, Sarah Allen (Dead Zombies by lake). 101 min.

Battle of the Bone (2008) UK. Dir/Scr: George Clarke. Mus: Chris Logan. DP: George Clarke. Ed: Jonny Kirk. Cast: Phil Barnhill (Swat 2), Andrew Brown (Swat 3), Logan Bruce (Zombie), George Clarke (Thug), Roddy Conlon (Swat 1), Alan Crawford (Scott), John Gallagher (Zombie John). 90 min.

Battle of the Damned (2013) USA. Dir/Scr: Christopher Hatton. Mus: Joe Ng, Ting Si Hao. DP: Roger Chingirian. Ed: Danny Rafic. PD: Daniel Lim. Cast: Dolph Lundgren (Max Gatling), Esteban Cueto (Hernandez), Lydia Look (Lynn), Melanie Zanetti (Jude), David Field (Duke), Oda Maria (Anna), Jen Sung (Elvis). 88 min.

Battlefield Death Tales (*Nazi Zombie Death Tales*, *Nazi Zombie Battleground*, 2012) UK. Dir/Scr: James Eaves, Pat Higgins, Alan Ronald. Mus: Phil Sheldon. Ed: Debbie Attwell. Cast: Lara Lemon (Harriet Price), Jess-Luisa Flynn (Ruth), Cy Henty (PC Jones), David Wayman (George), Paul Kelleher (Maj. Kendricks). 87 min.

Beaver Lake Zombies (2003) USA. Dir/Scr/Ph/Ed: Mike C. Hartman. Cast: Mike C. Hartman, Sherrie Hartman, Frank J. Levanduski, Joe Saccone. 61 min.

Before Dawn (2012) UK. Dir: Dominic Brunt, Scr: Mark Illis, Joanne Mitchell. DP: Alex Nevill. Cast: Dominic Brunt (Alex), Joanne Mitchell (Meg), Eileen O'Brien (Eileen), Nicky Evans (Stephen), Alex Baldacci (Zombie), Alan French (Peter), Holly Illis (Sarah), David Nolan (Garage Zombie), Neale Myers (Zombie), Bryn Hammond (Zombie). 82 min.

The Beyond (*L'Aldila'*, 1981) Italy. Dir: Lucio Fulci. Scr: Dardano Sacchetti, Giorgio Mariuzzo, Lucio Fulci. Mus: Fabio Frizzi, Walter E. Sear. DP: Sergio Salvati. Ed: Vincenzo Tomassi. PD: Massimo Lentini. Cast: Catriona MacColl (Liza Merril), David Warbeck (Dr. John McCabe), Cinzia Monreale [as Sarah Keller] (Emily), Antoine Saint-John (Schweick), Veronica Lazar (Martha), Anthony Flees (Larry), Al Cliver (Dr. Harris). 87 min.

Beyond Re-Animator (2003) Spain. Dir: Brian Yuzna. Scr: Xavier Berraondo, José Manuel Gómez, Miguel Tejada-Flores and Brian Yuzna based on a story by H.P. Lovecraft. Mus: Xavier Capellas. DP: Andreu Rebés. Ed: Bernat Vilaplana. PD: Llorenç Miquel. Cast: Jeffrey Combs (Dr. Herbert West), Tommy Dean Musset (Young Howard Phillips), Jason Barry (Dr. Howard Phillips), Bárbara Elorrieta (Emily Phillips), Elsa Pataky (Laura Olney), Ángel Plana (Kitchen Zombie). 96 min.

Big Tits Dragon (*Big Tits Zombie*, *Zombie Stripper Apocalypse*, 2010) Japan. Dir: Takao Nakano. Scr: Rei Mikamoto, Takao Nakano, based on the manga series "Kyonyū doragon." DP: Kazuaki Yoshizawa. PD: Ken'ichi Sasaki. Cast: Sora Aoi (Lena Jodo), Risa Kasumi (Ginko), Mari Sakurai (Maria), Tamayo (Nene), Io Aikawa (Darna), Minoru Torihada (Blue Ogre). 83 min.

Biker Zombies from Detroit (2001) USA. Dir/DP: Todd

Brunswick. Scr: John Kerfoot. Mus: Jeffrey Michael. Ed: Brandon V. Blanchard. Cast: Tyrus Woodson (Ken Yargeau), Jillian Buckshaw (Courtney Goodwyn), Joshua Allan (Scott), Jeffrey Michael (Fritz), Rob Roth (Chad). 80 min.

Blood Lodge (2012) USA. Dir: Kevin Orosz. Scr: Ed McKeever, Kevin Orosz. DP: David Kappler. Ed: Jake Iannaco. Cast: Greg Greco (Steven), Matthew L. Imparato (Gus Pagano), Michael McFadden (Trent Huckleberry), Ed McKeever (Armageddon Ed), Jason Koerner (The Gooch), Ryan Loughney (Hook Up Kid), Kevin Orosz (Jigger), Julie Ann Hamolko (Amber).

Blood Moon Rising (2009) USA. Dir: Brian Skiba. Scr: Laurie Love, Brian Skiba. DP: Tyler Cadwell. Ed: Brian Skiba. Cast: Laurie Love (Lucy/Sadie), Ron Jeremy (Phil), Aaron Neal Trout (Darrell Lee), Kent Welborn (Sam), Jose Rosete (Sanchez). 94 min.

Blood of the Beast (2003) USA. Dir/Scr: Georg Koszulinski. Mus: Georg Koszulinski, Steven Landis, Mike Maines. DP: Brian White. Ed: Georg Koszulinski, Brian White. Cast: Georg Koszulinski (Jesse), Matt Devine (James), Sharon Chudnow (Alice). 74 min.

Blood Suckers from Outer Space (1984) USA. Dir/Scr: Glen Coburn. DP: Chad D. Smith. Ed: Karen D. Latham. AD: Rick Garlington. Cast: Robert Bradeen (Uncle Joe), Big John Brigham (Norman), Glen Coburn (Ralph Rhodes), Franny Coppenbarger (Dead Woman), Christine Crowe (President's Playmate), Joyce Dixon (Seductive Bloodsucker), Laura Ellis (Julie), Pat Paulsen (U.S. President). 79 min.

Bloodeaters (*Toxic Zombies*, 1980) USA. Dir/Scr: Charles McCrann. Scott Roberts. Mus: Ted Shapiro. DP: David Sperling. Ed: Charles McCrann. Cast: Charles McCrann [as Charles Austin] (Tom Cole), Beverly Shapiro (Polly Cole), Dennis Helfend (Hermit), Kevin Hanlon (Jimmy), Judith Brown (Amy), Pat Kellis (Mother), Roger Miles (Father). 89 min.

Bloody Border (2013) USA. Dir/Scr: Bryan C. Goff. DP: Eric Hays, Chiara Montonati, Rene Rivas. Ed: Rene Rivas. Cast: Nathan Staveley (Garrett/Biohazard Worker #5), Bear Vash (Pat), Diana Gomez (Christina), Edward Behle (Frank/Biohazard Worker #4), Jeremie Dalaba (West), Andrae Blissett Jr. (Terry), Austin Sanchez (Hugo), Cebronette Wade (Denise). 92 min.

Bloody New Year (1987) UK. Dir: Norman J. Warren. Scr: Frazer Pearce, Hayden Pearce, Norman J. Warren. Mus: Nick Magnus. DP: John Shann. Ed: Carl Thomson.

PD: Hayden Pearce. Cast: Suzy Aitchison (Lesley), Nikki Brooks (Janet), Colin Heywood (Spud), Mark Powley (Rick), Catherine Roman (Carol), Julian Ronnie (Tom), Steve Emerson (Dad). 90 min.

Blue Demon y Zovek en La invasión de los muertos (1973) Mexico. Dir/Scr: René Cardona. Mus: Raúl Lavista. DP: José Ortiz Ramos. Ed: Alfredo Rosas Priego. AD: Alberto Ladrón de Guevara. Cast: Armando Acosta, Guillermo Ayala, René Barrera, Eduardo Bonada, Blue Demon, Cesar Silva. 85 min.

Body Snatchers (1993) USA. Dir: Abel Ferrara. Scr: Stuart Gordon, Dennis Paoli, Nicholas St. John based on the adaptation by Larry Cohen and Raymond Cistheri of the novel by Jack Finney. Mus: Joe Delia. DP: Bojan Bazelli. Ed: Anthony Redman. Cast: Terry Kinney (Steve Malone), Meg Tilly (Carol Malone), Gabrielle Anwar (Marti Malone), Reilly Murphy (Andy Malone), Billy Wirth (Tim Young), Christine Elise (Jenn Platt), R. Lee Ermey (Platt), Forest Whitaker (Collins). 87 min.

Bone Sickness (2004) USA. Dir/Scr/Mus/Ed: Brian Paulin. Cast: Kevin Barbare (Inspector Seacrest), Griff Brohman (Zombie), Brian DeClercq (Swat & Zombie), Rich George (Alex McNetti). 90 min.

The Boneyard (1991) USA. Dir/Scr: James Cummins. Mus: John Lee Whitener. DP: Irl Dixon. AD: Carl Anderson. Cast: Ed Nelson (Jersey Callum), Deborah Rose (Alley Oates), Norman Fell (Shepard), James Eustermann (Gordon Mullen), Denise Young (Dana), Willie Stratford Jr. (Marty), Phyllis Diller (Miss Poopinplatz). 98 min.

Born Undead (*Garden of Love*, 2003) Germany. Dir: Olaf Ittenbach. Scr: Thomas Reitmair, Olaf Ittenbach. Mus: Thomas Reitmair, A.G. Striedl. DP: Holger Fleig. Ed: Eckart Zerzawy. PD: Torsten Mühlbach. Cast: Natacza Boon (Rebecca Verlaine), James Matthews-Pyecka (Thomas Munster), Daryl Jackson (David Riven), Bela B. Felsenheimer (Gabriel Verlaine), Donald Stewart (Don Creedon), Alexandra Thom-Heinrich (Barbara Creedon), Anika Julien (Young Rebecca), Jeff Motherhead (Roger), Kayla Motherhead (Melanie). 86 min.

Bowery at Midnight (1942) USA. Dir: Wallace Fox. Scr: Gerald Schnitzer based on a story by Sam Robins. DP: Mack Stengler. Ed: Carl Pierson. AD: Dave Milton. Cast: Bela Lugosi (Professor Brenner/Karl Wagner), John Archer (Richard Dennison), Wanda McKay (Judy Malvern), Tom Neal. Frankie Mills), Vince Barnett (Charley), Anna Hope (Mrs. Brenner), John Berkes (Fingers Dolan), J. Farrell MacDonald (Capt. Mitchell). 61 min.

Boy Eats Girl (2005) Ireland/UK. Dir: Stephen Bradley. Scr: Derek Landy. Mus: Hugh Drumm. Stephen Rennicks. DP: Balazs Bolygo. Ed: Dermot Diskin, Ben Yeates. PD: Anna Rackard. Cast: Samantha Mumba (Jessica), David Leon (Nathan), Tadhg Murphy (Diggs), Laurence Kinlan (Henry), Sara James (Cheryl), Mark Huberman (Samson), Sarah Burke (Charlotte). 80 min.

Brain Dead (2007) USA. Dir: Kevin Tenney. Scr: Dale Gelineau. Mus: Dennis Michael Tenney. DP: Patrick McGowan, Alex Simon. Ed: William Daniels. PD: Javiera Varas. Cast: Joshua Benton (Clarence Singer), Sarah Brendecke (Sherry Morgan), David Crane (Bob Jules), Andy Forrest (Reverend Farnsworth), Alexandra Goodman (Interviewer), Chad Guerrero (Deputy Jimmy Ray), Elizabeth Lambert (Candy), Greg Lewolt (Deputy Jimmy Bob), Tess McVicker (Ranger Sydney). 95 min.

Braindead (*Dead Alive*, 1992) New Zealand. Dir: Peter Jackson. Scr: Stephen Sinclair, Fran Walsh, Peter Jackson. DP: Murray Milne. Ed: Jamie Selkirk. PD: Kevin Leonard-Jones. Cast: Timothy Balme (Lionel Cosgrove), Diana Peñalver (Paquita Maria Sanchez), Elizabeth Moody (Mum, Vera Cosgrove), Ian Watkin (Uncle Les), Brenda Kendall (Nurse McTavish), Stuart Devenie (Father McGruder), Jed Brophy (Void), Stephen Papps (Zombie McGruder), Murray Keane (Scroat). 104 min.

Bride of Re-Animator (1989) USA. Dir: Brian Yuzna. Scr: Rick Fry, Woody Keith, Brian Yuzna based on a story by H.P. Lovecraft. Mus: Richard Band. DP: Rick Fichter. Ed: Peter Teschner. PD: Philip Duffin. Cast: Jeffrey Combs (Dr. Herbert West), Bruce Abbott (Dr. Dan Cain), Claude Earl Jones (Lt. Leslie Chapham), Fabiana Udenio (Francesca Danelli), David Gale (Dr. Carl Hill), Kathleen Kinmont (Gloria), Mel Stewart (Dr. Graves), Irene Cagen (Nurse Shelley), Michael Strasser (Ernest), Mary Sheldon (Meg Halsey). 96 min.

Buffy the Vampire Slayer (1998, television series, Season 3, Episode 2: "Dead Man's Party") USA. Creator: Joss Whedon. Dir: James Whitmore Jr. Tel: Marti Noxon. Mus: Christophe Beck. DP: Michael Gershman. Ed: Skip MacDonald. Cast: Sarah Michelle Gellar (Buffy), Nicholas Brendon (Xander Harris), David

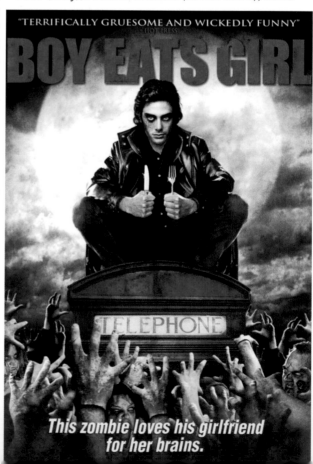

"TERRIFICALLY GRUESOME AND WICKEDLY FUNNY"

BOY EATS GIRL

TELEPHONE

This zombie loves his girlfriend for her brains.

Boreanaz (Angel), Alyson Hannigan (Willow Rosenberg), Charisma Carpenter (Cordelia Chase), Seth Green (Oz), Kristine Sutherland (Joyce Summers), Nancy Lenehan (Pat), Armin Shimerman (Principal Snyder), Danny Strong (Jonathan Levinson), Scott Duthie (Zombie). 42 min.

El buque maldito (*The Ghost Galleon, Horror of the Zombies*, 1974) Spain. Dir/Scr: Amando de Ossorio. Mus: Antón García Abril. DP: Raúl Artigot. Ed: Petra de Nieva. PD: Eduardo Torre de la Fuente. Cast: Maria Perschy (Lillian), Jack Taylor (Howard Tucker), Bárbara Rey (Noemi), Carlos Lemos (Professor Grüber), Manuel de Blas (Sergio), Blanca Estrada (Kathy), Margarita Merino (Lorena Kay). 89 min.

C.H.U.D. II, Bud the Chud (1989) USA. Dir: David Irving. Scr: Ed Naha [as M. Kane Jeeves]. Mus: Nicholas Pike. DP: Arnie Sirlin. Ed: Barbara Pokras. Cast: Brian Robbins (Steve Williams), Bill Calvert (Kevin), Tricia Leigh Fisher (Katie), Gerrit Graham (Bud Oliver/Bud the C.H.U.D.), Robert Vaughn (Col. Masters), Larry Cedar (Graves), Bianca Jagger (Velma). 84 min.

Cadaverella (2007) USA. Dir: Timothy Friend. Scr: Jennifer Friend, Timothy Friend. Mus: Joseph Allen. DP: Todd Norris. Ed: Timothy Friend. Cast: Megan Goddard (Cinder), Ryan Seymour (Cash/Justin), Kieran Hunter (Lenore/Donna), Santiago Vasquez (Baron Samedi), Mackenzie Montes (Young Cinder), Christopher Booth (Frank), Jena Bright, Kylie Jussel (the Twins). 71 min.

Carmilla, the Lesbian Vampire (*Vampires vs. Zombies*, 2004) USA/Canada. Dir: Vince D'Amato. Scr: Vince D'Amato based on the novella by J. Sheridan Le Fanu. Mus: Mikael Jacobson. DP: Damien Foisy. Ed: Vince D'Amato, Nicole Hancock. Cast: Bonny Giroux (Jenna Fontaine), C.S. Munro (Travis Fontaine), Maritama Carlson (Carmilla), Brinke Stevens (Julia/State Trooper), Peter Ruginis (The General), Melanie Crystal (Tessa Briggs). 85 min.

El Castillo de las momias de Guanajuato (*The Castle of Mummies of Guanajuato*, 1973) Mexico. Dir: Tito Novaro. Scr: Rogelio Agrasánchez, Laura Marchetti, Tito Novaro. Mus: Bernardo Serrano. DP: Antonio Ruiz. Ed: Ignacio Chiu. Set Decoration by Jaime Mota. Cast: Superzan, Blue Angel, Tinieblas (Themselves), Zulma Faiad (Nora), María Salomé (Lita). 85 min.

Un cazador de zombis (*A Zombie Hunter*, 2008) Argentina. Dir/Scr/Ed: Germán Magariños. Mus: Eduardo Cariglino. Cast: Leandro De la Torre (Toro),

MARIA PERSCHY   JACK TAYLOR
CARLOS LEMOS   BARBARA REY
MANUEL DE BLAS   BLANCA ESTRADA

EASTMANCOLOR

EL BUQUE MALDITO

director: AMANDO DE OSSORIO   UNA PRODUCCION ANCLA CENTURY FILMS PARA BELEN FILMS

Ezequiel Hansen (El Gorno), Verónica Fernandez (Stripper), Francisco Pérez Laguna (Padre), Fernando Giangiacomo (Blade), Lloyd Kaufman (Lloyd). 70 min.

Cementerio del terror (*Zombie Apocalypse*, 1985) Mexico. Dir/Scr: Rubén Galindo Jr. Mus: Chucho Zarzosa. DP: Rosalío Solano. Ed: Carlos Savage. Cast: Hugo Stiglitz (Dr. Cardan), José Gómez Parcero (Devlon), Bety Robles (Mujer 1), Leo Villanueva (Official Pineda), Raúl Meraz (Captain Ancira), René Cardona III (Oscar), Servando Manzetti (Jorge). 88 min.

The Child (1977) USA. Dir: Robert Voskanian. Scr: Ralph Lucas. Mus: Rob Wallace. DP: Mori Alavi. Ed: Robert Dadashian. Robert Voskanian. AD: Mori Alavi. Cast: Laurel Barnett (Alicianne Del Mar), Rosalie Cole (Rosalie Nordon), Frank Janson (Nordon), Richard Hanners (Len Nordon), Ruth Ballan (Mrs. Whitfield), Slosson Bing Jong (Gardener), Rod Medigovich (Priest/Creature). 82 min.

The Children (1980) USA. Dir: Max Kalmanowicz. Scr: Carlton J. Albright, Edward Terry. Mus: Harry

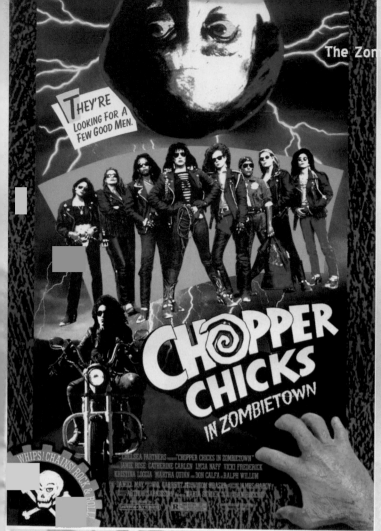

THEY'RE LOOKING FOR A FEW GOOD MEN.

The Zombie Film

WHIPS! CHAINS! ROCK & ROLL!

CHOPPER CHICKS IN ZOMBIETOWN

Chiller (1985) USA. Dir: Wes Craven. Scr: J.D. Feigelson. Mus: Dana Kaproff. DP: Frank Thackery. Ed: Duane Hartzell. Cast: Michael Beck (Miles Creighton), Beatrice Straight (Marion Creighton), Laura Johnson (Leigh Kenyon), Dick O'Neill (Clarence Beeson), Alan Fudge (Dr. Stricklin), Craig Richard Nelson (Dr. Collier), Paul Sorvino (Reverend Penny), Jill Schoelen (Stacey), Anne Seymour (Mrs. Bunch), Russ Marin (Dr. Sample). 104 min.

Chillers (1987) USA. Dir/Scr: Daniel Boyd. Mus: Michael Lipton. DP: Bill Hogan. PD: Steve Gilliland, Cast: Jesse Emery (Mason), Marjorie Fitzsimmons (Lindsey), Laurie Pennington (Sharon), Jim Wolfe (Ron), David Wohl (Conrow), Gary Brown (Scoutmaster Bob). 87 min.

The Chilling (1989) USA. Dir: Deland Nuse, Jack A. Sunseri. Scr: Guy Messenger, Jack A. Sunseri. Mus: William Ashford. DP: Deland Nuse. Ed: Beth Conwell. AD: Dave Bundtzen, Daryl Privette. Cast: Linda Blair (Mary Hampton), Dan Haggerty (Sgt. Vince Marlow), Troy Donahue (Dr. Miller), Jack De Rieux (Joseph Davenport Sr.), Ron Vincent (Joe Davenport, Jr.), Michael Jacobs (Mark Evans). 90 min.

Choking Hazard (2004) Czech Republic. Dir: Marek Dobes. Scr: Stepan Kopriva, Martin Pomothy. Mus: Frantisek Fuka, Daniel Krob. DP: Martin Preiss. Ed: Michal Hýka. PD: Katerina Koutská. Cast: Jan Dolanský (Verner), Jaroslav Dusek (Prof. Reinis), Eva Nádazdyová (Hanusova), Anna Fialkova (Lefnerova), Kamil Svejda (Nedobyl). 81 min.

Chopper Chicks in Zombietown (*Chrome Hearts*, 1989) USA. Dir/Scr: Dan Hoskins. Mus: Daniel May. DP: Tom Fraser. Ed: W.O. Garrett. AD: Timothy Baxter. Cast: Jamie Rose (Dede), Catherine Carlen (Rox), Lycia Naff (T.C.), Vicki Frederick (Jewel), Kristina Loggia (Jojo), Gretchen Palmer (Rusty). 86 min.

Christmas with the Dead (2012) USA. Dir: T.L. Lankford. Scr: Joe R. Lansdale, Keith Lansdale. Mus: Lance Treviño. DP: Bil Arscott. Ed: Ryan Blackburn, Dan Golden. PD: Marion Arscott. Cast: Damian Maffei (Calvin), Brad Maule (G.M.), Chet Williamson (Reverend Mac), Clyde Williams (Driver). 88 min.

Cinque Tombe per un medium (*Terror-Creatures from the Grave*, 1965) Italy/USA. Dir: Massimo Pupillo [as Ralph Zucker]. Scr: Ruth Carter, Cesare Mancini, Romano Migliorini, Roberto Natale. Mus: Aldo Piga. DP: Carlo Di Palma [as Charles Brown]. Ed: Mariano Arditi

Manfredini. DP: Barry Abrams. Cast: Martin Shakar (John Freemont), Gil Rogers (Sheriff Billy Hart), Gale Garnett (Cathy Freemont), Shannon Bolin (Molly), Tracy Griswold (Deputy Harry Timmons), Joy Glaccum (Suzie MacKenzie). 93 min.

Children of the Living Dead (2001) USA. Dir: Tor Ramsey. Scr: Karen L. Wolf. Mus: Alan Howarth. DP: S. William Hinzman. Ed: Lewis Schoenbrun. AD: Robert V. Michelucci. Cast: Tom Savini (Deputy Hughs), Damien Luvara (Matthew Micheals), Jamie McCoy (Laurie Danesi), Sam Nicotero (Dusty), Heidi Hinzman (Candy Danesi), Philip Bower (Joseph Michaels). 90 min.

Children Shouldn't Play with Dead Things (1973) USA. Dir: Bob Clark [as Benjamin Clark]. Scr: Alan Ormsby, Bob Clark. Mus: Carl Zittrer. DP: Jack McGowan. Ed: Gary Goch. AD: Forest Carpenter. Cast: Alan Ormsby (Alan), Valerie Mamches (Val), Jeff Gillen (Jeff), Anya Ormsby (Anya), Paul Cronin (Paul), Jane Daly (Terry), Roy Engleman (Roy), Robert Philip (Emerson). 87 min.

[as Robert Ardis]. Cast: Walter Brandi (Albert Kovac), Mirella Maravidi (Corinne Hauff), Barbara Steele (Cleo Hauff), Alfredo Rizzo (Dr. Nemek [as Alfred Rice]), Riccardo Garrone (Joseph Morgan [as Richard Garrett]), Luciano Pigozzi (Kurt, the servant), Tilde Till (Louise, the maid). 85 min.

Cockneys vs. Zombies (2012) UK. Dir: Matthias Hoene. Scr: James Moran, Lucas Roche. DP: Daniel Bronks. Ed: Neil Farrell, John Palmer. PD: Matthew Button. Cast: Rasmus Hardiker (Terry), Harry Treadaway (Andy), Michelle Ryan (Katy), Jack Doolan (Davey Tuppence), Georgia King (Emma), Ashley Thomas (Mental Mickey), Tony Gardner (Clive), Alan Ford (Ray), Honor Blackman (Peggy). 88 min.

Colin (2008) UK. Dir/Scr/DP/Ed: Marc Price. Mus: Jack Elphick, Dan Weekes. Cast: Alastair Kirton (Colin), Daisy Aitkens (Linda, Colin's Sister), Kate Alderman (False Laura), Leanne Pammen (Laura), Tat Whalley (Marlen, Linda's Friend), Kerry Owen (Colin's Mother). 97 min.

Convention of the Dead (2013) UK. Dir/Scr/Ed: Kelvin Beer. DP: Ken Clay. PD: Daniel Spencer. Cast: Christopher Rithin (Errol), Ashleigh Lawrence (Ashleigh), Jonathan Hansler (Steven Sinclair), Dani Thompson (Slave Girl Zombie), Chris Knight (Rickles), Ellie Torrez (Hotel Receptionist Zombie), Nadine Gorman (Purple Zentai Zombie), Paul Draper (Hotel Reception Zombie), Jay Oliver Yip (Cooper), Frank Osborne (Barry), William Wallace (Rock Star Zombie), Adam Millbrook (Zombie), Andy Pierce (Herbie).

Corpse Bride (2005) USA. Dir: Tim Burton, Mike Johnson. Scr: John August, Caroline Thompson, Pamela Pettler based on characters by Tim Burton, Carlos Grangel. Mus: Danny Elfman. DP: Pete Kozachik. Ed: Chris Lebenzon, Jonathan Lucas. PD: Alex McDowell. Cast: Johnny Depp (Victor Van Dort, voice), Helena Bonham Carter (the Corpse Bride, voice), Emily Watson (Victoria Everglot, voice). 77 min.

Corpses (2004) USA. Dir/Scr: Rolfe Kanefsky. DP: Rick Lamb, Andrew Parke. Ed: Lewis Schoenbrun. Cast: Jeff Fahey (Captain Winston), Tiffany Shepis (Rhonda Winston), Stephen W. Williams (Jerry Gordon), Robert Donavan (Fred Withers), Melinda Bonini (Helen), Khris Kaneff (Christopher Barnes). 90 min.

Corpses Are Forever (2003) USA. Dir/Scr: Jose Prendes. Mus: Thomas Park, Jose Prendes. DP: Alvaro Rangel. Ed: Brandon Dumlao. Cast: Richard Lynch (Gen. Morton), Jose Prendes (Malcolm Grant/Quint

Barrow), Brinke Stevens (Dr. Emily Thesiger), Bill Perlach (Father James Mason), Debbie Rochon (Marguerite), Linnea Quigley (Elli Kroger). 92 min.

The Crazies (1973) USA. Dir/Ed: George A. Romero. Scr: Paul McColloughand, George A. Romero. Mus: Bruce Roberts. DP: S. William Hinzman. Cast: Lane Carroll (Judy), Will MacMillan (David), Harold Wayne (Clank), Lloyd Hollar (Col. Peckem), Lynn Lowry (Kathy), Richard Liberty (Artie), Richard France (Dr. Watts), Harry Spillman (Maj. Ryder), Will Disney (Dr. Brookmyre), Edith Bell (Lab Technician). 103 min.

The Crazies (2010) USA. Dir: Breck Eisner. Scr: Scott Kosar, Ray Wright, George A. Romero. Mus: Mark Isham. DP: Maxime Alexandre. Ed: Billy Fox. PD: Andrew Menzies. Cast: Timothy Olyphant (David), Radha Mitchell (Judy), Joe Anderson (Deputy Russell Clank), Danielle Panabaker (Becca), Christie Lynn Smith (Deardra Farnum), Brett Rickaby (Bill Farnum), Preston Bailey (Nicholas Farnum). 101 min.

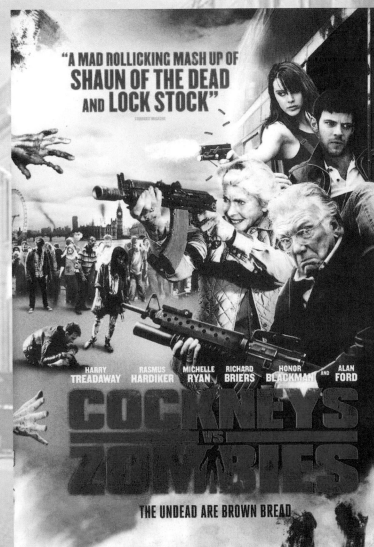

The Zombie Film

Creature with the Atom Brain (1955) USA. Dir: Edward L. Cahn. Scr: Curt Siodmak. DP: Fred Jackman Jr. Ed: Aaron Stell. AD: Paul Palmentola. Cast: Richard Denning (Dr. Chet Walker), Angela Stevens (Joyce Walker), S. John Launer (Capt. Dave Harris), Michael Granger (Frank Buchanan), Gregory Gaye (Dr. Wilhelm Steigg), Linda Bennett (Penny Walker), Tristram Coffin (Dist. Atty. MacGraw). 69 min.

Creepshow (1982, "Father's Day" segment) USA. Dir: George A. Romero. Scr: Stephen King. Mus: John Harrison. DP: Michael Gornick. Ed: Michael Spolan. PD: Cletus Anderson. Cast: Carrie Nye (Sylvia Grantham), Viveca Lindfors (Aunt Bedelia), Ed Harris (Hank Blaine). 120 minute [full feature].

Curse of the Blue Lights (1988) USA. Dir/DP/Ed: John

Henry Johnson. Scr: John Henry Johnson, Bryan Sisson. Mus: Randall Crissman. Cast: Brent Ritter (Loath), Bettina Julius (The Witch), Clayton A. McCaw (Paul), Deborah McVencenty (Sandy), Becky Golladay (Alice). 104 min.

Curse of the Buxom Strumpet (2014) UK. Dir: Matthew Butler. Scr: Matthew Butler, Tori Hart. Mus: Tom Kane. DP: Pete Wallington. Cast: Gillian Anderson (Betsy Foxer), Ian McKellen (Gerald Macklin), Imelda Staunton (Mrs. Halfpint), Andrew Buchan (Richard Filthe), Mark Williams (Father Thomas), Tori Hart (Vanity Banks).

Curse of the Maya (*Evil Grave*, 2004) USA. Dir/Scr: David Heavener. DP: Joseph Rubinstein. Ed: Christopher Roth. PD: Sally Sherwood. Cast: David Heavener (Michael), Amanda Bauman (Renee), Joe Estevez (Jeffrey), Todd Bridges (Herardo), Steven Bracy (Daniel), Carrie Gonzalez (Trisha). 90 min.

The Curse of the Screaming Dead (1982) USA. Dir: Tony Malanowski. Scr: Lon Huber based on a story by Tony Malanowski [as Tony Stark]. Mus: Charlie Barnett. Cast: Steve Sandkuhler (Wyatt), Christopher Gummer (Mel), Rebecca Bach (Sarah), Judy Dixon (Lin), Jim Ball (Bill), Bumb Roberts (Deputy Franklin). 91 min.

Dance of the Dead (2008) USA. Dir: Gregg Bishop. Scr: Joe Ballarini. Mus: Kristopher Carter. DP: George Feucht. Ed: Gregg Bishop. PD: James Jarrett. Cast: Jared Kusnitz (Jimmy Dunn), Greyson Chadwick (Lindsey), Chandler Darby (Steven), Carissa Capobianco (Gwen), Randy McDowell (Jules Reiner), Michael Mammoliti (George), Mark Lynch (Rod). 87 min.

Dark Echoes (1977) Yugoslavia. Dir/Scr: George Robotham. Mus: Sanja Ilic, Slobodan Markovic. DP: Bozidar Miletic. Ed: Pierre Jalbert. PD: Vladislav Lasic. Cast: Karin Dor (Lisa Bruekner), Joel Fabiani (Bill Cross), Wolfgang Brook (Inspector Woelke), Hanna Hertelendy (Frau Ziemler), John Robotham (Dieter Beckmann), Norman Marshall (Captain Gohr). 91 min.

The Dark Power (1985) USA. Dir/Scr: Phil Smoot. Mus: Christopher Deane, Matt Kendrick. DP: Paul Hughen. Ed: Sherwood Jones. AD: Dean Jones. Cast: Lash La Rue (Ranger Girard), Anna Lane Tatum (Beth), Cynthia Bailey (Tammie), Mary Dalton (Mary), Paul Holman (Uncle Earl Coleman), Cynthia Farbman (Lynn Evans). 78 min.

Dark Shadows (television series, 1966–1971) USA. Creator: Dan Curtis. Recurring cast: David Selby (Quentin, zombie).

Dating a Zombie (2012) USA. Dir/Scr: Jack Abele. Mus: Jonathon Cox. DP: Aaron Moorhead. Ed: Bo Buckley. Cast: Jack Abele (Clarence), Claudia Andrejuk (Sally Stevens), Glenn Balli (Psychologist), John Bard (Sally's Father), Tabatha Beshears (Kate), Brendan Boyce (IRS Agent Zombie), Meagan Brownell (Hot Chick Friend), Jaclyn Courter (Hot Chick), Emily Daigneault (Hot Chick Friend), Lora Lee Ecobelli (Princess Betty). 80 min.

Dawn of the Dead (1978) USA/Italy. Dir/Scr: George A. Romero. Mus: Dario Argento. DP: Michael Gornick. Ed: George A. Romero, Dario Argento. Cast: David Emge (Stephen), Ken Foree (Peter), Scott H. Reiniger (Roger), Gaylen Ross (Francine), David Crawford (Dr. Foster), David Early (Mr. Berman), Richard France (Scientist), Howard Smith (TV Commentator). 127 min.

Dawn of the Dead (2004) USA/Canada/Japan/France. Dir: Zack Snyder. Scr: James Gunn based on the script by George Romero. Mus: Tyler Bates. DP: Matthew F. Leonetti. Ed: Niven Howie. PD: Andrew Neskoromny. Cast: Sarah Polley (Ana), Ving Rhames (Kenneth), Jake Weber (Michael), Mekhi Phifer (Andre), Ty Burrell (Steve), Michael Kelly (CJ). 101 min.

The Day It Came to Earth (1979) USA. Dir: Harry Thomason. Scr: Paul Fisk. Mus: Joe Southerland. DP: Mike Varner. Ed: LeRoy Slaughter. PD: Mike Frey. Cast: Wink Roberts (Eddie Newton), Roger Manning (Ronnie McGuire), Robert Ginnaven (Lt. Kelly), Delight De Bruine (Sally Baxter), George Gobel (Prof. Bartholomew), Rita Wilson (Debbie), Lyle Armstrong (Sgt. Larry Pinkerton), Ed Lover (Ed Love/The Creature/Lou Jacoby). 88 min.

Day of the Dead (1985) USA. Dir/Scr: George A. Romero. Mus: John Harrison, Jim Blazer, Spotzy Sparacino. DP: Michael Gornick. Ed: Pasquale Buba. PD: Cletus Anderson. Cast: Lori Cardille (Sarah), Terry Alexander (John), Joseph Pilato (Rhodes), Jarlath Conroy (McDermott), Anthony Dileo Jr. (Miguel), Richard Liberty (Logan), Sherman Howard (Bub), Gary Howard Klar (Steel). 102 min.

Day of the Dead (2008) USA. Dir: Steve Miner. Scr: Jeffrey Reddick based on the script by George Romero. Mus: Tyler Bates. DP: Patrick Cady. Ed: Nathan Easterling. PD: Carlos Da Silva, Cast: Mena Suvari (Sarah Bowman), Nick Cannon (Salazar), Michael Welch (Trevor Bowman), AnnaLynne McCord (Nina), Stark Sands (Bud Crain), Matt Rippy (Dr. Logan), Pat Kilbane (Scientist), Taylor Hoover (Local Girl), Christa Campbell (Mrs. Leitner), Ian McNeice (Paul, DJ), Ving Rhames (Captain Rhodes). 86 min.

Day of the Dead 2: Contagium (2005) USA. Dir: Ana Clavell, James Glenn Dudelson. Scr: Ryan Carrassi, Ana Clavell. Mus: Chris Anderson. DP: James M. LeGoy. Ed: Ana Clavell. PD: Suzanne Rattigan. Cast: Laurie Baranyay (Emma), Stan Klimecko (Boris), John F. Henry II (Jackie), Justin Ipock (Isaac), Julian Thomas (Sam), Stephan Wolfert (Donwynn). 103 min.

Days of Darkness (2007) USA. Dir: Jake Kennedy. Scr: Joey Gaynor, Jake Kennedy. Mus: Jamey Scott. DP: Brandon Trost. Ed: William Daniels. Cast: Tom Eplin (Chad), Sabrina Gennarino (Lin), Travis Brorsen (Steve),

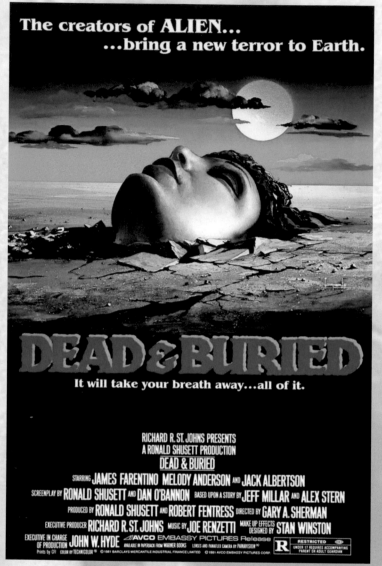

The creators of ALIEN…
…bring a new terror to Earth.

DEAD & BURIED

It will take your breath away…all of it.

RICHARD R. ST. JOHNS PRESENTS
A RONALD SHUSETT PRODUCTION
DEAD & BURIED
STARRING JAMES FARENTINO MELODY ANDERSON AND JACK ALBERTSON
SCREENPLAY BY RONALD SHUSETT AND DAN O'BANNON BASED UPON A STORY BY JEFF MILLAR AND ALEX STERN
PRODUCED BY RONALD SHUSETT AND ROBERT FENTRESS DIRECTED BY GARY A. SHERMAN
EXECUTIVE PRODUCER RICHARD R. ST. JOHNS MUSIC BY JOE RENZETTI MAKE UP EFFECTS DESIGNED BY STAN WINSTON
EXECUTIVE IN CHARGE OF PRODUCTION JOHN W. HYDE AVCO EMBASSY PICTURES Release
R RESTRICTED

Roshelle Baier (Mimi [as Roshelle Pattison]), John Lee Ames (Trent), Bryan Rasmussen (Slasher), Eric Stuart (DJ). 89 min.

Days of Infection (2012) UK. Dir/DP: Ranjeet S. Marwa, Tom Nicholls. Scr: Tom Nicholls. Ed: Dan Everton. Cast: Elizabeth Arends (Claire), Mark Braun (Infected), Ranjeet S. Marwa (Infected), Kim Irene Merchant (Infected), Tom Nicholls (Infected), Jago North (Rob), Jay O'Connor (Infected), Liz Smith (Infected). 83 min.

The Dead (2010) UK. Dir/Scr: Howard J. Ford, Jon Ford. Mus: Imran Ahmad. DP: Jon Ford. PD: Daniel Gomme. Cast: Rob Freeman (Lt. Brian Murphy), Prince David Oseia (Sgt. Daniel Dembele (as Prince David Osei),

David Dontoh (The Chief), Ben Crowe (Mercenary Leader), Glenn Salvage (Mercenary), Dan Morgan (James), Julia Scott-Russell (James' Fiance). 105 min.

Dead & Breakfast (2004) USA. Dir/Scr: Matthew Leutwyler. Mus: Brian Vander Ark. DP: David Scardina. Ed: Peter Devaney Flanagan. PD: Don Day. Cast: Jeremy Sisto (Christian), Erik Palladino (David), Bianca Lawson (Kate), Oz Perkins (Johnny), Ever Carradine (Sara), Gina Philips (Melody), Zach Selwyn (Randall Keith Randall). 88 min.

Dead & Buried (1981) USA. Dir: Gary Sherman. Scr: Ronald Shusett, Dan O'Bannon based on a story by Jeff Millar, Alex Stern. Mus: Joe Renzetti. DP: Steven Poster. Ed: Alan Balsam. AD: Joe Aubel. William Sandell. Cast: James Farentino (Sheriff Dan Gillis), Melody Anderson (Janet Gillis), Jack Albertson (William G. Dobbs), Dennis Redfield (Ron), Nancy Locke (Linda), Lisa Blount (Girl on the Beach/Nurse Lisa), Robert Englund (Harry), Bill Quinn (Ernie), Michael Currie (Herman). 94 min.

Dead & Deader (2006) USA. Dir: Patrick Dinhut. Sreenplay: Mark A. Altman, Steven Kriozere. Mus: Joe Kraemer. DP: Raymond Stella. Cast: John Billingsley (Langdon), Dean Cain (Lt. Bobby Quinn), Colleen Camp (Mrs. Wisteria), Greg Collins (Captain Niles), Ellie Cornell (Dr. Adams), Affion Crockett (Pvt. Connery). 89 min.

The Dead and the Damned (*Cowboys vs. Zombies*, 2010) USA. Dir/Scr/Ed: Rene Perez. Mus: Mattia Borrani, Rene Perez. DP: Paul Nordin. Cast: David A. Lockhart (Mortimer), Camille Montgomery (Rhiannon), Rick Mora (Indian/Brother Wolf), Robert Amstler (The German), Autumn Harrison (Lucinda). 82 min.

Dead City (2008) UK. Dir/Scr/Ph/Ed: James Kennedy. Mus: Rusty Apper. Cast: Rusty Apper (Gary), Daniel Bush (Mark), Anna Cade (Samantha), Kate Armstrong Clark (Beth), Nikita Heaney (Amanda), James Kennedy (John), Sean Mason (McReady), Greg Norton (Tarantino), Jennifer Oates (Sarah), Jo Rayner (Amy). 90 min.

Dead Clowns (2004) USA. Dir/Scr/Mus: Steve Sessions, Carol Riordan. Cast: Lucien Eisenach (Spree Killer/Clown), Jeff Samford (Lou), Eric Spudic (Timmy/Clown), Debbie Rochon (Tormented Woman), Brinke Stevens (Lillian, Storyteller), William Riordan (Darrin). 95 min.

Dead Crazy (2011) UK. Dir/Scr/Ed: Frank Scantori. DP: Marcus Alexander. Art Dir: Bonnie Paddle. Cast: Bonnie

Adair (Jennifer Ford), Andrew Lewis (Adam Carr), Matt Houlihan (Jason Nunn), Wendy Cooper (Stephanie Carr), Eva Gray (Sophie), Anna Wilde (Trish Taylor), Ellie Dickens (Margaret Poole), Danny George (Colin Pearse), Natalie Hall (Wendy), Lucy Bruegger (Nurse Renn). 90 min.

Dead Creatures (2001) UK. Dir/Scr/Mus/Ed: Andrew Parkinson. DP: Jason Shepherd. AD: Jennifer Clapcott. Cast: Beverley Wilson (Jo), Antonia Beamish (Ann), Brendan Gregory (Reece), Anna Swift (Sian), Bart Ruspoli (Christian), Fiona Carr (Zoe). 95 min.

The Dead Don't Die (1975) USA. Dir: Curtis Harrington. Scr: Robert Bloch. Mus: Robert Prince. DP: James Crabe. Ed: Ronald J. Fagan. AD: Robert Kinoshita. Cast: George Hamilton (Don Drake), Linda Cristal (Vera LaValle), Joan Blondell (Levenia), Ralph Meeker (Police Lt. Reardon), James McEachin (Frankie Specht), Reggie Nalder (Perdido), Ray Milland (Jim Moss), Jerry Douglas (Ralph Drake), Yvette Vickers (Miss Adrian). 74 min.

Dead Down Under (2013) Australia. Dir/Ed: Jason Carthew. Scr: Jason Carthew, David Leys, Scott Francis Sowter. PD: Cassandra Jamcotchian. Cast: Amelia Foxton (Amanda Devine), Charlie Hopkins (Barry Bradman), Alexia Kelly (Maggie), Bianca Jade Mauceri (Lucy), Alistair Milne (Michael), Brigid O'Sullivan (Deborah), Robin Queree (Doc), David Sutton (Steve), Nicholas Gledhill (Carlisle), Kiara Thomas (Natalie).

The Dead Hate the Living! (2000) USA. Dir/Scr: Dave Parker. DP: Thomas L. Callaway. Ed: Dave Parker, Harry James Picardi. Cast: Eric Clawson (David Poe), Jamie Donahue (Topaz), Brett Beardslee (Paul), Wendy Speake (Shelly Poe), Benjamin P. Morris (Eric). 90 min.

Dead Heat (1988) USA. Dir: Mark Goldblatt. Scr: Terry Black. Mus: Ernest Troost. DP: Robert D. Yeoman. Ed: Harvey Rosenstock. PD: Craig Stearns. Cast: Treat Williams (Det. Roger Mortis), Joe Piscopo (Det. Doug Bigelow), Lindsay Frost (Randi James), Darren McGavin (Dr. Ernest McNab), Vincent Price (Arthur P. Loudermilk), Clare Kirkconnell (Dr. Rebecca Smythers), Keye Luke (Mr. Thule), Linnea Quigley (Dancer). 86 min.

Dead in the Head (2010) USA. Dir/Scr: Amazon Bob Carter. DP: Andrew Giannetta. Ed: Douglas Rennie. Cast: Brad Milne (Demon Jones), Estephania LeBaron (The Babe), William D. Caldwell (Bo), Vito La Morte (Reese Crowley), Laura Buckles (Dr. Moreaux), Chas Mitchell (Professor Bruce Campbell). 147 min.

The Dead Inside (2012) USA. Dir/Ed: Travis Betz. Mus: Michael Brake, Joel Van Vliet. DP: Shannon Hourigan. Cast: Sarah Lassez (Fi/Emily/Harper), Dustin Fasching (Wes/Max), Jediah Brown (Matthew), Aaron Gaffey (Dennis), Melisa McCawley (Phone Operator). 98 min.

The Dead Inside (2013) UK. Dir: Andrew Gilbert. Scr: Andrew Gilbert, Julian Hundy. Mus: Stephen Currell. DP: Julian Hundy, James Mann. Ed: Julian Hundy. Cast: Luke Hobson (Adam), Nicky Paul Barton (Tom), Roger Fowler (Darren), Samuel Hogarth (Aidan), David Wayman (PTE Paul Bradburn), James Harrison (Sgt. Faulkner), Simon Mathews (Pvt. Mark Dowling), Elizabeth Quinn (Rachel), Abby Simpson (Jenny), Simon Nader (Wayne Andrews), James Callàs Ball (Lee), Stuart J. Prowse (Gary). 116 min.

Dead Life (2005) USA. Dir: William Victor Schotten. Scr: William Victor Schotten. DP: David Caleris. Cast: Michael Hanton (Maxx), Ashleigh Holeman (Brianna), Jayson Garity (Rick), Lindsay Gerish (Kim). 90 min.

Dead Meat (2004) Ireland. Dir/Scr/Ed: Conor McMahon. Mus: John Gillooley. DP: Andrew Legge. PD:

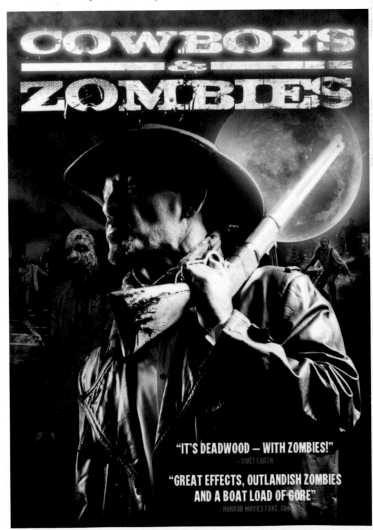

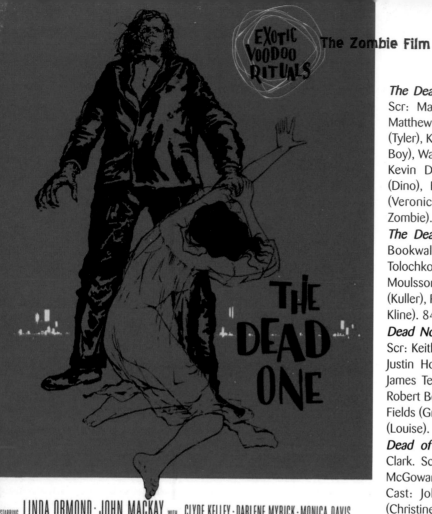

EXOTIC VOODOO RITUALS

STARRING LINDA ORMOND · JOHN MACKAY WITH CLYDE KELLEY · DARLENE MYRICK · MONICA DAVIS
PRODUCED AND DIRECTED BY BARRY MAHON   EXECUTIVE PRODUCER BRANDON CHASE
A PRESENTATION OF MARDI GRAS PRODUCTIONS, INC. ULTRASCOPE EASTMAN COLOR

Cornelius Browne. Cast: Marian Araujo (Helena), David Muyllaert (Desmond), Erin Whelan (Cathal Cheunt), David Ryan (Martin), Amy Redmond (Francie). 80 min.

Dead Men Don't Die (1990) USA. Dir/Scr: Malcolm Marmorstein. Mus: Mark Koval, David C. Williams. DP: Tom Fraser. Ed: Michael D. Ornstein. PD: Diane Hughes, Phillip Vasels. Cast: Elliott Gould (Barry Baron), Melissa Anderson (Dulcie Niles), Jack Betts (Alex Cavanaugh), Philip Bruns (Nolan), Robert Dryer (Mungo). 94 min.

Dead Men Walking (2005) USA. Dir: Peter Mervis. Scr: Mike Watt. Mus: Mel Lewis. DP: Mark Atkins. Ed: Peter Mervis. PD: Kurt Altschwager. Cast: Bay Bruner (Samantha Beckett), Griff Furst (Johnny [as Brick Firestone]), Chriss Anglin (Sweeny), Bobby James (Warden Mahler), Brandon Stacy (Travis), James Ferris (Jenkins). 82 min.

The Dead Mile (2012) Canada. Dir/Ed: K.J. Kleefeld. Scr: May Charters, Mark Hug, K.J. Kleefeld. Mus: Matthew Bonnyman. DP: Michael Rye. Cast: Shawn Roe (Tyler), Krystle Mintonye (Krystle), Sean Dykink (Johnny Boy), Wade Sun (Kevin Wong), Julia Kruis (Jessie Black), Kevin Davey (Skogan), Connor Harvey-Derbyshire (Dino), Bobby Sparrow (Nick), Jacqueline Breakwell (Veronica), Veronica Pocza (Rachel/Daisy Duke Zombie).

The Dead Next Door (1989) USA. Dir/Scr/Ed: J.R. Bookwalter. Mus: J.R. Bookwalter. DP: Michael Tolochko. Cast: Pete Ferry (Raimi), Bogdan Pecic (Dr. Moulsson), Michael Grossi (Mercer), Jolie Jackunas (Kuller), Robert Kokai (Rev. Jones), Floyd Ewing Jr. (Capt. Kline). 84 min.

Dead Noon (2007) USA. Dir/DP/Ed: Andrew Wiest. Scr: Keith Suta, Matthew Taggart, Andrew Wiest. Mus: Justin Hosford, Aaron Nielson, Tim Schoessler. AD: James Teague. Cast: Kane Hodder (Undead Cowboy), Robert Bear (Frank), Robert Milo Andrus (Stuart), Lillith Fields (Grace), Dixon Phillips (Logan), Elizabeth Mouton (Louise). 85 min.

Dead of Night (*Deathdream*, 1972) USA. Dir: Bob Clark. Scr: Alan Ormsby. Mus: Carl Zittrer. DP: Jack McGowan. Ed: Ronald Sinclair. AD: Forest Carpenter. Cast: John Marley (Charles Brooks), Lynn Carlin (Christine Brooks), Richard Backus (Andy Brooks), Henderson Forsythe (Dr. Philip Allman), Anya Ormsby (Cathy Brooks), Jane Daly (Joanne), Michael Mazes (Bob), Arthur Anderson (Postman), Bob Clark (Officer Ted). 88 min.

The Dead One (*Blood of the Zombie*. 1961) USA. Dir/Scr: Barry Mahon. DP: Mark Dennis. Ed: Alan Smiler. PD: Stanley Raines. Cast: John McKay (John Carlton), Linda Ormond (Linda Carlton), Monica Davis (Monica), Clyde Kelly (Jonas), Darlene Myrick (Bella Bella), Lacey Kelly (Lacey), Paula Maurice (Kooch Club Proprietress). 71 min.

The Dead Outside (2008) UK. Dir: Kerry Anne Mullaney. Scr: Kris R. Bird, Kerry Anne Mullaney. DP: Kris R. Bird. Cast: Sandra Louise Douglas (April), Alton Milne (Daniel), Sharon Osdin (Kate), Vivienne Harvey (Eleanor), John Erskine (April's Grandfather), Phylis Douglas (April's Grandmother), Robin Morris (Daniel's Son), Max Adair (April's Brother). 86 min.

Dead Season (2012) USA. Dir: Adam Deyoe. Scr: Adam Deyoe, Joshua Klausner, Loren Semmens. Mus:

Louis Chalif. DP: Jeffrey Peters. Ed: Adam Deyoe, Loren Semmens. Scott Peat (Elvis), Marissa Merrill (Tweeter), James C. Burns (Kurt Conrad), Corsica Wilson (Rachel Conrad), Marc L. Fusco (Tommy), Todd Pritchett (Todd), Grant Beijon (Alex Waterman). 85 min.

Dead Snow (2009) Norway. Dir: Tommy Wirkola. Scr: Tommy Wirkola, Stig Frode Henriksen. Mus: Christian Wibe. DP: Matthew Weston. Ed: Martin Stoltz. PD: Liv Ask. Cast: Vegar Hoel (Martin), Stig Henriksen (Roy), Charlotte Frogner (Hanna), Lasse Valdal (Vegard), Evy Kasseth Røsten (Liv). 91 min.

Dead Summer (2005) USA. Dir/DP: Eddie Benevich. Scr: Robert Brewer. Cast: Amy Liszka (Amanda). Peter Blessel (Brody), John Pierce (Army Officer/Zombie). 71 min.

The Dead 2: India (2013) UK. Dir/Scr: Howard J. Ford, Jon Ford. Mus: Imran Ahmad. DP: Jon Ford. Ed: Howard J. Ford. Art Dir: Sanjay Sujitabh. Cast: Joseph Millson (Nicholas Burton), Meenu Mishra (Ishani Sharma), Anand Gopal (Javed), Sandip Datta Gupta (Ishani's Father), Poonam Mathur (Ishani's Mother), Niharika Singh (Mystery Woman), Coulsom Sujitabh (Mourning Wife)

The Dead Undead (2010) USA. Dir: Matthew R. Anderson, Edward Conna. Scr: Edward Conna. Mus: Steve Benton, Scott James. DP: Jon Myers. Ed: Nancy Brindley Bhagia, Patrea Patrick, Jack Tucker. PD: Nadia Reed. Cast: Luke Goss (Jack), Matthew R. Anderson (Viper), Spice Williams-Crosby (Gabrielle), Luke LaFontaine (Aries), Edward Conna (Doc), Laura Chinn (Megan), Joshua Alba (Curtis), America Young (Shelly), Cameron Goodman (Summer). 89 min.

Dead Walkers Rise of the 4th Reich (2013) UK. Dir/Scr/Ed: Philip Gardiner. DP: Jack Burrows. Art Dir: John R. Sullivan. Cast: Philip Berzamanis (Alpha One), Jane Haslehurst (Private Anael Sraosha), Rudy Barrow (Alpha Five), Bob Lee (Dr. Gavreel), Nathan Head (Professor Mastema), Eirian Cohen (Captain Oriax).

Deadgirl (2008) USA. Dir: Marcel Sarmiento, Gadi Harel. Scr: Trent Haaga. DP: Harris Charalambous. Ed: Phillip Blackford. PD: Diana J. Zeng. Cast: Shiloh Fernandez (Rickie), Noah Segan (JT), Candice Accola (Joann), Eric Podnar (Wheeler), Jenny Spain (Deadgirl), Andrew DiPalma (Johnny), Nolan Gerard Funk (Dwyer), Michael Bowen (Clint), David Alan Graf (Mr. Harrison). 101 min.

DeadHeads (2011) USA. Dir/Scr: Brett Pierce, Drew T.

Pierce. Mus: Devin Burrows. DP: Robert Toth. Ed: Kevin O'Brien. PD: Steven Milosavleski. Cast: Michael McKiddy (Mike Kellerman), Ross Kidder (Brent Guthrie), Markus Taylor (Cheese), Thomas Galasso (Thomas Jeremiah), Natalie Victoria (Ellie Masterson), Eden Malyn (Emily). 100 min.

Deadhunter: Sevillian Zombies (2003) Spain. Dir/Scr/Ed: Julián Lara. DP: Daniel Ordóñez. Cast: Beatriz Mateo, María Miñagorri, Julián Lara, José Manuel Gómez (Deadhunters). 75 min.

Deadlands: The Rising (2006) USA. Dir/Scr/Ed: Gary Ugarek. Mus: Gary Ugarek, Brian Wright. DP: Thomas Fant. Cast: Dave Cooperman (Dave), Gary Ugarek (Gary), Michelle Wright (Michelle), Brian Wright (Brian), Connor Brandt (Connor). 72 min.

Deadlands 2: Trapped (2008) USA. Dir/Scr/Ed: Gary Ugarek. Mus: Marq-Paul La Rose, Gary Ugarek, Brian Wright. DP: Krystian Ramlogan. Cast: Jim Krut (Dr. Robert Mitchell), Joseph D. Durbin (Sean), Chris L. Clark (Chris), Josh Davidson (Jack), Ashley Young (Casey), Corrine Brush (Shelly). 87 min.

Death Becomes Her (1992) USA. Dir: Robert Zemeckis. Scr: Martin Donovan, David Koepp. Mus: Alan Silvestri.

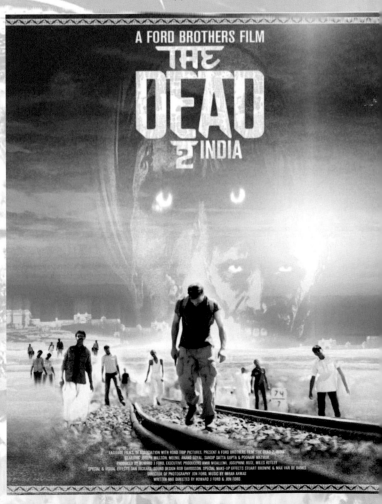

DP: Dean Cundey. Ed: Arthur Schmidt. PD: Rick Carter. Cast: Meryl Streep (Madeline Ashton), Bruce Willis (Ernest Menville), Goldie Hawn (Helen Sharp), Isabella Rossellini (Lisle Von Rhuman), Ian Ogilvy (Chagall), Adam Storke (Dakota), Nancy Fish (Rose). 104 min.

Death House (*Zombie Death House*, 1987) USA. Dir: John Saxon. Scr: William Selby, David S. Freeman, Kate Wittcomb, Devin Frazer. Mus: Chuck Cirino. DP: John V. Fante. Ed: Fred Roth, Gary Blair. Cast: Dennis Cole (Derek Keillor), Anthony Franciosa (Vic Moretti), Dino Paskas (Jimmy), Dana Lis Mason (Genelle Davis), Ron O'Neal (Tom Boyle), Salvatore Richichi (Tony), John Saxon (Col. Gordon Burgess). 90 min.

Death Valley: The Revenge of Bloody Bill (2004) USA. Dir: Byron Werner. Scr: John Yuan, Matt Yuan. Mus: Ralph Rieckermann. DP: Byron Werner. Ed: David Michael Latt, Leigh Scott. Cast: Chelsea Jean (Gwen), Gregory Bastien (Earl), Denise Boutte (Mandy), Scott Carson (Avery), Matt Marraccini (Jerry), Kandis Erickson

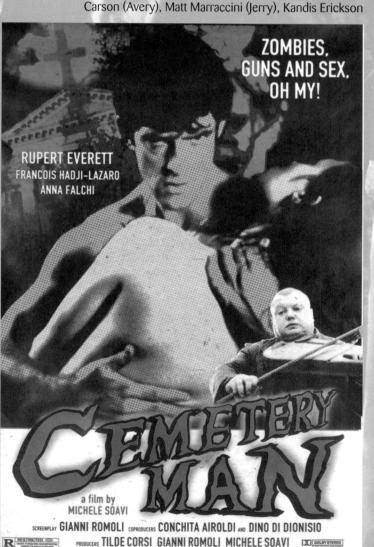

(Sondra), Steven Glinn (Buck), Jeremy Bouvet (Bloody Bill). 82 min.

Decay (2012) UK. Dir/Scr: Luke Thompson. Ed: Burton De Wilde. Cast: Zoë Hatherell (Amy), Tom Procter (Connor), Stewart Martin-Haugh (James), Sara Mahmoud (Kate), William P. Martin (Matt), Eduard Friesen (Director General), Kurt Rinnert (Dr. Niven), Jenn Strauss (Lisa). 80 min.

Degenerates (2013) USA. Dir/Scr/DP/Ed: Carlos Suarez. Mus: Blake Pichon. Cast: Alyssa Belen (Zoe), Blake Pichon (Haggard), Dustin Reeves (Animal), Jayce Wierzbicki (Loonie), Jimmy Moreno (Razack), Jonathon Delgado (Slug), Joshua Mathis (Liam Russo), Joshua Wilkins (Odie), Justin Whitney (Don Barret) 105 min.

Dellamorte Dellamore (*Cemetery Man*, 1994) Italy. Dir: Michele Soavi. Scr: Gianni Romoli based on the novel by Tiziano Sclavi. Mus: Riccardo Biseo, Manuel De Sica. DP: Mauro Marchetti. Ed: Franco Fraticelli. PD: Massimo Geleng. Cast: Rupert Everett (Francesco Dellamorte), François Hadji-Lazaro (Gnaghi), Anna Falchi (She), Mickey Knox (Marshall Straniero), Fabiana Formica (Valentina Scanarotti), Clive Riche (Dr. Verseci), Katja Anton (Claudio's Girlfriend), Barbara Cupisti (Magda). 105 min.

Demon's Rook (2013) USA. Dir/PD: James Sizemore. Scr: James Sizemore, Akom Tidwell. DP/Ed: Tim Reis. Cast: Ashleigh Jo Sizemore (Eva), James Sizemore (Roscoe), John Chatham (Dimwos), Melanie Richardson (Barbara), Josh Adam Gould (Owrefewl/Ogrom/Zombie/Barbara's Admirer), Sade Smith (Valurga), Dustin Dorough (Rolmortus). 103 min.

Demoni 3 (*Black Demons*, 1991) Italy. Dir: Umberto Lenzi. Scr: Umberto Lenzi, Olga Pehar. Mus: Franco Micalizzi. DP: Maurizio Dell'Orco. Ed: Vanio Amici. PD: Guliana Bertuzzi. Cast: Keith Van Hoven (Kevin), Joe Balogh (Dick), Sonia Curtis (Jessica), Philip Murray (Jose). 88 min.

Detention of the Dead (2012) USA. Dir: Alex Craig Mann. Scr: Alex Craig Mann based on the play by Rob Rinow. Mus: Cody Westheimer. DP: Noah Rosenthal. PD: Danika Von Gesjen. Cast: Jacob Zachar (Eddie), Alexa Nikolas (Willow), Christa B. Allen (Janet), Jayson Blair (Brad), Justin Chon (Ash), Max Adler (Jimmy), Joseph Porter (Mark), Michele Messmer (Mrs. Rumblethorp), Jonathan Coogan (Guidance Counselor Zombie), Richard Jewell (Colonel).

The Devil's Daughter (1939) USA. Dir: Arthur H. Leonard. Scr: George Terwilliger. Mus: John Killam. DP: Jay Rescher. Ed: Samuel Datlowe. Cast: Nina Mae McKinney (Isabelle Walton), Jack Carter (Philip Ramsay), Ida James (Sylvia Walton), Hamtree Harrington. Percy Jackson), Emmett Wallace (John Lowden), Willa Mae Lang (Elvira). 52 min.

Devil's Playground (2010) UK. Dir: Mark McQueen. Scr: Bart Ruspoli. Mus: James Edward Barker. DP: Jason Shepherd. Ed: Robert Hall. PD: Sophie Wyatt. Cast: Craig Fairbrass (Cole), Danny Dyer (Joe), MyAnna Buring (Angela Mills), Jaime Murray (Lavinia), Shane Taylor (Geoffrey), Bart Ruspoli (Matthew Mills). 92 min.

The Devil's Tower (2013) UK. Dir: Owen Tooth. Scr: Adam J. Marsh. DP: Karl Poyzer, Ben Lewis Turner. Ed: Robert Higson, Jon Walmsley. PD: Felix Coles. Cast: Roxanne Pallett (Sarah), Frances Ruffelle (Kim), Jessica-Jane Stafford (Kate), Emma Buckley (Lucy).

Diary of the Dead (2007) USA. Dir/Scr: George A. Romero. Mus: Norman Orenstein. DP: Adam Swica. Ed: Michael Doherty. PD: Rupert Lazarus. Cast: Michelle Morgan (Debra Moynihan), Joshua Close (Jason Creed), Shawn Roberts (Tony Ravello), Amy Lalonde (Tracy Thurman), Joe Dinicol (Eliot Stone), Scott Wentworth (Andrew Maxwell), Philip Riccio (Ridley Wilmott), Chris Violette (Gordo Thorsen). 95 min.

Die You Zombie Bastards! (2005) USA. Dir: Caleb Emerson. Scr: Haig Demarjian, Caleb Emerson. Mus: Christopher Beal, Paul Leary. Tony Milano, Smokey Miles, Ian Ross. DP: Jarred Alterman. Ed: Daniel Strange. Cast: Tim Gerstmar (Red/Coconut Head Face Man/Mother Nefarious/Thierry), Geoff Mosher (Baron Nefarious), Pippi Zornoza (Violet), Jamie Gillis (Stavros). 97 min.

Die-ner (Get It?) (2009) USA. Dir/Scr: Patrick Horvath. DP: Jonathan Rigattieri. Ed: David Fishel, Patrick Horvath. Cast: Joshua Grote (Ken), Liesel Kopp (Kathy), Parker Quinn (Rob), Maria Olsen (Rose), Larry Purtell (Duke), Daniel Schweiger (Jessie), Jorge Montalvo (Fred), Scott Fish (Zombie Trucker), Brodrick Thornsberry (Ken, age 5), Richard Thornsberry (Zombie Cowboy), Stephen Nelson (Zombie with head wound), Eric Johnson (Getaway Zombie), Jill Black (Ken's Mother. 75 min.

The Disembodied (1957) USA. Dir: Walter Grauman. Scr: Jack Townley. Mus: Marlin Skiles. DP: Harry Neumann. Ed: William Austin. AD: Dave Milton. Cast: Paul Burke (Tom Maxwell), Allison Hayes (Tonda Metz), John Wengraf (Dr. Carl Metz), Eugenia Paul (Mara, Wife of Suba), Joel Marston (Norman), Robert Christopher (Joe), Dean Fredericks (Suba [as Norman Frederic]), A.E. Ukonu (Lead Voodoo Drummer), Paul Thompson (Gogi), Otis Greene (Kabar). 66 min.

Doctor Blood's Coffin (1961) USA. Dir: Sidney J. Furie. Scr: Nathan Juran, James Kelley, Peter Miller. Mus: Buxton Orr. DP: Stephen Dade. Ed: Antony Gibbs. AD: Scott MacGregor. Cast: Kieron Moore (Dr. Peter Blood),

징후 2. 깨달음을 얻은 로봇
피조물인 인간, 신의 영역을 넘보다! 〈천상의 피조물〉

멸망의 3가지 징후

인류멸망보고서

〈천상의 피조물〉 김지운 감독 〈멋진 신세계〉×〈해피 버스데이〉 임필성 감독

류승범 김강우 송새벽 송영창 김규리 고준희 진지희 김서형 박해일(목소리출연) (우정출연) 배두나 류승수 이영은

www.doomsdaybook.kr

2012.4.11

Hazel Court (Nurse Linda Parker), Ian Hunter (Dr. Robert Blood, Peter's Father), Kenneth J. Warren (Sgt. Cook), Gerald Lawson (Mr. G. F. Morton), Fred Johnson (Tregaye), Paul Hardtmuth (Prof. Luckman), Paul Stockman (Steve Parker, Linda's Husband), Andy Alston (George Beale, the Tunnel Expert). 92 min.

Doghouse (2009) UK. Dir: Jake West. Scr: Dan Schaffer. Mus: Richard Wells. DP: Ali Asad. Ed: Julian Gilbey, Will Gilbey, Jake West. PD: Matthew Button. Cast: Danny Dyer (Neil), Noel Clarke (Mikey), Emil Marwa (Graham), Lee Ingleby (Matt), Keith-Lee Castle (Patrick), Christina Cole (Candy). 89 min.

Don't Wake the Dead (2008) Germany. Dir: Andreas Schnaas. Scr: Klaus Dzuck, Ted Geoghegan. Mus: Marc Trinkhaus. Cast: Ralph Fellows (Vincent), Sonja Kerskes (Lana), Fiana de Guzman (Beth), Carolin Schmidt (Jessie), Cristiane Malia (Shannon), Sarah Plochl (Iris). 78 min.

Doomed (2007) USA. Dir/DP: Michael Su. Scr: Patrick

McManus, Sean O'Bannon. Mus: Tom Hiel. Ed: Maui Toca. PD: Anita Naylor. Cast: Drew Russell (Conrad), Kara Schaaf (Kyra), Edwin Villa (Benny), Aaron Gaffey (Wes), Mary Brown (Sybil), Steve Cryen (Reese), Ward Roberts (Boyle). 76 min.

Doomsday (2008) UK. Dir/Scr: Neil Marshall. Benedict Carver, Steven Paul. Mus: Tyler Bates. DP: Sam McCurdy. Ed: Andrew MacRitchie, Neil Marshall. PD: Simon Bowles. Cast: Rhona Mitra (Maj. Eden Sinclair), Bob Hoskins (Bill Nelson), Alexander Siddig (Prime Minister Hatcher), Adrian Lester (Norton), Nora-Jane Noone (Read), Emma Cleasby (Sinclair), David O'Hara (Michael Kanaris), Sean Pertwee (Dr. Talbot), Malcolm McDowell (Marcus Kane), Craig Conway (Sol Kane). 105 min.

Doomsday Book (2012) Korea. Dir: Pil-Sung Yim, Kim Jee-Woon. Scr: Kim Jee-Woon, Pil-Sung Yim. DP: Sung-min Ha, Ji-yong Kim. Cast: Yoon Se Ah (Min-Seo's Mother), Doona Bae (Min-seo), Joon-ho Bong (Joon-ho, lee), Ji-hee Jin (Min-seo), Yun-hie Jo (Ji-Eun), Gyu-ri Kim (Bodhisattva Hye-Joo), John D. Kim (Former NASA Researcher), Kang-woo Kim (Robot Repairman Park Do-won). 115 min.

Dorm of the Dead (2006) USA. Dir/Scr: Donald Farmer. DP: Donald Farmer, Chris Watson. Ed: Allan McCall. Cast: Ciara Richards (Sarah), Adrianna Eder (Allison), Jackey Hall (Clare), Tiffany Shepis (Amy), Andrea Ownbey (Julie), Christopher Slade (Xander). 75 min.

Dorm of the Dead (2012) USA. Dir: Tobias Canto Jr., Tyrel Good. Scr: Tobias Canto Jr., Jimmy Anthony Donahue, Michael Joyner, John Strong. DP: Oscar Rivera. Ed: Tobias Canto Jr., Michael Joyner. Cast: Chelsea Bowdren (Gaylen), Christi Cordova (Zombie), Ryan DeLuca (Cory), Dana DiRado (Tina), Jimmy Donahue (Derrick), Corie Johnson (Zombie). 86 min.

Ed, His Dead Mother (1993) USA. Dir: Jonathan Wacks. Scr: Chuck Hughes. Mus: Mason Daring. DP: Francis Kenny. Ed: Lisa Day. PD: Eve Cauley. Cast: Eric Christmas (Mr. Abner), Steve Buscemi (Ed Chilton), Harper Roisman (Judge Fearson), Sam Jenkins (Storm Reynolds), Ned Beatty (Uncle Benny), Gary Farmer (Big Lar), Robert Harvey (Mr. Anderson), John Glover (A.J. Pattle), Miriam Margolyes (Mabel Chilton). 93 min.

Edges of Darkness (2008) USA. Dir/Scr: Blaine Cade, Jason Horton. Mus: Pakk Hui. DP: James L. Bills. Ed: Jason Horton. PD: Lauren Henne. Cast: Alonzo F. Jones (Stan), Shamika Ann Franklin (Stellie), Annemarie

Pazmino (Natalie), Lee Perkins (Paul), Michelle Rose (Heather), Xavier Jones (Marcus). 87 min.

Electric Zombies (2006) USA. Dir: John Specht. Scr: Richard M. Novosak, John Specht. Cast: Nicole Ashmore, Trudy Lynn Barr, Jim Keith. 90 min.

The Eschatrilogy: Book of the Dead (2012) UK. Dir/Scr/Ed: Damian Morter. DP: Brett Chapman, Dean Hinchliffe, Ben Saffer, Matt Thomas. Cast: Stuart Wolfenden (The Leader), Sarah Jane Honeywell (Beth), Damian Morter (Cal), Sam Cullingworth (Big S), Tim Mcgill Grieveson (Matthew), Paul Collin-Thomas (Alex), Zoe Simone (Laura), Clay Whitter (Daniel), Brooklyn Baker (Baker), Neil Adams (Wes), Anna Batho (Joanne), Chris Knight (Grunt). 103 min.

The Evil Dead (1981) USA. Dir/Scr: Sam Raimi. Mus: Joseph LoDuca. DP: Tim Philo. Ed: Edna Ruth Paul. Cast: Bruce Campbell (Ashley J. Williams), Ellen Sandweiss (Cheryl), Richard DeManincor (Scott [as Hal Delrich]), Betsy Baker (Linda), Theresa Tilly (Shelly [as Sarah York]), Ted Raimi (Fake Shemp), Sam Raimi (Hitchhiking Fisherman/Evil Force), Robert G. Tapert (Local Yokel). 85 min.

Evil Dead (2013) USA. Dir: Fede Alvarez. Scr: Fede Alvarez, Rodo Sayagues based on the script by Sam Raimi. Mus: Roque Baños. DP: Aaron Morton. Ed: Bryan Shaw. Cast: Jane Levy (Mia), Shiloh Fernandez (David), Lou Taylor Pucci (Eric), Jessica Lucas (Olivia), Elizabeth Blackmore (Natalie), Phoenix Connolly (Teenager), Jim McLarty (Harold), Sian Davis (Old Woman). 91 min.

Evil Dead II (1987) USA. Dir: Sam Raimi. Scr: Sam Raimi, Scott Spiegel. Mus: Joseph LoDuca. DP: Peter Deming. Ed: Kaye Davis. AD: Randy Bennett, Philip Duffin. Cast: Bruce Campbell (Ashley J. Williams), Sarah Berry (Annie Knowby), Dan Hicks (Jake), Kassie Wesley (Bobby Joe), Ted Raimi (Possessed Henrietta), Denise Bixler (Linda), Richard Domeier (Ed Getley), John Peakes (Professor Raymond Knowby), Lou Hancock (Henrietta Knowby). 84 min.

Evil Town (1977) USA. Dir: Curtis Hanson [as Edward Collins], Larry Spiegel, Peter S. Traynor, Mardi Rustam. Scr: Robert Bassing, Richard Benson, Larry Spiegel based on a story by Royce D. Applegate. Mus: Charles Bernstein, Michael Linn. DP: Isidore Mankofsky, Bill Manning. Ed: David Blangsted, Jess Mancilla, Peter Parasheles. AD: Richard Gillis. Cast: James Keach (Christopher Fuller), Dean Jagger (Dr. Schaeffer), Robert Walker Jr. (Mike Segal), Doria Cook-Nelson (Julie), Michele Marsh (Linda), Christie Houser (Terrie), Dabbs Greer (Lyle Phelps), Lurene Tuttle (Mildred Phelps), Regis Toomey (Doc Hooper). 88 min.

Exhumed (2003) Canada. Dir/Scr/Ph/Ed: Brian Clement. Mus: Justin Hagberg. Cast: Masahiro Oyake (Ryuzo), Hiroaki Itaya (Zentaro), Bettina May (Jane Decarlo [as Claire Westby]), Moira Thomas (Vivian Von Prowe), Chelsey Arentsen (Cherry), Chantelle Adamache (Zura). 87 min.

Exquisite Corpse (2010) USA. Dir/Scr: Scott David Russell. Mus: Jonathan Licht. DP: Nikolas Smith. Ed: Matt Tegtmeier. Cast: Steve Sandvoss (Nicholas), Nicole Vicius (Sophia), Guillermo Díaz (Henry), Tessa Thompson (Liz), Larry Cedar (Dr. Waldman), David H. Lawrence (Officer Kirwin).

MONOGRAM PICTURES presents "THE FACE of MARBLE"

starring

JOHN CARRADINE

with

CLAUDIA DRAKE · ROBERT SHAYNE
MARIS WRIXON · WILLIE BEST

Directed by WILLIAM BEAUDINE
Screenplay by Michel Jacoby
Original story by William Thiele and Edmund Hartmann

The Face of Marble (1946) USA. Dir: William Beaudine. Scr: Edmund L. Hartmann, Michael Jacoby based on a story by Wilhelm Thiele. Mus: Edward J. Kay. DP: Harry Neumann. Ed: William Austin. Cast: John Carradine (Dr. Charles Randolph), Claudia Drake (Elaine Randolph), Robert Shayne (Dr. David Cochran), Maris Wrixon (Linda Sinclair), Willie Best (Shadrach), Thomas E. Jackson (Inspector Norton), Rosa Rey (Maria). 72 min.

Feeding the Masses (2004) USA. Dir: Richard Griffin. Scr: Trent Haaga. Mus: Daniel Hildreth. DP: Andrew Vellenoweth. Ed: Richard Griffin. Cast: Billy Garberina (Torch), Rachel Morris (Shelly), Patrick Cohen (Roger), Michael Propster (James). 85 min.

A Few Brains More (2012) USA. Dir: Christine Parker.

Scr: Bill Mulligan, Christine Parker. Mus: Greg Putnam. DP: Ryan Malham, Christine Parker. Cast: Emlee Vassilos (Lily), Michael Ray Williams (Jack), Edward Warner (Dead Eye), Zachary Edgerton (Smiley), Jessie Walley (Jasmine), Bill Mulligan (Doctor Versavius), Kevin Teachey (Tyrone), Paul Cardullo (John Dumas), Amber Teachey (Sylvia).

Fido (2006) Canada. Dir: Andrew Currie. Scr: Robert Chomiak, Andrew Currie, Dennis Heaton. Mus: Don MacDonald. DP: Jan Kiesser. Ed: Roger Mattiussi. PD: Rob Gray. Cast: Kesun Loder (Timmy Robinson), Alexia Fast (Cindy Bottoms), Henry Czerny (Mr. Bottoms), Billy Connolly (Fido), Aaron Brown (Roy Fraser), Brandon Olds (Stan Fraser), Jennifer Clement (Dee Dee Bottoms), Tim Blake Nelson (Mr. Theopolis), Carrie-Anne Moss (Helen Robinson), Dylan Baker (Bill Robinson). 93 min.

Fistful of Brains (2006) USA. Dir/Scr: Christine Parker. Mus: Greg Putnam. DP: Bill Mulligan, Christine Parker. Cast: Jaqueline Martini (Lily), Conrad Osborne (Jack), Edward Warner (Lazarus/Dead Eye), Darrell Parker (T.W. Earp), Wayne Bates (Pastor John), Heidi Martinuzzi (Daisy), Pericles Lewnes (Frank), Jessie Walley (Katie), Angela Giddings (Theresa). 78 min.

Flesh Freaks (2000) Canada. Dir/Scr/Ed: Conall Pendergast. Scr: Conall Pendergast. Mus: Steven Kado. DP: G. Gillard Golen. Cast: Eshe Mercer-James (Jane), Etan Muskat (Stan), Conall Pendergast (Barry [as Ronny Varno]), Erica Goldblatt (Lea). 79 min.

FleshEater (1988) USA. Dir: S. William Hinzman. Scr: S. William Hinzman, Bill Randolph. Mus: Erica Portnoy. DP: Simon Manses. Ed: S. William Hinzman, Paul McCollough. Cast: S. William Hinzman (FleshEater), John Mowod (Bob), Leslie Ann Wick (Sally), Kevin Kindlin (Ralph), Charis Acuff (Lisa), James J. Rutan (Eddie), Lisa Smith (Kim). 88 min.

Flight of the Living Dead (2007) USA. Dir: Scott Thomas. Scr: Sidney Iwanter, Mark Onspaugh, Scott Thomas. Mus: Nathan Wang. DP: Mark Eberle. Ed: Wilton Cruz. Cast: David Chisum (Truman), Kristen Kerr (Megan), Kevin J. O'Connor (Frank), Richard Tyson (Paul Judd), Erick Avari (Dr. Bennett), Derek Webster (Long Shot), Todd Babcock (Co-Pilot Randy), Siena Goines (Anna). 94 min.

Forever Dead (2007) USA. Dir/DP/Mus/Ed: Christine Parker. Scr: Bill Mulligan, Christine Parker. Mus: Greg Putnam. Cast: Bill Mulligan (Adam Dumas), Libby Lynn

(Tracy Dick), Jessie Walley (Mary Lupus), Ryan Williams (Teddy Schwartzenneger), Brian Chippewa (Todd Scout), Jaqueline Martini (Alice), Liesl Owle (Eve Lupus/Zombie Mom). 100 min.

The 4th Reich (2014) UK. Dir/Scr: Shaun Robert Smith. Mus: James Edward Barker. DP: Peter Hannan. Ed: Robert Hall. Cast: Sean Bean (Gordon), Doug Bradley (Gast), Tom Savini (Dirlewanger), Craig Conway (Smith), Simon Bamford (Kraus), Andreas Schnaas (Willhelm). 97 min.

Frankenstein's Army (2013) Czech Republic/USA. Dir: Ryan Bellgardt. Scr: Ryan Bellgardt, Josh McKamie, Andy Swanson based on characters by Mary Shelley. Mus: David S. Hamilton. DP: Josh McKamie. Ed: Andy Swanson. PD: Dustin Faust. Cast: Jordan Farris (Alan Jones), Christian Bellgardt (Igor), John Ferguson (Dr. Tanner Finski), Eric Gesecus (Frankenstein), Rett Terrell (Solomon Jones), Raychelle McDonald (Virginia), Lucas Ross (Herbert Henry Swanson), Thomas Cunningham (Robert E. Walto).

Frost Bite (2012) USA. Dir/Scr: Joe Davison. Mus: Lucas Quinn. DP: Beth Skabar. Ed: Daniel Brienza. PD: Gayle Heathrow. Cast: David Bond (Jim), Cheyenne Buchanan (Regis), Travis Busse (Corn Bread), Ben Charles (Yukon Charlie), Joe Davison (Luke), Duey Essex (Choked-out Raider), Luke Hobbs (Hills Have Eyes Raider), David Koepfinger (Joe), Cassandre Leigh (Reagan), Erik Martin (Tyler).

The Frozen Dead (1966) USA. Dir/Scr: Herbert J. Leder. Mus: Don Banks. DP: Davis Boulton. Ed: Tom Simpson. PD: Scott MacGregor. Cast: Dana Andrews (Dr. Norberg), Anna Palk (Jean Norburg), Philip Gilbert (Dr. Ted Roberts), Kathleen Breck (Elsa Tenney), Karel Stepanek (Gen. Lubeck), Basil Henson (Dr. Tirpitz), Alan Tilvern (Karl Essen), Anne Tirard (Mrs. Schmidt). 95 min.

Gallery of Horror (*Alien Massacre,* "Monster Raid" episode, 1967) USA. Dir: David L. Hewitt. Scr: David L. Hewit, Gary R. Heacock based on stories by Russ Jones. Mus: Marlin Skiles. DP: Austin McKinney. Ed: Tim Hinkle. AD: Ray Dorn. Cast: John Carradine (Narrator). 83 min.

Gallowwalkers (2013) USA/UK. Dir: Andrew Goth. Scr: Andrew Goth, Joanne Reay. Mus: Stephen Warbeck. DP: Henner Hofmann. Ed: Rudolf Buitendach, Steven Forrester. PD: Laurence Borman. Cast: Wesley Snipes (Aman), Kevin Howarth (Kansa), Riley Smith (Fabulos),

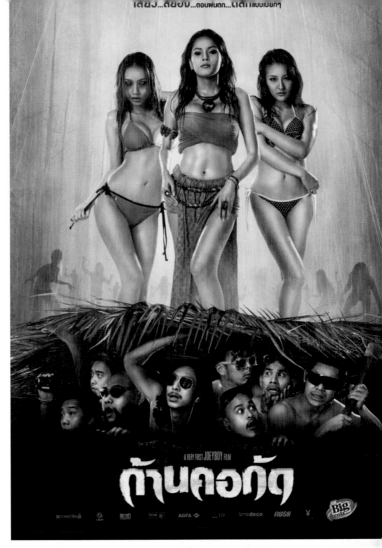

Tanit Phoenix (Angel), Simona Brhlikova (Kisscut), Steven Elder (Apollo Jones), Patrick Bergin (Marshall Gaza), Jay Grant (Slip Knot), Hector Hank (Hool), Alyssa Pridham (Sueno), Dallas Page (Skullbucket). 90 min.

Game of Thrones (television series) USA. Creators: David Benioff, D.B. Weiss based on the novels by George R.R. Martin.

Gangcore Gud (*Dead Bite,* 2011) Thailand. Dir: Apisit Opasaimlikit. Cast: Apisit Opasaimlikit (Joey Boy), Natee Aekwijit (Ui), Suranan Chumtaratorn (Tong), Kittipong Khamsat (Aim), Nattawat Srimawk (Golf). 94 min.

Gangster, Guns, & Zombies (2012) UK. Dir: Matt Mitchell. Scr: Matt Mitchell, Taliesyn Mitchell. Mus: Simon Woodgate. DP: Jamie Burr. Ed: David Davidian. Cast: Vincent Jerome (Q), Huggy Leaver (Tony), Fabrizio Santino (Crazy Steve), Cassandra Orhan (Cassie), Frank Rizzo (Pat), Charlie Rawes (Muscles), Jennie Lathan (Grandma), Simon Mathews (Danny). 88 min.

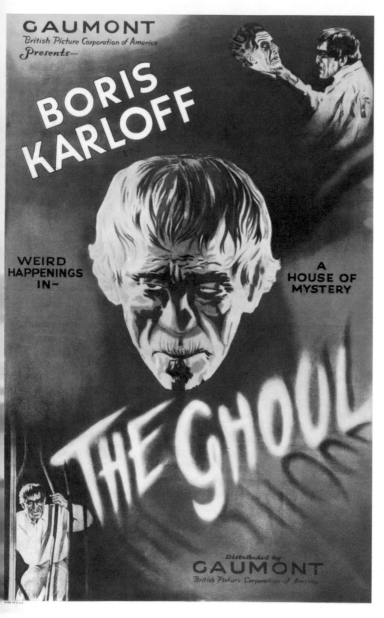

(Jack), Tim Downie (Dweeb), Todd Boyce (Morgan), Stacey Daly (Malleeta), John Jenner (Harris). 80 min.

George: A Zombie Intervention (2009) USA. Dir: J.T. Seaton. Scr: Brad Hodson, J.T. Seaton. Mus: Joel J. Richard. DP: Jason Raswant. Ed: Tyler Earring. PD: David Nicholson. Cast: Peter Stickles (Ben), Michelle Tomlinson (Sarah), Lynn Lowry (Barbra), Carlos Larkin (George), Shannon Hodson (Francine), Eric Dean (Steve), Vincent Cusimano (Roger), Adam Fox (Tom), Brian Nolan (John), Matthew Stephen Herrick (William), Angela Landis (Foxy), Victoria De Mare (Mouse). 93 min.

Germ (2013) USA. Dir/Scr: J.T. Boone, John Craddock. Mus: Siddhartha Barnhoorn. DP: Gus Sacks. Ed: Randy Paik. Cast: Marguerite Sundberg (Brooke), Michael Flores (Max), Mark Chiappone (Stu), Beth Pratt (Karen), Zoe Miller (Steph), Bernard Setaro Clark (Davidson), Jody Pucello (Cooper).

The Ghost Breakers (1940) USA. Dir: George Marshall. Scr: Walter DeLeon based on a play by Charles Goddard, Paul Dickey. Mus: Ernst Toch, Victor Young. DP: Charles Lang. Ed: Ellsworth Hoagland. AD: Hans Dreier, Robert Usher. Cast: Bob Hope (Larry Lawrence), Paulette Goddard (Mary Carter), Richard Carlson (Geoff Montgomery), Paul Lukas (Parada), Willie Best (Alex), Pedro de Cordoba (Havez), Virginia Brissac (Mother Zombie), Noble Johnson (The Zombie). 85 min.

The Ghoul (1933) USA. Dir: T. Hayes Hunter. Scr: Rupert Downing, Roland Pertwee, John Hastings Turner based on a play by Leonard Hines, Frank King. Mus: Louis Levy, Leighton Lucas. DP: Günther Krampf. Ed: Ian Dalrymple, Ralph Kemplen. AD: Alfred Junge. Cast: Boris Karloff (Henry Morlant), Cedric Hardwicke (Broughton), Ernest Thesiger (Laing), Dorothy Hyson (Betty Harlon), Anthony Bushell (Ralph Morlant), Kathleen Harrison (Kaney), Harold Huth (Aga Ben Dragore), D.A. Clarke-Smith (Mahmoud), Ralph Richardson (Nigel Hartley). 77 min.

Go Goa Gone (2013) India. Dir: Krishna D.K., Raj Nidimoru. Scr: Krishna D.K, Kunal Khemu, Sita Menon. Raj Nidimoru, Raja Sen. Mus: Jigar, Sachin. DP: Dan Macarthur, Lukasz Pruchnik. Ed: Arindam Ghatak. PD: Clara Álvarez. Cast: Saif Ali Khan (Boris), Kunal Khemu (Hardik), Vir Das (Luv), Anand Tiwari (Bunny), Puja Gupta (Luna), Hardik Malaviya (Hardik). 111 min.

Gore Whore (1994) USA. Dir/Scr: Hugh Gallagher. Cast: Audrey Street (Dawn), Brady Debussey (Chase),

Garden of the Dead (*Tomb of the Undead*, 1972) USA. Dir: John Hayes. Scr: Daniel Cady, Jack Matcha. Mus: Jaime Mendoza-Nava. DP: Paul Hipp. AD: Earl Marshall. Cast: Philip Kenneally (Warden), Duncan McLeod (Dr. Saunders [as Duncan McCloud]), John Dullaghan (Sgt. Burns), John Dennis (Jablonski), Marland Proctor (Paul Johnson), Tony Vorno (Mitchell). 59 min.

The Gatekeeper (2008) UK. Dir/Scr: Darren Ripley. DP: Graham Horder. Ed: Viv Mainwaring. Cast: Craig Kelly

D'Lana Tunnell (Pat), Paul Woodard (Witman). 89 min.

Gou hun jiang tou (*Revenge of the Zombies,* 1976) Hong Kong. Dir: Meng Hua Ho [as Horace Mengwa]. Scr: Kuang NiMus: Yung-Yu Chen. DP: Hui-chi Tsao. Ed: Hsing-lung Chiang. PD: Ching-Shen Chen. Cast: Lung Ti, Ni Tien, Lili Li, Feng Lin. 89 min.

A Grave for Corpses (2008) UK. Dir/Scr/Ph/Ed: Steven N. Sibley. Cast: William Scott Johnson (Davro), Ken Mood (Axel Falcon), Chris Moad (Wayne), Richard Thorn (Zombie), Lee Nicholson (Lamburto), Richard Scott (Necromancer), Cain Thomason (Partner). 89 min.

Grave Mistake (2008) USA. Dir/Scr/Ed: Shawn Darling. Cast: Seth Darling (Alex King/Zombie), Wendy Andrews (Monica Dickinson), James Blackburn (Mike Shaw), Stephen W. Eckles (Karl King/Zombie), David Lionbarger (Phil Baker/Richard Long). 90 min.

Grave of the Zombie Antelope (2013) USA. Dir/Scr: A.D. Gerhardt. DP: Zander Gerhardt. Ed: Michael Yingst. Cast: Lynette Zumo (Geraldine), Tyler Kodet (Tyler), Rebecca Cornwallis (Danielle), Tiffany Bishop (Jessica), Mark Serry (Mr. Martin), Danielle Apolo (Mrs. Martin), Buti Buckcha (Professor Lawal). 92 min.

Grave Reality (2013) USA. Dir/Scr/Ed: Oliver Tosh. Mus: Jason Hawkins, Kevin MacLeod, Gunnar Valdimarsson. PD: John Elias. Cast: Erika Avery (Groupie), Elijah Beckett (Charlie), Kelli Cayman Cozlin (Rachel), Kenny Forthun (Metal Head), Peter Harper (Franklin), Jason Hawkins (Dean), Elaine Hoxie (Kirsten). 75 min.

Hard Rock Zombies (1985) USA. Dir: Krishna Shah. Scr: David Allen Ball, Krishna Shah. Mus: Paul Sabu. DP: Tom Richmond. Ed: Amit Bose. AD: Cynthia Sowder. Cast: E.J. Curse (Jessie), Sam Mann (Bobby), Lisa Toothman (Elsa), Jennifer Coe (Cassie), Ted Wells (Ron), Jack Bliesener (Hitler), Richard Vidan (Sheriff), Phil Fondacaro (Mickey). 98 min.

Harold's Going Stiff (2011) UK. Dir/Scr/Ed: Keith Wright. Mus: Tom Kane. Cast: Stan Rowe (Harold Gimble), Sarah Spencer (Penny Rudge), Andy Pandini (Jon Grayson), Phil Gascoyne (Norbert Shuttleworth), Lee Thompson (Mike Jacksmith), Richard Harrison (Colin), Liz Simmons (June Peterson), Michaela Anne Rowe (Grace Mathews). 77 min.

Heaven Is Hell (2012) USA. Dir/Ed: Mike Meyer, Chris Sato. Scr: Mike Meyer. Mus: Eric D. Morrison. DP: Jason Kraynek. Ed: Michael Tsirtsis. Cast: Lindsey Marks (Faith), Christopher Marcum (Judas), Ethan Henry (Zerach), Mark ViaFranco (Jesus), Jack Schultz (Lucifer), Danny Heeter (Jake), Tierza Scaccia (Junia), David Bertucci (Thomas). 115 min.

Hellgate (1990) USA. Dir: William A. Levey. Scr: Michael O'Rourke. Mus: Barry Fasman, Dana Walden. DP: Peter Palmér. Ed: Mark Baard, Chris Barnes, Max Lemon. Cast: Ron Palillo (Matt), Abigail Wolcott (Josie), Carel Trichardt (Lucas), Petrea Curran (Pam), Evan J. Klisser (Chuck). 91 min.

Hide, Creep (2004) USA. Dir: Chuck Hartsell, Chance Shirley. Scr: Chance Shirley. Mus: Eric McGinty. DP: Robert Rugan. AD: Michael Benson. Cast: Chuck Hartsell (Chuck), Michael Shelton (Michael/Lee), Kyle Holman (Keith), Chris Garrison (Ted), Eric McGinty (Ned). 85 min.

Honky Holocaust (2013) USA. Dir/Scr/Ed: Paul McAlarney. DP: Nick Norrman. Ed: Thomas Delcarpio, Nick Norrman. AD: Thomas Delcarpio. Cast: Maria Natapov (Kendra Manson), Lucas Fleming (Dan Masucci), Krisoula Varoudakis (Fiona), Constantine Taylor (Lucius), Blake Rickerson (Mayor), Nick Caliendo (Judd). 110 min.

Hood of the Living Dead (2005) USA. Dir/Scr: Eduardo Quiroz, Jose Quiroz. Cast: Chris Angelo (Scott), Jaysun Barr (Guy in Park), Johanna Christensen (Josie), Al Daniels (Coroner #2), Brandon Daniels (Jermaine). 90 min.

A FILM BY KEITH WRIGHT
HAROLD'S GOING STIFF

FRISSON FILM PRESENTS HAROLD'S GOING STIFF
STARRING STAN ROWE SARAH SPENCER
PHILIP GASCOYNE ANDY PANDINI
MUSIC TOM KANE PRODUCER RICHARD GUY
WRITTEN & DIRECTED BY KEITH WRIGHT
© FRISSON FILM 2011

frisson film

La Horde (2009) France. Dir: Benjamin Rocher, Yannick Dahan. Scr: Arnaud Bordas, Yannick Dahan, Stephane Moissakis, Benjamin Rocher. Mus: Christopher Lennertz. DP: Julien Meurice. Ed: Dimitri Amar. Cast: Claude Perron (Aurore), Jean-Pierre Martins (Ouessem), Eriq Ebouaney (Adewale Markudi), Aurélien Recoing (Jimenez), Doudou Masta (Bola Markudi), Antoine Oppenheim (Tony), Jo Prestia (José), Yves Pignot (René), Adam Pengsawang (Le Tchèque). 86 min.

The Horror of Party Beach (1964) USA. Dir: Del Tenney. Scr: Richard Hilliard, Lou Binder, Ronald Gianettino. Mus: Wilford L. Holcombe. DP: Richard Hilliard. Ed: Gary Youngman, Leonard De Munde, David Simpson. AD: Robert Verberkmoes. Cast: John Scott (Hank Green), Alice Lyon (Elaine Gavin), Allan Laurel (Dr. Gavin), Eulabelle Moore (Eulabelle), Marilyn Clarke

(Tina), Agustin Mayor (Mike), Damon Kebroyd (Lt. Wells). 78 min.

Hot Wax Zombies on Wheels (1999) USA. Dir: Michael Roush. Scr: Elizabeth Bergholz. DP: Mark Combs. Ed: Kenn Kashima. PD: Robert E. Poe. Cast: Jill Miller (Sharon), Gwen Somers (Yvonne Wayne), Trevor Lovell (Sven), Jon Briddell (Mick), Kimberly St. John (Carrie), Renee Stewart (Martin), Randall St. George (Obadiah). 90 min.

House of the Dead (2003) USA/Germany/Canada. Dir: Uwe Boll. Scr: Dave Parker, Mark A. Altman. DP: Mathias Neumann. Ed: David M. Richardson. Cast: Jonathan Cherry (Rudy), Tyron Leitso (Simon), Clint Howard (Salish), Ona Grauer (Alicia), Ellie Cornell (Casper), Will Sanderson (Greg), Enuka Okuma (Karma), Kira Clavell (Liberty), Sonya Salomaa (Cynthia), Michael Eklund (Hugh), David Palffy (Castillo), Jürgen Prochnow (Kirk), Erica Durance (Johanna). 90 min.

House of the Dead 2 (2005) USA. Dir: Michael Hurst. Scr: Mark A. Altman, Michael Roesch, Peter Scheerer. Mus: Joe Kraemer. DP: Raymond Stella. Ed: Joseph Gutowski. PD: Denise Pizzini. Cast: Emmanuelle Vaugier (Alexandra Morgan), Ed Quinn (Ellis), Sticky Fingaz (Dalton), Steve Monroe (O'Conner), Victoria Pratt (Henson), James Parks (Bart), Dan Southworth (Nakagawa). 95 min.

Humans VS Zombies (2011) USA. Dir/Scr: Brian T. Jaynes. Scr: Devan Sagliani. Mus: Maigin Blank. DP: François Frizat. Ed: Justin Purser. PD: Matthew Englebert. Cast: Christine Bently (Megan), Cody Callahan (Chris), David Blackwell (Dr. Alan Bridgman), Chip Joslin (Brad), Frederic Doss (Frank). 93 min.

Hysterical (1983) USA. Dir: Chris Bearde. Scr: Bill Hudson, Brett Hudson, Mark Hudson, Trace Johnston. Mus: Bob Alciva,. Robert O. Ragland. DP: Thomas Del Ruth. Ed: Stanley Frazen. Cast: Bill Hudson (Frederic Lansing/Casper), Mark Hudson (Dr. Paul Batton), Brett Hudson (Fritz), Cindy Pickett (Kate), Richard Kiel (Captain Howdy), Julie Newmar (Venetia), Robert Donner (Ralph), Murray Hamilton (Mayor), Clint Walker (Sheriff), Franklyn Ajaye (Leroy), Charlie Callas (Dracula). 87 min.

I Walked with a Zombie (1943) USA. Dir: Jacques Tourneur. Scr: Curt Siodmakand Ardel Wray based on a story by Inez Wallace. Mus: Roy Webb. DP: J. Roy Hunt. Ed: Mark Robson. AD: Albert S. D'Agostino, Walter E. Keller. Cast: James Ellison (Wesley Rand), Frances Dee

(Betsy Connell), Tom Conway (Paul Holland), Edith Barrett (Mrs. Rand), James Bell (Dr. Maxwell), Christine Gordon (Jessica Holland), Theresa Harris (Alma, Maid), Sir Lancelot (Calypso Singer), Darby Jones (Carrefour), Jeni Le Gon (Dancer). 69 min.

I Was a Teenage Zombie (1987) USA. Dir: John Elias Michalakis. Scr: James Aviles Martin, Steve McKoy, George Seminara. DP: Peter Lewnes. Ed: John Elias Michalakis. AD: Dora Katsoulogiannakis. Cast: Michael Rubin (Dan Wake), Steve McCoy (Mussolini), George Seminara (Gordy), Robert C. Sabin (Chuckie), Peter Bush (Rosencrantz), Allen Rickman (Lieberman). 90 min.

I Was a Zombie for the F.B.I. (1982) USA. Dir/Scr: Marius Penczner. DP: Rick Dupree. Cast: Larry Raspberry (Ace Evans), John Gillick (Bart Brazzo), James Raspberry (Rex Armstrong). 105 min.

I, Zombie: The Chronicles of Pain (1998) USA. Dir/Scr/Mus: Andrew Parkinson. DP: Jason Shepherd. Ed: Gary Hewson, Andrew Parkinson. Cast: Ellen Softley (Sarah), Dean Sipling (David), Claire Griffin (Sarah's Friend), Kate Thorougood (Prostitute). 79 min.

Idle Hands (1999) USA. Dir: Rodman Flender. Scr: Terri Hughes, Ron Milbauer. Mus: Graeme Revell. DP: Christopher Baffa. Ed: Stephen E. Rivkin. Cast: Devon Sawa (Anton Tobias), Seth Green (Mick), Elden Henson Pnub), Jessica Alba (Molly), Vivica A. Fox (Debi LeCure), Christopher Hart (the Hand), Jack Noseworthy (Randy). 92 min.

In the Flesh (2013, television series, 3 episodes) UK. Dir: Jonny Campbell. Tel: Dominic Mitchell. Mus: Edmund Butt. DP: Tony Slater-Ling. Ed: Jamie Pearson. PD: Sami Khan. Cast: Luke Newberry (Kieren Walker), Emily Bevan (Amy Dyer), Harriet Cains (Jem Walker), Steve Cooper (Steve Walker), Kenneth Cranham (Vicar Oddie), Marie Critchley (Sue Walker), Juliet Ellis (Patty Lancaster), Steve Evets (Bill Macy), Steve Garti (Duncan Lancaster), Karen Henthorn (Janet Macy), Sandra Huggett (Shirley Wilson). Episodes: 55 min.

Incubo sulla città contaminata (*Nightmare City*, 1980) Italy/Spain. Dir: Umberto Lenzi. Scr: Antonio Cesare Corti, Luis María Delgado, Piero Regnoli. Mus: Stelvio Cipriani. DP: Hans Burman. Ed: Daniele Alabiso. AD: Mario Molli. Cast: Hugo Stiglitz (Dean Miller), Laura Trotter (Dr. Anna Miller), Maria Rosaria Omaggio (Sheila Holmes), Francisco Rabal (Maj. Warren Holmes), Sonia Viviani (Cindy), Eduardo Fajardo (Dr. Kramer), Stefania

D'Amario (Jessica Murchison), Mel Ferrer (Gen. Murchison), Umberto Lenzi (News Reporter). 88 min.

Infected (2013) USA. Dir: Glenn Ciano. Scr: Glenn Ciano, Robert Rotondo Jr. Mus: Eric Masunaga. DP: Ben DeLuca. Ed: Jedidiah Burdick, Tom DeNucci, Kathryn E. Prescott. PD: Robert Rotondo Jr. Cast: Christy Romano (Kelly), Michael Madsen (Louis Hartley), William Forsythe (Dr. Edward Dennehey), Johnny Cicco (Seth), Tracey Sheldon (Call Girl), Kristi Lynn (Infected), Tom DeNucci (Andrew Hartley), Michael Nicolosi (Matt), Carlyne Fournier (Pregnant Zombie), Tom Paolino (Sera's Father). 95 min.

Insane in the Brain (2007) USA. Dir/Scr/Ed: Chad Hendricks. DP: Bernardo Santana. Cast: John W. Sloan (Sloan), Rhynell Brumfield (Goldie), Bernicia Womack (Shay Shay), JoKisha Brown (Cookie). 78 min.

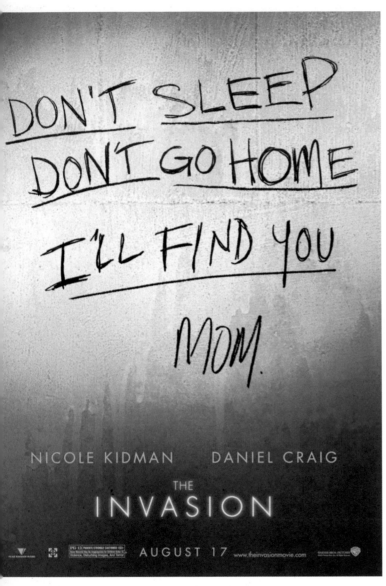

Haworth. Cast: Kevin McCarthy (Dr. Miles J. Bennell), Dana Wynter (Becky Driscoll), Larry Gates (Dr. Dan Kauffman), King Donovan (Jack Belicec), Carolyn Jones (Theodora Belicec), Jean Willes (Nurse Sally Withers), Ralph Dumke (Police Chief Nick Grivett), Virginia Christine (Wilma Lentz), Tom Fadden (Uncle Ira Lentz), Kenneth Patterson (Stanley Driscoll), Guy Way (Officer Sam Janzek). 80 min.

Invasion of the Body Snatchers (1978) USA. Dir: Philip Kaufman. Scr: W.D. Richter based on the novel by Jack Finney. Mus: Denny Zeitlin. DP: Michael Chapman. Ed: Douglas Stewart. PD: Charles Rosen. Cast: Donald Sutherland (Matthew Bennell), Brooke Adams (Elizabeth Driscoll), Jeff Goldblum (Jack Bellicec), Veronica Cartwright (Nancy Bellicec), Leonard Nimoy (Dr. David Kibner), Art Hindle (Dr. Geoffrey Howell, DDS), Lelia Goldoni (Katherine Hendley), Kevin McCarthy (Dr. Miles J. Bennell), Don Siegel (Taxi Driver). 115 min.

Invisible Invaders (1959) USA. Dir: Edward L. Cahn. Scr: Samuel Newman. Mus: Paul Dunlap. DP: Maury Gertsman. AD: William Glasgow. Cast: John Agar (Maj. Bruce Jay), Jean Byron (Phyllis Penner), Philip Tonge (Dr. Adam Penner), Robert Hutton (Dr. John Lamont), John Carradine (Dr. Karol Noymann), Hal Torey (The Farmer), Paul Langton (Lt. Gen. Stone), Eden Hartford (WAAF Secretary). 67 min.

Jennifer's Body (2009) USA. Dir: Karyn Kusama. Scr: Diablo Cody. Mus: Stephen Barton, Theodore Shapiro. DP: M. David Mullen. Ed: Plummy Tucker. PD: Arvinder Grewal. Cast: Megan Fox (Jennifer), Amanda Seyfried (Needy), Johnny Simmons (Chip), Adam Brody (Nikolai), Sal Cortez (Chas), Ryan Levine (Mick). 102 min.

Jigoku Koshien (*Battlefield Baseball*, 2003) Japan. Dir: Yudai Yamaguchi. Scr: Isao Kiriyama, Ryuichi Takatsu, Yudai Yamaguchi based on the manga by Gatarô Man. Mus: Daisuke Yano. Ed: Shûichi Kakesu. 87 min.

The Invasion (2007) USA/Australia. Dir: Oliver Hirschbiegel, James McTeigue. Scr: David Kajganich based on the novel by Jack Finney. Mus: John Ottman. DP: Rainer Klausmann. Ed: Hans Funck, Joel Negron. PD: Jack Fisk. Cast: Nicole Kidman (Carol Bennell), Daniel Craig (Ben Driscoll), Jeremy Northam (Tucker Kaufman), Jackson Bond (Oliver), Jeffrey Wright (Dr. Stephen Galeano), Veronica Cartwright (Wendy Lenk), Josef Sommer (Dr. Henryk Belicec). 99 min.

Invasion of the Body Snatchers (1956) USA. Dir: Don Siegel. Scr: Daniel Mainwaring, Richard Collins based on the novel by Jack Finney. Mus: Carmen Dragon. DP: Ellsworth Fredericks. Ed: Robert S. Eisen. PD: Ted

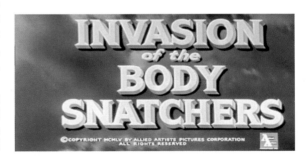

The Jitters (1989) USA/Japan. Dir: John Fasano. Scr: Sonoko Kondo, Jeff McKay. Mus: Tom Borton, Daniel Linck. DP: Paul Mitchnick. Ed: John Fasano. Cast: Sal Viviano (Michael Derrick), Marilyn Tokuda (Alice Lee), Randy Atmadja (Frank Lee), James Hong (Tony Yang Sr.), Doug Silberstein (Leach), Frank Dietz (Rat), John Quincy Lee (Tony Yang Jr.). 80 min.

Johnny Sunshine Maximum Violence (2008) USA. Dir: Matt Yeager. Scr: Sean-Michael Argo. Mus: Dan Robinson. DP: Leo Smith. Ed: Eric Halsell, Leo Smith. Cast: Ian Argo (Dennis), Sean-Michael Argo (Raid), Shey Bland (Johnny Sunshine), Casey Halsell (Dez), Eric Halsell (Max), Jason Hurley (Zombie #1), John P. McCauley (Stein). 78 min.

Joshikyôei hanrangun (*Undead Pool*, 2007) Japan. Dir: Kôji Kawano. Scr: Satoshi Ôwada. Mus: Hideto Takematsu. DP: Mitsuaki Fujimoto. Cast: Sasa Handa (Aki), Yuria Hidaka (Sayaka), Ayumu Tokitô (Mariko), Mizuka Arai, Hiromitsu Kiba, Hidetomo Nishida, Sakae Yamazaki. 78 min.

Juan de los Muertos (2011) Cuba. Dir/Scr: Alejandro Brugués. Mus: Julio de la Rosa. DP: Carles Gusi. Ed: Mercedes Cantero. Art Dir: Derubín Jácome. Cast: Alexis Díaz de Villegas (Juan), Jorge Molina (Lazaro), Andrea Duro (Camila), Andros Perugorría (Vladi California), Jazz Vilá (La China), Eliecer Ramírez (El Primo), Blanca Rosa Blanco (Sara), Susana Pous (Lucía), Antonio Dechent (Father Jones), Eslinda Núñez (Berta), Elsa Camp (Yiya). 92 min.

Junk: Shiryô-gari (*Battlefield Baseball*, 2000) Japan. Dir/Scr: Atsushi Muroga. Mus: Goro Yasukawa. DP: Takanobu Kato. Cast: Nobuyuki Asano (Jun), Shū Ehara (Akira), Tate Gouta (Ramon), Yuji Kishimoto (Nakada), Miwa (Kyôko/Zombie Queen). 83 min.

Karla contra los jaguares (1974) Mexico. Dir/DP: Juan Manuel Herrera. Scr: Sergio Álvarez Acosta. Mus: Albert Lévy. Cast: Marcela López Rey (Karla), Gilberto Puentes, María Eugenia Dávila, Wayne Geroloman, King Bryner. 71 min.

Khun krabii hiiroh (*Sars Wars*, 2004) Thailand. Dir: Taweewat Wantha. Scr: Sommai Lertulan, Kuanchun Phemyad, Taweewat Wantha, Adirek Wattaleela. DP: Art Srithongkul. Ed: Doctor Head. PD: Rachata Panpayak. Cast: Suthep Po-ngam (Master Thep), Supakorn Kitsuwon (Khun Krabii), Phintusuda Tunphairao (Liu), Lena Christensen (Dr. Diana), Andrew Biggs (Sars zombie). 95 min.

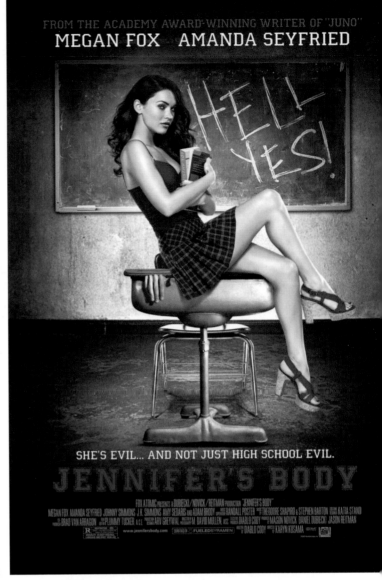

Killing Spree (1987) USA. Dir/Scr: Tim Ritter. Mus: Perry Monroe. DP: Mark L. Pederson. Ed: Robert Williams. Cast: Asbestos Felt (Tom Russo), Courtney Lercara (Leeza Russo), Raymond Carbone (Ben Seltzer), Bruce Paquette (Delivery Man), Joel D. Wynkoop (TV Repairman), Kieran Turner (Lawn Man). 88 min.

King of the Zombies (1941) USA. Dir: Jean Yarbrough. Scr: Edmond Kelso. Mus: Edward J. Kay. DP: Mack Stengler. Ed: Richard C. Currier. AD: Charles Clague. Cast: Dick Purcell (James McCarthy), Joan Woodbury (Barbara Winslow), Mantan Moreland (Jeff Jackson), Henry Victor (Dr. Miklos Sangre), John Archer (Bill

Summers), Patricia Stacey (Alyce Sangre), Guy Usher (Adm. Arthur Wainwright), Madame Sul-Te-WanTahama (the Cook, High Priestess), James Davis (Lazarus, a Zombie), Laurence Criner (Dr. Couillie). 67 min.

Kiss Daddy Goodbye (*Revenge of the Zombie*, 1981) USA. Dir: Patrick Regan. Scr: Alain Silver, Patrick Regan, Ronald Abrams, Mary Stewart. Mus: David Spear. DP: Peter Jensen [as George Bakken]. Ed: Glenn Erickson. Cast: Fabian Forte (Deputy Tom Blanchard), Marilyn Burns (Nora Dennis), Jon Cedar (Wally Stanton), Marvin Mille (Bill Morris), Chester Grimes (Snake, Biker Gang Leader), Jed Mills (Jesse, Biker), Gay French (Nicky, Biker Chick)), Robert Dryer (Billy, Biker), Bill Randa (Guy Nicholas), Nell Regan (Beth Nicholas), Patrick Regan III (Michael Nicholas). 92 min.

Knight of the Dead (2013) UK. Dir/DP: Mark Atkins. Scr: Jeffrey Giles, Mark Atkins. DP: Mark Atkins. Ed: Mark Atkins, Orlando Ordonez, Erica Steele. PD: Carl Waters. Cast: Feth Greenwood (Leuthar), Vivien Vilela (Badriyah), Lee Bennett (Anzo), Dylan Jones (Bjorn), Jason Beeston (Raphael), Alan Calton (Gabriel), George

McCluskey (Calon), Alf Thompson (Cybron), Dennis Carr (Priest), Eva Morgan (Gwendolyn), Kevin Smith (Big Zombie). 82 min.

Knight of the Living Dead (2005) Iceland. Dir/DP: Bjarni Gautur. Scr: Höddi Björnsen, Bjarni Gautur. Mus: Changer, Einar Darri, Doghorse, Hammer-Craft, Haukur Möller. Ed: Siggi Jökull, Donald Wilkinsen. Cast: Höddi Björnsen (The Knight/Thomas), Andri Kjartan (The Viking/Jónas), Steinar Geirdal (Dean), Bjarni Gautur (Clark), Viktor Aron (Charlie), Andri Valur (Gary). 86 min.

Kung bakit dugo ang kulay ng gabi (*Night of the Zombies*, 1973) Philippines. Dir: Celso Ad. Castillo. Scr: Celso Ad. Castillo, Mary Abelardo. Mus: Jose Mari Chan. DP: Loreto Isleta. Cast: Rita Gomez, Celia Rodriguez, George Estregan, Liza Lorena, Ronaldo Valdez, Alona Alegre. 69 min.

Kyûketsu Shôjo tai Shôjo Furanken (*Vampire Girl vs. Frankenstein Girl*, 2009) Japan. Dir: Yoshihiro Nishimura, Naoyuki Tomomatsu. Scr: Naoyuki Tomomatsu based on the manga by Shungiku Uchida. Mus: Kou Nakagawa. DP: Shu G. Momose. Ed: Yoshihiro Nishimura. PD: Nori Fukuda. Cast: Yukie Kawamura (Monami/Vampire Girl), Takumi Saitô (Jyogon Mizushima), Eri Otoguro (Keiko/Frankenstein Girl), Sayaka Kametani (Midori), Jiji Bû (Igor). 84 min.

Le lac des morts vivants (*La Nuit des Traquées, Zombie Lake*, 1981) France/Spain. Dir: Jean Rollin [as J.A. Laser]. Scr: Julián Esteban [as Julius Valery], Jesús Franco [as A.L. Mariaux]. Mus: Daniel White. DP: Max Monteillet. Ed: Claude Gros, María Luisa Soriano. Cast: Howard Vernon (The Mayor), Pierre-Marie Escourrou (German Soldier), Anouchka (Helena), Antonio Mayans [Robert Forster] (Morane), Nadine Pascal (Helena's Mother), Youri Radionow (Chanac). 90 min.

Ladrones de tumbas (*Grave Robbers*, 1990) Mexico. Dir: Rubén Galindo Jr. Scr: Rubén Galindo Jr., Carlos Valdemar. Mus: Jon Michael Bischof, René Castillo, Ricardo Galindo. DP: Antonio de Anda. Ed: Antonio López Zepeda. Cast: Fernando Almada (Capt. Lopez), Edna Bolkan (Olivia), Erika Buenfil (Rebeca de la Huerta), Ernesto Laguardia Manolo (Andrade), María Rebeca (Diana). 87 min.

Land of the Dead (2005) USA/Canada/France. Dir/Scr: George A. Romero. Mus: Reinhold Heil, Johnny Klimek. DP: Miroslaw Baszak. Ed: Michael Doherty. PD: Arvinder Grewal. Cast: Simon Baker (Riley Denbo), John Leguizamo (Cholo DeMora), Dennis Hopper

(Kaufman), Asia Argento (Slack), Robert Joy (Charlie), Eugene Clark (Big Daddy), Joanne Boland (Pretty Boy). 93 min.

The Last Flesh & Blood Show (2012) USA. Dir/Scr/DP/Ed: Scout Tafoya. Cast: Stephie Ulm, Jack Farrell, Taryn Hipp, Scout Tafoya, Lina Pearson, Becca Savana. 125 min.

The Last Man(s) on Earth (2012) USA. Dir/Scr: Aaron Hultgren. Mus: Kevin G. Lee. DP: Eric Dove. Cast: Charan Prabhakar (Kaduche), Brady Bluhm (Wynn), Darin Southam (Marcus), Andrea Ciliberti (Violet), Rick Macy (Oracle), Elizabeth Knowelden (Violet the Intern Scientist). 86 min.

Last of the Living (2009) New Zealand. Dir/Scr/Ed: Logan McMillan. Mus: Ben Edwards, Kurt Preston. DP: Kirk Pflaum. Cast: Morgan Williams (Morgan), Robert Faith (Johnny), Ashleigh Southam (Ash), Stacey Stevens (Zombie Girl), Becky Truscott (Sandy). 88 min.

Last Rites (2006) USA. Dir: Duane Stinnett. Scr: Duane Stinnett, Krissann Shipley based on a story by Patrick Gleason, Todd Ovcirk. Mus: Ceiri Torjussen. DP: Yasu Tanida. Ed: Keith Henderson. PD: Brian Ollman. Cast: Noel Gugliemi (Caesar), Howard Alonzo (Jerome), Ethan Ednee (Mac T), Ryan Hanna King (Snake Dog), Dayana Jamine (Latasha). 90 min.

Last Rites of the Dead (*Zombies Anonymous*, 2006) USA. Dir/Scr/Ed: Marc Fratto. Mus: Andy Ascolese, Marc Fratto, Frank Garfi. Cast: Gina Ramsden (Angela), Joshua Nelson (Josh), Mary Jo Verruto (Solstice), Shannon Moore (Chris), JoCastia Bryan (Frankie), Kelly Ray (Melinda), Constantine Taylor (Malcolm), J. Scott Green (Richie), Christa McNamee (Commandant). 118 min.

The Last Zombi Hunter (2010) UK. Dir/Scr/Ph/Ed: Steven N. Sibley. Mus: Alex Campbell. Cast: Chris J. Allan (Zombie), Cate Beattie (Zombie), Simon Craig (Nazi Zombie), Tony Hickson (William Scott Johnson (Davro), Lloyd Kaufman (Uncle Lloydy), Ken Mood (Axel Falcon). 75 min.

The Laughing Dead (1989) USA. Dir/Scr/Mus: Somtow Sucharitkul. DP: David Boyd. Ed: Rose Anne Weinstein. PD: Diane Hughes, Phillip Vasels. Cast: Tim Sullivan (Father O' Sullivan), Wendy Webb (Tessie), Premika Eaton (Laurie), Patrick Roskowick (Ivan), Larry Kagen (Wilbur). 103 min.

Life Is Dead (2012) Japan. Dir: Kôsuke Hishinuma. Scr: Kôsuke Hishinuma based on the manga by Tomohiro Koizumi. DP: Tomohiko Tsuji. PD: Jun Terao. Cast: Shintarô Akutsu, Atsushi Arai, Aya Enjôji, Rino Higa, Ryôsuke Kawamura, Susumu Kobayashi.

A Little Bit Zombie (2012) Canada. Dir: Casey Walker. Scr: Trevor Martin, Christopher Bond. DP: Kevin C.W. Wong. Ed: Michael P. Mason. PD: Peter Mihaichuk. Cast: Kristopher Turner (Steve), Crystal Lowe (Tina), Shawn Roberts (Craig), Kristen Hager (Sarah), Stephen McHattie (Max), Emilie Ullerup (Penelope Pendleton), George Buza (Capt'n Cletus), Robert Maillet (Terry "Terror" Thompkins), Neil Whitely (The Professor), Melanie Rainville (Bearded Lady). 87 min.

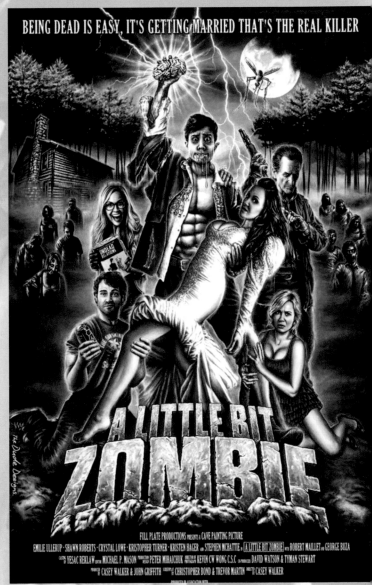

Living A Zombie Dream (1996) USA. Dir/Scr: Todd Reynolds. Mus: Clark Carter. DP: Steve Cochran. Ed: Steve Cochran, Ronnie Sortor. Cast: Amon Elsey (Man), Michelle White (Girlfriend/Other Zombie), Mike Smith (Brother/Zombie), Frank Alexander (Psycho/Zombie Lord), Ronnie Sortor, Steve Cochran (Workers), Lacramioara (Girl on the Street/Other Zombie), Todd Reynolds (2x4 Man), Mike Strain Jr. (Trash Man/Other Zombie), Dan Rowland (Yellow Zombie), Chris Cochran (Leg Zombie), Brian Streible (Big Zombie), Paul Rousselot (Weird Zombie), Lora Robinson (Rocking Zombie). 69 min.

Machine Head (2000) USA. Dir/Scr: Leonard Murphy, Michael Patrick. Cast: Jessica Bartz (Little Girl), Ginger Blanchatt (Principal Brown), Rich Cowden (Machine Head). 79 min.

The Mad Ghoul (1943) USA. Dir: James P. Hogan. Scr: Brenda Weisberg, Paul Gangelin based on a story by Hans Kraly. DP: Milton R. Krasner. Ed: Milton Carruth. AD: John B. Goodman, Martin Obzina. Cast: David Bruce (Ted Allison), Evelyn Ankers (Isabel Lewis), George Zucco (Dr. Alfred Morris), Robert Armstrong (Ken McClure), Turhan Bey (Eric Iverson), Milburn Stone (Macklin), Andrew Tombes (Eagan), Rose Hobart (Della). 65 min.

The Man They Could Not Hang (1939) USA. Dir: Nick Grinde. Scr: Karl Brown, George Wallace Syre, Leslie T. White. Mus: Morris Stoloff. DP: Benjamin H. Kline. Ed: William A. Lyon. Cast: Boris Karloff (Dr. Henryk Savaard), Lorna Gray (Janet Savaard), Robert Wilcox ("Scoop" Foley), Roger Pryor (District Attorney Drake), Don Beddoe (Police Lt. Shane), Ann Doran (Betty Crawford). 64 min.

Mark of the Astro-Zombies (2002) USA. Dir/Scr: Ted V. Mikels. DP: Siria Tena. Cast: Sean Morelli (Jeff LanCaster), Tura Satana (Malvira Satana), Liz Renay (Crystal Collins), Brinke Stevens (Cindy Natale), Anton Funtek (Zekith), Ted V. Mikels (Dr. Mikacevich), Donna Hamblin (Laura), Volmar Franz (Dr. Randolph West). 86 min.

Masters of Horror (2005, television series) USA. Creator: Mick Garris. "Dance of the Dead" Dir: Tobe Hooper. Tel: Richard Christian Matheson based on the story by Richard Matheson. Cast: Robert Englund (MC), Jessica Lowndes (Peggy). "Homecoming" Dir: Joe Dante. Scr: Sam Hamm based on a story by Dale Bailey. Cast: Thea Gill (Jane), Jon Tenney (David Murch).

Meat Market (2000) USA/Canada. Dir/Ed: Brian Clement. Scr: Brian Clement based on a story by Nick Sheehan, Tania Willard. Mus: Justin Hagberg. Cast: Bettina May (Argenta [as Claire Westby]), Paul Pedrosa (Shahrokh), Alison Therriault (Nemesis), Teresa Simon (Valeria). 90 min.

Meat Market 2 (2001) USA/Canada. Dir/Scr/Ed: Brian Clement. Mus: Justin Hagberg. Cast: Bettina May (Argenta [as Claire Westby]), Alison Therriault (Nemesis), Stephan Eng (Ferriden), Terra Thomsen (Lt. Janet Hapsburg), Rob Nesbitt (Bill Wilhelm), Chuck Depape (Dr. Gehlen). 80 min.

Midget Zombie Takeover (2013) USA. Dir/Scr: Glenn Berggoetz. DP: Orion Metzger. Ed: Erik Lassi. Cast: Kristi McKay (Amanda), Matt "Goose" Goosherst (Billy), Kedryn Carpenter (Maggie), Daniel G. Cramer (Steve), Cassandra Crawford (Molly), Anita Nicole Brown (Katie), Brian Johnson Jr. (Sam), Jayson L. Hicks (Tony), Cody Strack (Randy), Jonathan Hodges (Crazy Guy), Travis Greene, Jewell Kurtz, Kristen Tobey (Zombies). 72 min.

The Midnight Hour (1985) USA. Dir: Jack Bender. Scr: William Bleich. Mus: Brad Fiedel, Philip Giffin. DP:

BORIS KARLOFF in THE MAN THEY COULD NOT HANG

WEIRD! HORRIFYING! FASCINATING!

with LORNA GRAY ROBERT WILCOX ROGER PRYOR

Screen play by KARL BROWN Directed by NICK GRINDE

A COLUMBIA PICTURE

Rexford L. Metz. Ed: David A. Simmons. PD: Charles L. Hughes. Cast: Lee Montgomery (Phil Grenville), Shari Belafonte (Melissa Cavender), LeVar Burton (Vinnie Davis), Peter DeLuise (Mitch Crandall), Dedee Pfeiffer (Mary Masterson), Jonna Lee (Sandy Matthews), Jonelle Allen (Lucinda Cavender), Kevin McCarthy (Judge Crandall), Cindy Morgan (Vicky Jensen), Dick Van Patten (Martin Grenville). 94 min.

The Monkey's Paw (1923) UK. Dir: H. Manning Haynes. Scr: Lydia Hayward based on the story by W.W. Jacobs. Cast: Moore Marriott (John White), Marie Ault (Mrs. White), Charles Ashton (Herbert White), Johnny Butt (Sgt. Tom Morris).

The Monkey's Paw (1933) USA. Dir: Wesley Ruggles, Ernest B. Schoedsack. Scr: Graham John based on the story by W.W. Jacobs. Mus: Max Steiner. DP: Edward Cronjager. Jack MacKenzie, J.O. Taylor, Leo Tover. Ed: Charles L. Kimball. Cast: Ivan F. Simpson (Mr. White), Louise Carter (Mrs. White), C. Aubrey Smith (Sgt. Maj. Morris), Bramwell Fletcher (Herbert), Betty Lawford (Rose). 58 min.

The Monkey's Paw (1948) UK. Dir: Norman Lee. Scr: Norman Lee, Barbara Toy based on the story by W.W Jacobs. Mus: Stanley Black. DP: Bryan Langley. Ed: Inman Hunter. AD: Victor Hembrow, George Ward. Cast: Milton Rosmer (Mr. Trelawne), Megs Jenkins (Mrs. Trelawne), Michael Harvey (Kelly), Eric Micklewood (Tom Trelawne), Brenda Hogan (Beryl). 64 min.

The Monkey's Paw (2013) USA. Dir: Brett Simmons. Scr: Macon Blair based on the story by W.W. Jacobs. Mus: Bobby Tahouri. DP: Scott Winig. Ed: Jon Mendenhall, Brett Simmons. Cast: C.J. Thomason (Jake Titlton), Stephen Lang (Tony Cobb), Michelle Pierce (Olivia), Daniel Hugh Kelly (Gillespie). 84 min.

La morte vivante (*The Living Dead Girl*, 1982) France. Dir: Jean Rollin. Scr: Jacques Ralf, Jean Rollin. Mus: Philippe d' Aram. DP: Max Monteillet. Ed: Janette Kronegger. Cast: Marina Pierro (Hélène), Françoise Blanchard (Catherine Valmont), Mike Marshall (Greg), Carina Barone (Barbara Simon), Fanny Magier (6th Victim), Patricia Besnard-Rousseau, Jean Rollin (Salesman). 86 min.

Mortuary (2005) USA. Dir: Tobe Hooper. Scr: Jace Anderson, Adam Gierasch. Mus: Joseph Conlan. DP: Jaron Presant. Ed: Andrew Cohen. PD: Rob Howeth. Cast: Dan Byrd (Jonathan Doyle), Denise Crosby (Leslie Doyle), Rocky Marquette (Grady), Stephanie Patton (Jamie Doyle), Alexandra Adi (Liz), Courtney Peldon (Tina). 94 min.

Motocross Zombies from Hell (2007) USA. Dir: Gary Robert. DP: Don Thiel, Trevor Xavier. Ed: Trevor Xavier. Cast: Dave Competello (Tom), Rachel Diana (Lori), Juan Flabio (Satan's Voice), James A.E. Fuentez (Zombie #13). 78 min.

Mulberry Street (2006) USA. Dir/Ed: Jim Mickle. Scr: Nick Damici, Jim Mickle. Mus: Andreas Kapsalis. DP: Ryan Samul. PD: Beth Mickle. Cast: Nick Damici (Clutch), Kim Blair (Casey), Ron Brice (Coco), Bo Corre (Kay), Tim House (Ross). 84 min.

Mulva: Zombie Ass Kicker! (2001) USA. Dir/Sc/Ed: Chris Seaver. DP: Mike Nicolia, Doug Sakmann, Chris Seaver. Cast: Missy Donatuti (Mulva), Chris Seaver (Mr. Bonejack), Mike Nicolai (McLargehuge), Joe Anime (Takateru). 59 min.

Mutant Vampire Zombies from the 'Hood! (2008) USA. Dir: Thunder Levin. Scr: Thunder Levin, George Saunders. Mus: Kurt Oldman. DP: Eric Billman. Ed: Karl Armstrong. Cast: C. Thomas Howell (David), Tyshawn Bryant (G-Dog), Rachel Montez Collins (Latiffa), Johanna Watts (Lisa), Robert Wu (Dragon), KB Holland (Larson). 90 min.

Mutants (2009) France. Dir: David Morlet. Scr: Louis-Paul Desanges, David Morlet. DP: Nicolas Massart. PD: Jérémy Streliski. Cast: Hélène de Fougerolles (Sonia), Francis Renaud (Marco), Dida Diafat (Virgile), Marie-Sohna Conde (Perez). 95 min.

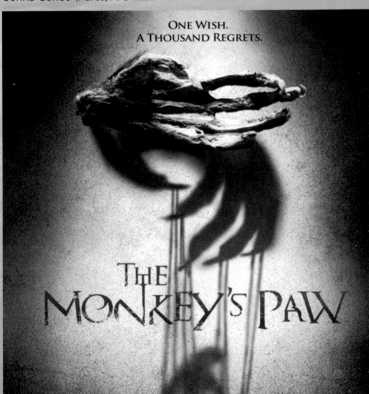

ONE WISH.
A THOUSAND REGRETS.

THE MONKEY'S PAW

My Boyfriend's Back (1993) USA. Dir: Bob Balaban. Scr: Dean Lorey. Mus: Harry Manfredini. DP: Mac Ahlberg. Ed: Michael Jablow. PD: Michael Z. Hanan. Cast: Andrew Lowery (Johnny), Traci Lind (Missy McCloud), Danny Zorn (Eddie), Edward Herrmann (Mr. Dingle), Mary Beth Hurt (Mrs. Dingle), Jay O. Sanders (Sheriff McCloud), Libby Villari (Camille McCloud), Matthew Fox (Buck Van Patten), Philip Seymour Hoffman (Chuck Bronski), Cloris Leachman (Maggie, the Zombie Expert). 85 min.

My Dead Girlfriend (2006) Canada. Dir: Brett Kelly. Scr: John Muggleton based on a story by Brett Kelly. Mus: Howard Sonnenburg. DP: Nicole Thompson. Ed: Brett Kelly. PD: Chance Wayne. Cast: Brett Kelly (Steve), Caitlin Delaney (Amy), Jody Haucke (Garry), John Muggleton (Carl), Anastasia Kimmett (Vanessa), Jason Daley (Ziggy). 73 min.

My Fair Zombie (2013) Canada. Dir: Brett Kelly. Scr: Brett Kelly. Trevor Payer. DP: Jera Kenez. Cast: Sacha Gabriel (Eliza Dolittle), Lawrence Evenchick (Henry Higgins), Barry Caiger (Colonel Pickering), Jennifer

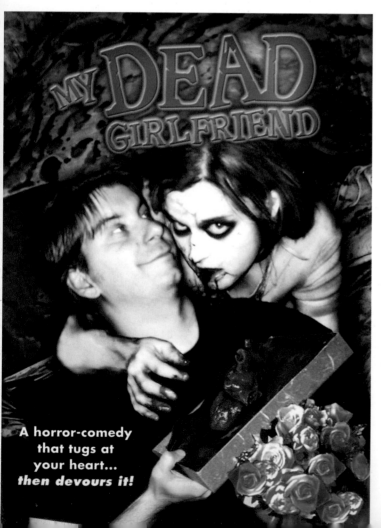

A horror-comedy that tugs at your heart... then devours it!

Vallance (Mrs. Pearce), Jason Redmond (Freddy Eynesford-Hill), Trevor Payer (Neppomuck), Gabrielle MacKenzie (Mrs. Eynesford-Hill), Penelope Goranson (Mrs. Higgins).

Die Nacht der lebenden Loser (*Night of the Living Dorks*, 2004) Germany. Dir/Scr: Mathias Dinter. Mus: Andreas Grimm. DP: Stephan Schuh. Ed: Cornelie Strecker. Cast: Tino Mewes (Philip), Manuel Cortez (Wurst), Thomas Schmieder (Konrad), Collien Fernandes (Rebecca), Hendrik Borgmann (Wolf), Nadine Germann (Uschi). 89 min.

The Necro Files (1997) USA. Dir/Mus/DP: Matt Jaissle. Scr: Todd Tjersland. Ed: Matt Jaissle, Todd Tjersland. Cast: Isaac Cooper (Logan/Zombie Sex Fiend/That Scumbag Garcia), Steve Sheppard (Detective Martin Manners), Gary Browning (Detective Orville Sloane), Christian Curmudgeon (Jack), Jason McGee (Barney), Theresa Bestul (Shower Girl), Jenn O. Cide (S&M Amazon), Drew Burymore (Camping Girl). 72 min.

Necro Files 2 (2003) USA. Dir: Ron Carlo, Matt Jaissle, Greg Lewis, Todd Tjersland. Scr: Todd Tjersland. Mus: Toshiyuki Hiraoka. Ed: Ron Carlo, Roger Lewis. Cast: Isaac Cooper (Logan/Zombie), Steve Sheppard (Detective Manners), Gary Browning (Detective Sloane), Greg Lewis (Greg Logan), Rod Fontana (Porn King), Taylor St. Clair (Taylor). 69 min.

Nederdood (2012) Netherlands. Dir/Scr/Ed: Vincent Bouritius. Ed: Mark Honsbeek. AD: Mellanie Naaijen. Cast: Erik Jasper Spithoven, Merel Spithoven, Robin van der Steen (Zombies), Jan-Willem Vos (Giant Zombie). 70 min.

The Neighbor Zombie (*Yieutjib jombi* 2010) Korea. Dir/Scr: Young-geun Hong, Youn-jung Jang, Young-doo Oh, Hoon Ryoo. Cast: Ji-hun Bae, Yong-geun Bae, Eun-Jung Ha, Young-geun Hong, Hyeon-tae Kim, Yeo-jini Kim, Gyu-seop Lee. 89 min.

Night Life (1989) USA. Dir: David Acomba. Scr: Keith Critchlow. Mus: Roger Bourland. DP: Roger Tonry. Ed: Michael John Bateman. PD: Phillip G. Thomas. Cast: Scott Grimes (Archie Melville), John Astin (Verlin Flanders), Cheryl Pollak (Charly Dorn), Anthony Geary (John Devlin), Alan Blumenfeld (Frank). 89 min.

Night of the Comet (1984) USA. Dir/Scr: Thom E. Eberhardt. Mus: David Richard Campbell. DP: Arthur Albert. Ed: Fred Stafford. PD: John Muto. Cast: Robert Beltran (Hector), Catherine Mary Stewart (Regina), Kelli Maroney (Samantha), Sharon Farrell (Doris), Mary

Woronov (Audrey), Geoffrey Lewis (Carter), Peter Fox (Wilson), John Achorn (Oscar). 95 min.

Night of the Creeps (1986) USA. Dir/Scr: Fred Dekker. Mus: Barry De Vorzon. DP: Robert C. New. Ed: Michael N. Knue. PD: George Costello. Cast: Jason Lively (Chris), Steve Marshall (J.C.), Jill Whitlow (Cynthia), Tom Atkins (Ray Cameron), Wally Taylor (Detective Landis), Bruce Solomon (Sgt. Raimi), Vic Polizos (Coroner), Allan Kayser (Brad). 88 min.

Night of the Dead: Leben Tod (2006) USA. Dir/Scr: Eric Forsberg. Mus: Robert Bayless. DP: Jon Bickford, David Frank. Ed: Mary Ann Skweres. AD: Daniel Lavitt. Cast: Louis Graham (Dr. Gabriel Schreklich), Joey Jalalian (Anais Sturben), Gabriel Womack (Peter Sturben), Deirdre V. Lyons (Schatzi), Lola Forsberg (Christi), David Reynolds (Gunther). 89 min.

Night of the Ghouls (1959) USA. Dir/Scr/Ed: Edward D. Wood Jr. DP: William C. Thompson. AD: Kathy Wood. Cast: Kenne Duncan (Dr. Acula), Duke Moore (Police Lt. Daniel Bradford), Tor Johnson (Lobo), Valda Hansen (The White Ghost), Johnny Carpenter (Police Captain Robbins), Paul Marco (Patrolman Kelton), Don Nagel (Crandel), Bud Osborne (Darmoor), Jeannie Stevens (the Black Ghost). 69 min.

Night of the Living Babes (1987) USA. Dir: Gregory Hippolyte [as Jon Valentine]. Scr: Anthony R. Lovett [as Veronica Cinq-Mars]. DP: Junior "Speedy" Bodden. Ed: Christopher Wilde. AD: Buddy Del Fuego. Cast: Michelle Bauer (Sue [as Michelle McClellan]), Andy Nichols (Chuck), Louie Bonanno (Buck), Connie Woods (Lulu), Forrest Witt (Madame Mondo), Cynthia Glegg (Igor). 60 min.

Night of the Living Dead (1968) USA. Dir/DP/Ed: George A. Romero. Scr: John A. Russo, George A. Romero. Cast: Duane Jones (Ben), Judith O'Dea (Barbra), Karl Hardman (Harry), Marilyn Eastman (Helen), Keith Wayne (Tom), Judith Ridle (Judy), Kyra Schon (Karen Cooper), Charles Craig (NewsCaster/Zombie), Bill Hinzman (Graveyard Zombie). 96 min.

Night of the Living Dead (1990) USA. Dir: Tom Savini. Scr: John A. Russo, George Romero. Mus: Paul McCollough. DP: Frank Prinzi. Ed: Tom Dubensky. PD: Cletus Anderson. Cast: Tony Todd (Ben), Patricia Tallman (Barbara), Tom Towles (Harry Cooper), McKee Anderson (Helen Cooper), William Butler (Tom), Katie Finneran (Judy Rose), Bill Moseley (Johnnie), Heather Mazur (Sarah Cooper), David W. Butler (Hondo),

Zachary Mott (Bulldog), Pat Reese (Mourner). 92 min.

Night of the Living Dead 3D (2006) USA. Dir: Jeff Broadstreet. Scr: George A. Romero, John A. Russo, Robert Valding. Mus: Jason Brandt. DP: Andrew Parke. Ed: Robert Valding. PD: Chris Davis. Cast: Brianna Brown (Barb), Joshua DesRoches (Ben), Sid Haig (Gerald Tovar, Jr.), Greg Travis (Henry Cooper), Johanna Black (Hellie Cooper), Adam Chambers (Owen), Ken Ward (Johnny), Alynia Phillips (Karen Cooper). 80 min.

Night of the Living Dead 3D: Re-Animation (2012) USA. Dir/Scr: Jeff Broadstreet. Story: Robert Valding. Mus: Jason Brandt. DP: Andrew Parke. Ed: Robert Valding. Cast: Andrew Divoff (Gerald Tovar, Jr.), Jeffrey Combs (Harold Tovar), Sarah Lieving (Cristie Forrest), Robin Sydney (DyeAnne), Adam Chambers (Russell), Melissa Bailey (Aunt Lou). 88 min.

Night of the Living Dead: Resurrection (2012) USA. Dir: James Plumb. Scr: Andrew Jones, James Plumb. Music/DP: James Morrissey. Ed: James Morrissey, James Plumb. PD: Jeff Butler. Cast: Sarah Louise (Madison Eve), Sabrina Dickens (Bonnie), Sule Rimi (Ben), Sousila Pillay (Broadcaster), Rorie Stockton (Slugger), Richard Goss (Red), Johnathon Farrell (Hess), S.J. Evans (Rhodes). 86 min.

YOU WON'T STAY DEAD.

NIGHT OF THE LIVING DEAD RESURRECTION

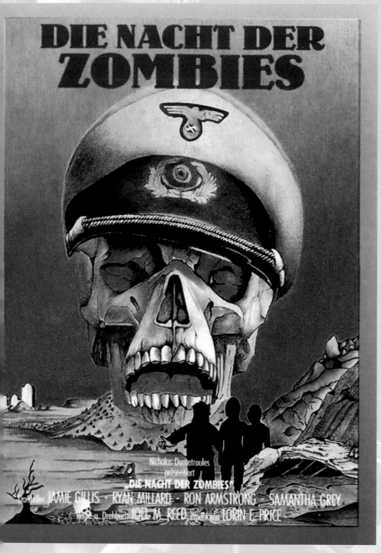

Night of the Living 3D Dead (2013) UK. Dir/Scr/Ph/Ed: Samuel Victor. Mus: Kane'd, Kevin MacLeod, Samuel Victor. Cast: Gemma Atkinson (Barbara), Nathaniel Francis (Ben), Gregory Caine (Harry), Joel Berg (Tom), Hannah May Wood (Karen), Rachel Doherty (Judy), Lara Duke (Helen), Martin Ashley Jones (Chief McClelland), Elana Di Troya (Rose McClelland), David Bruce Taylor (Dr. Victor). 96 min.

Night of the Zombies (*Night of the SS Zombies, Night of the Wehrmacht Zombies, Battalion of the Living Dead*, 1981) USA. Dir/Scr: Joel M. Reed. Mus: Goblin. DP: Ron Dorfman. Ed: Samuel D. Pollard. Cast: Jamie Gillis (Nick Monroe), Samantha Grey (Susan Proud), Ryan Hilliard (Dr. Clarence Proud), Ron Armstrong (Police Capt. Fleck), Joel M. Reed (CIA Informer). 88 min.

Night Shadows (1984) USA. Dir: John Cardos, Mark Rosman. Scr: Michael Jones, John C. Kruize, Peter Z. Orton. Mus: Richard Band. DP: Alfred Taylor. Ed: Michael J. Duthie. AD: Tony Kupersmith. Cast: Wings Hauser (Josh Cameron), Bo Hopkins (Sheriff Will Stewart), Jody Medford (Holly Pierce), Lee Montgomery (Mike Cameron), Marc Clement (Albert Hogue), Cary Guffey (Billy), Jennifer Warren (Dr. Myra Tate), Danny Nelson (Jack), Mary Nell Santacroce (Mrs. Mapes). 99 min.

Nightmare Weekend (1986) USA/UK/France. Dir: Henri Sala. Scr: George Faget-Benard, Robert Seidman. Mus: Martin Kershaw. DP: Robert M. Baldwin, Denis Gheerbrant. Ed: David Gilbert. PD: George Faget-Bernard. Cast: Debbie Laster (Julie Clingstone), Dale Midkiff (Ken), Debra Hunter (Jessica Brake), Lori Lewis (Annie), Preston Maybank (Bob), Wellington Meffert (Edward Brake), Kim Dossin (Mary-Rose), Andrea Thompson (Linda), Kimberley Stahl (Pamela). 85 min.

Ninjas vs. Zombies (2008) USA. Dir/Scr/Mus/DP/Ed: Justin Timpane. Cast: Daniel Ross (Kyle), Cory Okouchi (Cole), Carla Okouchi (Lily), P.J. Megaw (Eric), Dan Guy (Randall). 86 min.

Ninja Zombies (2011) USA. Dir/Ed: Noah Cooper. Scr: Michael Castro, Noah Cooper. DP: Michal Trzaska. Cast: Michael Castro (Luke), Pamela Chan (Dameon's Mom/Kage Ninja), Adam Discko (Truck Driver), Kylie Gellatly (Trish), Sang Kim (Shoju), Bernie Kuan (Albert/Kage Ninja), Chris Kulmann (Larry), Michael Lee (Dameon/Tenshu). 90 min.

La noche de las gaviotas (*Night of the Seagulls*, 1975) Spain. Dir/Scr: Amando de Ossorio. Mus: Antón García Abril. DP: Francisco Sánchez. Ed: Pedro del Rey. Cast: Víctor Petit (Dr. Henry Stein), María Kosty (Joan Stein), Sandra Mozarowsky (Lucy), José Antonio Calvo (Teddy), Julia Saly (Tilda Flanagan), Javier de Rivera (Doctor), María Vidal (Mrs. Flanagan). 89 min.

La noche del terror ciego (*Tombs of the Blind Dead*, 1972) Spain. Dir: Amando de Ossorio. Scr: Amando de Ossorio, Jesús Navarro Carrión. Mus: Antón García Abril. DP: Pablo Ripoll. Ed: José Antonio Rojo. PD: Jaime Duarte De Brito. Cast: Lone Fleming (Betty Turner), César Burner (Roger Whelan), María Elena Arpón (Virginia White), José Thelman, (Pedro Candal), Rufino Inglés (Insp. Oliveira), Verónica Llimera (Nina), Simón Arriaga (Morgue Keeper), Francisco Sanz (Prof. Candal), Juan Cortés (Coroner). 86 min.

Non si deve profanare il sonno dei morti (*Let Sleeping Corpses Lie, Living Dead at Manchester Morgue*, 1974)

Spain/Italy. Dir: Jorge Grau. Scr: Juan Cobos, Sandro Continenza, Marcello Coscia, Miguel Rubio. Mus: Giuliano Sorgini. DP: Francisco Sempere. Ed: Domingo García, Vincenzo Tomassi. PD: Carlo Leva. Cast: Cristina Galbó (Edna), Ray Lovelock (George), Arthur Kennedy (The Inspector), Aldo Massasso (Kinsey), Giorgio Trestini (Craig), Roberto Posse (Benson), José Lifante (Martin), Jeannine Mestre (Katie), Gengher Gatti (Keith), Fernando Hilbeck (Guthrie). 95 min.

Le notti del terrore (*Burial Ground: The Nights of Terror*, 1981) Italy. Dir: Andrea Bianchi. Scr: Piero Regnoli. DP: Gianfranco Maioletti. AD: Giovanni Fratalocchi. Cast: Karin Well (Janet), Gianluigi Chirizzi (Mark), Simone Mattioli (James), Antonella Antinori (Leslie), Roberto Caporali (George), Peter Bark (Michael), Claudio Zucchet (Nicholas), Anna Valente (Kathryn), Raimondo Barbieri (Professor), Mariangela Giordano (Evelyn). 85 min.

O.A.Z: Nan from Hell (2013) UK. Dir/Scr/DP/Ed: Tudley James. Mus: Jason Pesticcio. Cast: Marcus Carroll (Ed), Nia Ann (Gemma), Sabrina Dickens (Ceri), Josh Wood (PC Harris), Tudley James (Corey), Steve Purbrick (The Postman), Kathy Saxondale (Mum), Victor Ptak (Dad), Linda Bailey (Mother Zombie). 95 min.

O.C. Babes, the Slasher of Zombietown (2008) USA. Dir/Scr/Mus/DP: Creep Creepersin. Ed: Creep Creepersin, Gary Griffith. Cast: Elissa Dowling (Madison), Noelle Balfour (Ashley), Genna Bravo (Zombie), Allyson Clark (Tori), Cody Cowell (Mike), Creep Creepersin (Dick Fister). 70 min.

Oltre la morte (*After Death, Zombie Flesh Eaters 3, Zombi 4*, 1989) Italy. Dir: Claudio Fragasso [as Clyde Anderson]. Scr: Rossella Drudi. Mus: Al Festa. DP: Luigi Ciccarese. Ed: Maurizio Baglivo. AD: Mimmo Scavia. Cast: Jeff Stryker (Chuck), Candice Daly (Jenny), Massimo Vanni (David), Jim Gaines (Dan), Don Wilson (Tommy), Adrianne Joseph (Louise), Jim Moss (Mad). 84 min.

One Dark Night (1982) USA. Dir: Tom McLoughlin. Scr: Tom McLoughlin, Michael Hawes. Mus: Bob Summers. DP: Hal Trussell. Ed: Michael Spence, Charles Tetoni. PD: Craig Stearns. Cast: Meg Tilly (Julie Wells), Melissa Newman (Olivia McKenna), Robin Evans (Carol Mason), Leslie Speights (Kitty), Donald Hotton (Dockstader), Elizabeth Daily (Leslie Winslow), David Mason Daniels (Steve), Adam West (Allan), Leo Gorcey Jr (Barlow). 89 min.

Onechanbara: The Movie (2008) Japan. Dir: Yôhei Fukuda. Scr: Yôhei Fukuda, Yasutoshi Murakawa based

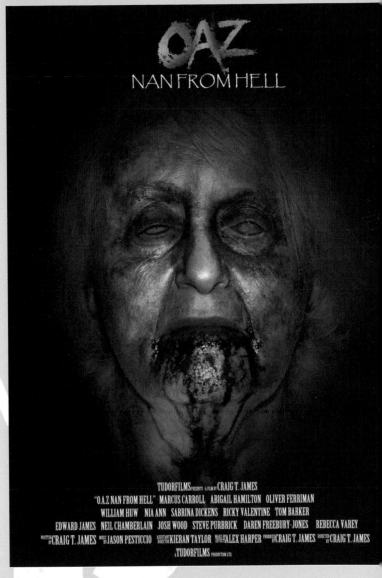

on the video game. Mus: Chika Fujino, Hideki Ikari. DP: Yôhei Fukuda. Ed: Tsuyoshi Wada. PD: Tomoya Imai. Cast: Eri Otoguro (Aya), Tomohiro Waki (Katsuji), Tarô Suwa (Dr. Sugita), Manami Hashimoto (Reiko), Chise Nakamura (Saki), Ai Hazuki (Maria), Sari Kurauchi (Asami). 80 min.

Onechanbara: The Movie–Vortex (2009) Japan. Dir: Tsuyoshi Shôji. Scr: Fukushima Yoshiki. Ed: Tsuyoshi Shôji. Cast: Chika Arakawa, Kumi Imura, Rika Kawamura, Akari Ozawa, Yû Tejima, Satoshi Yamamoto, Hoshina Youhei. 85 min.

Operation Nazi Zombies (*Maplewoods*, 2003) USA. Dir/Scr/Mus: David B. Stewart III. DP: Sean Hutcheon. John Martineau. Ed: David B. Stewart III. Cast: Thomas

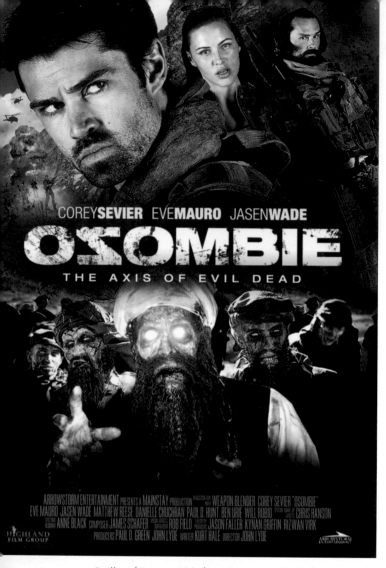

Reilly (Gen. Gibbs), Elissa Mullen (Lt. Myer), Christopher Connolly (Chaplain Johnson), John Weidemoyer (Maj. O' Malley), John Martineau (Sgt. Lake). 87 min.

La orgia de los muertos (*Terror of the Living Dead, The Hanging Woman, Les Orgies Macabres* 1973) Spain/Italy. Dir: José Luis Merino. Scr: Enrico Colombo, José Luis Merino. Mus: Francesco De Masi. DP: Modesto Rizzolo. Ed: Sandro Lena. AD: Francesco Di Stefano, Eduardo Torres. Cast: Stelvio Rosi [as Stan Cooper] (Serge Chekov), Maria Pia Conte (Nadia Mihaly), Dyanik Zurakowska (Doris Droila), Pasquale Basile (the Detective), Gérard Tichy (Professor Leon Droila), Aurora de Alba (Mary), Paul Naschy (Igor). 91 min.

Osombie (2012) USA. Dir: John Lyde. Scr: Kurt Hale. Mus: Jimmy Schafer. DP: Airk Thaughbaer. Ed: Kurt Hale, Airk Thaughbaer. Cast: Corey Sevier (Chip), Eve Mauro (Dusty), Jasen Wade (Derek), Danielle Chuchran (Tomboy), William Rubio (Chapo).

Ouanga (*The Love Wanga*, 1936) USA. Dir: George Terwilliger. Scr: George Terwilliger based on his story "Drums in the Night." DP: Carl Berger. Cast: Fredi Washington (Klili Gordon), Philip Brandon (Adam Maynard), Marie Paxton (Eve Langley), Sheldon Leonard (LeStrange, the Overseer), Winifred Harris (Aunt Sarah), Babe Joyce (Susie), George Spink (Johnson), Sidney Easton (Jackson). 56 min.

Outpost (2007) UK. Dir: Steve Barker. Scr: Rae Brunton. Mus: James Seymour Brett. DP: Gavin Struthers. Ed: Chris Gill, Alastair Reid. PD: Max Berman, Gordon Rogers. Cast: Ray Stevenson (DC), Julian Wadham (Hunt), Richard Brake (Prior), Paul Blair (Jordan), Brett Fancy (Taktarov), Enoch Frost (Cotter). 90 min.

Outpost: Black Sun (2012) UK. Dir: Steve Barker. Scr: Steve Barker, Rae Brunton. Mus: Theo Green. DP: Darran Tiernan. Ed: Bill Gill, Chris Gill. PD: James Lapsley. Cast: Richard Coyle (Wallace), Clive Russell (Marius), Catherine Steadman (Lena), Michael Byrne (Neurath), David Gant (Klausener), Nick Nevern (Carlisle). 101 min.

Outpost: Rise of the Spetsnaz (2013) UK. Dir: Kieran Parker. Scr: Rae Brunton. Mus: Al Hardiman, Patrick Jonsson. DP: Carlos De Carvalho. Ed: Naysun Alae-Carew. PD: James Lapsley (Bryan Larkin (Dolokhov), Iván Kamarás (Fyodor), Michael McKell (Strasser), Velibor Topic (Arkadi), Laurence Possa (Osakin), Ben Lambert (Rogers), Alec Utgoff (Kostya), Vince Docherty (Klotz), Gareth Morrison (Potrovsky), Leo Horsfield (Surgeon), Vivien Taylor (Nurse).

Ozone! Attack of the Redneck Mutants (1986) USA. Dir: Matt Devlen. Scr: Brad Redd. Mus: Kim Davis, Richard Davis, John Hudek,. Lasalo Murr. DP: Guy Rafferty, Charlene Vallenti. Ed: Tedrick Kureishi. Cast: Scott Davis (Kevin), Barbara Dow [as Ashley Nevada] (Loretta Lipscomb), Brad McCormick (Wade), Blue Thompson (Arlene).

ParaNorman (2012) USA. Dir: Chris Butler, Sam Fell. Scr: Chris Butler. Mus: Jon Brion. DP: Tristan Oliver. Ed: Christopher Murrie. Cast (voices): Kodi Smit-McPhee (Norman Babcock), Tucker Albrizzi (Neil), Anna Kendrick (Courtney Babcock), Casey Affleck (Mitch), Christopher Mintz-Plasse (Alvin), Leslie Mann (Sandra Babcock), Jeff Garlin (Perry Babcock), Elaine Stritch (Grandma). 93 min.

Parasitic (2012) USA. Dir/Scr/Ed: Tim Martin. Mus:

Brian Wherry. DP: Will Barratt. Cast: Julie Anne (Go go), Camille Balsamo (Grace Gillis), Amanda Beck (Renee), Carrie Carnes (Tiffany), Miguel de la Rosa (Tim), Isle Gallagher (Amber). 79 min.

Paura nella città dei morti viventi (*City of the Living Dead, Gates of Hell*, 1980) Italy. Dir: Lucio Fulci. Scr: Lucio Fulci, Dardano Sacchetti. Mus: Fabio Frizzi. DP: Sergio Salvati. Ed: Edward Brizio, Vincenzo Tomassi. PD: Massimo Antonello Geleng. Cast: Christopher George (Peter Bell), Catriona MacColl (Mary Woodhouse), Carlo De Mejo (Gerry), Antonella Interlenghi (Emily Robbins), Giovanni Lombardo Radice (Bob), Daniela Doria (Rosie Kelvin), Fabrizio Jovine (Father William Thomas), Luca Venantini (John-John Robbins), Michele Soavi (Tommy Fisher), Lucio Fulci (Dr. Joe Thompson). 93 min.

La perversa caricia de Satán (*Devil's Kiss, Wicked Caresses of Satan,* 1976) Spain. Dir/Scr: Jordi Gigó. Mus: Alberto Argudo. DP: Julio Pérez de Rozas. Ed: Albert Gasset Nicolau. Cast: Silvia Solar (Claire Grandier), Olivier Mathot (Professor Gruber), José Nieto (Duke de Haussemont), Evelyne Scott (Loretta), Daniel Martín (Richard), María Silva (Susan), Carlos Otero (Joseph), Víctor Israel (Baron de Clanchart), José Lifante (Charles), Moisés Rocha (Zombie). 89 min.

Pet Sematary (1989) USA. Dir: Mary Lambert. Scr: Stephen King based on his novel. DP: Peter Stein. Ed: Daniel P. Hanley, Mike Hill. PD: Michael Z. Hanan. Cast: Dale Midkiff (Louis Creed), Fred Gwynne (Jud Crandall), Denise Crosby (Rachel Creed), Brad Greenquist (Victor Pascow), Michael Lombard (Irwin Goldman), Miko Hughes (Gage Creed), Blaze Berdahl (Ellie Creed). 103 min.

Pet Sematary II (1992) USA. Dir: Mary Lambert. Scr: Richard Outten based on Stephen King's novel. Mus: Mark Governor. DP: Russell Carpenter. Ed: Tom Finan. PD: Michelle Minch. Cast: Edward Furlong (Jeff Matthews), Anthony Edwards (Chase Matthews), Clancy Brown (Sheriff Gus Gilbert), Jared Rushton (Clyde Parker), Darlanne Fluegel (Renee Hallow), Jason McGuire (Drew Gilbert), Sarah Trigger (Marjorie Hargrove). 100 min.

Pirates of the Caribbean: On Stranger Tides (2011) USA. Dir: Rob Marshall. Scr: Ted Elliott, Terry Rossio. Mus: Hans Zimmer. DP: Dariusz Wolski. Ed: David Brenner, Wyatt Smith. PD: John Myhre. Cast: Johnny Depp (Jack Sparrow), Penélope Cruz (Angelica Teach), Geoffrey Rush (Barbossa), Ian McShane (Blackbeard), Kevin McNally (Joshamee Gibbs), Sam Claflin (Philip), Astrid Bergès-Frisbey (Syrena), Stephen Graham (Scrum), Keith Richards (Captain Teague). 136 min.

Plaga Zombie (1997) Argentina. Dir/Ph/Ed: Pablo Parés, Hernán Sáez. Scr: Berta Muñiz, Pablo Parés, Hernán Sáez. Mus: Pablo Vostrouski. Cast: Berta Muñiz (John West), Pablo Parés (Bill Johnson), Hernán Sáez (Max Giggs), Walter Cornás (Mike Taylor). 69 min.

Plaga Zombie: Zona mutante (2001) Argentina. Dir/Scr: Pablo Parés, Hernán Sáez. Mus: Alejandro D'Aloisio, Paulo Soria, Hernán Sáez, Pablo Vostrouski. Ed: Hernán Sáez. Cast: Berta Muñiz (John West), Pablo Parés (Bill Johnson), Hernán Sáez (Max Giggs), Paulo Soria (Max Fan). 101 min.

Plaga Zombie: Zona Mutant. Revolución Tóxica (2011) Argentina. Dir/Scr/Ed: Pablo Parés, Hernán Sáez. Mus: Pablo Vostrouski. DP: Diego Echave. Cast: Hernán Sáez (Max Giggs), Pablo Parés (Bill Johnson), Berta Muñiz (John West), Paulo Soria (Junior), Walter Cornás (Jack Taylor). 100 min.

il nuovo film di LUCIO FULCI

PAURA NELLA CITTÀ DEI MORTI VIVENTI

CHRISTOPHER GEORGE · KATHERINE MAC COLL · CARLO DE MEJO
ANTONELLA INTERLENGHI · GIOVANNI LOMBARDO RADICE
DANIELA DORIA · FABRIZIO JOVINE · e con JANET AGREN nel ruolo di SANDRA
Regia di LUCIO FULCI
Fotografia SERGIO SALVATI · Musiche FABIO FRIZZI · Colore LV LUCIANO VITTORI
Produzione DANIA FILM · MEDUSA DISTRIBUZIONE · NATIONAL CINEMATOGRAFICA

The Plague of the Zombies (1966) UK. Dir: John Gilling. Scr: Peter Bryan. Mus: James Bernard. DP: Arthur Grant. Ed: Chris Barnes. PD: Bernard Robinson. Cast: André Morell (Sir James Forbes), Diane Clare (Sylvia Forbes), Brook Williams (Dr. Peter Tompson), Jacqueline Pearce (Alice Mary Tompson), John Carson (Squire Clive Hamilton), Alexander Davion (Denver), Michael Ripper (Sgt. Jack Swift), Marcus Hammond (Tom Martinus), Dennis Chinnery (Constable Christian). 90 min.

Plan 9 from Outer Space (1959) USA. Dir/Scr/Ed: Edward D. Wood Jr. DP: William C. Thompson. Cast: Gregory Walcott (Jeff Trent), Mona McKinnon (Paula Trent), Duke Moore (Lt. Harper), Tom Keene (Col. Edwards), Carl Anthony (Patrolman Larry), Paul Marco (Patrolman Kelton), Tor Johnson (Inspector Clay), Dudley Manlove (Eros), Joanna Lee (Tanna), John Breckinridge (Ruler), Lyle Talbot (General), Vampira (Vampire Girl), Bela Lugosi (Ghoul Man), Tor Johnson (Zombie), Criswell (Narrator/Himself). 79 min.

Planet Terror (2007) USA. Dir/Scr/Mus/DP: Robert Rodriguez. Scr: Robert Rodriguez. Ed: Ethan Maniquis, Robert Rodriguez. PD: Steve Joyner. Cast: Rose McGowan (Cherry Darling), Freddy Rodríguez (Wray), Josh Brolin (Dr. William Block), Marley Shelton (Dr. Dakota Block), Jeff Fahey (J.T.), Michael Biehn (Sheriff Hague), Rebel Rodriguez (Tony Block), Bruce Willis (Lt. Muldoon). 105 min.

Platoon of the Dead (2009) USA. Dir/Scr/Ed: John Bowker. Mus: Steve Sessions. DP: Joe Sherlock. Cast: Ariauna Albright (Heather), Tom Stedham (Sgt. Butler), Chris Keown (Lt. Roberts), Tyler David (Pvt. Dillon), Amanda Bounds (Jill). 82 min.

Pretty Dead (2013) USA. Dir: Benjamin Wilkins. Scr/Ed: Joe Cook, Benjamin Wilkins. Mus: Chanda Dancy. DP: Joshua Grote. AD: Allison Kin. Cast: Carly Oates (Regina Stevens), Ryan Shogren (Ryan), Quantae Love (Dr. Daniel Romera), Heather Anne Wood (Cooper), Emily Button (Nurse Boyle), Dave Matos (Joe), Joshua Grote (Quint Fitzgerald), Daesha Lynn (Virginia). 77 min.

Pro Wrestlers vs. Zombies (2013) USA. Dir/Scr: Cody Knotts. DP: Joseph Russio. Cast: Roddy Piper (Himself), Adrienne Fischer (Sarah Schuman), Matt Hardy (Himself), Jim Duggan (Himself), Kurt Angle (Himself), Shane Douglas (Himself), Taya Parker (Herself), Shannon M. Hart (Serena).

Purulent (2013) USA. Dir: Jerad Ashworth. Scr: Randy Robinson. Mus: Toshiyuki Hiraoka. Cast: Tara McIntosh, Randy Robinson (Adam), Reuben Rox (Gary), Jesi Smith (Astrid).

Quarantine (2008) USA. Dir: John Erick Dowdle. Scr: John Erick Dowdle, Drew Dowdle. DP: Ken Seng. Ed: Elliot Greenberg. PD: Jon Gary Steele. Cast: Jennifer Carpenter (Angela Vidal), Steve Harris (Scott Percival), Jay Hernandez (Jake), Johnathon Schaech (George Fletcher), Columbus Short (Danny Wilensky), Andrew Fiscella (James McCreedy). 89 min.

Quarantine 2: Terminal (2011) USA. Dir/Scr: John Pogue. DP: Matthew Irving. Ed: William Yeh. Cast: Mercedes Masöhn (Jenny), Josh Cooke (Henry), Mattie Liptak (George), Ignacio Serricchio (Ed), Noree Victoria (Shilah), Bre Blair (Paula). 89 min.

Quella villa accanto al cimitero (*The House by the Cemetery*, 1981) Italy. Dir: Lucio Fulci. Scr: Elisa

YOU MIGHT FEEL A LITTLE PRICK.

ROBERT RODRIGUEZ'S
PLANET TERROR

Briganti, Lucio Fulci, Giorgio Mariuzzo, Dardano Sacchetti. Mus: Walter Rizzati. DP: Sergio Salvati. Ed: Vincenzo Tomassi. PD: Massimo Lentini. Cast: Catriona MacColl (Lucy Boyle), Paolo Malco (Dr. Norman Boyle), Ania Pieroni (Ann, the babysitter), Giovanni Frezza (Bob Boyle), Silvia Collatina (Mae Freudstein), Dagmar Lassander (Laura Gittleson), Giovanni De Nava (Dr. Jacob Tess Freudstein), Daniela Doria (First Female Victim). 87 min.

The Quick and the Undead (2006) USA. Dir/Scr: Gerald Nott. Mus: Brian Burns Beardsley, Pieter A. Schlosser. DP: Scott Peck. Ed: Jeff Murphy. Cast: Clint Glenn Hummel (Ryn Baskin), Toar Campbell (Toar Zombie), Dion Day (Jackson), Nicola Giacobbe (Hans Tubman), Brian Koehler (Zombie). 90 min.

Les raisins de la mort (*The Grapes of Death*, 1978) France. Dir: Jean Rollin. Scr: Jean-Pierre Bouyxou, Christian Meunier, Jean Rollin. Mus: Philippe Sissman. DP: Claude Bécognée. Ed: Dominique Saint-Cyr, Christian Stoianovich. Cast: Marie-Georges Pascal (Élisabeth), Félix Marten (Paul), Serge Marquand (Lucien), Mirella Rancelot (Lucie), Michel Herval (Elisabeth's Fiancé), Brigitte Lahaie (Tall Blonde), Paul Bisciglia (Lucas). 85 min.

Rape Zombie: Lust of the Dead (2012) Japan. Dir: Naoyuki Tomomatsu. Scr: Jirô Ishikawa, Naoyuki Tomomatsu. DP: Takehiko Tamiya. PD: Chris Ryô Kaihara. Cast: Rina Aikawa, Yui Aikawa, Kazuyoshi Akishima, Asami, Norman England, Hiroshi Fujita. 73 min.

Rape Zombie: Lust of the Dead 2, 3 (2013) Japan. Dir: Naoyuki Tomomatsu. Scr: Yûko Momochi, Naoyuki Tomomatsu. DP: Takehiko Tamiya. PD: Chris Ryô Kaihara. Cast: Yui Aikawa, Maki Aoyama, Asami, Hiroshi Fujita, Fuzuki, Yutaka Ikejima, Hiroyuki Kaneko. 67 min (2)/68 min (3).

Rapture Palooza (2013) USA. Dir: Paul Middleditch. Scr: Chris Matheson. Mus: Joachim Horsley. DP: Robert C. New. PD: Joe Cabrera. Cast: Anna Kendrick (Lindsey), John Francis Daley (Ben House), Craig Robinson (Anti-Christ), Ken Jeong (God), Thomas Lennon (Mr. Murphy), Rob Corddry (Mr. House). 85 min.

Re-Animator (1985) USA. Dir: Stuart Gordon. Scr: Dennis Paoli, William Norris, Stuart Gordon based on a story by H.P. Lovecraft. Mus: Richard Band. DP: Mac Ahlberg. Robert Ebinger. Ed: Lee Percy. AD: Robert A. Burns. Cast: Jeffrey Combs (Herbert West), Bruce Abbott (Dan Cain), Barbara Crampton (Megan Halsey), David Gale (Dr. Carl Hill), Robert Sampson (Dean

Halsey), Gerry Black (Mace), Carolyn Purdy-Gordon (Dr. Harrod), Peter Kent (Melvin the Re-Animated), Barbara Pieters (Nurse). 95 min.

La rebelión de las muertas (*Vengeance of the Zombies*, 1973) Spain. Dir: León Klimovsky. Scr: Paul Naschy [as Jacinto Molina]. Mus: Juan Carlos Calderón. DP: Francisco Sánchez. Ed: Antonio Ramírez de Loaysa. Cast: Paul Naschy (Krisna/Kantaka/Satán), Carmen "Romy" Romero (Elvire Irving), Mirta Miller (Kala), María Kosty (Elsie), Aurora de Alba (Olivia), Luis Ciges (MacMurdo), Pierre Besari (Ti Zachary). 90 min.

[Rec] (2007) Spain. Dir: Jaume Balagueró, Paco Plaza. Scr: Jaume Balagueró, Manu Díez, Paco Plaza. DP: Pablo Rosso. Ed: David Gallart. Art Dir: Gemma Fauria. Cast: Manuela Velasco (Ángela Vidal), Ferrán Terraza (Manu), Jorge-Yaman Serrano (Young Policeman), Pablo Rosso

AVRAI
IL CORAGGIO
DI TORNARCI?

[∙ REC]²

Un Film di **Jaume Balagueró & Paco Plaza**

(Pablo), David Vert (Álex), Vicente Gil (Policemen), Martha Carbonell (Mrs. Izquierdo), Carlos Vicente (Guillem Marimón). 78 min.

*[Rec]² * (2009) Spain. Dir: Jaume Balagueró, Paco Plaza. Scr: Jaume Balagueró, Manu Díez, Paco Plaza. DP: Pablo Rosso. Ed: Xavi Gimenez. Art Dir: Gemma Fauria. Cast: Jonathan D. Mellor (Dr. Owen), Óscar Zafra (Jefe), Ariel Casas (Larra), Alejandro Casaseca (Martos), Pablo Rosso (Rosso), Pep Molina (Padre Jennifer), Andrea Ros (Mire), Àlex Batllori (Ori), Pau Poch (Tito), Juli Fàbregas (Bombero), Ferran Terraza (Manu), Claudia Silva (Jennifer). 85 min.

[Rec]³ Genesis (2012) Spain. Dir: Paco Plaza. Scr: Paco Plaza, Luiso Berdejo. Mus: Mikel Salas. DP: Pablo Rosso. Ed: David Gallart. Cast: Leticia Dolera (Clara), Diego Martín (Koldo), Ismael Martínez (Rafa), Àlex Monner (Adrián), Sr. B (Atun), Emilio Mencheta (Tio Pepe Victor). 81 min.

[Rec]⁴ Apocalypse (2014) Spain. Dir: Jaume Balagueró. Scr: Jaume Balagueró, Manu Díez. DP: Pablo Rosso. Ed: David Gallart. Cast: Manuela Velasco (Ángela Vidal),

Paco Manzanedo (Guzmán), Héctor Colomé (Dr. Ricarte), Ismael Fritschi (Nic), Críspulo Cabezas (Lucas), Paco Obregón (Dr. Ginard).

Red Victoria (2008) USA. Dir/Scr/Ph/Ed: Tony Brownrigg. Mus: Desha Dunnahoe. Cast: Tony Brownrigg (Jim), Arianne Martin (Victoria), Edward Landers (Carl), Joshua Morris (Peter), Christian Taylor (Blake). 89 min.

Redneck Zombies (1989) USA. Dir: Pericles Lewnes. Scr: Fester Smellman. Mus: Adrian Bond. DP: Ken Davis. Ed: Edward Bishop. Cast: Stan Morrow (Dr. Kildare), Brent Thurston-Rogers (Dr. Casey), Lisa M. DeHaven (Lisa Dubois), Tyrone Taylor (Tyrone), Anthony Burlington-Smith (Bob), James H. Housely (Wilbur), Martin J. Wolfman (Andy), Boo Teasedale (Sally), Darla Deans (Theresa). 84 min.

Resident Evil (2002) USA/UK/Germany/France. Dir: Paul W.S. Anderson. Scr: Paul W.S. Anderson based on the video game. Mus: Marco Beltrami, Marilyn Manson. DP: David Johnson. Ed: Alexander Berner. PD: Richard Bridgland. Cast: Milla Jovovich (Alice), Eric Mabius (Matt), Colin Salmon (One), Martin Crewes (Kaplan), Pasquale Aleardi (J.D.), Michelle Rodriguez (Rain). 100 min.

Resident Evil: Apocalypse (2004) USA/Germany /France/UK. Dir: Alexander Witt. Scr: Paul W.S. Anderson. Mus: Jeff Danna. DP: Derek Rogers, Christian Sebaldt. Ed: Eddie Hamilton. PD: Paul D. Austerberry. Cast: Milla Jovovich (Alice), Sienna Guillory (Jill Valentine), Oded Fehr (Carlos Olivera), Thomas Kretschmann (Maj. Tom Cain), Sophie Vavasseur (Angie Ashford), Razaaq Adoti (Sgt. Wells), Jared Harris (Dr. Ashford), Mike Epps (L.J.). 94 min.

Resident Evil: Extinction (2007) USA/France/UK/ Germany/Australia. Dir: Russell Mulcahy. Scr: Paul W.S. Anderson. Mus: Charlie Clouser. DP: David Johnson. Ed: Niven Howie. PD: Eugenio Caballero. Cast: Milla Jovovich (Alice), Oded Fehr (Carlos Olivera), Ali Larter (Claire), Iain Glen (Dr. Isaacs), Ashanti (Betty), Christopher Egan (Mikey), Spencer Locke (K-Mart), Matthew Marsden (Slater), Mike Epps (L.J.). 94 min.

Resident Evil: Afterlife (2010) USA/Germany/France/ Canada. Dir/Scr: Paul W.S. Anderson. Mus: tomandandy. DP: Glen MacPherson. Ed: Niven Howie. PD: Arvinder Grewal. Cast: Milla Jovovich (Alice), Ali Larter (Claire Redfield), Kim Coates (Bennett), Shawn Roberts (Albert Wesker), Sergio Peris-Mencheta (Angel Ortiz), Spencer Locke (K-Mart), Boris Kodjoe (Luther West), Wentworth Miller (Chris Redfield), Sienna Guillory (Jill Valentine). 97 min.

Resident Evil: Retribution (2012) USA/Germany/ Canada. Dir/Scr: Paul W.S. Anderson. Mus: tomandandy. DP: Glen MacPherson. Ed: Niven Howie. PD: Kevin Phipps. Cast: Milla Jovovich (Alice), Sienna Guillory (Jill Valentine), Michelle Rodriguez (Rain), Aryana Engineer (Becky), Bingbing Li (Ada Wong), Boris Kodjoe (Luther West), Johann Urb (Leon S. Kennedy). 96 min.

Resident Evil: Damnation (2012, animation) Japan. Dir: Makoto Kamiya. Scr: Shotaro Suga. 100 min.

Retardead (2008) USA. Dir: Rick Popko, Dan West. Scr: Rick Popko, Dan West. Mus: Marshall Crutcher. Ed: Ken Dashner, Rick Popko, Dan West. PD: Dan West. Cast: Rick Popko (Deputy Rick/Porn Actress/Doctor/Ripper Detective), Tony Adams (Agent Russo), Michael Allen (Institute Director), Shamika Baker (Living Dead Girl), Jello Biafra (Mayor Anton Sinclaire). 100 min.

The Return of the Living Dead (1985) USA. Dir: Dan O'Bannon. Scr: Dan O'Bannon based on a story by Rudy Ricci, Russell Streiner. Mus: Matt Clifford. DP: Jules Brenner. Ed: Robert Gordon. PD: William Stout. Cast: Clu Gulager (Burt), James Karen (Frank), Don Calfa (Ernie), Thom Mathews (Freddy), Beverly Randolph (Tina), John Philbin (Chuck), Jewel Shepard (Casey), Miguel A. Núñez Jr (Spider), Brian Peck (Scuz), Linnea Quigley (Trash). 91 min.

Return of the Living Dead II (1988) USA. Dir/Scr: Ken Wiederhorn. Mus: J. Peter Robinson. DP: Robert Elswit. Ed: Charles Bornstein. AD: Dale Allen Pelton. Cast: Michael Kenworthy (Jesse Wilson), Thor Van Lingen (Billy Crowley), Jason Hogan (Johnny), James Karen (Ed), Thom Mathews (Joey), Suzanne Snyder (Brenda), Marsha Dietlein (Lucy Wilson). 89 min.

Return of the Living Dead III (1993) Japan/USA. Dir: Brian Yuzna. Scr: John Penney. Mus: Barry Goldberg. DP: Gerry Lively. Ed: Christopher Roth. PD: Anthony Tremblay. Cast: Kent McCord (Col. John Reynolds), James T. Callahan (Col. Peck), Sarah Douglas (Col. Sinclair), Melinda Clarke (Julie Walker), Abigail Lenz (Mindy), J. Trevor Edmond (Curt Reynolds), Jill Andre (Chief Scientist), Michael Decker (Science Technician), Billy Kane (Sentry), Mike Moroff (Santos). 97 min.

Return of the Living Dead: Necropolis (2005) USA. Dir: Ellory Elkayem. Scr: William Butler, Aaron Strongoni. Mus: Robert Duncan. DP: Gabriel Kosuth. Ed: James Coblentz. Cast: Aimee-Lynn Chadwick (Becky), Cory Hardrict (Cody). 88 min.

Return of the Living Dead: Rave to the Grave (2005) USA. Dir: Ellory Elkayem. Scr: William Butler, Aaron Strongoni. Mus: Aimee-Lynn Chadwick, Robert Duncan, Ralph Rieckermann. DP: Gabriel Kosuth. PD: Calin Papura. Cast: Aimee-Lynn Chadwick (Becky), Cory Hardrict (Cody), John Keefe (Julian Garrison), Jenny Mollen (Jenny), Peter Coyote (Uncle Charles), Claudiu Bleont (Aldo Serra), Sorin Cocis (Gino). 86 min.

The Returned (2013) Spain/Canada. Dir: Manuel Carballo. Scr: Hatem Khraiche. Mus: Jonathan Goldsmith. DP: Javier Salmones. PD: Gavin Mitchell. Cast: Emily Hampshire (Kate), Kris Holden-Ried (Alex), Claudia Bassols (Amber), Shawn Doyle (Jacob).

La revanche des mortes vivantes (*The Revenge of the Living Dead Girls*, 1987) France. Dir: Pierre B. Reinhard [as Peter B. Harsone]. Scr: John Kingbased on a story by

Edgar Wallace. Mus: Christopher Ried. DP: Henry Frogers. Cast: Véronique Catanzaro, Kathryn Charly, Sylvie Novak. 76 min.

Revenge of the Zombies (1943) USA. Dir: Steve Sekely. Scr: Edmond Kelso, Van Norcross. DP: Mack Stengler. Ed: Richard C. Currier. AD: Dave Milton. Cast: John Carradine (Dr. Max Heinrich von Altermann), Gale Storm (Jennifer Rand), Robert Lowery (Larry Adams), Bob Steele (United States Agent), Mantan Moreland (Jeff), Veda Ann Borg (Lila von Altermann), Barry Macollum (Dr. Harvey Keating), Mauritz Hugo (Scott Warrington), Madame Sul-Te-Wan (Beulah). 61 min.

Revolt of the Zombies (1936) USA. Dir: Victor Halperin. Scr: Victor Halperin, Howard Higgin, Rollo Lloyd. DP: Arthur Martinelli. Ed: Douglass Biggs. AD: Leigh Smith. Cast: Dorothy Stone (Claire Duval), Dean Jagger (Armand Louque), Roy D'Arcy (Gen. Mazovia), Robert Noland (Clifford Grayson), George Cleveland (Gen. Duval), E. Alyn Warren (Dr. Trevissant), Teru Shimada (Buna), Adolph Mila (Gen. von Schelling), Sana Rayya (Dancer), Bela Lugosi (The Eyes). 65 min.

The Revolting Dead (2003) USA. Dir: Michael Su. Scr: Daniel Benton, Michael Su. Mus: Ross Wright. DP: Michael Su. Ed: Noah Nelson. PD: Patrick Russo. Cast: Shelley Delayne (Marissa Drue), Aaron Gaffey (Duke Malone), Bokahra Robinson (Millicent Crain), Michael Falls (Cedric Crain), Lindsey Lofaso (Betsy Crain). 87 min.

Rise of the Undead (2005) USA. Dir/Scr/Ed: Jason Horton, Shannon Hubbell. Mus: Maximilian Kabong. DP: Shannon Hubbell, Ryan Martin. PD: Blaine Cade. Cast: Chrystal Skye Jordan (Buffy), Mark Karem (Wound), Chantal Koerner (Screaming Woman), Blaine

Cade (Naked Zombie), Sunshine Bond (Thrice Zombie). 89 min.

Rise of the Undead (2013) USA. Dir/Scr/Ed: Nick Woltersdorf. Mus: Hans Zimmer. Cast: Dietrich Hanson (Adam), Nick Woltersdorf (Jake), Annie Jacobs (Jessica), Nathanial Walker (Brett), Emma Walker (Colonel Pankov). 70 min.

Rise of the Zombie (2013) India. Dir: Luke Kenny, Devaki Singh. Scr: Devaki Singh. DP: Murzy Pagdiwala. Cast: Benjamin Gilani (Dr. Dave Parker), Luke Kenny (Neil Parker), Kirti Kulhari (Vinny Rao), Ashwin Mushran (Anish Kohli), Prem Thapa (Thapa Ji).

Rise of the Zombies (2012) USA. Dir: Nick Lyon. Tel: Keith Allan, Delondra Williams. Mus: Chris Ridenhour. DP: Alexander Yellen. Ed: James Kondelik. PD: Mark Macauley. Cast: Mariel Hemingway (Lynn Snyder), Ethan Suplee (Marshall), LeVar Burton (Dr. Dan Halpern), Danny Trejo (Captain Caspian), Heather Hemmens (Ashley), French Stewart (Dr. Arnold), Chad Lindberg (Kyle), Madonna Magee (Vivian). 89 min.

Roadside Massacre (2012) USA. Dir/Scr: Scott Kirkpatrick. Mus: Christopher Haynes. DP: Shane Foster. Ed: Michael Prince. AD: Julianne Loof. Cast: Marina Resa (Karen), Elio Mardini (Nick), Dusty Probert (Gus), Matthew Schiltz (Vince), Fragino M. Arola (Tommy), Summer Lima (Courtney), Master Dave Johnson (Jimmy). 83 min.

Roaming Hungry (2013) Canada. Dir/Scr/DP/ED: Julian Figueroa. Cast: Kyle Brogan (Wreath), Cassidy Clayton (Wreath's Mother), Connor Desharnais (Carl), Alexa Houle (Clown Zombie), Rosi Hunter (Stella). 109 min.

El robo de las momias de Guanajuato (*Robbery of the Mummies of Guanajuato*, 1972) Mexico. Dir: Tito Novaro. Scr: Rogelio Agrasánchez, Francisco Morayta, Miguel Morayta. Mus: Rafael Carrión. DP: Antonio Ruiz. Ed: Ángel Camacho. Cast: Mil Máscaras (Mil Máscaras), Blue Angel (himself), Julio César Agrasánchez, El Rayo de Jalisco. Mabel Luna. Tito Novaro (Conde Cagliostro). 86 min.

Rockabilly Zombie Weekend (2013) Dir: Jaime Velez Soto. Scr: Tammy Bennett. Mus: Dani Donadi. DP: Andy S. Montejo. Ed: Paul Steward. PD: Joseph E. Stone. Cast: J. LaRose (Curtis), Christina Bach (Becky), Michelle Elise (Micca), Scott Singer (Pete), Randy Molnar (Bo), Gary B. Gross (Zombie Cop #1). 88 min.

Roma contro Roma (*War of the Zombies*, 1964) Italy. Dir: Giuseppe Vari. Scr: Piero Pierotti, Marcello Sartarelli based on a story by Ferruccio De Martino, Massimo De Rita, Piero Pierotti, Marcello Sartarelli. Mus: Roberto Nicolosi. DP: Gábor Pogány. PD: Giorgio Giovannini. Cast: John Drew Barrymore (Aderbad), Susy Andersen (Tullia), Ettore Manni (Gaius), Ida Galli (Rhama), Mino Doro (Lutetius), Ivano Staccioli (Sirion), Philippe Hersent (Azer). 98 min.

The Roost (2005) USA. Dir/Scr/Ed: Ti West. Mus: Jeff Grace. DP: Eric Robbins. Ed: Ti West. PD: David Bell. Cast: Tom Noonan (Horror Host), Karl Jacob (Trevor), Vanessa Horneff (Allison), Sean Reid (Brian), Wil Horneff (Elliot), Barbara Wilhide (May), Richard Little (Elvin).

Santo contra los zombies (1962) Mexico. Dir: Benito Alazraki. Scr: Benito Alazraki, Antonio Orellana, Fernando Osés. DP: José Ortiz Ramos. Ed: José W. Bustos. PD: Roberto Silva. Cast: Santo (Santo), Armando Silvestre (Lt. Sanmartin), Jaime Fernández (Det. Rodriguez), Dagoberto Rodríguez (Det. Chief Almada), Irma Serrano (Det. Isabel), Carlos Agostí (Genaro), Ramón Bugarini (Rogelio), Fernando Osés (Dorrell, Zombified Wrestler), Lorena Velázquez (Gloria Sandoval). 85 min.

Le nouveau film du réalisateur des "Griffes de la Nuit".

Ne m'enterrez pas...
je ne suis pas mort!

L'EMPRISE des TÉNÈBRES
"THE SERPENT AND THE RAINBOW"
KEITH BARISH ROB COHEN/DAVID LADD
L'EMPRISE DES TÉNÈBRES BILL PULLMAN—CATHY TYSON · ZAKES MOKAE · PAUL WINFIELD
RICHARD MAXWELL · A.R. SIMOUN WADE DAVIS BRAD FIEDEL DAVID NICHOLS
GLENN FARR ROB COHEN · KEITH BARISH DAVID LADD · DOUG CLAYBOURNE
WES CRAVEN

Scooby-Doo on Zombie Island (1998, animation) USA. Dir: Hiroshi Aoyama. Kazumi Fukushima, Jim Stenstrum. Scr: Glenn Leopold. Mus: Steven Bramson. Ed: Paul Douglas. 77 min.

The Scotland Yard Mystery (*The Living Dead,* 1934) UK. Dir: Thomas Bentley. Scr: Frank Miller based on a play by Wallace Geoffrey. DP: James Wilson. Ed: Walter Stokvis. PD: David Rawnsley. Cast: Gerald du Maurier (Commissioner Stanton), George Curzon (Dr. Charles Masters), Grete Natzler (Irene Masters), Belle Chrystall (Mary Stanton), Leslie Perrins (John Freeman), Frederick Peisley (Kenneth Bailey), Wally Patch (Detective Sgt. George). 72 min.

The Second Death (2005) USA. Dir/Ed: Joe Wilson. Scr: Christine Parker. Mus: Matt Carey. Cast: Bill Mulligan (Adam), Libby Lynn (Tracy), Jessie Walley (Mary), Ryan Williams (Teddy), Brian Chippewa (Todd).

The Serpent and the Rainbow (1988) USA. Dir: Wes Craven. Scr: Richard Maxwell, Adam Rodman inspired by the book by Wade Davis. Mus: Brad Fiedel. DP: John Lindley. Ed: Glenn Farr. PD: David Nichols. Cast: Bill Pullman (Dennis Alan), Cathy Tyson (Marielle Duchamp), Zakes Mokae (Dargent Peytraud), Paul Winfield (Lucien Celine), Brent Jennings (Louis Mozart), Conrad Roberts (Christophe), Badja Djola (Gaston), Theresa Merritt (Simone), Michael Gough (Schoonbacher), Paul Guilfoyle (Cassedy). 98 min.

Severed (2005) Canada. Dir: Carl Bessai. Scr: Carl Bessai, Travis McDonald based on a story by McDonald, Julian Clarke. DP: James Liston. Ed: Julian Clarke. Cast: Paul Campbell (Tyler), Sarah Lind (Rita), Julian Christopher (Mac), JR Bourne (Carter), Michael Teigen (Luke), Leanne Adachi (Stacey). 93 min.

Shadow: Dead Riot (2006) USA. Dir: Derek Wan. Scr: Michael Gingold, Richard Siegel. Mus: Vernon Reid. DP: Derek Wan. Ed: Ki-hop Chan, Joanna Or, Andrew Sterling. PD: Dave Barnes. Cast: Tony Todd (Shadow), Carla Greene (Solitaire), Nina Hodoruk (Warden Danvers), Michael Quinlan (Swann), Cat Miller (Emily), Andrea Langi (Elsa), Tatianna Butler (Mondo), Misty Mundae (Crystal). 81 min.

Shadows of the Dead (2004) USA. Dir/Scr/Ed/PD: Carl Lindbergh. Mus: Antonio Underwood. DP: Roderick E. Stevens. Cast: Jonathan Flanigan (John), Beverly Hynds (Jennifer). 92 min.

Shatter Dead (1994) USA. Dir/Scr: Scooter McCrae. Mus: Geek Messiah, Steven Rajkumar. DP: Matthew M. Howe. Cast: Stark Raven (Susan), Flora Fauna (Mary), Daniel Johnson (Dan), Robert Wells (Preacher). 84 min.

Shaun of the Dead (2004) UK/France/USA. Dir: Edgar Wright. Scr: Simon Pegg, Edgar Wright. Mus: Dan Mudford, Pete Woodhead. DP: David M. Dunlap. Ed: Chris Dickens. PD: Marcus Rowland. Cast: Simon Pegg (Shaun), Kate Ashfield (Liz), Nick Frost (Ed), Lucy Davis (Dianne), Dylan Moran (David), Nicola Cunningham (Mary). 99 min.

Sheng hua te jing zhi sang shi ren wu (*Bio-Cops*, 2000) Hong Kong. Dir: Wai-Man Cheng. Scr: Cheuk-Hon Szeto. Cast: Stephen Fung (Marco), Sam Lee (Brother Cheap), Alice Chan (Bell). 89 min.

Shikabane hime aka (*Corpse Princess*, 2008–2009, television series, animated) Japan.

Shock Waves (1977) USA. Dir: Ken Wiederhorn. Scr: John Kent Harrison, Ken Pare, Ken Wiederhorn. Mus: Richard Einhorn. DP: Reuben Trane. Ed: Norman Gay. Cast: Peter Cushing (SS Commander), Brooke Adams

(Rose), Fred Buch (Chuck), Jack Davidson (Norman), Luke Halpin (Keith), John Carradine (Captain), Clarence Thomas (Fisherman). 85 min.

Sick (2012) Canada. Dir: Ryan M. Andrews. Scr: Ryan M. Andrews., Chris Cull. Mus: Andrew Lauzon. DP: Michael Jari Davidson. Ed: Navin Ramaswaran. PD: Josh Heisie. Cast: Christina Anne Aceto (Dr. Leigh Rozetta), Richard Roy Sutton (Seph Copeland), Robert Nolan (Mckay Jacobs), Jennifer Polansky (Claudia Silveira), Debbie Rochon (Dr. Joselda Fehmi), Sandra DaCosta (Betsy). 95 min.

Sick, the Dead (2009) USA. Dir: Jordy Dickens, Brockton McKinney. Mus: Amy Banks Fader, Bo Fader. Cast: Travis G. Allen (Rock & Roll High School Zombie 5), Amy Banks (Ellen), Southey Blanton (Andy), Nathan Boreiko (Alex), Brian T. Coe (Rock & Roll High School Zombie 2). 90 min.

Silent Night, Zombie Night (2009) USA. Dir/Scr/Ed: Sean Cain. Mus: Mario Salvucci. DP: Jim Wright. Cast: Jack Forcinito (Frank Talbot), Andy Hopper (Nash Jackson), Nadine Stenovitch (Sarah Talbot), Lew Temple (Jeffrey Hannigan), Vernon Wells (Paul Irwin), Felissa Rose (Elsa Lansing), Timothy Muskatell (Raccoon). 83 min.

The Slaughter (2006) USA. Dir/Scr/Ph/Ed: Jay Lee. Mus: Chauncey Mahan. PD: Sara Kugelmass. Cast: Jessica Custodio (Dana), Zak Kilberg (Iggy), Terry Erioski (Tyler), Laura Sabbia (Heather), Travis Wood (Brandon), Jen Alex (Alexandra). 96 min.

Slither (2006) USA. Dir/Scr: James Gunn. Mus: Tyler Bates. DP: Gregory Middleton. Ed: John Axelrad. PD: Andrew Neskoromny. Cast: Don Thompson (Wally), Nathan Fillion (Bill Pardy), Gregg Henry (Jack MacReady), Xantha Radley (Uptight Mom), Elizabeth Banks (Starla Grant), Tania Saulnier (Kylie Strutemyer). 95 min.

Sole Survivor (1983) USA. Dir/Scr: Thom E. Eberhardt. Mus: David F. Anthony. DP: Russell Carpenter. Ed: Thom E. Eberhardt. Cast: Anita Skinner (Denise Watson), Kurt Johnson (Brian Richardson), Robin Davidson (Kristy Cutler), Caren L. Larkey (Karla Davis), Andrew Boyer (Blake), Daniel Cartwell (Lt. Patterson), Wendy Dake (Roxie). 85 min.

Space Zombie Bingo!!! (1993) USA. Dir: George Ormrod. Scr: George Ormrod, John Sabotta. DP: Alan Halfhill. Cast: William Darkow (Maj. Kent Bendover), Ramona Provost (Barbie Que), Hugh Crawford (Gen. Herpes Simplex), Mike Milligan (Soldier). 75 min.

Stacy: Attack of the Schoolgirl Zombies (2001) Japan. Dir: Naoyuki Tomomatsu. Scr: Chisato Ôgawara based on a novel by Kenji Otsuki. DP: Masahide Iioka. Cast: Norman England (Jeff), Tomoka Hayashi (Nozomi), Yukijirô Hotaru, Ryôichi Inaba, Natsuki Katô (Eiko), Toshinori Omi (Shibukawa), Ryûki Kitaoka, Shirô Misawa, Masayoshi Nogami (Father). 80 min.

Stalled (2013) UK. Dir: Christian James. Scr: Dan Palmer. DP: Sashi Kissoon. Ed: Mark Gilleece. PD: Antony Haylock. Cast: Dan Palmer (W.C.), Antonia Bernath (Heather), Tamaryn Payne (Evie), Mark Holden (Jeff From I.T), Giles Alderson (Nick Shanks), Sarah Biggins (Debbie), Victoria Broom (Holly), Marcus Kelly (Charlie), Victoria Eldon (Samantha), Chris R. Wright (Mikey).

State of Emergency (2011) USA. Dir/Scr/Ed: Turner Clay. DP: Tony Oberstar. Cast: Jay Hayden (Jim), Andy Stahl (Pivens), Tori White (Ix), Scott Lilly (Scott), Kathryn Todd Norman (Julie), McKenna Jones (Emilie), Loren Albanese (Jeremy). 90 min.

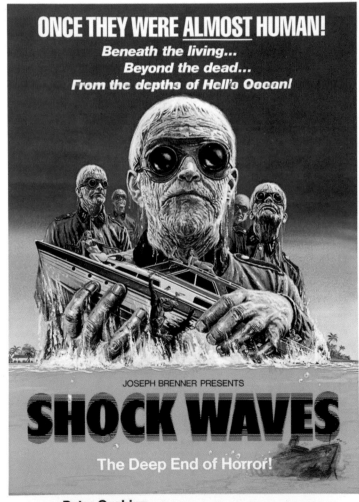

ONCE THEY WERE **ALMOST** HUMAN!
Beneath the living...
Beyond the dead...
From the depths of Hell's Ocean!

JOSEPH BRENNER PRESENTS

SHOCK WAVES

The Deep End of Horror!

starring **Peter Cushing** · with Brooke Adams · Fred Buch · Jack Davidson
Luke Halprin · D.J. Sidney · Don Stout · and **John Carradine**
A Zopix Presentation · screenplay by John Harrison, Ken Wiederhorn
music by Richard Einhorn · produced by Reuben Trane · directed by Ken Wiederhorn
Released by JOSEPH BRENNER ASSOCIATES, INC. · in EASTMANCOLOR   PG PARENTAL GUIDANCE SUGGESTED

The Stink of Flesh (2005) USA. Dir/Scr/Ed: Scott Phillips. Mus: Chris Alexander, Carrie Eliza. DP: Richard Griffin. PD: Israel Wright. Cast: Kurly Tlapoyawa (Matool), Ross Kelly (Nathan), Diva (Dexy), Billy Garberina (Mandel). 85 min.

Storm of the Dead (2006) USA. Dir/Scr: Bob Cook. Mus: Jason Solowsky. DP: Francis Grumman. Ed: Ginger Brigham Cook. AD: George Siplin. Cast: Bob Cook (Reporter), Carlos Guity (Looter/Zombie), Todd Terry (Sgt. Barnes), Jim Pacitti (Cpl. Jackson), Laurence Chavez (Pvt. Sanchez), Yvone Williamson (Older Yvonne), Debra Cassano (Cpl. Dani Stevens). 88 min.

Stripperland (2011) USA. Dir: Sean Skelding. Scr: Brad McCray, Shawn Justice. DP: Michael Lindberg. Ed: David Wester. PD: Jeff Seats. Cast: Benjamin Sheppard (Idaho), Jamison Challeen (Frisco), Maren McGuire (Virginia), Ileana Herrin (West), Hank Cartwright (Guy Gibson), Daniel Baldwin (Double D), Linnea Quigley (Grambo). 103 min.

Strippers vs. Zombies (*Zombies Zombies Zombies*, 2008) USA. Dir: Jason Murphy. Scr: Anthony Steven Giordano. Mus: Chris Lott. DP: Kenny Beaumont. Ed: Anthony Steven Giordano, Brad Tremaroli. Cast: Lyanna Tumaneng (Dallas), Jessica Barton (Dakota), Hollie Winnard (Harley), Sean Harriman (Chris), Anthony Headen (Johnny Vegas), Valensky Sylvain (Clive). 82 min.

The Stuff (1985) USA. Dir/Scr: Larry Cohen. Mus: Anthony Guefen. DP: Paul Glickman. Ed: Armond Lebowitz. AD: Marleen Marta, George Stoll. Cast: Michael Moriarty (David "Mo" Rutherford), Andrea Marcovicci (Nicole), Garrett Morris (Charlie W. Hobbs), Paul Sorvino (Col. Malcolm Grommett Spears), Scott Bloom (Jason), Danny Aiello (Vickers), Patrick O'Neal (Fletcher). 93 min.

Sugar Hill (1974) USA. Dir: Paul Maslansky. Scr: Tim Kelly. Mus: Dino Fekaris, Nick Zesses. DP: Robert C. Jessup. Ed: Carl Kress. Cast: Marki Bey (Diana "Sugar" Hill), Robert Quarry (Morgan), Don Pedro Colley (Baron Samedi), Betty Anne Rees (Celeste), Richard Lawson (Valentine), Zara Cully (Mama Maitresse), Charles Robinson (Fabulous), Larry Don Johnson (Langston). 91 min.

Sun faa sau si (*Biozombie*, 1998) Hong Kong. Dir: Wilson Yip. Scr: Matt Chow, Siu Man Sing, Wilson Yip. Mus: Peter Kam. DP: Kwok-Man Keung. Ed: Ka-Fai Cheung. AD: Stanley Cheung. Cast: Jordan Chan (Woody Invincible), Emotion Cheung (Loi), Sam Lee (Crazy Bee), Yiu-Cheung Lai (Kui), Angela Tong (Rolls). 94 min.

The Supernaturals (1986) USA. Dir: Armand Mastroianni. Scr: Joel Soisson, Michael S. Murphey. Mus: Robert O. Ragland. DP: Peter Lyons Collister. Ed: John R. Bowey. PD: Alexandra Kicenik. Cast: Maxwell Caulfield (Pvt. Ray Ellis), Nichelle Nichols (Sgt. Leona Hawkins), Talia Balsam (Pvt. Angela Lejune), Bradford Bancroft (Pvt. Tom Weir), LeVar Burton (Pvt. Michael Osgood), Bobby Di Cicco (Pvt. Tim Cort), Scott Jacoby (Pvt. Chris Mendez). 91 min.

Surf II: the End of the Trilogy (1984) USA. Dir/Scr: Randall M. Badat. Mus: Peter Bernstein. DP: Álex Phillips Jr. Ed: Jacqueline Cambas. PD: Jeff Staggs. Cast: Eddie Deezen (Menlo), Morgan Paull (Chuck's Dad), Ruth Buzzi (Chuck's Mom), Lyle Waggoner (Chief Boyardie), Cleavon Little (Daddy O), Linda Kerridge (Sparkle), Carol Wayne (Mrs. O'Finlay), Eric Stoltz (Chuck), Jeffrey Rogers (Bob). 91 min.

Survival of the Dead (2009) USA/Canada. Dir/Scr: George A. Romero. Mus: Robert Carli. DP: Adam Swica.

Ed: Michael Doherty. PD: Arvinder Grewal. Cast: Alan Van Sprang (Sgt. Crockett), Kenneth Welsh (Patrick O'Flynn), Kathleen Munroe (Janet/Jane O'Flynn), Devon Bostick (Boy), Richard Fitzpatrick (Seamus Muldoon), Athena Karkanis (Tomboy). 90 min.

Swamp Zombies!!! (2005) USA. Dir/Scr: Len Kabasinski. Mus: Russ Castella. Ed: J.R. Hubbard. Cast: Brian Heffron (The Hermit), Jasmin St. Claire (Lillian Carter), Pamela Sutch (Monica), Dan Severn (Police Captain), Shannon Solo (Dr. Phillips). 90 min.

Tales from the Crypt (1972) USA/UK. Dir: Freddie Francis. Scr: Milton Subotsky based on the comic books. Mus: Douglas Gamley. DP: Norman Warwick. Ed: Teddy Darvas. Cast: Joan Collins (Joanne Clayton), Peter Cushing (Arthur Edward Grimsdyke), Roy Dotrice (Charles Gregory), Richard Greene (Ralph Jason), Ian Hendry (Carl Maitland), Patrick Magee (George Carter), Barbara Murray (Enid Jason), Nigel Patrick (Maj. William Rogers), Robin Phillips (James Elliot), Ralph Richardson (The Crypt Keeper). 92 min.

Tales from the Crypt (1989–1996, television series) USA. (1992, Season 4, Episode 7: "The New Arrival") Dir: Peter Medak. Tel: Ron Finley. Mus: Michael Kamen. DP: John R. Leonetti. Ed: Stanley Wohlberg. PD: Gregory Melton. Cast: David Warner (Dr. Alan Gertz), Joan Severance (Rona), Zelda Rubinstein (Nora), Twiggy (Bonnie), Robert Patrick (Lothar). 25 min. (1996, Season 6, Episode 7: "Cold War") Dir: Andrew Morahan, Robin Bextor. Tel: Scott Nimerfro. Mus: J. Peter Robinson. DP: Robin Vidgeon. Ed: Jeremy Strachan. PD: Peter Mullins. Cast: Ewan McGregor (Ford), Jane Horrocks (Cammy), Colin Salmon (Jimmy Picket), John Salthouse (Cutter), Willie Ross (Barman). (1996, Season 7, Episode 2: "Last Respects") Dir: Freddie Francis. Tel: Scott Nimerfro. Mus: Frank Becker. DP: Alan Hume. Ed: Jeremy Strachan. PD: Gregory Melton. Cast: Emma Samms (Yvonne), Kerry Fox (Dolores), Julie Cox (Marlys), Michael Denison (Richard), Dulcie Gray (Mrs. Wilde).

Tales of Terror (1962, "The Case of M. Valdemar" segment) USA. Dir: Roger Corman. Scr: Richard Matheson based on the stories of Edgar Allan Poe. Mus: Les Baxter. DP: Floyd Crosby. Ed: Anthony Carras. PD: Daniel Haller. Cast: Vincent Price (Ernest Valdemar), Basil Rathbone (Carmichael), Debra Paget (Helene), David Frankham (Dr. James). 89 min.

Theater of the Dead (2013) Australia. Dir/Scr: Patrick J. Gallagher. DP: Miguel Gallagher. Ed: Dallas Bland, Rafael Perez. PD: Joshua Zeigler. Cast: Emma Gleeson (Cassie), Rob Baird (Mike), Andy Minh Trieu (Ritchie), Matt Butcher (Zach), Kirsten Haussmann (Val), Kat Bramston (Kristine).

Thriller (1983) USA. Dir: John Landis. Scr: John Landis, Michael Jackson. Mus: Elmer Bernstein. DP: Robert Paynter. Ed: Malcolm Campbell, George Folsey Jr. Cast: Michael Jackson (Michael), Ola Ray (Michael's Girl), Vincent Price (Narration), Forrest J Ackerman (Man in Movie Theater). 13 min.

To kako (*Evil*, 2005) Greece. Dir/Scr/Ed: Yorgos Noussias. DP: Claudio Bolivar, Petros Nousias. Mus: Grigoris Grigoropoulos, Thanos Karabatziakis, Petros Nousias. Cast: Meletis Georgiadis (Meletis), Argiris Thanasoulas (Argyris), Pepi Moschovakou (Marina), Stavroula Thomopoulou (Dimitra). 83 min.

Tokyo Zombie (2005) Japan. Dir: Sakichi Satô. Scr: Sakichi Satô based on the manga by Yûsaku Hanakuma. Mus: Hiroshi Futami. DP: Isao Ishii. Ed: Yasushi Shimamura. PD: Hisao Inagaki. Cast: Tadanobu Asano (Fujio), Shô Aikawa (Mitsuo), Erika Okuda (Yoko), Arata Furuta (Ishihara), Hina Matsuoka (Fumiyo). 103 min.

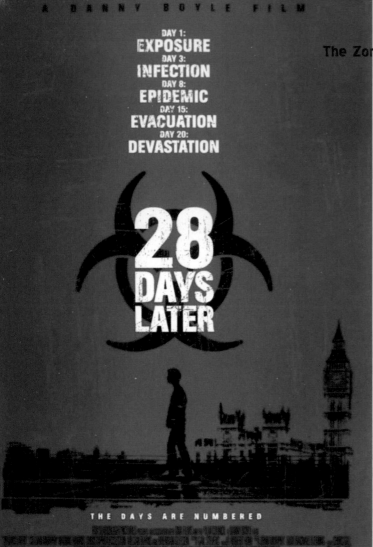

A DANNY BOYLE FILM

DAY 1:
EXPOSURE
DAY 3:
INFECTION
DAY 8:
EPIDEMIC
DAY 15:
EVACUATION
DAY 20:
DEVASTATION

28 DAYS LATER

THE DAYS ARE NUMBERED

Sloane Smith (Sarah, CDC Boss). 86 min.

La tumba de los muertos vivientes (*L'Abime des Morts Vivants, The Treasure of the Living Dead, Oasis of the Living Dead, Oasis of the Zombies* 1982) France. Dir/Scr: Jesús Franco [as A.M. Frank]. Mus: Daniel White. DP: Max Monteillet. Ed: Claude Gros. Cast: Manuel Gélin (Robert Blabert), France Lomay (Erika), Jeff Montgomery (Ben), Myriam Landson (Kurt's Wife), Eric Viellard (Ronald), Caroline Audret (Sylvie), Henri Lambert (Kurt). 82 min.

The Turning (*Zombie Lover*, 2011) UK. Dir/Scr DP/Ed: Jason Impey. Mus: Ralph Cardell. Cast: Kemal Yildirim (Dillon Slater), Lianne Robertson (Stacey Gallagher), Rami Hilmi (Quaid Hess), Eileen Daly (Ilsa), Max Fellows (Michael Gallagher), Jason Impey (Leon), Rachael Stewart, Joanne Pettit (Zombies). 91 min.

28 Days Later (2002) UK. Dir: Danny Boyle. Scr: Alex Garland. Mus: John Murphy. DP: Anthony Dod Mantle. Ed: Chris Gill. PD: Mark Tildesley. Cast: Cillian Murphy (Jim), Naomie Harris (Selena), Noah Huntley (Mark), Brendan Gleeson (Frank), Megan Burns (Hannah), Luke Mably (Pvt. Clifton), Stuart McQuarrie (Sgt. Farrell), Ricci Harnett (Cpl. Mitchell), Leo Bill (Pvt. Jones), Junior Laniyan (Pvt. Bell), Ray Panthaki (Pvt. Bedford), Christopher Eccleston (Maj. Henry West), Sanjay Rambaruth (Pvt. Davis). 113 min.

28 Weeks Later (2007) UK/Spain. Dir: Juan Carlos Fresnadillo. Scr: Rowan Joffe, Juan Carlos Fresnadillo, Enrique López Lavigne, Jesús Olmo. Mus: John Murphy. DP: Enrique Chediak. Ed: Chris Gill. PD: Mark Tildesley. Cast: Robert Carlyle (Don), Rose Byrne (Scarlet), Jeremy Renner (Doyle), Harold Perrineau (Flynn), Catherine McCormack (Alice), Idris Elba (Stone), Imogen Poots (Tammy), Mackintosh Muggleton (Andy), Amanda Walker (Sally), Shahid Ahmed (Jacob), Garfield Morgan (Geoff). 100 min.

Two Evil Eyes ("The Facts in the Case of Mr. Valdemar" segment, 1990) Italy/USA. Dir: George A. Romero (segment "The Facts in the Case of Mr. Valdemar"). Scr: Romero based on the story by Edgar Allan Poe. Mus: Pino Donaggio. DP: Peter Reniers. Cast: Adrienne Barbeau (Jessica Valdemar), Ramy Zada (Dr. Robert Hoffman), Bingo O'Malley (Ernest Valdemar), Jeff Howell (Policeman). 120 min.

Uccelli Assassini (*Zombie 5: Killing Birds*, 1987) Italy. Dir: Claudio Lattanzi, Joe D'Amato. Scr: Claudio Lattanzi, Sheila Goldberg, Daniele Stroppa. Mus: Carlo Maria Cordio. DP: Joe D'Amato [as Fred Sloniscko Jr]. Ed: Kathleen Stratton [as Rosanna Landi]. Cast: Lara Wendel (Anne), Robert Vaughn (Dr. Fred Brown),

Towers of Terror (2013) USA. Dir/Scr: Matt Gibson. Ed: Nick Gibson. Cast: Aleksander D'Avignon (William), Shannon Lark (Kendra), Erik Cram (Captain Nicholas Menagerie), Vic May (Stellan), Jason Kaye (Corey), Brett Robert Culbert (Chad), Kevin Bradel (Dirk), Jimmy Seargeant (J). 84 min.

Trailer Park of Terror (2008) USA. Dir: Steven Goldmann. Scr: Timothy Dolan based on the Imperium comic book series. Mus: Alan Brewer. DP: Jeff Venditti. Ed: Jarred Buck. Cast: Nichole Hiltz (Norma), Lew Temple (Marv), Jeanette Brox (Bridget), Myk Watford (Roach), Michelle Lee (Miss China), Ed Corbin (Sgt. Stank), Ricky Mabe (Michael), Cody McMains (Jason), Hayley Marie Norman (Amber). 98 min.

True Love Zombie (2012) USA. Dir/Scr/DP/Ed: Paul Blevins. Cast: Paul Blevins (Paul), Rhonda Blevins (Rhonda), Steve Snyder (Stan), Jeff Merrill (Roger),

Timothy W. Watts (Steve Porter), Leslie Cummins (Mary), James Villemaire (Paul), Sal Maggiore (Brian). 92 min.

Undead (2003) Australia. Dir/Scrs/Ed: Michael Spierig, Peter Spierig. Mus: Cliff Bradley. DP: Andrew Strahorn. Cast: Felicity Mason (René Chaplin), Mungo McKay (Marion), Rob Jenkins (Wayne), Lisa Cunningham (Sallyanne), Dirk Hunter (Harrison). 97 min.

Undead or Alive: A Zombedy (2007) USA. Dir/Scr: Glasgow Phillips. Mus: Ivan Koutikov. DP: Thomas L. Callaway. Ed: Larry Madaras. PD: Mark Alan Duran. Cast: Lew Alexander (Geronimo), Chris Coppola (Cletus), James Denton (Elmer Winslow), Leslie Jordan (Padre), Chris Kattan (Luke Rudd), Cristin Michele (Kate), Navi Rawat (Sue), Chloe Russell (Ruby). 90 min.

Utopia (2013) Norway. Dir: Daniel William Bones. Scr: Daniel William Bones, Bjørn Alexander Brem. Mus: Bjørn Alexander Brem, DP: Tor Eigil Scheide. Ed: Patrick Bernhardt. AD: Jane Levick. Cast: Fie Baro (Zombie, Dead Bride), Unni Bendigtsen (The Little Girl), Geir Bratland (Himself), Bjørn Alexander Brem (Gothminister), Linda Cecilie Stoea Buckholm (Lady Zombie), Alena Chechyk (Nurse), Hanna Duna (Zombie Fire-Breather). 72 min.

The Vanguard (2008) USA. Dir/Scr: Matthew Hope. Mus: Mark Delany. DP: David Byrne. Ed: Simon Adams, Larry Trybec. Cast: Karen Admiraal (Linda), Jack Bailey (Lead Biosyn), Ray Bullock Jr. (Max), Emma Choy (Rachael), Terry Cole (Tracker). 89 min.

The Video Dead (1987) USA. Dir/Scr: Robert Scott. Mus: Leonard Marcel, Kevin McMahon, Stuart Rabinowitsh. DP: Greg Becker. Ed: Bob Sarles. PD: Katalin Rogers. Cast: Michael St. Michaels (Henry Jordan), Rocky Duvall (Jeff Blair), Sam David McClelland (Joshua Daniels), Jennifer Miro (The Woman), Victoria Bastel (April Ellison), Libby Russler (Maria). 90 min.

Violent Shit 3: Infantry of Doom (*Zombie Doom*, 1999) Germany. Dir/Scr: Andreas Schnaas. Mus: Gregor Adolf Hartz. DP: Steve Aquilina. Ed: Steve Aquilina, Alexander Jurkat, A.J. Simpson. Cast: Andreas Schnaas (Karl the Butcher), Marc Trinkhaus (Karl Sr.), Matthias Kerl (Dr. Senius). 85 min.

Virus (*Hell of the Living Dead, Night of the Zombies*, 1980) Italy/Spain. Dir: Bruno Mattei [as Vincent Dawn], Claudio Fragasso. Scr: Claudio Fragasso, José María Cunillés, Rossella Drudi, Bruno Mattei. Mus: Goblin. DP: John Cabrera. Ed: Claudio Borroni. PD: Antonio Belart. Cast: Margit Evelyn Newton (Lia Rousseau), Franco Garofalo (Zantoro), Selan Karay (Vincent), José

Gras (Lt. Mike London), Gabriel Renom (Pierre), Josep Lluís Fonoll (Osborne). 101 min.

Virus Undead (2008) Germany. Dir: Wolf Wolff, Ohmuthi. Scr: Wolf Jahnke. Mus: Dominik Schultes, Max Würden. DP: Heiko Rahnenführer. Ed: Robert Kummer. PD: Anna Misch, Jan Wünsche. Cast: Philipp Danne (Robert Hansen), Birthe Wolter (Marlene Vogt), Anna Breuer (Vanessa Lux), Nikolas Jürgens (Eugen Friedrich), Marvin Gronen (Patrick Schubert). 95 min.

Voodoo Island (1957) USA. Dir: Reginald Le Borg. Scr: Richard H. Landau. Mus: Les Baxter. DP: William Margulies. Ed: John F. Schreyer. PD: Jack T. Collis. Cast: Boris Karloff (Phillip Knight), Beverly Tyler (Sarah Adams), Murvyn Vye (Barney Finch), Elisha Cook Jr. (Martin Schuyler), Rhodes Reason (Matthew Gunn), Jean Engstrom (Claire Winter), Friedrich von Ledebur (Native Chief). 76 min.

Voodoo Man (1944) USA. Dir: William Beaudine. Scr: Robert Charles. DP: Marcel Le Picard. Ed: Carl Pierson. AD: Dave Milton. Cast: Bela Lugosi (Dr. Richard Marlowe), John Carradine (Toby), George Zucco (Nicholas), Wanda McKay (Betty Benton), Louise Currie (Stella Saunders), Tod Andrews (Ralph Dawson), Ellen Hall (Mrs. Evelyn Marlowe), Terry Walker (Alice), Mary Currier (Mrs. Benton). 61 min.

Vudú Sangriento (*Voodoo Black Exorcist*, 1974) Spain. Dir: Manuel Caño. Scr: Santiago Moncada. Mus: Fernando García Morcillo. DP: Roberto Ochoa. Ed: Antonio Ramírez de Loaysa, Frederic Vich. Cast: Aldo Sambrell (Gatanebo), Tanyeka Stadler (Kenya), Alexander Abrahan, Fernando Sancho (Inspector Dominguez), Alfredo Mayo (Dr. Kessling), Eva León (Sylvia), Ricardo Rodríguez, Enrique del Río, María Antonia del Río. 88 min.

The Walking Dead (1936) USA. Dir: Michael Curtiz. Scr: Ewart Adamson, Peter Milne, Robert Hardy Andrews,

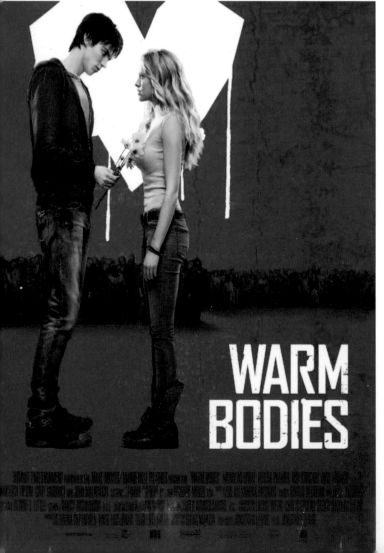

Lillie Hayward based on a story by Adamson, Joseph Fields. DP: Hal Mohr. Ed: Thomas Pratt. AD: Hugh Reticker. Cast: Boris Karloff (John Ellman), Ricardo Cortez (Nolan), Edmund Gwenn (Dr. Beaumont), Marguerite Churchill (Nancy), Warren Hull (Jimmy), Barton MacLane (Loder), Henry O'Neill (Werner), Joe King (Judge Shaw), Addison Richards (Warden). 66 min.

The Walking Dead (2010–present, television series) USA. Creator: Frank Darabont based on the comic book series by Robert Kirkman. Cast: Andrew Lincoln (Rick Grimes), Jon Bernthal (Shane Walsh), Sarah Wayne Callies (Lori Grimes), Laurie Holden (Andrea), Jeffrey DeMunn (Dale Horvath), Steven Yeun (Glenn Rhee), Chandler Riggs (Carl Grimes), Norman Reedus (Daryl Dixon), Melissa McBride (Carol Peletier). Episodes: 42–45 min.

War of the Dead (2006) Canada. Dir: Sean Cisterna. Mus: Frank Adriano. DP: Eduardo Arregui. PD: Arlene Stewart. Cast: Camille Djokoto (Special Agent Kelly Conda), Talia Schwebel (Vampire Girl), Daniel Wener (Security Guard), Lauren Kurtz (Tracy), Myer Gordon (Vincent), Andrea Korac (Waitress), Colin Nash (Zombie Gotz), Mihkel Ranniste (Zombie Fritz), Jayme Kalino (Zombie Klaus). 88 min.

War of the Dead (2012) Italy/Finland. Dir: Marko Mäkilaakso. Scr: Marko Mäkilaakso, Barr B. Potter. Mus: Neal Acree, Joel Goldsmith. DP: Hannu-Pekka Vitikainen. Ed: Michael J. Duthie. PD: Algis Garbaciauskas. Cast: Andrew Tiernan (Capt. Martin Stone), Jouko Ahola (Capt. Niemi), Samuel Vauramo (Kolya), Mikko Leppilampi (Lt. Laakso), Andreas Wilson (Assistant), Antti Reini (Sgt. Halonen), Magdalena Górska (Dasha), Mark Wingett (David Selzman), Andrius Paulavicius (Russian Soldier), Geoffrey T. Bersey (Old Man), Tomas Ereminas (Nazi Zombie Soldier). 86 min.

Warm Bodies (2013) USA. Dir: Jonathan Levine. Scr: Jonathan Levine based on the novel by Isaac Marion. Mus: Marco Beltrami, Buck Sanders. DP: Javier Aguirresarobe. Ed: Nancy Richardson. PD: Martin Whist. Cast: Nicholas Hoult (R), Teresa Palmer (Julie), Analeigh Tipton (Nora), Rob Corddry (M), Dave Franco (Perry), John Malkovich (Grigio), Cory Hardrict (Kevin). 98 min.

Wasting Away (*Zombie Town, Aaah! Zombies!!*, 2007) USA. Dir: Matthew Kohnen. Scr: Matthew Kohnen, Sean Kohnen. Mus: The Newton Brothers. DP: Allan Fiterman. Ed: Emily Chiu, Michael Schwartz. PD: Jasmin Graham. Cast: Matthew Davis (Mike), Julianna Robinson

(Vanessa), Michael Grant (Tim), Betsy Beutler (Cindy). 90 min.

When Good Ghouls Go Bad (2001, television movie) USA. Dir: Patrick R. Johnson. Tel: Patrick R. Johnson, John Lau based on a story by R.L. Stine. Mus: Christopher Gordon. DP: Brian J. Breheny. Ed: Robert Gibson. PD: Leslie Binns. Cast: Christopher Lloyd (Uncle Fred Walker), Tom Amandes (James Walker), Roy Billing (Mayor Churney), Brittany Byrnes (Dayna), Jose Element (Mike Kankel). 93 min.

White Zombie (1932) USA. Dir: Victor Halperin. Scr: Garnett Weston. DP: Arthur Martinelli. Ed: Harold McLernon. AD: Ralph Berger. Cast: Bela Lugosi (Legendre), Madge Bellamy (Madeline Short Parker), Joseph Cawthorn (Dr. Bruner), Robert Frazer (Charles Beaumont), John Harron (Neil Parker), Brandon Hurst (Silver), George Burr Macannan (Von Gelder), Frederick Peters (Chauvin), AJohn Printz (Ledot). 69 min.

White Zombie (2014) USA. Dir/Scr/Mus: Creep Creepersin based on the script by Garnett Weston. DP: Jeff Galyan. Ed: Milo Chibata, Andrew Crandall. Cast: Elina Madison (Madeline), Creep Creepersin (Murder Legendre), Tony Slade (Mr. Charles Beaumont), Johnno Wilson (Neil), Dean Mounir (Dr. Bruner), Myles Cranford (Silver).

Wicked Little Things (2006) USA. Dir: J.S. Cardone. Scr: Ben Nedivi. Mus: Tim Jones. DP: Emil Topuzov. Ed: Alain Jakubowicz. PD: Carlos Silva Da Silva. Cast: Lori Heuring (Karen), Scout Taylor-Compton (Sarah), Chloë Grace Moretz (Emma), Geoffrey Lewis (Harold), Ben Cross (Aaron Hanks), Craig Vye (Tim), Chris Jamba (Sean), Julie Rogers (Lisa). 94 min.

The Wickeds (2005) USA. Dir: John Poague. Scr: David Zagorski. Mus: Bill Rogers. DP: Joe O'Ferrel. Ed: Charlie Puritano. AD: Kristian Hickman. Cast: Ron Jeremy (Gus), Justin Alvarez (Jake), Anna Bridgforth (Julie), Kelly Sue Roth (Alyssa), Bradford Sikes (Bailey), Bryan Donoghue (Billy). 94 min.

Wild Zero (1999) Japan. Dir: Tetsuro Takeuchi. Scr: Satoshi Takagi, Tetsuro Takeuchi. Mus: Guitar Wolf. DP: Motoki Kobayashi. Ed: Tomoe Kubota. PD: Akihiko Inamura. Cast: Guitar Wolf (himself), Drum Wolf (himself), Bass Wolf (himself), Masashi Endô (Ace). 98 min.

Woke Up Dead (2009, Web series) USA. Creator: John Fasano. Dir: Tim O'Donnell. Tel: John Fasano, Kevin Bonani, Jenn Lloyd, Michael Ludy. Mus: Sam Winans. DP: Theo Angell. Ed: Richard LaBrie, Benjamin Meyer. Cast: John Heder (Drex), Krysten Ritter (Cassie), Josh Gad (Matt), Daniel Roebuck (Shadow Man), Wayne Knight (Andrew Batten), Meital Dohan (Aurora). Episodes: 4 min.

Working Stiffs (1989) USA. Dr/Scr/DP/Ed: Michael Legge. Mus: Bruce Mattson. Cast: Beverly Epstein (Lacey Shannon), Bruce Harding (Carl Worm), Tony Ferreira (Larry Shannon). 61 min.

World War Z (2013) USA. Dir: Marc Forster. Scr: Matthew Michael Carnahan, Drew Goddard, Damon Lindelof based on a story by Carnahan, J. Michael Straczynski and the novel by Max Brooks. Mus: Marco Beltrami. DP: Ben Seresin. Ed: Roger Barton, Matt Chesse. PD: Nigel Phelps. Cast: Brad Pitt (Gerry Lane), Mireille Enos (Karin Lane), Daniella Kertesz (Segen), James Badge Dale (Captain Speke), Ludi Boeken (Jurgen Warmbrunn), Fana Mokoena (Thierry Umutoni), Elyes Gabel (Andrew Fassbach). 116 min.

Wu long tian shi zhao ji gui (*Kung-Fu Zombie*, 1982) Hong Kong. Dir/Scr: Yi-Jung Hua. DP: Yung Hu. Cast: Billy Chong (Pang), Lau Chan, Kang-Yeh Cheng, Kei Ying

"Wicked Little Things"

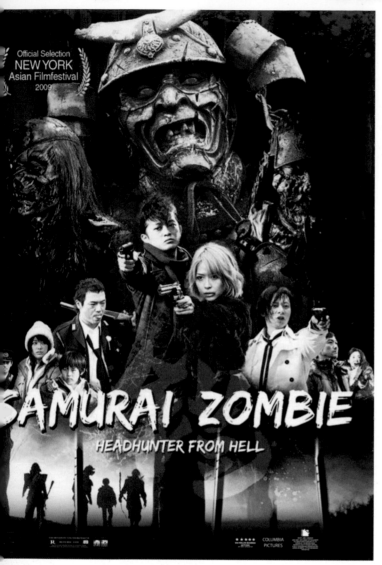

Cheung, Wei Hu, Yeong-mun Kwon. 99 min.

The Year After Infection (2012) USA. Dir/Scr/DP/Ed: Antonio E. Greco. DP: Maria Brack, Kelly Gorman. Cast: Trinka (Anna), Stan Davis (Roy), James Eason (Gary), Nichole Fischer (Madison), Joe Hammerstone (Harold), Ben Bovee (Glenn), Dennis Dashley (Thomas), Christopher M. Johnson (Richard), Eric Warrington (Andy), Timothy Lantz (Doc), Rhonda Husak (Marianne), Julian Thomas (Marcus). 130 min.

Yeogo goedam 3: Yeowoo gyedan (*Wishing Stairs*, 2003) South Korea. Dir: Jae-yeon Yun. Scr: Soyoung Lee. DP: Jeong-min Seo. Cast: Ji-hyo Song (Yun Jin-seong), Han-byeol Park (Kim Sohee), An Jo (Eom Hye-ju), Ji-Yeon Park (Han Yun-ji). 97 min.

Yoroi: Samurai zonbi (*Samurai Zombie*, 2008) Japan. Dir: Tak Sakaguchi. Scr: Ryûhei Kitamura. Mus: Nobuhiko Morino. DP: Kôji Kanaya. Cast: Mitsuru Fukikoshi, Issei Ishida, Tak Sakaguchi, Airi Nakajima, Shintarô Matsubara. 91 min.

Zeder (*Revenge of the Dead, Revenge of the Zombies*, 1983) Italy. Dir: Pupi Avati. Scr: Pupi Avati, Maurizio Costanzo, Antonio Avati. Mus: Riz Ortolani. DP: Franco Delli Colli. Ed: Amedeo Salfa. PD: Giancarlo Basili, Leonardo Scarpa. Cast: Gabriele Lavia (Stefano), Anne Canovas (Alessandra), Paola Tanziani (Gabriella Goodman), Cesare Barbetti (Dr. Meyer), Bob Tonelli (Mr. Big), Ferdinando Orlandi (Giovine), Enea Ferrario (Mirko). 89 min.

Zima mertvetsov. Metelitsa (*Winter of the Dead*, 2012) Russia. Dir/Scr: Nikolai Pigarev. DP: Vladislav Aravenkov, Ivan Egorov. AD: Irina Surikova. Cast: Mikhail Borzenkov (Konstantin), Tatyana Zhevnova (Iskra), Aleksandr Abramovich (Otets Mikhail), Sergey Shirochin (Khan), Dmitriy Kozhuro (Capitan Igor Knyazev), Yuliya Yudintseva (Dariya), Andrey Karako (Serega), Ilya Cherepko (Fotograf Vladik). 90 min.

Zombi 3 (*Zombie Flesh Eaters 2*, 1988) Italy. Dir: Lucio Fulci, Claudio Fragasso, Bruno Mattei. Scr: Rossella Drudi, Claudio Fragasso. Mus: Stefano Mainetti. DP: Richard Grassetti. Ed: Alberto Moriani, Bruno Mattei. AD: Mimmo Scavia. Cast: Deran Sarafian (Ken), Beatrice Ring (Patricia), Ottaviano Dell'Acqua (Roger), Massimo Vanni (Bo), Ulli Reinthaler (Nancy), Marina Loi (Carole). 84 min.

Zombie (*Zombi 2*, 1979) Italy. Dir: Lucio Fulci. Scr: Elisa Briganti, Dardano Sacchetti. Mus: Giorgio Cascio, Fabio Frizzi, Adriano Giordanella, Maurizio Guarini. DP: Sergio Salvati. Ed: Vincenzo Tomassi. PD: Walter Patriarca. Cast: Tisa Farrow (Anne Bowles), Ian McCulloch (Peter West), Richard Johnson (Dr. David Menard), Al Cliver (Brian Hull), Auretta Gay (Susan Barrett), Stefania D'Amario (Menard's Nurse), Olga Karlatos (Paola Menard), Leo Gavero (Fritz), Lucio Fulci (Newspaper Editor). 91 min.

Zombie A-Hole (2011) USA. Dir/Scr/DP/Ed: Dustin Mills. Mus: Jared Kaelber. Cast: Jessica Daniels (Mercy), Josh Eal (Frank Fulci), Brandon Salkil (Castor/Pollux/Zombie). 108 min.

Zombie Apocalypse (2010) USA. Dir/Ph/Ed: Ryan Thompson. Scr: Adam Goron, Kenny James, Ryan Thompson. Mus: David Fienup, Steve Longworth. Cast: Kenny James (Dwight Miller), Michael Empson (Mark),

Michael Harthen (Tom), Kelly Knoll (Raven), Scott Watson (Kevin). 90 min.

Zombie Apocalypse (2011) USA/UK. Dir: Nick Lyon. Tel: Craig Engler, Brooks Peck. Mus: Chris Ridenhour. DP: Pedja Radenkovic. Ed: James Kondelik. PD: Alexa Roland. Cast: Ving Rhames (Henry), Taryn Manning (Ramona), Johnny Pacar (Julien), Gary Weeks (Mack), Lesley-Ann Brandt (Cassie), Eddie Steeples (Billy). 87 min.

Zombie Apocalypse: Redemption (2011) USA. Dir/DP: Ryan Thompson. Scr: Ryan Lieske, Matthew O'Day, Ryan Thompson, John Tillotson. Mus: Steve Longworth. Ed: James Collins, George Smock, Ryan Thompson. Cast: Johnny Gel (Knox), Fred Williamson (Moses), Joseph Scott Anthony (Robert), Tommy Beardmore (Lucas), Jerry Lynch (Rome), Alicia Clark (Sarah), Tokkyo Faison (Lawrence), Didrik Davis (Billy). 101 min.

Zombie Army (1991) USA. Dir: Betty Stapleford. Scr: Roger Scearce. Mus: Skip Davis, Joseph Kerr, Gregg Kirk. Cast: Cindie Lou Acker, Jody Amato, Michelle Anderson, Jack Armstrong. 67 min.

Zombie Babies (2011) USA. Dir/Scr/Ed: Eamon Hardiman. Mus: Mark Shaw. DP: Dave Russell. Cast: Rob Cobb (Teddy), Ford Austin (Reginald), Missy Dawn (Jami Lynn), Brian Gunnoe (Burt Fleming), Eamon Hardiman (Kevin), Lee Harrah (Razor), Lauren Landers (Motorboat Girl #2), Ruby Larocca (Veronica), Shawn C. Phillips (Louis), Sam Qualiana (Blade). 95 min.

Zombie Beach Party (*Enter...Zombie King*, 2003) Canada. Dir: Stacey Case. Scr: Bill Marks, Sean K. Robb. Mus: Stephen Skratt. DP: Adam Swica. Ed: Jason Winn Bareford, Sandy Pereira. PD: Naomi Allen. Cast: Jules Delorme (Ulysses), Jennifer Thom (Mercedes), Raymond Carle (Blue Saint), Rob Etcheverria (Tiki), Sean K. Robb (Mister X), Nick Cvjetkovich (Zombie King), Jason Winn Bareford (Murdelizer). 76 min.

Zombie Bloodbath (1993) USA. Dir: Todd Sheets. Scr: Jerry Angell, Todd Sheets, Roger Williams. Mus: Astoroth, T.J. Erhardt, Enochian Key. DP: Andrew Appell, Scott Jolley, Todd Sheets. Cast: Chris Harris (Joey Talbott), Auggi Alvarez (Mike Walsh), Frank Dunlay (Ralph Walsh), Jerry Angell (Larry Talbott), Cathy Metz (Gwen Talbott), Cheryl Metz (Beth Talbott). 70 min.

Zombie Bloodbath 2: Rage of the Undead (1995) USA. Dir: Todd Sheets. Scr: Dwen Doggett, Todd Sheets. Mus: Enochian Key, Todd Sheets, Matthew Jason Walsh. PD: Roger Williams. Cast: Dave Miller (Jimmy), Kathleen McSweeney (Donna), Gena Fischer (Sarah), Nick Stodden (Bart), Jody Rovick (Jodie), Jerry Angell (Joe Bob), Matthew Jason Walsh (Shiner). 98 min.

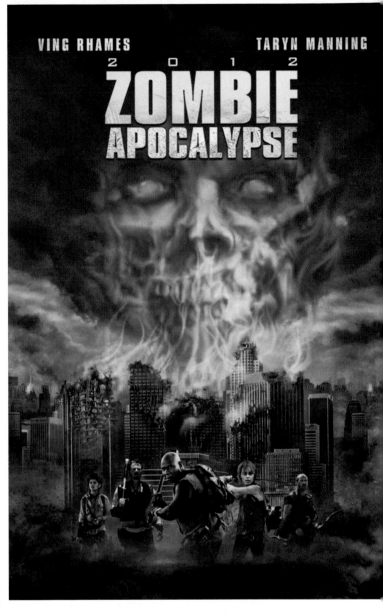

VING RHAMES   TARYN MANNING
2012
ZOMBIE APOCALYPSE

Zombie Bloodbath 3: Zombie Armageddon (2000) USA. Dir: Todd Sheets. Scr: Brian Eklund. Mus: John Stone. Cast: Abe Dyer (Brian Travis), Curtis Spencer (Steve Jones), Blake Washer (Gavin), Jolene Durrill (Rachel), Jen Davis (Andrea). 90 min.

Zombie Brigade (1986) Australia. Dir/Scr: Carmelo Musca, Barrie Pattison. Mus: John Charles, Todd Hunter. DP: Alex McPhee. PD: Julieanne Mills. Cast: John Moore (Jimmy), Khym Lam (Yoshie), Geoffrey Gibbs (Mayor Ransom), Adam A. Wong (Kinoshita). 92 min.

Zombie Busters: Outlive the Undead (2012, television special) USA. Dir/Scr: Scot Kuchta. Cast: B.C. Furtney (John), Jennifer Halbrook-Furtney (Debbie), Lacretia Lyon (Courtney Hale), Rob Young (Sam).

Zombie Campout (2002) USA. Dir/Scr: Joshua D. Smith. Mus: Richard Gunnar Nelson. DP: Lindsay Perry, Joshua D. Smith. Ed: Chad Briggs, Hunter Nolen, Joshua D. Smith, Rex Winfrey. PD: Carol Smith. Cast: Misty Orman (Bunny), Tiffany Black (Tammy), John M. Davis (Steve), Jeremy Schwab (Trevor), Alecia Peterman (Lora). 91 min.

The Zombie Christ (2012) USA. Dir: Christopher Bryan. Scr: Ryan Darbonne, Allan Traylor. Mus: Andrew Manson. DP: Austin Trotter. Ed: Adam Henderson. Cast: Ernest James (Thomas), Justin Arnold (Harelip), Philip Elder (The Zombie Christ), Sherman Allen (Tinker), Ken Rucker (Paul), Ally Hoffmann (Ali), Jonathan Povoski (Fat Biker), Adam Henderson

(Meltface), Mallory Carrick (P.L.), Christopher Bryan, Casey Barteau (Apostles), Jack Montgomery (Rothchilde/Joker).

Zombie Chronicles (2002) USA. Dir: Brad Sykes. Scr: Garrett Clancy. DP: Jeff Leroy. Ed: John Polonia, Mark Polonia. Cast: Greg Brown (Pvt. Wilson), Garrett Clancy (Sgt. Ben Draper), Mike Coen (Jason), Brian C. Donnelly (Main Zombie), Matt Emery (Man #1), John Kyle Grady (Buzz), Joe Haggerty (Ebenezer Jackson). 71 min.

Zombie Chronicles Infected Survivors (2013) USA. Dir/Scr/Ph/Ed: Marvin Suarez. Cast: Jeff Moffitt (Rick), Katie Maguire (Michelle), Michael Chmiel (Jason), Steven Gaswirth (Steve), Deja Aramburu (Deja), Matthew L. Imparato (Jack), Brice Foster (Officer Foster), Andrew Tarek (News Reporter).

Zombie Cop (1991) USA. Dir/Ed: J.R. Bookwalter. Scr: J.R. Bookwalter [as Lance Randas], Matthew Jason Walsh. Mus: Matthew Jason Walsh. DP: Brock N. Lenz. Cast: James Black (Dr. Death), Christina Bookwalter (Elementary School Xtudent), J.R. Bookwalter [as Darryl Squatmpump] (Reverend), David DeCoteau (Guy Driving Car), James L. Edwards (Sculley), Michael Kemper (Zombie Cop). 90 min.

Zombie Dawn (2012) Chile. Dir: Lucio A. Rojas, Cristian Toledo. Scr: Alex Hurtado, Lucio A. Rojas, Cristian Toledo. Mus: Alejandro Urrutia. DP: Javiera Farfán, Nicolás Ugarte. Ed: Cristian Toledo. Cast: Cristian Ramos (Col. Rainoff), Guillermo Alfaro (Sgt. Mondaca), Pablo Tournelle (Spc. Kimura), Pamela Rojas (Sc.D. Elisa), Felipe Lobos (Spc. Charlie), Christopher Offermann (Sc.D Cornellius), Maximo Yanez (Spc. Dag), Sebastian Accorsi (Lt. Brushnell), Jorge Magni (Gen. Campbell). 82 min.

Zombie Dearest (2009) USA. Dir: David Kemker. Scr: David Kemker, Mark Cavanagh. Mus: Slater Jewell-Kemker, David Kemker. DP: Michel Bisson. Ed: Mark Hajek. PD: Pierre Bonhomme. Cast: David Kemker (Gus Lawton), Shauna Black (Deborah), David Sparrow (Quinto, The Zombie), John Jarvis (Donny), Derek McGrath (Uncle Pete). 85 min.

The Zombie Diaries (2006) UK. Dir/Scr/Ed: Michael Bartlett, Kevin Gates. Mus: Stephen Hoper. DP: George Carpenter. Cast: Russell Jones (Goke), Jonnie Hurn (John), James Fisher (Geoff), Anna Blades (Vanessa), Craig Stovin (Andy), Imogen Church (Sue), Alison Mollon (Elizabeth). Kyle Sparks (Greg), Victoria Naldin (Leeann), Juliet Forester (Sharon Buckley), Leonard Fenton (Bill). 85 min.

Zombie Diaries 2 (2011) UK. Dir: Michael Bartlett, Kevin Gates. Scr: Kevin Gates. Mus: Pete Renton. DP: George

Carpenter. Ed: Drew Cullingham, Mark Tehnsuko. PD: Michael Bell. Cast: Philip Brodie (Maddox), Alix Wilton Regan (Leeann), Rob Oldfield (Jonesy), Vicky Araico (Kayne), Toby Bowman (Nicholson). 88 min.

Zombie Dream (2012) USA. Dir/Scr: Blair Murphy. DP: Jaemi Elia. Cast: Manuel Abberra (Manuel), Kevin Bean (The Alien), Phat Man Dee (Mandy), Bill Eggert (Bill), Deanna Dolges Kane (Deanna).

Zombie Driftwood (2010) UK. Dir: Bob Carruthers. Scr: Phil Eckstein. Mus: October File. DP: Bruno Breil, Gil Letourneau. Ed: Chris Gormlie. Cast: Brian Braggs (Gordon), Rita Estevanovich (Jackie), Peter Kosa (Dan), Kaz B. (Vampella/Marianne), Colin G. Wilson (Tom), Lucy Darkness (Zombie), Malcolm Ellis (Ron), Sue Howe (Gwen). 75 min.

Zombie Ed (2013) USA. Dir/Scr: Ren Blood. DP: Shaun Dallas. Ed: Scotty Baldwin, Russell Parks. Cast: William Cutting (Ed), Kelly Petering (Teddy Bare), Myles McLane (Tommy Bone), Trista Robinson (Barbie), Melissa R. Bacelar (Glamorilla), Kim Sønderholm (News Anchor), Pedro Mendoza (Pedro), Tom Nyman (Harry). 104 min.

Zombie eXs (2012) USA. Dir: George Smith. Scr: Jean Cohen, George Smith. DP: Paul J. Manoogian. Ed: Paul J. Manoogian, George Smith. Cast: Alex Hammel Shavor (Zach), Madison Hart (Lilly), Scott Keebler (Dan), Kendall Valerio (Felecia), Brandy Bryant (Irene), Gabrielle Martinez (Jolene), Jessica Sullivan (Monica).

Zombie Farm (2007) USA. Dir/Scr: B. Luciano Barsuglia. Mus: Adam MacDonald. DP: B. Luciano Barsuglia, Richard Chamberlin. Ed: Jennifer Noonan. Cast: Bobby Field (Bill), Javier Morga (Rob), Kimberly Fisher (Linda), Danielle De Luca (Jennifer), John Philbin (Agent Richardson), Joe Estevez (Anchor Man), Christine Cowden (Agent Spaulding), Daron McFarland (Agent Maxson), Shawn Hauser (J.T. Hauser), Stephen Peirick (Sheriff Boyd), Rachel Riley (Sweet Thing), Jed Rowen (Inbred Jed), Klatann Thomas (Inbred Ned), Chris Leone (Inbred Ted). 81 min.

Zombie Farm (2009) USA. Dir/Scr: Ricardo Islas. Mus: Aritz Villodas. DP: Christian Herrera. PD: Brian Michael Crutchfield. Art Dir: Virginia Fuselier. Cast: Adriana Cataño (Pilar Franco), Nadia Rowinsky (Mana Luna), Khotan (Antonio), Monika Munoz (Ana Maria), Roberto Montesinos (Roque), Eduardo Ibarrola (Senor Augustin), Mariana Da Silva (Sonia), Nair Kuzmik (Ligia), Eric Le (Asian Zombie), Eugene Kwarteng (Zombie for Mama Luna). 90 min.

Zombie Ferox (2002) UK. Dir/Scr/Ph/Ed: Jonathon

Ash. Mus: Il Kommander Gelatinoso Ninja. Cast: Jimmy Alder (Photographer), Gavin Ash (Game Player), Jonathon Ash (Doctor Fogger), Steven Ash (Stash), Kimberly Kensington (Kim). 70 min.

Zombie Ferox Zero (2002) UK. Dir/Scr/Ph/Ed: Jonathon Ash. Mus: Il Kommander Gelatinoso Ninja. Cast: Jonathon Ash (Doctor Fogger), Steven Ash (Stash), Kimberly Kensington (Kim). 61 min.

Zombie Ferox 2, *Zombie Ferox 3* (2003) UK. Dir/Scr/DP: Jonathon Ash. Mus: Il Kommander Gelatinoso Ninja. Ed: Bob Note. Cast: Jonathon Ash (Doctor Fogger), Bob Note (Sam 'Fox' Seven). (2) 74/(3) 77 min.

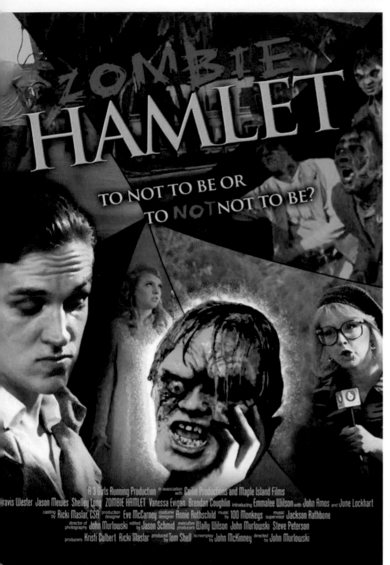

Zombie Graveyard (2004) UK. Dir/Scr/DP: Jonathon Ash. Mus: Il Kommander Gelatinoso Ninja. Ed: Bob Note. Cast: Jonathon Ash (Zombie Hunter), Paul Fletcher (Jack Flash), Bob Note (Zombie). 90 min.

Zombie Hamlet (2012) USA. Dir/Scr/DP: John Murlowski. Mus: Jackson Rathbone. Ed: Jason Schmid, Joy Zimmerman. PD: Eve McCarney. Cast: John Amos (Edgar Mortimer), A.J. Buckley (Marvin), K.C. Clyde (Dan Dover), Kim Collins (Pig Man), Brendan Michael Coughlin (Lester), Kristi Culbert (Pesky Nun). 90 min.

Zombie High (1987) USA. Dir: Ron Link. Scr: Tim Doyle, Aziz Ghazal, Elizabeth Passarelli. Mus: Daniel May. DP: Brian Coyne, David Lux. Ed: Shawn Hardin, James Whitney. PD: Matt Kozinets. Cast: Virginia Madsen

(Andrea), Paul Feig (Emerson), Sherilyn Fenn (Suzi), Clare Carey (Mary Beth), Scott Coffey (Felner), Richard Cox (Philo), Kay E. Kuter (Dean Eisner), Paul Williams (Ignatius), Henry Sutton (Bell). 93 min.

Zombie Holocaust (*Dr. Butcher*, 1980) Italy. Dir: Marino Girolami. Scr: Fabrizio De Angelis, Romano Scandariato. Mus: Nico Fidenco, Walter E. Sear. DP: Fausto Zuccoli. Ed: Alberto Moriani. PD: Walter Patriarca. Cast: Ian McCulloch (Dr. Peter Chandler), Alexandra Delli Colli (Lori Ridgeway), Sherry Buchanan (Susan Kelly), Peter O'Neal (George Happer), Donald O'Brien (Dr. Obrero/Dr. Butcher), Dakar (Molotto), Walter Patriarca (Dr. Drydock). 84 min.

Zombie Honeymoon (2004) USA. Dir/Scr: David Gebroe. Mus: Michael Tremante. DP: Thomas Browning Jr., Ken Seng. Ed: Gordon Grinberg. PD: Barbara Pietsch. Cast: Tracy Coogan (Denise Zanders), Graham Sibley (Danny Zanders), Tonya Cornelisse (Nikki Boudreaux), David M. Wallace (Buddy Cooper), Neal Jones (Officer Carp), Maria Iadonisi (Phyllis Catalano). 83 min.

Zombie Hood (2013) UK. Dir/Scr/Ed: Steve Best. Mus: Darren Maffucci, David 'dwyz' Wayman. DP: David 'dwyz' Wayman. Cast: Edward Nudd (Dermott), Jade Blocksidge (Candi), Tom Murton (Sam), Richard Lee O'Donnell (Rik), Harry Keeling (Bill), Alexandra Lyon (Kelly), Alice Joyce (Melanie), Adelle Overton (Ella), Daniela Tlumacova (Claire), Dean Tate (Luke), Marcus Akin (Mitch), Sarah Astill (Georgina), Ian Hitchens (Ross), Sophie Hyde (Kate), Sue Prunty (Brenda), Lauren Marie (Rach). 89 min.

Zombie Hunter (2013) USA. Dir: K. King. Scr: K. King, Kurt Knight. Mus: Christian Davis. DP: Ephraim Smith. PD: Kurt Knight. Cast: Martin Copping (Hunter), Danny Trejo (Jesús), Clare Niederpruem (Alison), Terry Guthrie (Jerry), Shona Kay (Female Reporter), Jeff Kirkham (Funny Man), Michael Monasterio (Casanova), Jarrod Phillips (Bill).

A Zombie Invasion (2012) USA. Dir: Matt Green. Scr: Brendan Vogel. Mus: Steven Grove. DP: Brad Garris. Ed: Janlatae Mullins, Dylan Wintersteen. Cast: Robert Pralgo (Sheriff Long), Ted Huckabee (Tucker), Stephen Caudill (Thadeus), Geoff McKnight (Crazy Earl), Courtney Hogan (Sarah Long), Vince Canlas (Ed), Lynn Talley (Vickie).

Zombie Island Massacre (1984) USA. Dir/Ed: John N. Carter. Scr: Logan O'Neill, William Stoddard. Mus: Harry Manfredini. DP: Robert M. Baldwin. AD: Srecko Gall. Cast: David Broadnax (Paul), Rita Jenrette (Sandy),

Tom Cantrell (Steve), Diane Clayre Holub (Connie), George Peters (Whitney), Ian McMillan (Joe), Dennis Stephenson (Tour Guide), Debbie Ewing (Helen). 95 min.

The Zombie King (2013) UK. Dir: Aidan Belizaire. Scr: Rebecca-Clare Evans, Jennifer Chippindale, George McCluskey, Lisa Cachia. Mus: Andrew Phillips. DP: Ismael Issa. Ed: Andrew McKee. PD: Tabitha Quitman. Cast: Edward Furlong (Samuel Peters, The Zombie King), Corey Feldman (Kalfu), George McCluskey (Ed Wallace), David McClelland (Munch), Michael Gamarano (Boris), Seb Castang (Simo), Rebecca-Clare Evans (Danny), Jennifer Chippindale (Tara), Jon Campling (Father Lawrence). 85 min.

A Zombie Love Song (2013) Canada. Dir/Scr: William Morrison. Mus: Thomas Burchell. DP: Ahmad Askoul. Ed: William Morrison. Cast: William Morrison (Jason), Gideon More (Freddy), Tessa Johnson (Amanda), Charity More (Frankie), Connor Amond (Eric), Cassy Schutz (Jessica).

Zombie Massacre (2002) Canada. Dir/Scr/Ed: Eric Weller. Cast: Sara Boyer (Beth), Matthew Henry (Matt), Kurt Martell (Kurt), Kol McKay (Hoover), Gary Halstead (Moose), Chris Hamilton (Mort). 86 min.

Zombie Massacre (2013) Italy/USA. DirScr: Luca Boni, Marco Ristori. DP: Mirco Sgarzi. Ed: Marco Ristori. Cast: Christian Boeving (Jack Stone), Mike Mitchell (John "Mad Dog" McKellen), Tara Cardinal (Eden Shizuka), Ivy Corbin (Sam Neumann), Carl Wharton (General Carter), Jon Campling (Doug Mulligan), Daniel Vivian (Dragan Ilic), Gerry Shanahan (Doctor Neumann). 87 min.

Zombie Massacre: Army of the Dead (2012) Canada. Dir: Gary Ugarek. Cast: Christopher L. Clark, Josh Davidson, Joseph D. Durbin, Jim Krut. 80 min.

Zombie Massacre III (2014) Canada. Dir/Scr: Stefan Popescu. Cast: Jimmy Nguyen (Wolfe Von Hofferloff), Kathryn Foran (Vixen Velvet), Nathan Bragg (Hector). 90 min.

Zombie Mutation (2012) UK. Dir/Scr/Ed: Adam A. Park. Music/DP: Robert Kitson. Cast: Kevin James (Ben), Harmony Hex (Stacy), Chris Greensmith (George), Robert Kitson (Chainsaw), Samantha Alexandra (Amanda) 80 min.

Zombie Nation (2004) USA. Dir/Scr: Ulli Lommel. Mus: Robert J. Walsh. DP: Jürg V. Walther. Ed: Christian Behm. Cast: Gunter Ziegler (Joe Singer), Brandon Dean (Vitalio), Axel Montgomery (Det.

McQueen), Phil Lander (Scott), Martina Bottesch (Romy), Szilvi Naray-Davey (Holly), Karen Maxwell (Virginia). 81 min.

Zombie Night (2003) Canada. Dir: David J. Francis. Scr: Amber Lynn Francis, David J. Francis. Mus: Kevin Eamon, Rich Hamelin. Ed: Chris Bellio. Cast: Danny Ticknovich (Dave), Sandra Segovic (Shelley), Dwayne Moniz (Derek), Steve Curtis (Keith), Andrea Ramolo (Amber). 93 min.

Zombie Nightmare (1987) Canada. Dir: Jack Bravman. Scr: David Wellington. Mus: Jon Mikl Thor. DP: Roger Racine. Ed: David Franko. AD: David Blanchard. Cast: Adam West (Capt. Tom Churchman), Jon Mikl Thor (Tony Washington), Tia Carrere (Amy), Manuska Rigaud (Molly Mokembe), Frank Dietz (Frank Sorrell), Linda Singer (Maggie). 89 min.

Zombie '90: Extreme Pestilence (1991) Germany. Dir: Andreas Schnaas. Scr: Andreas Schnaas. Mus: Gregg Parker. DP/Ed: Steve Aquilina. Cast: Matthias Kerl, Ralf Hess, Mathias Abbes. 75 min.

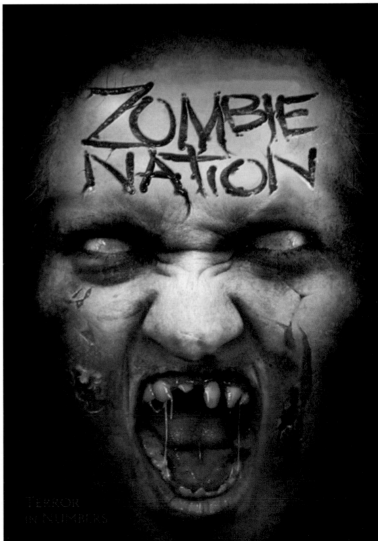

Zombie 108 (2012) Taiwan. Dir/Scr: Joe Chien. Scr: Joe Chien. Cast: Shiang Rung, Morris Rong, Yvonne Yao, Sona Eyambe. 88 min.

Zombie Planet (2004) USA. Dir/Scr: George Bonilla. Mus: Klevin Scott. DP: Billy W. Blackwell, Todd Burrows, Jon Shelton, Roy M. White. Ed: Sven Granlund, Matthew Perry. Cast: Frank Farhat (T.K. Kane), Rebecca Minton (Julie), Matt Shorr (Tom), Karl Lindstrom (Frank), Christopher Rose (Warren), Fran Rabe (Mary). 119 min.

Zombie Resurrection (2013) UK. Dir/Scr: Jake Hawkins, Andy Phelps. Mus: Dale Sumner. DP: Jake Hawkins. Ed: Marcelo Vianna. PD: Jaimie Lloyd-Anderson. Cast: Eric Colvin (Sykes), Jim Sweeney (Mac), Danny Brown (Beaumont), Simon Burbage (Gandhi), Jade Gatrell (Harden), Joe Rainbow (Gibson), Rachel Nottingham (Becca), Shamiso Mushambi (Esther), Georgia Winters (Asher), Rupert Phelps (Messiah), Jamie Frampton (Soldier), Kate Korbel (Hostage). 86 min.

Zombie Strippers! (2008) USA. Dir/Scr/Ph/Ed: Jay Lee.

"THE MUST SEE ZOMBIE FILM... GIRLS, GORE AND GROSS-OUT GAGS"

"FUNNY, IMAGINAT... AND VERY GOF IN THE TRADITIC SUCH FILMS A EVIL DEAD BAD TAST

A Film by Warren Speed & Steve O'Brien

ZOMBIE WOMEN OF SATAN

Drop dead good looks.

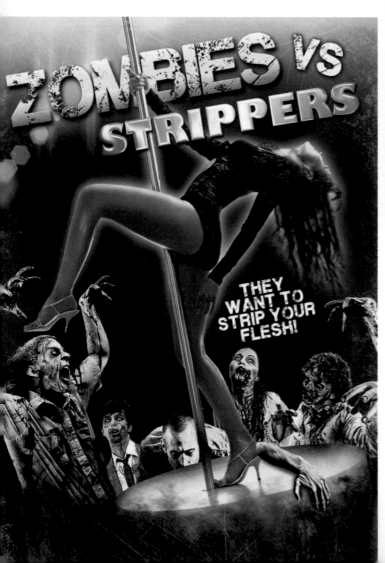

THEY WANT TO STRIP YOUR FLESH!

Mus: Billy White Acre. Cast: Jenna Jameson (Kat), Robert Englund (Ian), Roxy Saint (Lilith), Penny Drake (Sox), Whitney Anderson (Gaia), Jennifer Holland (Jessy), Shamron Moore (Jeannie), Jeannette Sousa (Berenge), Carmit Levité (Blavatski). 94 min.

Zombie Town (2007) USA. Dir/Scr: Damon Lemay. DP: George Lyon. PD: Neal Giberti. Cast: Adam Hose (Jake), Brynn Lucas (Alex), Dennis Lemoine (Randy), Phil Burke (Denton), James Aspden (Fred), Keith Boylan Baudreau (Bobby), Carol Benson II (Renee). 95 min.

Zombie Undead (2010) UK. Dir: Rhys Davies. Scr: Kris Tearse. Mus: David Fellows, Kris Tearse. DP: Neill Phillips. Ed: Rhys Davies, Kris Tearse. Cast: Ruth King (Sarah), Kris Tearse (Jay), Barry Thomas (Steve),

Christopher J. Herbert (Phil), Steven Dolton (Farmer), Sandra Wildbore (Mary). 79 min.

Zombie vs. Ninja (*Zombie Revival,* 1989) Hong Kong. Dir: Godfrey Ho [as Charles Lee]. Scr: Godfrey Ho. Mus: Stephen Tsang. DP: Raymond Chang. Ed: Homer Kwong. PD: Jimmy Chu. Cast: Pierre Kirby (Duncan), Edowan Bersmea (Villain Ninja), Dewey Bosworth (Mason), Thomas Hartham, Patrick Frzebar (Ira).

Zombies vs. Strippers (2011) USA.Dir: Alex Nicolaou. Scr: Nick Francomano, Alex Nicolaou, Kent Roudebush. Mus: William Levine, Ryan McGuffin. DP: Ben Demaree. Ed: Danny Draven. PD: Molly McIntosh. Cast: Circus-Szalewski (Spider), Eve Mauro (Sugar Hills), Victoria Levine (Bambi), Adriana Sephora (Jasmine), J. Scott (Marvin), Don Baldaramos (Bobby), Tanner Horn (DJ Bern), Brittany Gael Vaughn (Vanilla), Adam Brooks (Spike), Patrick Lazzara (Richard), Brad Potts (Red Wings). 75 min.

Zombie Wars (*War of the Living Dead,* 2007) USA. Dir/Scr: David A. Prior. Mus: David M. Poole. DP: Frédéric Chaignat. Ed: David Alan, Alan Roberts. Cast: Adam Mayfield (David), Alissa Koenig (Star), Jim Hazelton (Brian), Kristi Pearce (General), Jonathan Badeen (Sliver), Billy Hayes (George/Zombie King), Loretta Norton (Josh). 80 min.

Zombie Women of Satan (2009) UK. Dir: Steve O'Brien, Warren Speed. Scr: Seymour Leon Mace, Steve O'Brien, Warren Speed. Mus: Dan Bewick. DP: Steve O'Brien. Ed: Richard Johnstone. Cast: Warren Speed (Pervo the Clown), Victoria Hopkins (Skye Brannigan), Victoria Broom (Rachel Brannigan/Cult Girl M), Marysia Kay (Red Zander), Peter Bonner (Zeus), Kate Soulsby (Harmony Starr). 85 min.

Zombiechrist (2010) USA. Dir/Scr/Ph/Ed: Bill Zebub. Cast: Caitlin Burdi (Mary Magdeline), Jordana Leigh (Nun), Jessica Green (Mary), Julie Anne Hamolke (Detective), Adam Kuligowski (Druid). 100 min.

Zombiegeddon (2003) USA. Dir/Scr: Chris Watson. DP: Damon Abraham, Jim Siebert. Ed: Damon Abraham, Sean Cain. Cast: Mark Adams (Det. Mark Argento), Ari Bavel (Cage), Uwe Boll (himself), J.R. Bookwalter (Crazed Professor), Conrad Brooks (Dean Martinson), Josh Christofferson (Grocery Guy), Joe

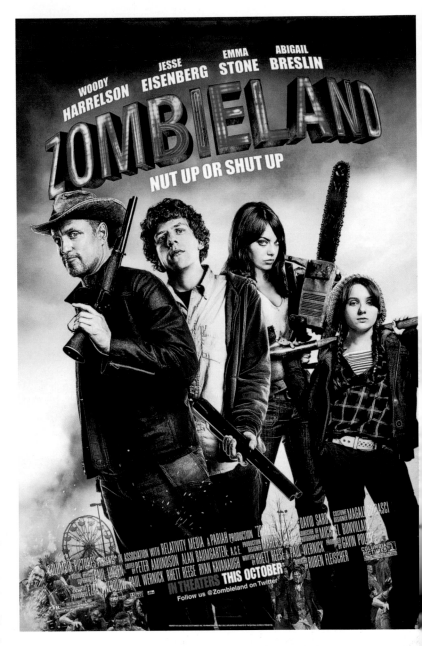

Estevez (Brooks), Linnea Quigley (Principal Russo). 81 min.

Die Zombiejäger (2005) Sweden. Dir: Jonas Wolcher. Scr: Petter Hörberg, Jonas Wolcher. Mus: Aardia. Cast: Martin Brisshäll (Heinrich Rummel), Nick Holmquist (Dieter Höss), Christian van Caine (Ivo Reinharth), Margareta Strand (Ewa Weiss), Erich Silva (The Zombie Master). 85 min.

Wally **BROWN** · Alan **CARNEY** · Bela **LUGOSI**

in

Zombies on Broadway

RKO RADIO PICTURES

WITH

ANNE JEFFREYS

SHELDON LEONARD · **FRANK JENKS**

PRODUCED BY **BEN STOLOFF** DIRECTED BY **GORDON DOUGLAS**

SCREEN PLAY BY LAWRENCE KIMBLE

1A Copyright 1945 RKO Radio Pictures Inc. Country of Origin U.S.A.

44/478

Zombieland (2009) USA. Dir: Ruben Fleischer. Scr: Rhett Reese, Paul Wernick. Mus: David Sardy. DP: Michael Bonvillain. Ed: Alan Baumgarten. PD: Maher Ahmad. Cast: Jesse Eisenberg (Columbus), Woody Harrelson (Tallahassee), Emma Stone (Wichita), Abigail Breslin (Little Rock), Amber Heard (406), Bill Murray (himself), Derek Graf (Clown Zombie). 88 min.

Zombieland (2013, Web series) USA. Dir: Eli Craig. Scr: Rhett Reese, Paul Wernick. Ed: Catherine Haight. PD: Eric Weiler. Cast: Kirk Ward (Tallahassee), Tyler Ross (Columbus), Maiara Walsh (Wichita), Izabela Vidovic (Little Rock). 29 min.

Zombienation Dead by Dawn (2009). Dir/Ed: Víctor Méndez. Scr: Magnus Mefisto, Víctor Méndez. DP: Gastón García. Art Dir: Gastón García, Magnus Mefisto. Cast: Lara Aldana, Juan Manuel Paradiso, Pablo Avendano.

Zombienation Hail to the Führer (2009) Argentina. Dir/Ed: Víctor Méndez. Scr: Magnus Mefisto, Víctor Méndez. DP: Gastón García. Art Dir: Gastón García, Magnus Mefisto. Cast: Magnus Mefisto (Dr. Akula/Adolf Hitler), Víctor Méndez (John Mc Hutter), Nayla Perez Knees (Lucy Quanto), Fernando Tulián (Gral. Warsteiner). 82 min.

Zombies (*I Eat Your Skin*, 1964) USA. Dir/Scr: Del Tenney. Mus: Lon E. Norman. DP: François Farkas. Ed: Lawrence C. Keating. Cast: William Joyce (Tom Harris), Heather Hewitt (Jeannie Biladeau), Betty Hyatt Linton (Coral Fairchild), Dan Stapleton (Duncan Fairchild), Walter Coy (Charles Bentley), Robert Stanton (Dr. Biladeau). 84 min.

Zombies: A Living History (2011, television special) USA. Dir: David V. Nicholson. Scr: Andre Abramowitz, John Palakas, Ted Schillinger, David Sampliner. DP: Piotr Jagninski, David Krebelj, Marshall Stief. Ed: Bill Glenn, Ian Johnson, Doug Morrione, Rob Tobin. PD: Rory Mulholland, Cast: Peter Outerbridge (Narrator), Josh Ford (Ben/Lead Zombie), Rachael Platt (Wife), Eden Marryshow (Orderly), Pei Pei Lin (Jiang Shi/Nurse), Jono Hustis, Jared Miller (Revenants/Soldiers, Chester Jones III (Soldier), Jillian Morgese (Ghoul), Elliott Brooks (Ghoul/Female Reporter), Tracy Infield (Infected Refugee). 87 min.

Zombies from Ireland (2013) UK. Dir/Scr(s)/Ph/Ed: Ryan Kift, Sian Davies. Mus: Duncan Black. Rheon Jones (Mclugwy). 83 min.

Zombies Gone Wild (2007) USA. Dir/Scr: Gary Robert. Mus: The Vankmans. DP: Patrick Smith. Ed: Jim Sevin. Cast: Dave Competello (Marty), Chris Saphire (Randy), Dominique Rochelle (LeRoy), Giselle Lopez (Sue), Summer Morgan (Betty). 102 min.

Zombies of Mora Tau (1957) USA. Dir: Edward L. Cahn.

Scr: Bernard Gordon aka Raymond T. Marcus based on a story by George Plympton. Mus: Mischa Bakaleinikoff. DP: Benjamin H. Kline. Ed: Jack Ogilvie. AD: Paul Palmentola. Cast: Gregg Palmer (Jeff Clark), Allison Hayes (Mona Harrison), Autumn Russell (Jan Peters), Joel Ashley (George Harrison), Morris Ankrum (Dr. Jonathan Eggert), Marjorie Eaton (Grandmother Peters), Gene Roth (Sam, the Chauffeur), Leonard P. Geer (Johnny). 70 min.

Zombies on Broadway (1945) USA. Dir: Gordon Douglas. Scr: Lawrence Kimble, Robert E. Kent based on a story by Robert Faber, Charles Newman. Mus: Roy Webb. DP: Jack MacKenzie. Ed: Philip Martin. AD: Albert S. D'Agostino, Walter E. Keller. Cast: Wally Brown (Jerry Miles), Alan Carney (Mike Strager), Bela Lugosi (Professor Paul Renault), Anne Jeffreys (Jean La Danse), Sheldon Leonard (Ace Miller), Frank Jenks (Gus), Russell Hopton (Benny), Joseph Vitale (Joseph), Ian Wolfe (Prof. Hopkins), Louis Jean Heydt (Douglas Walker), Darby Jones (Kalaga–the Zombie), Sir Lancelot (Calypso Singer). 69 min.

Zombiez (2005) USA. Dir/Scr: John Bacchus. DP: Paul Swan. Cast: Jenicia Garcia (Josephine), Jackeem Sellers (DR), Randy Clarke (Steve), Raymond Spencer (Terry). 83 min.

Zonbi jieitai (*Zombie Self-Defense Force*, 2006) Japan. Dir: Naoyuki Tomomatsu. Scr: Naoyuki Tomomatsu, Chisato Ōgawara. Ed: Masaru Ikeda. Cast: Kenji Arai, Norman England, Masayuki Hase, Yū Machimura. 75 min.

Zonbi rōn (*Zombie Loan*, 2007, television series, animation) Japan. Dir: Akira Nishimori. Scr: Banri Sendo, Shibuko Ebara based on their manga.

Contributors

<u>The Authors</u>

Alain Silver wrote and edited the books listed on page 2. His articles have appeared in *Film Comment, Movie, Wide Angle,* anthologies on *The Philosophy of Film Noir, The Hummer,* and *Akira Kurosawa* as well as the on-line magazines *Images* and *Senses of Cinema*. His produced screenplays include *Time at the Top, White Nights* (from Dostoyevsky), and *Nightcomer* (which he also directed). He has also produced a score of independent feature films (including *Palmer's Pick-up, Beat, Cyborg 2,* and *Crashing*) and forty soundtrack albums. His commentaries may be heard and seen on numerous DVDs discussing Raymond Chandler, the gangster film, the classic period of film noir from *Murder My Sweet* to most recently *He Walked by Night*. His Ph.D. in Theater Arts/Motion Pictures, Critical Studies is from the University of California, Los Angeles.

James Ursini also wrote and edited the books listed on page 2 and provided text for the Taschen Icon series on Bogart, Dietrich, Elizabeth Taylor, Mae West, and De Niro. His early study of Preston Sturges was reprinted in a bilingual edition by the San Sebastián Film Festival. His film noir DVD commentaries (often with Alain Silver) include *Out of the Past, The Dark Corner, Nightmare Alley, Lady in the Lake, Kiss of Death, Brute Force, Crossfire, The Lodger, The Street with No Name, Where Danger Lives,* and *Kiss Me Deadly* and such other titles as *Hobson's Choice* and the recent limited edition of *The Egyptian*. He has been a producer on features and documentaries, and lectured on filmmaking at UCLA, from which he holds a Masters degree, and other colleges in the Los Angeles area where he works as an educator.

<u>Contributors</u>

Linda Brookover is a researcher and writer who works in the field of multi-cultural education and holds Masters degrees from Texas A&M and UCLA. She has written on a variety of American Indian/ethnographic subjects for *oneWorld,* an on-line magazine which she co-edited. Her essays, most notably the two-part "What is This Thing Called Noir," appear in *Film Noir Reader* series and *Horror Film Reader*. Other work includes side-bars on Weegee for *The Noir Style* and *True Blood* for *The Vampire Film* and entries in *Film Noir the Encyclopedia*. She co-wrote the Showtime family feature *Time at the Top* and was a production executive on the independent feature *Beat*.

John Edgar Browning has contracted or co-written a dozen books on Dracula, vampires, Bram Stoker, or horror, most recently with *Speaking of Monsters: A Teratological Anthology* (with

Caroline J. S. Picart) and *The Forgotten Writings of Bram Stoker*, and is presently at work on *The Palgrave Literary Dictionary of Bram Stoker* and a book on *Dracula* for Cornell University Press. He is an Arthur A. Schomburg Fellow and Ph.D. student (American Studies) in the Department of Transnational Studies and an adjunct faculty member in the Department of English at the University at Buffalo (SUNY).

Paolo Durazzo is a graduate of Penn State University and worked in Pennsylvania producing local TV spots, shorts such as *Black Fu*, and as a firefighter/paramedic. He contributed several neo-noir entries to *Film Noir the Encyclopedia*. He has been a videographer, assistant director, and producer on independent features, such as *White Nights*, *Crashing*, and *Callers* and the television series *The Aquanauts*. His short films as director include *Rockboy*, *Getting through Security*, and *Really Fake*. He is a member of the Directors Guild of America and his production company is Scura Citta or "Dark City."

Eric Forsberg is a graduate of Tufts University and began his career as producer and director with performance pieces,over sixty plays, musicals, and comedy reviews in his native Chicago and the Midwest. In Los Angeles he has worked in independent production and television for more than a dozen years. His screenplays include *Clash of the Empires* and *Snakes on a Train*. His other exploitation features as writer/director are *Alien Abduction* (2005), *Torture Room* (2007), *Sex Pot* (2009), *Mega Piranha* (2010). He is a member of the Dramatists Guild, Writers Guild of America, and Directors Guild of America.

Todd K. Platts holds a Ph.D. from the University of Missouri and is an adjunct professor of sociology at Harrisburg Area Community College. His research focuses primarily on the production of zombie media in popular culture. His article on the sociology of zombies was recently published in *Sociology Compass*. Among his other published or forthcoming essays are an examination of production of zombie films in the 1930s and 1940s and a more detailed production history of AMC's *The Walking Dead*. He is currently transforming his dissertation, which examines the evolution of zombie cinema through shifting nexi of production, into a book.

Tony Williams is the author of *Body and Soul: the Cinematic Vision of Robert Aldrich*; *The Cinema of George A. Romero: Knight of the Living Dead*; *Jack London: the Movies*; *Structures of Desire: British Cinema 1949-1955*; and *John Woo's Bullet in the Head*. Forthcoming are new editions of *Hearths of Darkness: the Family in the American Horror Film* and *Larry Cohen: Radical Allegories of an American Filmmaker*. He edited *George A. Romero: Interviews*, co-wrote *Italian Western: Opera of Violence*, and co-edited *Vietnam War Films* and *Jack London's The Sea Wolf: A Screenplay by Robert Rossen*. His articles have appeared in *Cinema Journal, CineAction, Wide Angle, Jump Cut, Asian Cinema, Creative Filmmaking*, and several *Film Noir Reader*s. He is an Associate Professor and Area Head of Film Studies at Southern Illinois University, Carbondale.

Index of Film Titles

The Filmography, which is alphabetical for direct access, is not indexed. However, alternate titles that do not appear in the text are included below and reference the title used in the Filmography. Page numbers for scenes stills are in *italics*; posters are not indexed.

Index

BLACK DEATH WAS ONLY THE BEGINNING...

KNIGHT OF THE DEAD

ON MARCH 11, 2008 THE GOVERNMENT SEALED OFF AN APARTMENT COMPLEX IN LOS ANGELES.

THE RESIDENTS WERE NEVER SEEN AGAIN.

NO DETAILS.
NO WITNESSES.
NO EVIDENCE.

UNTIL NOW.

QUARANTINE

28 Weeks Later.

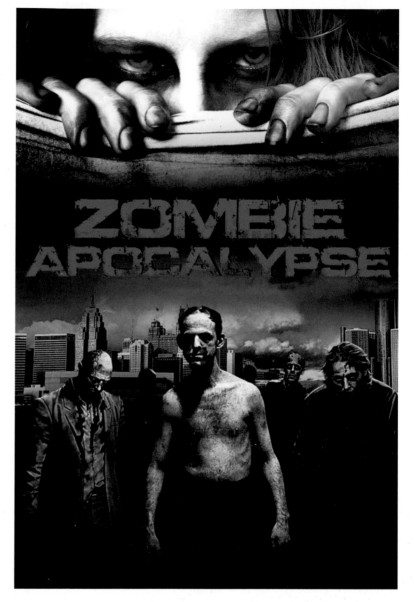

Zombie Strippers.